Cottrell

SAMARITAN OF SCIENCE

BY FRANK CAMERON

Foreword by Ernest O. Lawrence

COTTRELL: SAMARITAN OF SCIENCE is the biography of one of this century's outstanding figures: scientist, inventor and philanthropist Frederick Gardner Cottrell. Young Cottrell, a Tom Edison in academic gown, held values native to his era and the American frontier: they focused on hard work and education, on one's duty to society, and on the power of good works to change the world for the better. These values were expressed in the creation of Research Corporation, Cottrell's philanthropic foundation for the advancement of science and technology established in 1912 with the assistance of the Secretary of the Smithsonian Institution. One of the first U.S. foundations and the only one wholly devoted to science and its practical applications the nation over, Research Corporation has just completed its 80th year. This reissue of *Samaritan of Science* by Frank Cameron, first published in 1952, marks that anniversary. Although the book is unannotated, its accuracy has been well tested.

Born in Oakland, California in 1877, Cottrell revealed as a boy the intense curiosity and love of science that was to characterize his life. He was admitted to the University of California after four semesters of high school where, one acquaintance recalled, "he read textbooks like novels." Completing four years of college work in three, he was awarded a bachelor's degree in 1896 and a fellowship for graduate study, an honor he could not then afford to accept.

Taking a job teaching high school chemistry, Cottrell set his own course of research at the university until he could pursue graduate study. For this he voyaged to Germany, then at the frontiers of physics and chemistry, winning an advanced degree from the University of Berlin in 1901, and a Ph.D. from the University of Leipzig in 1902. A faculty post at the University of California awaited his return.

Several years later he undertook to solve a pressing public nuisance and supplement the modest salary of an assistant professor of chemistry by finding a way to collect the pollutants that belched from turn-of-the-century smelters, chemical, cement and power plants. After several false starts, he hit upon electrical precipitation as a means of collecting acid mists, fly ash, dust and fumes. His first successful device led to a gas cleaning industry in which the electrostatic precipitator—still very much in use today—became a primary means for controlling industrial air pollution. The device imparts an electrical charge to drops and particulate matter, collecting them on oppositely-charged electrodes.

The precipitator won him fame, and its rapid acceptance promised him a fortune. One fallout was a 1911 job offer from the fledgling U.S. Bureau of Mines. In abandoning the precipitator to accept it, Dr. Cottrell, then just 34, resolved that science would be the principal beneficiary of his invention. He persuaded those associated with him in developing the precipitator to accept this highly unusual idea, and offered the patent rights to the Smithsonian Institution.

Although the Smithsonian's Board of Regents decided that it should not become the owner of the patents, it agreed that it *could* accept the *income* from the precipitation process earned by an independent organization. The ball was back in Cottrell's court, but he had a vital ally in the person of Smithsonian Secretary Charles Doolittle Walcott. Together the two of them–the Smithsonian's distinguished administrator-geologist and the young chemist-inventor from California–blitzed New York and Boston to recruit men prominent in academe and industry for the board of directors of a new organization to be called "Research Corporation." With the backing of the Smithsonian, they were successful. A charter was filed and the board assembled, and Walcott found himself serving not only as spark plug, but overseer of Research Corporation until funds and assistance could be secured to put the foundation on a solid footing.

The purposes of the organization, in the words of its charter, were to make inventions and patent rights "more available in the useful arts and manufactures . . ." and to provide means for "technical and scientific investigation, research and experimentation by contributing the net earnings of the corporation . . . to the Smithsonian Institution and other scientific and educational institutions and societies. . . ."

Dr. Cottrell served the U.S. Bureau of Mines in several capacities, including a brief stint as director. His heart was in the laboratory, however, and he played a vital role in making possible helium production during World War I. After a decade with the Bureau, he assumed posts with the National Research Council and the U.S. Department of Agriculture's Fixed Nitrogen Laboratory. As scientist and statesman, he was highly regarded, and acquainted with the outstanding academic and industrial scientists of the day. He was especially well known for his ability to spark new ideas, and "Ask Cot" became a byword in Washington and other capitals. His awards ranged from the Le Conte fellowship and an honorary degree from the University of California to the highest awards of a variety of professional societies, and he was elected to the National Academy of Sciences in 1939.

Those who honored him spoke not only of his contributions to scientific knowledge, but of his dedicated efforts to enlist science in the service of society. "There is," Frederick Cottrell once told an audience of engineers, "the crying need and splendid opportunity for the young engineer of creative imagination and moral courage to join forces with his brother specialists from the humanitarian side and thus insure a really comprehensive picture of what Homo sapiens should be driving at as the immediate and conscious goal for the species."

His influence continues to be felt as Research Corporation approaches the 21st century. The foundation meets pressing needs for funds to advance research and education in the natural sciences as it did in earlier eras. Since 1912 it has contributed well over $100 million to the best research projects independently proposed by young academic scientists–some 22 of whom later won Nobel Prizes. Many other former Research Corporation grantees are prominent in industry and government as well as the academic community. In the area of "making inventions and patent rights more available and effective. . . ." the foundation has patented and licensed to industry hundreds of inventions from nearly 20,000 evaluated. Included have been vitamins, pharmaceuticals, research instruments, the laser concept, computer technology and others comprising much of modern-day technology.

"The things we look ahead to as ends, when accomplished, often disappoint us, while the steps by the way stand out in refreshing contrast as real points of satisfaction," Frederick Gardner Cottrell once wrote to his prospective bride, Jessie Mae Fulton. "The end should be far enough ahead of possibilities never to be really reached. This chasing the will o'the wisp and purposely pinning your faith to a phantom, almost which you never expect to catch, simply to keep yourself at the highest working pressure, takes nerve and courage and backbone. The person who pursues personal happiness as an end in itself is taking the greatest chance of all of losing it. If we can work together for the world's good and beyond ourselves and our own direct personal pleasure and keep this ideal steadily before us as the end, we will accomplish both."

March, 1993

John P. Schaefer, President
Research Corporation

FOREWORD

THE LIFE of Frederick Gardner Cottrell was distinguished not only by his own scientific contributions but even more by his generous spirit and his devotion to helping others along the paths of scientific progress.

His early interest and substantial help in the development of the cyclotron are examples of his fine influence in the promotion of science. I remember so well one of his visits to his alma mater when I had the pleasure of conducting him through the physics laboratory and showing him our work on the development of means for accelerating charged particles to high velocities. He immediately appreciated the possibilities of the cyclotron principle and with infectious enthusiasm volunteered to help in any way he could. The result was a grant from Research Corporation which was the first of many which played such a vital role in the development of the cyclotron in the ensuing years.

Whenever I reminded him of his first visit to our laboratory with all its beneficent consequences, as well as the many succeeding happy occasions when we enjoyed his company, he would laughingly remark that it only served to show he was only a catalyst and that sometimes catalysts are helpful in chain reactions.

It is always an inspiration to oncoming generations to read about the lives of good men who, through their spirit as well as their works, make contributions of lasting importance.

ERNEST O. LAWRENCE

Radiation Laboratory
University of California
Berkeley, California

Cot'trell precipitator (kŏt'rĕl). *Physical Chem.* An apparatus consisting of a wire at high potential in a chimney of opposite charge, for precipitating suspended particles.

Cottrell process. [After the inventor, Frederick Gardner Cottrell (b. 1877).] A process in which dust and suspended particles are removed from gases by a Cottrell precipitator.

—*Webster's New International Dictionary*
Second Edition. 1949. Unabridged.

Cot'trell or Cottrell', n. [After the prototype, Frederick Gardner Cottrell (b. 1877; d. 1948).] A type of scientist, inventor, and man of good will, loosely defined in the pages that follow.

COTTRELL / Samaritan of Science

IN THE YEAR 1890 the state of California was still an ultima Thule to much of the rest of the country and Oakland, its colorless third city, stood in the same relation to San Francisco—culturally, economically, and in some ways geographically—as Brooklyn to New York. Oakland was, indeed, the butt of jokes on the vaudeville stages of San Francisco—jokes which had originated on Broadway and, with a hardihood and adaptability peculiar to clichés and insect pests, spanned the continent. Oakland commuters shuttled across an unbridged bay on ferryboats that, while swift, were still ferryboats; a source of pleasure on bright sunny days and of irritation, delay, and even danger when the fog, spilling in through the Golden Gate, overflowed and piled up against the hills that ring the bay.

Many of the more prosperous commuters gravitated toward Oakland's western section to streets with names familiar the country over: Chestnut, Linden, Filbert, Myrtle; streets which were intersected at precise intervals by others sounding less arboreal but equally native: Tenth, Twelfth, Fourteenth, Sixteenth. For reasons that are trade secrets to city planners the odd-numbered streets failed to penetrate this area although they survived their interrupted existence to the northwest and southeast. By all conventional standards it was a district of solid citizens and one of Oakland's best. In it lived professional men, some clergy, a judge or two, and well-to-do businessmen with offices in The City, as San Francisco was known throughout much of California. In its tacit approval of San Francisco's presumptive right to such a title Oakland acknowledged its own civic shortcomings and with quiet self-acceptance took pride in its fast-growing population and its position as the terminus of several transcontinental rail lines.

The houses around Myrtle and Filbert streets in the neighborhood of Twelfth were of wood construction, homely both in the sense that they bespoke home life and in that they were completely innocent of beauty by any functional standards. Amply proportioned, they were far, far from baronial. Some of their exteriors gave evidence of an overfondness for scrollwork but that was, after all, an era in which such decorative touches found favor—a hitching-post era in which gas or carbon-arc lamps gave a fitful light to unpaved residential streets. But whatever the errors in the eyes of modern designers, the houses sat at restful sovereign ease. Separated from each other by yards and vacant lots, they were enhanced by the presence of occasional live oaks from which their city took its name and which were depended upon for shade duty most of the year in the Mediterranean-like climate.

It was, in short, a good place to be born in, to live in (providing one paid obeisance to San Francisco by beatifying its civic status with the upper-case C), and, if death proved inevitable, to die in. Many of its 48,700 residents in the early 1890s thought so and at least one of them found it a suitable milieu for a startling variety of business enterprises that were embryonic of what was later to be called, with both favor and abuse, "rugged individualism."

The house at 1019 Filbert Street differed little in character from others in the vicinity. To the stranger it was anonymous. To the adults in the neighborhood it housed "the Cottrells." But to the teen-aged males, still young enough to think as intolerantly of all girls as they did of their sisters, it was a storm center of furious activity dominated by a thirteen-year-old boy named Fred. Fred was a tall boy well on the way to the six-foot-two-inch terminal he was eventually to achieve. He was, moreover, large and weighed at that time close to 160 pounds yet successfully avoided an appearance of heaviness. He had brown hair and he had brown eyes. His features, pleasantly regular, were obviously destined to mature into a plain and unspectacular handsomeness during young manhood. It was a face that seemed incapable of deviousness as indeed it was. It was a face that smiled frequently, openly, and honestly. It was, then and later, a purposeful countenance difficult to dislike.

Since the stereotype of the tall, muscular, well-built boy, pleasing of face ("clean-cut" is perhaps the most frequently used term), has long held a place in national advertising and literary mores as typically American, Fred was not in this sense unique. He conformed physically but there were other differences so marked that even his contemporaries were aware of some of them. Certainly his elders were. For one thing, there was his possession of a furious energy that seemed to have its wellspring in some deep-seated force, as vital as it was secret. It was something for which youthfulness alone could scarcely be held accountable. Whatever its source, it was seemingly limitless and recognized as such by his immediate family, who with uncommon wisdom adjusted themselves accordingly. Twin to this energy was an equal fund of enthusiasm that swelled and fixed itself to any new concept that challenged, then ebbed into a passive neutrality once fulfillment became possible. There was a keen, flexible intelligence, an itching mind forever wanting to be scratched with fresh ideas. There were other things too, but chiefly evident was a strange maturity, as though he had passed from boyhood to manhood with only the briefest of transitions.

In his early teens his play was not the play of games nor during his later life was there ever to be a sharp distinction between his recreation and his work. Perhaps the best early evidence of this is a glimpse of what went on behind the placid façade of 1019 Filbert around the early 1890s. A neatly printed business card announced this address as the headquarters of *F. G. Cottrell, Landscape Photographer. Real Estate Work A Specialty. All Orders Receive Prompt Attention.* Now *Cottrell the Landscape Photographer* might, if one were a stranger to the neighborhood, forgivably have been confused with *F. G. Cottrell, Artistic Job Printer,* whose address was the same, who promised the same prompt attention although this time to *Cards, Envelopes, Bill Heads, Letter Heads, Programmes, Etc.,* and whose artistry was attested to by a type face that utilized as many flourishes as anything that must have been available west of the Rockies at that time.

As with all good job printers, this one kept specimen copies of his work available for inspection. These included handbills of plays with which his older brother, Harry, an actor and playwright, was connected; office stationery of one sort or another for the Arctic Oil Works, a San Francisco firm for which his father worked; dance programs where the name of one's partner was written alongside such exotic numbers as schottisches, lancers, yorks, and mazurkas, to say nothing of polkas and waltzes; miscellaneous business cards for other than Cottrell enterprises; labels and a large assortment of Etcs. Whatever the outlook at that time for a landscape photographer, there is good reason to believe that an alert and artistic job printer could command a respectable amount of business.

The printer/photographer shared the same address with one *F. G. Cottrell, Electrician,* a versatile man, if one were to have faith in his printed billhead which made a bid for *All Kinds of Contract Work— Electrical Bells, Gas Lighting, Door Openers, Annunciators, Burglar Alarms,* and *Repairing in Everything Electrical (All Orders Promptly Executed).* This new thing, electricity, was fast catching on, and the mother of the electrician, in spite of his sop tossed to gas lighting, could write to her Eastern relatives that he was earning his spending money installing doorbells.

As a printer/photographer/electrician Fred had by no means exhausted his possibilities. There were *Engs & Cottrell, Chemists,* who operated a surprisingly well-equipped laboratory in the Engs barn with rows of neatly identified bottles, each label bearing the names of the partners in a type face easily traceable to a Filbert Street printer. Work here reached its highest pitch on Saturdays when experiments already performed in school were repeated and elaborated. There were times when they became too elaborate. One with cyanogen gas, both poisonous and inflammable, ended in an explosion. The neighbors complained, and the Engs family reclaimed its barn to be used henceforth for its God-given purpose.

The dissolution of this partnership was apparently not a sufficiently moving experience to dampen Fred's eternal enthusiasm, for the printing samples later show labels and billheads of a *Horswill & Cottrell, Chemists,* with a Chestnut Street address. What went on there is neither a matter of record nor part of the folklore of Oakland. One can only be certain that it was an interesting order of chemistry.

Somewhere about this time the *Occidental Telegraph Co.* was formed in which Fred had a guiding hand. Its membership consisted of neighborhood boys with homemade telegraph sets connected by wires strung between their houses. Here again the printing samples give the best clues to the organization's activities. It had printed message blanks of a Western Union yellow about one fourth the size of those now in use. Printed dues receipts make it clear that it was a membership affair with monthly assessments of twenty-five cents. There were also receipts for the payment of monthly fines. These ranged from five cents, levied against one operator's interrupting another, to fifteen cents for violation of Regulation 16—a stern prohibition against using vulgar and profane language over any part of the line. There were nineteen rules and regulations.

Under the by-line of Putnam and Cottrell, the Occidental Telegraph Company began an ambitious work (with illustrations) entitled *Electrical Apparatus, How Made and How Used. For Amateurs.* Of this, Chapter I ("The Battery") survives in longhand and begins, "A very simple battery may be made by placing a strip of zinc upon one side of the tongue and a piece of silver upon the other side, then by bringing the two ends in contact, a slight current of electricity will be experienced through the end of the tongue." It is conceivable that such suggestions in conjunction with the system of fines may have discouraged the less persevering members of the company and account for the scarcity of Occidentiana.

By and large, the venture which best expresses the character of its thirteen-year-old entrepreneur (landscape photography and job printing, however artistic, were potboiling activities at best) was the *Boys' Workshop.* A publication consisting of four pages no larger than a boy's hand, it was mailed out to subscribers every Monday. It is significant to note that under the title of each issue the following appeared in italics: *"Dedicated to the public in general and boys in particular."*

The date of Vol. I, No. I was April 28, 1890, or roughly about the time another, and more dedicated writer, named Jack London was becoming a familiar figure around the raffish edges of Oakland's waterfront a mile or so to the west. The *Boys' Workshop,* however, instead of plumbing the seamier side of life, stated its policy in a lead article:

Having dedicated this to "the public in general and boys in particular" we wish to say that it will be devoted chiefly to the descriptively of easily and cheaply constructed apparatus.

There will be space reserved for the use of subscribers wishing to exchange specimines or other articles with others.

There will also be a space reserved for any questions, and the answers thereto, that subscribers may wish to ask concerning the matter treated of in this paper.

Respectivly requesting the assistance of the public sustaining this sheet we remain. Yours sincerely. The Boys' Workshop.

The masthead on page two listed F. G. Cottrell and W. Wigginton and bracketed them together as "Props." Here, also, were the rates. A six months' subscription was quoted at fifty cents and advertising a dollar an inch. The first issue contained over a half page of the latter, five advertisers being represented. These were the agents for an oil engine in San Francisco; a hardware dealer; an "electritian" in Oakland; the *Penny Whistle* Publishing Company (a rival sheet and job-printing firm run by the Oliver boys on Twelfth Street), and, lastly, one which gave the editors trouble long familiar to older and wiser heads. It was for the "Artic Oil Works" where Fred's father was employed and which dealt in whale and sperm oils. With a tolerance now rare among advertisers, the oil works again in the second issue selected this medium for their message. Here they became the "Artcic Oil Works" but, since it takes dauntless spirits to pursue whales, they still persevered and in the third issue came out with all "*c's*" and "*t's*" properly distributed.

If the publishers showed vacillation in their spelling, the tone of the editorial matter was all firmness and resolution. The first issue, logically enough, gave instructions for setting up a workshop with a list of the necessary tools. It also told how to make a camera obscura from a cigar box which "although probably not as fine looking as those in the stores will certainly do as good work as any." To meet the exigencies of editorial composition a squib was inserted at the bottom of page two which at first glance appeared to be a strange recipe for boys, but which on closer inspection revealed that by dissolving ordinary glue in whiskey and keeping it well corked, liquid glue would be readily at hand.

That the editors were not insensitive to merchandising their paper was indicated in the second issue. Just above an ad for the competitive *Penny Whistle* they made "AN OFFER!!!" which finer type showed to be open only until May 15. Generous enough in its way, it threw in a dozen calling cards with each six months' subscription at the regular price.

In mid-May the *Workshop* sensibly suspended publication for the summer and by the time it resumed in early August, W. Wigginton had gone on to other pursuits, leaving Fred the sole Prop. Here he began a series concerning the construction and use of electrical apparatus, Chapter I dealing with the telegraph. Supplementing these articles were descriptions of simple chemical experiments such as How To bleach ink, How To crystallize the surface of glass, and How To detect alum in bread (boil the bread in water, filter the liquid and, when cold, add chloride of barium. "If either alum or plaster of Paris are present, white powder will be thrown down"). Regrettably, this piece of information left unanswered the challenging question of what neighborhood mothers did when their inquisitive offspring nagged at them to test their home-baked bread.

As promised at the outset, a lively query column went along with each issue. While some of the questions no doubt represented a thirst for precise knowledge on the part of the askers, others were suspiciously academic and of a nature not usually thought of in connection with either the public in general or boys in particular. Whether of popular or editorial-chair origin, the answers were uniformly of a clarity and conciseness that could well have been imitated by more ambitious publications. For example, one B.E.R. asked: "Will an electric battery run an induction coil to good advantage?" The reply, to quote the *Workshop* fully, was: "Yes."

Perhaps the greatest journalistic recognition the *Workshop* received was to be entered at the Oakland Post Office as second-class matter. Having achieved this stature, the *Workshop* sought to measure the field by establishing itself on an exchange list with other technical publications. These latter were of some importance nationally and no doubt the *Workshop* editors were willing to concede a certain superiority—quantitatively if not qualitatively. Rapport was established without difficulty with the *Electrical World*, published in New York. Another, the *Electrical Review*, which also had the advantage of a New York-Park Row address over an Oakland one, failed miserably to grasp the spirit of the thing. While the secretary of the *Review* replied courteously in the affirmative to Fred's preliminary query regarding the exchange, higher echelons treated it as a plain case of lèse-majesté, for the first issue to reach New York was dispatched back to Oakland in irate haste and bore the following message from the *Review's* publisher (an obviously unhappy man whose recollections of his own boyhood could have been tinged only with bitterness): "Mr. Cottrell, I would thank you to quit your insults. It may be a funny joke to you and your friend but you and your friend will be shown up as the damned idiots you are in a friend of mine daily paper there if not discontinued at once." At least the *Workshop* editors could take satisfaction in the knowledge that it was better to be damned than to be ignored. In his lifetime, few people ignored Fred Cottrell, and it is unlikely that he was ever again damned as an idiot.

The Christmas number in 1890 was noteworthy on several counts. An editorial described the growth of the *Workshop* and mentioned, without giving figures, that the subscription list had twice doubled itself since the founding. It exuded bright hopes for the future. The editors (Fred had been joined in October by a W. A. Starr) then went on to announce a slight shift in policy. Although the original intention had been to devote the paper exclusively to scientific matters, experience had taught them that the reading public demanded more varied fare and that henceforth one page would be given over to matters of general interest. While the editors were ready to meet the public halfway, they made it clear that in so doing there would be no reckless letting down of any bars, for in their coverage of these other subjects they would refrain from "those of a sensational nature."

By an odd coincidence the Christmas issue of the *Workshop* contained the briefest of statements which could, if Fred recalled it fifteen years later, have been the genesis of one of his most im-

portant contributions to science and technology—electrical precipitation of dust, fumes, and smoke. There is reason to doubt that
he did remember it. At any rate in that number he did run a story
on "The Progress of Science" in which readers were brought up to
date on such things as the Eiffel Tower, cheap aluminum, and
"two very important applications of electricity." The first of these
applications concerned welding. The second was "the deposition of
smoke and dust by electrical aid." With that single mention, the
matter was dispensed with. It was undoubtedly a reference to the
work of Sir Oliver Lodge in this field, but to what extent Fred
had probed the idea or whether he was merely condensing and para-
phrasing from another article, is a matter of speculation.

This same Christmas issue, already prophetic, burgeoned forth a
four-page supplement—three pages of which were devoted to a
biographical sketch of Thomas Edison. His life, the lead paragraph
stated, should "be an incentive to every young American boy. It is
one of the many instances where a poor boy has, by his own exer-
tions, risen to a position of distinction and honor." Looked at in
retrospect, there can be no doubt that this was no idle exhortation
but already a solid part of Fred's credo. It was neither lip service
nor cant repeated from elders who intended it only as advice to
others. It was something Fred himself had already taken to heart.

The other item in the supplement was a page devoted to a description of Girard College in Philadelphia. The opening paragraph here
again contains the wisp of an idea indicative of the fact that Fred
had positive ideas not usually associated with a thirteen-year-old
boy. "Among the men who have made the best use of their money,"
he states, "is Stephen Girard, who erected and endowed the noted
Girard College at Philadelphia, Pennsylvania." A further note on this
premature concern for money and its uses crops up several months
later when the Workshop, in a lead article, thus pays a tribute under
the title, "A Noble Man": "It is with the deepest regret that we learn
of the death of the well-known philanthropist Charles Pratt; the
founder of the Pratt Institute and the friend of every institution of
learning. When the Pratt Institute was first established there was no
other school where the scholars had the use of workshops. As a man,
he performed his work in life in such a manner that it left nothing
to be desired. He did his duty not in the restrictive sense of the word
but in its broadest and noblest meaning."

Here then, in rudimentary and unamplified form, were three twig-like indications of the early trend of Fred's thought, the more remarkable in that they did not materially change in principle for the rest of his life: there was the dedication of the *Workshop,* boyish as it was, to the "public in general"; there was the reverence for Edison and, by implication, for creative science; finally there was a concept of how money should be used which in later years formed the basis for an almost legendary reputation created by colleagues and the press that Fred Cottrell "had no use for money."

2

Frederick Gardner Cottrell was born January 10, 1877, at 706 Tenth Street in Oakland. It was an event left unrecorded by the Oakland *Evening Tribune,* which did, however, observe that rain was needed, that the public schools were crowded, and that San Francisco Bay was rough.

Fred's father, Henry Cottrell, was at that time paid secretary of the Union Club in San Francisco before that organization merged to form the sacrosanct Pacific Union Club. His mother had been Cynthia Durfee. His brother Harry (né Henry but nicknamed to distinguish father from son) had been born eight years earlier in Brooklyn before the family moved West. Harry was followed three years later by Paul, who died in infancy. Aside from Harry and Fred, there were no other children.

Both the Cottrells and the Durfees were of solid and mildly distinguished stock going well back into colonial times. The Rhode Island (as differentiated from the Virginia) Cottrells first enter the records in America in 1638. This was a Nicholas Cotterell (as it was then spelled) and whether he originated in England or Ireland is uncertain since the name in a variety of spellings was apparently native to both. Nicholas, at any rate, appears on the "Roule of ye freemen" admitted to the "Towne of Nieu Port," Rhode Island, in that year. By 1678 he was well enough along to buy seven hundred acres of land in Plymouth Colony where he died, leaving more land to Nicholas II in Westerly, Rhode Island, which then became the family headquarters for several generations. The Cottrells participated in Indian Wars, the Revolution, Colonial Assemblies, and until well into the nineteenth century gave their children such forthright names as Jabez, Joshua, Comfort, Lebbeus, Thankful, and John. The John Cottrell who appeared in the sixth generation married a Lydia Stillman, and their first child, Silas, born in 1809, was Fred's paternal grandfather. Silas eventually established himself in Newport, where the original Nicholas had been admitted as a freeman, while other direct descendants of Nicholas remained in Westerly to found the well-known firm of C. B. Cottrell and Sons, manufacturers of printing presses to which their inventions contributed many refinements.

Grandfather Silas married Abby Gardner, a cousin of Commodore Oliver Hazard Perry and a woman also of vintage stock going back, through the Potter family, to the Hazards who came to America in the 1600s and were instrumental in the founding of Newport. Silas prospered in the shipbuilding and shipping business, trading with the West Indies and the Southern states. A statement of the firm of Silas H. Cottrell and Company, dated March 1, 1851, shows assets of over $24,000, consisting of interests in various brigs and schooners as well as stock in the Cottrell shipyard. Outstanding obligations amounted to a little over $1000. Then the fortunes of Silas plummeted in one disastrous season when, for one reason or another, five ships in which he had an interest foundered in succession. On his death in 1880, at the age of seventy, the company's debt equaled the assets thirty years before with only $18,000 being realized from the sale of the firm. This latter went to the bank to satisfy indebtedness and the aging Abby was left with little more than a house and the devoted care of those of their five children who had survived.

The children of Silas and Abby were Anna, Charles, Robert, Gardner, and Henry. Only Henry married, fathering Harry and Fred. Gardner in some ways was the more interesting figure. At the age of nineteen he entered the Navy and by what his obituary termed his "vigorous energy" rose in rank with sufficient rapidity to command a squadron of Marines a year later. This vigor and energy took him into the thick of a skirmish on Sullivan's Island, off Charleston, in the unpeaceful year 1862, where he was twice wounded while two men at his side were killed. It was not the only time Gardner escaped violent death, for in the Battle of Mobile Bay, two years later, he barely missed entombment on the monitor *Tecumseh*. The

Tecumseh, newest and most formidable of the Union ironclads, was thought to be impervious to enemy shells, torpedoes, and possibly even acts of God, just as the *Titanic* was once considered unsinkable and the Maginot Line impregnable. Thirty minutes after firing the battle's first shot, the *Tecumseh* was blown up. The story of this, featuring Gardner's remarkable survival, was told as late as 1910 by a Rear Admiral Caspar F. Goodrich in the New York *Herald.*

Gardner, described by Admiral Goodrich as a "splendid handsome officer, full of energy and animated by the loftiest professional ideals," later went into the tea business in New York. When he died of consumption at the age of thirty-one, he left to his friends what the Newport *Mercury* called an "imperishable memory."

This was the Gardner for whom Fred was named and it seems to have been a fortuitous choice. A picture of Fred when only six months old moved Grandfather Philo Durfee to write: "The general striking resemblance is to me wonderfully like Gard's," and then he went on to congratulate the Cottrells for having bestowed on Fred such "good strong sensible names, with force and character befitting the nature of the noble little chap who bears it." When Henry Cottrell reported to his brother Charles some of Fred's bright sayings at the age of five, Charles replied that they were "very business-like for one so young" and added that they sounded "something like Gard." Abby (Gardner's mother) thought that at the age of six she could "trace a resemblance to Gard in Fred's face." Aunt Anna, four years later, found the likeness "remarkably strong." By the time he was twenty-three, Fred had met the Newport relatives, one of whom wrote back to California that there was a strong suggestion of his Uncle Gard in his "genial ease of manner and 'bon-hommie.'"

Although this theme had its variations—one here suggesting a nervous trait that seemed to stem from Fred's mother, another there seeing an expression in his eyes that reminded them of his father— such close harmony among relatives in this most controversial of family issues must stand in the records as fairly unique.

Compared with Gardner's career and dashing personality, the life of Henry Cottrell, Fred's father, was one of relative placidity. It was not without conflict but the skirmishes were of a type usually unmentioned in obituary dispatches.

Henry was born in Newport in 1840 when the Whigs won their first presidential election and the national debt stood at $3,500,000.

Although the town had never recaptured the thriving sea commerce lost during the blockades of the War of 1812, old Silas' ledgers were still showing up well in the black. This gave Henry what advantages there were, at the time, of a private-school education in Newport. An unidentified Cousin Martha, in writing to Fred years later of his father, thought it was a Mr. Leverett's school which was, she said, select and which the children of "the summer people" attended, presumably being allowed to mingle freely with offspring of the natives. Newport had not yet developed its full schizoid character which after the Civil War would be embodied in the personalities of Silas Cottrell, merchant, vis-à-vis Ward McAllister, social alp. In the year Henry was twelve, however, its reputation as a watering place was growing and twelve summer houses were erected although mostly by Boston people.

After Mr. Leverett's, Henry attended a Mr. Merret Lyon's school in Providence where he prepared to enter Brown University. (Although she apparently failed to go on record regarding this, it undoubtedly pleased Cousin Martha and was in keeping with her opinion of Fred's ancestors on his father's side as "men of scientific genius." Silas himself she claimed to be a "man of scientific taste with a perfect knowledge of history.") Somewhere about this time, however, Silas' shipping ventures were scourged with evil days and Henry went to New York City, where he found a clerical job. Here the Civil War intervened. Cousin Martha, who evidently found it distasteful to think of a member of the family in any but fastidious surroundings, considered Henry's "the most aristocratic regiment in New York." Patrician though it may have been, the regiment was not sufficiently standoffish to keep Henry from contact with typhoid, which invalided him out of the Army and back to New York.

After his recovery Henry turned to some phase of the shipping business. In this environment, where the clipper ships docked along South Street and pointed their sharp jib booms at the still squat New York sky line, it is possible that he came in contact with Philo Durfee, himself a heavy shipper of flour and grain. Somehow he met Philo's comely daughter Cynthia. Henry, who had now matured into a short-statured, gentle, and strikingly handsome man with soft, brooding eyes, courted Cynthia Durfee.

The Durfees were also early Rhode Island settlers, the first one, Thomas, coming to Portsmouth from England sometime in the seventeenth century. Here again the family Christian names had a strong Puritanical flavor, for among those given the descendants of the first Thomas were Job, Gideon, Pardon, and Philo. Some of these moved to Tiverton, Rhode Island, but after returning from the Revolutionary War found Tiverton too crowded for their taste. In the best American tradition, Gideon, Job, Edward, and Pardon Durfee loaded their families and, with what belongings could be stowed on oxcarts, headed west in 1791 through upstate New York. Not the least of their possessions was a leather satchel well filled with coin at a time when money was scarce. They came to rest in Palmyra (some thirty years before a report from Joseph Smith that the Angel Moroni appeared to him on the nearby hill of Cumorah with his revelation of the Book of Mormon) and here Gideon bought 1600 acres of land enabling a warranty deed of the town to be obtained. The marriage of Gideon's daughter Ruth to a Captain William Wilcox was said to be the first performed in Palmyra.

Philo Durfee (Fred's maternal grandfather) was born in Palmyra in 1809. The trend of the times was westward and while still a young man he moved on to the greater opportunities offered by Buffalo, where he became signally successful in the grain business and erected at least one flour mill. He is also credited in one account with building the first grain elevator in the country, although still another limits it to the first in Buffalo. He was enterprising and adventurous enough to make a business trip alone and on horseback from Buffalo to a trading post at the foot of Lake Michigan called Fort Dearborn, returning, since there was little choice in those days, in the same manner.

As he grew more successful Philo's range of contacts enlarged and he became a figure of some importance. He was among the first of the large shippers of grain over the Erie Canal, which had opened in 1825, and it is likely that he had some financial interest in the amalgamation of a group of small railroad lines that some years later became the New York Central. Like other members of the Durfee family at that time, Philo belonged to the Society of Friends. Either because of his religious beliefs or in addition to them, he was a man of scrupulous integrity. Several obituaries point to the fact that his credit was such that he could purchase large quantities of grain on his note. When currency was short (western New York State was still semi-frontier and banking in a wildcat era) his notes were solicited by banks and used as legal tender in the area. He was, according to another obituary, well thought of by President Andrew Johnson, who not only sought his advice when impeachment seemed likely but even offered him the secretaryship of the Treasury. Philo declined.

After the death of his wife Philo moved to New York in 1861 and settled down in a neighborhood of fine homes at Broadway and Twenty-first streets. (Two short blocks away at Madison Square, the newly opened Fifth Avenue Hotel had unflinchingly met the march of progress by installing an elevator described as a "perpendicular railway intersecting each story.") Accompanying Philo in his move were some of his children, including his daughters Mary, then age twenty-five, and Cynthia, eighteen. Mary, who, as the cycle of family relationships progressed, was to become Fred's "Aunt Mame," was a small, determined woman of a forceful and somewhat domineering personality—a compact flower of Victorian spinsterhood. It would be less taxing to go along with certain freethinkers of the time and doubt the existence of God than to question Mary Durfee's virtue. Along with her rectitude and strong will went a high order of intelligence. Had it not been that her thinking was circumscribed by the ladies-and-gentlemen concept of her generation, she might, by the proper exercise of her abilities, conceivably have been a strong champion of women's rights. Instead her role was to be one akin to that of foster motherhood.

Cynthia Durfee, Mary's junior by seven years, emerges only dimly as an Ibsen-like character. A friend to whom Cynthia served as bridesmaid once described hers as a "sweet face like a rose with its leaves yet folded." It was indeed an attractive face, yet one into which conflicting qualities might have been read. Mary, on the other hand, was homely in such a forthright fashion that it was easy to think of her as "sensible" and "having both feet on the ground." Anyone less purposeful and staunch could, by contrast, have been considered flighty. Cynthia, possessed of beauty, was.

The nature of the romance and courtship of Henry and Cynthia is as elusive as the manner of their first meeting. They were married in Stamford, Connecticut, in 1866, five years after Cynthia's arrival in New York. Their first child, Harry, was born in Brooklyn shortly after their second wedding anniversary. Paul, who died in infancy, came in 1872. Then followed an unsettling year in which, for reasons of either business or health, Henry moved to San Francisco, leaving the family temporarily in the East. His first work there was with a shipping and grain-exporting firm and he wrote back tender letters to Cynthia from his $30-a-month furnished rooms which he called "cozy" but difficult to be at ease in with his family so far away. But it was not a prolonged separation and apparently Henry prospered, for in a year Cynthia, her sister Mary, and Harry were able to undertake the costly overland journey, joining Henry in 1874.

Mary Durfee had by this time become the indomitable "Aunt Mame" and a figure to be reckoned with in the Cottrell household. At what specific point she took over complete control of the family's domestic arrangements it is not possible to say, but her influence was such that Cynthia refused to make the long and tedious transcontinental railroad trip without her. Aunt Mame came, and Aunt Mame remained.

For the home-loving man that he was, Henry had odd convictions about home ownership. He thought of it as restricting and giving him a "tied-down" feeling. As a result, the Cottrells put in a ten-year period of shuttling between boardinghouses, hotels, and rented houses in both Oakland and San Francisco, finally settling in Oakland. It was not, apparently, a question of money, for Henry's salary was such that he could afford the handsome sum of $100 a month as rent on the Tenth Street house in which Fred was born. After that event the moves were confined to the Linden-Filbert-Myrtle sector, thus providing a continuity of background in which Fred grew up.

In the growing up of Fred Cottrell two people played important roles—his father and his Aunt Mame. Henry Cottrell seems to have been a quiet, introspective man, intelligent and non-aggressive, with a strong pride and interest in Fred's aptitudes. He certainly had a prudish side. On one occasion the family received pictures of Cynthia's Los Angeles nieces who, Harry later wrote to Fred, "to father's horror were in low neck and short sleeves." The less conservative Cynthia was no whit abashed by this and stoutly defended their propriety by declaring, "Why, they don't even show the mere suggestion of a breast." The carnality of this compounded shamelessness was too much for Henry. He rose from the dinner table and left the room.

Henry Cottrell's great and probably only interest, aside from his work and his youngest son, was photography. Like many accomplished amateurs, he developed his own plates. For this he had a darkroom at home as well as an extensive assortment of such necessary chemicals as hyposulphite of soda and pyrogallic acid. His favorite subjects were flowers and the sailing ships then still an integral part of San Francisco Bay's picturesqueness. The results he obtained, even putting aside any consideration of the equipment available at the time, were amazingly fine. Since he was a man of patience and sensibility, he was able to achieve strikingly good composition and had a demonstrable feeling for form.

Not all of this was he able to transmute to Fred, for the latter's eagerness, particularly in his youth, was never subject to the rein and check which artistry in this field demanded. It did give Fred what for many years was to be one of his two serious hobbies (the other was hiking or "tramping" as he always called it, but both this and photography later succumbed to his insatiable desire for scientific novelty). It also gave him a very early introduction to chemicals, although these seem to have absorbed him less in pre-high school days than electrical apparatus and telegraphy.

Aware as was Henry Cottrell of budding, if undirected, talent in young Fred, Aunt Mame was equally so. Her devotion to both Harry and Fred was an all-consuming one, but for the latter she dreamed her more grandiose plans. It was she who saw to their clothes, mended and darned, warmed and laid out the nightshirts, watched over their diet, proclaimed the "don'ts," worried and fretted over wet feet, and even dispensed the discipline, although in the case of Fred it seems unlikely that much was required. At Aunt Mame's insistence (she was, it must be remembered, a sensible woman) Fred from an early age was subjected to a knee-length linen duster worn over his tight-fitting knee-pants suits that must easily have marked him among his playmates. Fifty years later Harry could recall it when writing to Fred of one time Aunt Mame took Fred shopping in downtown Oakland. As happens once in nearly every child's life, he became lost. While Aunt Mame "nearly went out of her mind," four-year-old Fred found his way home, where he was discovered by Harry in a backyard shed wedged under a wooden seat. "You were," Harry uncharitably reminded him, "scared stiff and crying and wouldn't come out. I remember perfectly your linen blouse or duster all over dirt and the little round felt hat you wore."

To Grace Gorrill, the little girl next door on Myrtle Street, Fred and the linen duster were still an incisive recollection almost seventy years later. For a year, about the time Fred was six, they were loyal playmates in the brief period that he ever expressed himself in play. Each day when he joined her to gather polliwogs in the gutter or dig a cave in a vacant lot, Aunt Mame would see that the large patch pockets of the duster were larders for crackers and lumps of sugar. Possibly even then Aunt Mame recognized in the intensity with which Fred played the necessity of sustaining the vast store of energy in this stocky, ruddy-cheeked boy.

Grace found in Fred a gifted and imaginative companion, artful in contriving things that would amuse them, yet mischievous enough to spice their daily and unsophisticated doings. He taught her how to draw circles with a compass, how to cut out paper lanterns and paste them with gum arabic, and how impractical it was to try sailing down the gutter in a slatted apple crate. He showed her how to model clay, although not too expertly. On one occasion when Aunt Mame forced him to remain in bed because of a childhood illness, he rigged up a double line of cord between their houses to which was attached a pulley. With a heavy paper shopping bag, this arrangement served to transport between their rooms all the unnecessary items that children find necessary at such times—pencils, notes, other momentarily important trivia. Possibly the only time in his life that he betrayed a trusted friend was the day he dispatched, via the bag and pulley, a small jar of apple jelly to Grace. Grace dipped into it hungrily, only to find that Fred had salted it heavily, and for the balance of the day relations between them were strained. To atone for this Fred installed a taut-cord-and-tin-can "telephone" familiar to all small boys. With the fancied aid of this device they carried on long conversations under greater strain and difficulty than they need have by the less glamorous method of simply leaning out the window to talk.

One of the brighter moments each day was the arrival of the Chinese fruit and vegetable vendors. These, in a timeless oriental fashion, carried heavily laden baskets suspended from each end of a long pole slung across one shoulder. They were a familiar sight in Oakland in those days, large numbers of them disembarking at the Mole from the San Francisco ferries each morning and fanning throughout the town. Known as the "Basket Brigade," they peddled their fresh and sometimes exotic wares, and to Fred of the voracious appetite they were an irresistible lure able to distract him from whatever he was engrossed in at the moment. Hovering around Aunt Mame, who herself did the purchasing at the back door rather than entrust it to the Cottrells' Chinese cook, he would beg to sample the strawberries, still so fresh that one could smell their red, ripe tartness, or plead for a taste of the yellow-golden peaches. Aunt Mame was not the one to refuse him.

Somewhere in the house, remote from the workaday world of peddlers, of a cook's complaints, of flies buzzing against a screen door and the clamor of children, Cynthia sat writing letters to her relatives back East. She told them of her boys and particularly of Fred. She wrote how bright and alert he was, of his agility with a fret saw, and that he was a good boy. Her pride in him was such that she may, as mothers do, have overstressed here or bragged there. Her letters gave a pleasing picture of a world she was in but, incomprehensibly, not of.

3

Before the University of California deserted Oakland for neighboring Berkeley in 1873, many residents felt that the presence of such an institution gave the city a certain éclat. Some of them went so far as to refer to Oakland publicly, although without any great conviction, as "the Athens of the West." It never could be said that this gentle and well-meant conceit caught the popular fancy, and one published historian of the period slurringly deflated any cultural pretentions by characterizing it as a city wherein "a good dogfight could draw an audience anywhere."

Fortunately for Frederick Cottrell, age six, a Miss Sarah Horton saw in the purlieus of Myrtle and Twelfth streets the need for an intellectual oasis for the boys and girls of the neighborhood, most of whose parents could afford a private-school education. On this well-founded assumption, in 1883—the same year Fred began his formal education—she opened the doors of a converted house on Adeline Street. A prospectus announced, with dignified simplicity, "The purpose of this school is to help its pupils to lay the foundation of a sound general culture."

Before entrusting the avid mind of Fred to an untested school, Aunt Mame investigated and found in Miss Horton a kindred spirit;

a woman with fourteen years' experience at Adelphi Academy in Brooklyn; a believer in educational fundamentals; a firm yet kindly and understanding woman who could appreciate individuality and be counted on to foster and encourage special aptitudes. She dressed neatly and austerely in long skirts, a high-collared basque which carried the suggestion of a uniform and which dispelled any ideas of loose living by clasping itself firmly with seventeen buttons lined in single file from neck to waist. Clearly Miss Horton was a woman of principle and as such won the stamp of Aunt Mame's approval—the prelude to a close and lifelong friendship that had as its focal point their mutual interest in Fred.

For school attendance he was allowed to dispense with the linen duster, which was replaced by a double-breasted jacket surmounted by an Eton collar and tie. Each daily session started with an inoffensively undenominational prayer followed by Psalms which Miss Horton read. The children then sang a song of some religious portent and classes were begun. This, as far as is known, was the extent of his youthful exposure to Christian orthodoxy, nor is there any evidence that this inspired him to seek further in the realm of theological dogma—yet oddly enough few men in his, or any other time, were better to exemplify the Christian ethic.

Miss Horton did indeed justify Aunt Mame's confidence in her. Within a surprisingly short time after its founding her school had acquired a solid reputation among Western educators as being one of the thoroughly efficient educational institutions on the Pacific Coast.

The school's curriculum, while conventionally elementary in most respects, did include both botany and German in Fred's fourth year and grades were cautiously dispensed. His report cards showed him to be a generally good student occasionally bordering on Miss Horton's highest accolade, which was "excellent." The same tenor existed in the categories of Behavior, Neatness, and Posture, although at one point in 1887, Miss Emma Wetherell, his fourth-year teacher, had occasion to annotate his report opposite Behavior, "Reported for Disorder three times." This was the only recorded blemish on his conduct in his elementary school career and showed a certain base ingratitude on the part of Miss Wetherell, whom Fred had remembered at Christmas with a present.

One thing that the combined efforts of Miss Horton, the Oakland

High School, and various universities of America and Europe could not give him was the gift of accepted spelling. In this, to the end, he was often the iconoclast and the phoneticist. In 1887 he began "central" with an *s* and in 1947 terminated "attic" with an added *k*.

If his days belonged to Miss Horton and Miss Wetherell, his evenings during his early school years were the treasured property of his father and Aunt Mame. While Fred did his homework Aunt Mame read to him from *Harper's Young People* and the *Scientific American*. His powers of maintaining divided attention probably surpassed those of most contemporary children who study to a radio, since he apparently absorbed both. He could, in fact, immediately prompt Aunt Mame on successive evenings as to the exact point where she had left off.

Harper's Young People of those days was of considerably different stature than the modern comic book. There were, to be sure, adventure and sentiment ("Silent Pete; or The Stowaways," as well as the "Little Match Girl") and the magazine occasionally delivered itself of such strong opinions as that the use of tobacco was a perverted taste. Mixed with this, however, were things a boy of Fred's temperament could and did put to use. In order to make a telephone, *Harper's* counseled its young readers to obtain two fresh beef bladders, two large gutta-percha overcoat buttons, strips of thin leather, and a flexible wire. Fred's adaptation of this omitted the beef bladders, but at one time or another he maintained contact with a half dozen of his neighborhood friends through an approximation of this system. The magazine, a weekly, also ran an "Amateur's Workshop" department (which later provided fodder for his own *Boys' Workshop*) and in one series of issues gave instructions on building a camera, going on into all the allied arts of taking pictures, developing, and printing. This was the genesis of F. G. Cottrell, Landscape Photographer, for Fred promptly presented his father with a cigar box and a watch crystal and suggested they build one. They not only succeeded but incorporated such relatively advanced refinements as a tripod and plateholders as well. By making "real estate work a specialty" (which probably meant photographing the house of an unsuspecting neighbor and then selling him a print), Fred was able to make enough to buy a better camera. It was the beginning of a hobby that survived the other few he ever attempted.

The success of the camera, however, almost automatically subordinated it to a place among the lesser interests. Fred's boyhood years coincided with the swift spread of applied electrical power. They were heady days for the inquiring mind, fresh with promise and pregnant with excitement. Bell had invented his telephone, Edison had developed the electric light. Kansas City and Cleveland sported electric trolley cars. There was electric welding, Berlin operated an electric train, and storage batteries were the newest thing. These were all reported in the *Scientific American*—reports devoured by Fred with avidity. In order to maintain a companion interest, his father kept pace. While the chief expression of Fred's temporary preoccupation with electricity seems to have been the Occidental Telegraph Company, snatches of correspondence in 1888, when he was eleven, indicate a more catholic interest. During the summer of that year Fred accompanied his mother and Aunt Mame on a vacation trip in the Santa Cruz Mountains, leaving his father in Oakland to keep abreast of all developments in the field. He reported to Fred that the supplements to the *Scientific American* had arrived and that there was enough to keep them both busy all winter and absorb all Fred's spare change. These supplements, he wrote Fred, covered instructions for making a dynamo, medical battery, induction coil, as well as experiments to be conducted with these after they were made. He then added with fatherly concern, "I will keep them here until you come up and you better rest quiet and enjoy yourself without troubling your head while there over electrical experiments." Fred's impatient intensity was apparently such, however, that Henry expressed his worry to Cynthia. "Hope Fred will get over his nervousness before he leaves. He must not crowd his brain as he has done heretofore." Then with a desperation of a man no longer able to pit his strength against strong tides, he wrote Cynthia, "Ask Fred who he wrote for circulars for they are coming from all directions. My pockets are full of them every night and they are over a foot deep in my room."

It was perhaps too early for Henry to know that his son's was a chronically restless brain and that no amount of gentle admonition could make it halt or even pause. It was a mind that had already begun to run and never after walked. Even then it held a glimmer of the enormity of the unknown to be encompassed, against which must be measured the pitiful inadequacy of time.

The discerning Miss Horton had also discovered Fred. In reply to what could only have been the Christmas gift of a self-portrait, she wrote him, "One thing in connection with your picture that I can't help saying is that whenever I look at it I say to myself with such pleasure and pride as I do not often feel, *This* boy of mine I never knew to say or do a cowardly thing, and I can't wish anything brighter or jollier for you and your friends in all the years to come than that this may be true of you always, and I believe it will."

It was, in all, an exciting year for Fred, this 1888. His interests were sure and the approach to them steady. It was perhaps the year, for such a year of departure came to him early, when he was no longer talked to as a boy, nor as a youth, but as an adult both at school and at home. The neighborhood boys regarded him with respect, imitated his scrollwork, or eagerly joined him in experiments. It was a year of experiments, not only electrical. He and Harry Torrey, a schoolmate at Miss Horton's, found a dead cat which they boiled until the flesh was removable, then strung it together with copper wire in an articulated skeleton. It was a year in which he was a money earner with his camera and the recipient of two windfalls from Eastern relatives. A jeweler's lathe belonging to his Uncle Charles, which had cost $75 when new, was shipped to him around the Horn in 144 days, accompanied by a complete box of tools. Grandmother Cottrell sent him Gardner's microscope, a handsome instrument big enough to require a mahogany case a foot long, half a foot deep, and ten inches wide. It was also the year he had mumps.

Oakland High School, which Fred entered when he was fourteen, was housed in an old building scarred by two fires but its scholastic reputation was sufficiently high to draw some pupils from the rest of the state and even a few from far-off Hawaii, still referred to as the Sandwich Islands. The boys of Oakland High School affected almost saucer-sized knots in their four-in-hand ties, referred to teasing jokes as "joshes," and in Senior "A" class, among girls as well as boys, the exchange of autographs (accompanied by a pat remark that would lose all meaning a year hence) was the rage.

In these non-essentials Fred showed a pattern of conformity with one—to the constant despair of Aunt Mame—plaguing exception. This was an almost complete inability to face the inactivity in a barber's chair necessary for a haircut. It was not a matter of affectation, for it was something, after a certain amount of insistent pressure on the part of others, he always meant to do. Things—just any number of things—had a way of intervening, with the result that all informal pictures taken then and throughout his life showed a tendency to shagginess from the rear or an elongated forelock before a mercifully receding hairline rendered the necessity of a haircut less obvious. This failing was in effect simply a testament to a set of values that, often through simple default, placed personal appearance in a negligible category.

These values, which could relegate such a matter as the length of a hair to sublime unimportance, he stated during his first high school year. One of his teachers, a Miss Hardy, for undisclosed reasons, had occasion to write him a series of questions to which he replied with almost a grim determination: "In answer to your questions I would say: First, my object in attending school is to gain such knowledge as is there taught, pertaining to both mental and moral improvement. Second, I hope to acquire the rudiments of the studies which I here take up, and to learn how to pursue my life work in the future in accordance with proper courses and principles of truth and honor. Third, my chief failings last term were, I believe, my poor spelling and writing and my readiness to talk with those about me during recitation time. . . ."

Miss Hardy was not the only one to consider this last point a fault. A note from another teacher, while complimenting him on his improvement in spelling, bluntly informed him in a schoolteacherish manner, "In every way I am pleased with you except one—and that you must know. I wish you would try in this too—for you are the one to overcome your overwhelming desire to talk. You know it is annoying to your teacher, troublesome to those about and worse that it tends to make one more and more underhand. Isn't it so? But I began this to say I am glad you have tried—and I am very truly your friend."

This desire to talk, confessed to Miss Hardy and criticized by the teacher who was truly his friend, was no ordinary garrulous chatter. It was rather the uninhibited outpouring of a mind too full of ideas to contain itself. He was a giver of these ideas to those who listened and when he departed into personalities it was in a spirit of speculative understanding and analysis and never in gossip.

Fred's serious-mindedness was more in the nature of earnestness than ponderous gravity, and happily it was leavened by a vast wealth of good-natured enthusiasm. He smiled often and engagingly, but it was a smile prompted less by humor than by a genuine pleasure quickly struck off by any kinship of interests or ideas. To all those able to recall him in those days, this, as much as his omnivorous pre-occupation with elementary science and gadgetry, was a dominant impression. There was, on meeting him, instantly evident a vivid warmth which his brown deep-set eyes expressed. There was an unmistakable eagerness to help and in his presence one felt that, even as a youth, here was a rare capacity for understanding and perception. Such ready sympathy carried with it the power to at-tract, and the more complex the problems of others, whether per-sonal or technical, the deeper Fred's interest. It is possible that just such an appeal first directed his attention toward Jessie May Fulton, a quiet, timid girl of fragile health and a classmate in Miss Wythe's botany course. Although their friendship at that time existed only on the level of tentative acquaintanceship, it was, twelve years and innumerable reams of letter paper later, to develop into an affection that culminated in their marriage.

If the nature of his adolescent feelings toward the shy Miss Fulton are a matter of speculation, his feeling for his scientific courses is not. In chemistry and physics Fred's instructor was Mr. S. P. Meads, a bearded and revered Mr. Chips of Oakland High, who proved almost equally indestructible. Although little stimulus was necessary, it was here that Fred's attention was weaned away from things pri-marily electrical and his interest fattened on the meatier fare of chemistry and physics. How directly Mr. Meads was responsible is not possible to say. The briefest of biographical notes in Fred's handwriting relative to this era simply states: "Chemistry ambitions, difficulty finding books suitable." Since his grades in science were of almost uniform excellence, and since he practiced chemistry with equal avidity at home, with Horswill (of Horswill & Cottrell, Chemists), and in the Engs barn, it is a reasonably safe conclusion that he found the texts too elemental. Fred was, in fact, even at that early teen-age so much the scientific sophisticate that he was wel-come in the laboratory of the family physician, Dr. Charles Fisher. In the doctor's downtown offices, during the evening hours when most high school boys diverted themselves with sports, amorphous wonderings about girls, or hunched themselves over cues at the Brunswick Temperance Billiard Parlor on Ninth Street, Fred scratched the surface of microscopy, using the good doctor's equipment to make up slides of diatomaceous soils.

Another course that commanded his interest was Miss Margaret Wythe's botany. Miss Wythe, like Mr. Meads, was beloved of all Oakland High alumni (although as pupils such mellow sentiment may not always have existed in their black little hearts). Both she and Mr. Meads were so highly thought of by Fred that he would, in later years, frequently pay them visits on his West Coast jaunts from Washington. In this botany course he was to discover that perfidy is where you find it, in scientists as much as spatted diplomats.

One bright Saturday morning he and a fellow student boarded a cable car and set out for the abundantly flowered Piedmont Hills in search of specimens. Slung from Fred's shoulder was a japanned tin case that even a professional botanist could have envied. It was two feet long, of Fred's own design, and one his father had had made to order for him. Outward bound it served as a lunchbox and on the return journey carried the plants and other fruits of the hunt. On this occasion both he and his companion were overjoyed to pick a very large and choice specimen which they thought to be *Zygadenus Fremontii*. Considerably elated, they laid it tenderly in the box. At that precise moment an upper-bracket professor of botany from the university in Berkeley spotted them and in their ingenuous enthusiasm they proudly showed off their prize, completely oblivious of the fact that even the pedagogical soul is sometimes shackled by cunning and lust. The professor eagerly begged the boys to let him take the specimen to his herbarium at the university, to which they, in good faith, consented. Whatever his intentions at the time, once locked in the fastness of his own laboratory he prepared a mounting in keeping with the plant's rarity, listening the while to a tempter's voice. Then, to the chagrin of two boys who still had faith in their elders, he gave it to the world as a newly discovered subspecies and named it after himself.

The interest of Fred's father in his son's work, both scholastic and extracurricular, was often the marvel and envy of other boys. In addition to the specimen box, Henry Cottrell built Fred a flower press and even co-ordinated his own hobby with Fred's studies by taking exquisite photographs of flowers as well as making remarkably fine photographic studies of insects under a microscope. While he was thus able to create bonds of mutual interest with Fred, no such firm rapprochement was possible with his elder son Harry. Henry's affection for both sons was great but Harry's temperament had taken a theatrical turn (in this some thought he was like his mother) and he was a young man quick with a pose, which he exercised by doing bit parts and writing skits for the Oakland theater and vaudeville houses. This Henry tolerated with an appreciable lack of enthusiasm, for it was a calling in those days considered a shade *that* side of reputable. Whatever interests Henry had once shared with Cynthia had long since turned arid, and while he appreciated Aunt Mame's capacities, it was only Fred of the immediate family who offered an outlet for one of Henry's studious turn of mind.

Early in the 1890s the Cottrells crated and packed once more, moving one street over from Myrtle to Filbert, to a house offering a clear gain of more room for less rent. These new quarters gave Henry and Fred the benefit of a first-floor study which they shared. Here the latter enjoyed the advantages of an adequate desk, an unabridged dictionary and other reference books, a terrestrial globe, a home-sized blackboard, his microscope, and assorted chemicals. The lathe, the printing press, his electrical apparatus, and even a vulcanizing outfit were relegated to the basement but, to the schoolmates who came to visit, all these represented a highly desirable set of equipment. With characteristic openhandedness Fred shared them.

In spite of some of these aids to study, high school English, spelling, and rhetoric continued to elude him and at one point he failed in English. It is easy to understand that, compared to science, he found the humanities dull and resented the theft of time from more exciting things. Nevertheless, it is difficult to understand why he failed, since in an English composition book remaining from this period he expressed himself passably well and an essay on the characters in *The Merchant of Venice* shows good analytical sense and perception. Sometimes the tenor of these compositions leaned toward a lofty morality that might be suspect of spuriousness were it not for the fact that present perspective shows that he validated the ideas there expressed during his lifetime. In one such composition entitled "Precept and Example," Fred stated: "The higher we aim, the nearer perfection we shall attain, but it is certain that no one ever surpasses his ideals, if they be what they should." Defensively aware that such sentiments might be lacking in popular appeal, he sternly admonished the reader—in an introduction to his composition book: "I wish it thoroughly understood that all these were written for my own advantage; therefore there will be no great harm done if they fail to interest others."

Rhetoric may have left him cold but his general zest for work was such that, while Fred's mother was away from home on a brief trip, his father wrote her, "Fred don't get much time to write. He is busy at his lessons all the time and analyzing to get his work up in time—tired out when through at night and up early in the morning again, generally about 6:30 A.M." The results of this application were such that Fred, impatient of time as always, decided that four semesters of Oakland High School were enough. Taking advantage of a system then in vogue at the University of California, he sat for the entrance examinations. In the fall of 1893, at the age of sixteen, he entered the university, passing chemistry with a first, or "highly creditable," grade although haunted by a "condition" in English.

4

Tucked away on an oak-studded plain at the foot of the Berkeley Hills, the University of California in the 1890s was a somnolent embryo as yet unaware of its destiny. It was warmed each year by the long summer sun, then, as autumn approached, bestirred itself into gentle activity to assimilate a thousand or so students before settling down to a routine wherein atoms still remained blissfully whole.

California's university was not, in those days, first-rate. It genuflected academically to older Eastern institutions which in turn deferred to those of England and the Continent. Its sole peer west of the Rockies was Leland Stanford Junior University at Palo Alto, but that, having opened only in 1891, gave even the Berkeley campus, by comparison, a patina of old parchment and ivy. Together they formed a Western cultural nucleus of only relative excellence— good, but still not by any means the best.

No different from people, universities base their own brand of snobbery on names, money, and age, and in all three the University of California at that time was short-suited. Its status as a university only dated back some twenty-odd years. Wealthy Westerners had not yet rallied to its support in any satisfactory numbers. Its faculty was drawn too largely from local sources, since it was difficult to induce first-rate men from the East to accept a lower salary and move several thousand miles to an area that had still to prove itself academically stimulating. It did have two notable assets—an exceptionally fine climate and a magnificent setting that not only looked out over much of San Francisco Bay but even peered out through the Golden Gate to the Pacific beyond. In the eyes of true scholars, however, these were not enough.

It might almost be said that the university—a group of five or six architecturally untidy buildings dreaming away in straw-colored fields among the oaks—was never again unaware of him after that day in 1893 when Fred Cottrell first strode its campus as a student. It might be said as an overstatement, yet in many respects it is true. By the end of his first year every member of the science faculty was aware of his presence. The students in all departments found him equally difficult to overlook. Most immediately noticeable was the curious pace with which this tall young man stalked the empty campus acres and, indoors, raced upstairs, taking a minimum of two steps at a time. He walked on the balls of his feet, his arms swinging freely at his sides, rushing with the air of one intolerant of the limitations of time. This often gave him the appearance of being slightly out of breath, an impression that was reinforced by the rapidity and ebullience of his speech. It sometimes seemed that he had so much he wanted to say that he couldn't pause to take a breath but must exhaust his lung capacity before inhaling to go on. At his side, leading a violent life of its own, was a book-filled briefcase attached to a strap slung over his shoulder, as familiar a part of him as his charging stride and his careless dress. Once adopted, the briefcase and its successors became as indispensable as a kangaroo's pouch, repositories for the ideas he was advocating at any one time in his life.

The impact of the dynamic young Cottrell on the science department in Berkeley was almost immediately apparent. Professors as well as instructors were competent but undistinguished and no great effort had ever been made to depart from the worn paths of textbooks into the uncertain fields of original research. To some of the faculty it must have come as a surprise that here was a young man to whom most of the routine experiments were old hat. They might also have been shocked had they known he was soon to think there were flaws in the second law of thermodynamics. Within the first month of the laboratory course of Chemistry I, a fellow student turned to Cottrell for help. To his surprise he found him wrapped up in a devious experiment that bore no relation to the work of the rest of the class.

"This," Cottrell explained with a disarming smile, "is just something I'm tinkering with."

"But what about the assignment?" the student asked. "Aren't you going to do it?"

"I've already finished that."

"Then why don't you go on to the next one?"

"Well," Cottrell said, "I've done that one too. The fact is," he went on to admit, "I've already finished all those laid out for the term."

Dr. H. B. Graham, the student who inquired, was one who could wistfully recall that Cottrell "read chemistry textbooks like novels." This was not far from the truth. In the second half of the 1894–95 term he had the rare courage to elect five different chemistry courses, and scored a 1, the highest grade given, in all of them. He found time in the same term for courses in German, physics, calculus, and zoology.

It is not surprising that those who, over fifty years later, were able to recall him during his undergraduate days still were impressed with his enormous capacity for work, as well as the way in which he drove himself unsparingly. Brilliance and resourcefulness alone were not enough. He worked like a man possessed, rising early enough each morning to get out to Berkeley between seven and eight, returning home sometimes for dinner and sometimes at midnight only to put in more hours in his study. On several occasions Aunt Mame found him there in the mornings, the student lamp still lit and its gas flame softly hissing while he slept hunched over his desk, his head pillowed on his arm. Strong-willed as she was, Aunt Mame found in Fred a determination that far surpassed hers and while she remonstrated, fearful that he was overtaxing his health, it was with little hope that he would pay heed.

The distance between the Berkeley campus and the house on Filbert Street was something over four miles of mostly open land given over to barley, wheat, and tomatoes. There were two means of transportation—the Telegraph Avenue horsecar, from which one changed to what was then called a steam "dummy," and the spanking new Grove Street electric line. During normal traffic hours the ride took about a half hour. Late at night the trip could consume double that time but that was no deterrent to Cottrell, whose zeal was such that he would sometimes walk the distance. He was known on more than one occasion to leave the house at midnight and make the eight-mile round trip to the laboratory for a temperature reading. Whether this was on foot, by horsecar or electric tram, he never considered it important enough to say.

This freedom to wander at will in and out of laboratories regardless of the hour was the rarest of undergraduate privileges and at that time accorded only one other student, George Louderback, a geology major, who was Cottrell's closest friend in those years. Nor was it an honor bestowed either early or lightly. It came to both in their senior year, although Cottrell was something of a classless student since he telescoped four years of college into three. To signal the occasion at the beginning of the fall term, the head of the College of Chemistry wrote him: "I wish to say to you that I consider your attainments in chemistry and your faithful devotion to the science worthy of some special recognition. I have accordingly, with the consent of the President of the University, designated you assistant to the professor of chemistry. While this is merely a name and carries with it few duties and few privileges, nevertheless it is meant to be an honorable title and is only given after mature deliberation. I shall be able to give you certain privileges in the laboratory which otherwise would hardly be possible."

This warming thought was soon followed by the official appointment from the secretary of the university. Cottrell and Louderback, who had been similarly notified, became the university's first Honorary (or salaryless) Student Assistants.

By an old collegiate custom, the student markedly devoted to his work has been set aside from his fellows by a name. In the patois of the undergraduate, the epithet employed has varied with the years and the locality but whenever the time and wherever the place, its descriptive brevity has never carried the same connotations as "Honorary Student Assistant." To better convey a broad flavor of opprobrium the long list of such terms has included "grind" and the even less delicate "greaseball." On the California campus before the turn of the century, the word was "dig."

By unanimous consent, Fred Cottrell was no ordinary dig, and his variations from the dig norm were such that it is doubtful whether he even merited the term at all. Just as a Don Juan could be forgiven his indiscretions because of the presumed overwhelming depth of his passions, so the obvious magnitude of Cottrell's fervor for science transcended ordinary titular cant. Even to some dullards it was apparent that here was a fellow whose interest was so wholehearted that it precluded selfishness. It was apparent because, despite the fact that he carried a heavily burdensome schedule, there was about him a disarming and winning anxiousness to help everyone else. It was a trait rendered the more remarkable by its sincerity. It sprang from no conscious eagerness to please, sired by uncertainty, but seemed rather to be born of an innate desire to give of himself, selflessly, wherever and whenever possible. It was an unpatronizing characteristic, unaffected and effortless, so striking that it remained for decades as a dominant impression in the minds of hundreds who knew him.

To many of the undergraduates he became known as "Cot" and to a half dozen on a more familiar level he was "Cottsy." But whether Cot, Cottsy, or Cottrell, it was to him that a student could turn if he wanted an idea on how to demonstrate why a salamander surfaced for air; by consulting him the less diligent could immediately have for the asking an obscure chemical formula; and even full professors were unhesitant in making use of his remarkable manual dexterity to improvise apparatus. When he gave, it was an outright gift quickly forgotten and for which he asked no credit. Of such stuff were the strands of confidence woven in both his ability and his integrity, and in the science departments of the university the phrase "Ask Cot" became almost a byword.

Among the few men on the faculty of whom the early university could boast were the brothers Le Conte, John and Joseph. Joseph's son, who came to be known as "Little Joe," followed his father to a place on the faculty, although he forsook the paternal interest in geology in favor of mechanical engineering. The fluidity with which the Cottrell personality seeped into all university work bordering even remotely on the scientific brought him inevitably in touch with the instructor, Little Joe. It was not a relationship that struck off great sparks but was chiefly notable because of the latter's ability to recall in detail some of the flair that gave Cottrell his peculiar (later to be dubbed "free-wheeling") laboratory style.

If there was one thing of which one could be certain in approaching Cottrell with a problem, it was that his answers or suggestions would have a distinctly original touch. His chronic lack of patience seldom allowed him time to search scientific literature to see what others had done. Instead, presented with a set of conditions, he relied largely on his intuitive acumen for possible conclusions. In somewhat the same way—if he thought of it at all—he held "catalogue engineering" in light contempt. Possibly in this he was in tune with his times, when it simply didn't occur to a good housewife to go out and buy bakery bread—a product markedly inferior to her own. Cottrell, the dexterous technician, when in need of a motor or just any piece of apparatus, more often than not ignored the catalogue even when funds were available. From it, it was true, one could order a conventional piece of equipment with a standard degree of efficiency. That, however, was scarcely the stuff of which pioneers were made. Why not, he could and did ask himself, strike out afresh with two good hands, the available material, and, unfettered by preconception, produce something even better—or, in the process, something altogether and excitingly different?

It was in the course of an experiment with Le Conte that Cottrell brought out the wonderful clarity and simplicity of this concept to Little Joe. They needed an oscillograph and the latter suggested trying to buy a good one then on the market.

"Let's make one," said Cottrell the student to Le Conte the instructor.

To Cottrell this represented a neatly effective solution about which little more need be said, but when Le Conte pressed him for suggestive details he elaborated by adding: "Why, you make the magnet and I'll make the mirror."

To get any kind of accurate measurement from a homemade oscillograph it is a prime requisite that both these integral parts be small and light. Cottrell began production of the mirror by silvering a thin piece of glass from a microscope cover. Then with a glass cutter he made two parallel cuts, a millimeter apart, and two of the same width at right angles to these. The tiny center was his mirror. This was set in the middle of Le Conte's minute magnet made out of soft iron. With this promising beginning, Cottrell next suggested they suspend the magnet and mirror on quartz. A fiber was drawn out from a piece of hot quartz melted over a carbon arc, which required a certain nimbleness, although Le Conte overlooked the effect of a carbon arc on unprotected eyes and came close to damaging his eyesight permanently. The experimenters, however, continued. The whole was then mounted under tension with hard rubber prongs and surrounded with a coil to create a magnetic field. In front of this, light from an arc lamp could enter through a long, thin slot, be reflected on the mirror, and shot out again. A final touch was the attachment of a photographic plate to trace the curve. It was, Le Conte remembered, a thoroughly satisfying job. How it compared with the illustrated catalogue specimen was unimportant. By their own ingenuity they had provided themselves with an adequate tool for their specific need.

While Le Conte and Cottrell fiddled with their oscillograph a physicist in Germany by the name of Röntgen discovered an amazing thing. Radiation from a vacuum tube, which he had covered with a black and opaque material, was causing a screen (prepared with chemicals and accidently lying near by) to glow. It was a puzzling as well as pulse-quickening reaction and it was eventually reported in the far-off San Francisco newspapers that this X ray of Röntgen's could pierce materials ordinarily thought impervious to light and even reveal bones through the flesh. This sensational news set aquiver the scientific laboratories, of Berkeley as it did those all over the world.

With the newspapers as their sole reference, Le Conte and Professor Clarence Cory, who headed the university's electrical engineering department, decided to duplicate the reported experiments. Afterward—neither of them could remember just how it happened—it seemed to both that their decision had scarcely been made when the scientifically ubiquitous Cottrell joined them in the venture. It was not that he thrust himself upon them or that he was in any sense unwelcome; it was, to them, an example of Cottrell's sense being attuned with infinite delicacy to anything of interest going on.

As reported in the papers, the most essential item for the X-ray experiment was an electric vacuum tube. Happily Cottrell knew exactly where to lay his hand on an old one which the physics department had acquired when the cathode ray was discovered in

England a decade earlier. It was a tube between eight and nine inches long and less than half that in diameter. The necessary high voltage was supplied by a 15,000-volt transformer making an interrupted current and which, after some homemade improvisations, was connected to each end of the tube. Underneath the latter was set a photographic plateholder on top of which were some nails in upright position. With the current on, the tube gave off a bluish flame, and by experimenting with the shadows cast by the nails, the amateur röntgenologists could tell from which electrode the X rays were coming. Once everything was working, the photographic plate dimly showed the shape of coins in a purse as well as the skeletal outline of the hands.

Secondhand though this was, it was nevertheless a thrilling demonstration of one of the nineteenth century's more important discoveries. Shortly after it had been put in working order, the son of a professor of electrical engineering was accidentally shot while at play, a .22-caliber bullet lodging itself in the fleshy part of his upper arm. The professor had heard of the activities of Le Conte, Cory, and Cottrell. Presumably his scientific curiosity had the upper hand and overrode any paternal apprehensions, for he asked them if this new device could locate the bullet. The fact that the three readily agreed is more than adequate indication that the nature of the X rays was only imperfectly perceived, and that they could inflict a dangerous burn was understood not at all. At any rate the lad was brought to the laboratory early one evening and the tube was set aglow. As a subject he proved unwilling and fractious, which in retrospect seems completely understandable. The operators, however, had an answer to that. Since they were in a laboratory they had access to ether, administering a light enough anesthetic to induce what they felt was only a reasonably co-operative attitude. After all, not every boy had such an opportunity. Once the patient, or subject, or client, was quieted, the apparatus was restarted and a photographic plate placed under his arm. In order to make certain that the exposure would prove effective it was continued for forty-five minutes. Nothing showed up. Since successful experimentation is often a matter of simple patience it was tried again, although how long the boy remained in his etherial state is not known. This time the experimenters practiced forbearance for a full hour and then, to eliminate any possibility of failure, another fifteen minutes beyond that. This time X rays triumphed and the hazy form of the bullet showed itself.

With the success of this experiment Cottrell's interest in X-ray application lay dormant for several years. In the meantime he graduated from the university with the class of '96, although he had entered with the class of '97. His scholastic stature at this time was such that he was awarded the prized Le Conte Fellowship (named for the father and uncle of his X-ray collaborator) and went on to a year of distinguished graduate work. He was again appointed Le Conte Fellow for the year 1897–98 but resigned it to become teacher of chemistry, at about $1200 a year, at Oakland High—a move dictated by economic considerations since his ambitions for further study reached out beyond the boundaries of California. Even this full-time position, however, failed to absorb all his energies, and he continued his contact with the university as a paid graduate assistant in electrochemistry, spending most of his week ends in the Berkeley laboratories. Whatever the title under which he functioned, those who were in touch with his work at the time report that his prestige was so great that he carried on with all the authority of a full professor. He had just turned twenty-one.

Oakland, at that time, put on an industrial exhibition which ran for several weeks in a large downtown building. It was in connection with this, probably about 1899, that Cottrell's interest in X rays was fanned into activity, this time in conjunction with two undergraduates in electrical engineering, Ralph Lohman and Ernest Dyer. Cottrell, Lohman, and Dyer felt that, in addition to the possibility of their earning some ready cash, the public was entitled to know its bone structure more intimately. In order to satisfy both these wants they contracted for a booth at the exposition. With the help of a San Francisco glass blower they produced an X-ray tube of modernized design costing in the neighborhood of seventy-five dollars. They built their own transformer, sometimes working over it entire nights through in order to meet the exposition's opening date. They built, although not without incident, a fluoroscope approximately eight by twelve inches, coated with calcium tungstate which became luminescent on contact with the X rays. In an effort to save time they tried to buy the tungstate ready-made but found not a single gram available in the entire San Francisco Bay area. To Cottrell the chemist fell the chore of producing some on the coal range in the Lohman's kitchen. Amidst feverish excitement, and under the eyes of Lohman and Dyer, he succeeded. In the ferment of the moment they looked impatiently for anything that could serve temporarily as a screen. So anxious were they to test the success of their efforts that they fastened on the first thing immediately available, which was Cottrell's derby hat. On the black surface of this they smeared the calcium tungstate, then dashed to the stable. Each of them had just enough time, after placing the hat under the X-ray tube, for a quick glance at his hand before the derby went up in flames.

In spite of this, they opened their exhibit on schedule and, with a ten-cent admission, handled a customer a minute. An improved screen was substituted for the derby hat and was housed in a light-tight box on top of which were two openings for the curious to peer through. Under this was space where the hand could be inserted and below this the X-ray tube which cast the shadows on the fluorescent screen. The device won instant popularity, and in order to keep the waiting customers amused they were allowed to first file past another curiosity of the day—an unattached tube which glowed without benefit of any apparent electrical connections. It was a gas-filled tube operating in an electrostatic field supplied by a Tesla coil and, like Japanese acrobats on a vaudeville bill, it served as a warming opener to the main X-ray act. Only one thing detracted from the smash-hit status of the latter. The next-door exhibit was put on by an Oakland ironworks and included an ammonia refrigerating machine which was somewhat less than worthy of public demonstration. Its flaws were such that at various times the escaping ammonia fumes seeped over into the X-ray booth, discomfiting the customers to such an extent that there was no choice except a refund of the ten-cent admission charge and an impatient wait for the air to clear.

Despite the fact that several years had elapsed since their discovery, X rays were still something of a mystery and if their potency was at all understood it was certainly not in the environs of Oakland. This almost resulted in placing a serious responsibility on the Cottrell-Lohman-Dyer partnership. In the same exhibition was a glass blower, a singularly gifted man who, as a tour de force, occasionally wrested gasps of startled awe from his audience by munching the more appetizing parts of his own products. Two skeptical Oakland doctors approached the proprietors of the X-ray exhibit and suggested that they examine the glass blower's stomach. In addition to being intestinally favored with the ability to tolerate sizable pieces of glass, this gentleman understood the law of supply and demand well enough to ask twenty dollars for the examination. The two doctors agreed to pay. When the exhibition closed, Cottrell, Lohman, and Dyer strapped an eighteen-by-twenty-inch screen to the glassblower's back and gave him an hour-and-a-half exposure. To the satisfaction of the doctors pieces of glass lamp chimney showed up somewhere along his alimentary canal. With this the examination ended.

Some weeks later each of the three X-ray technicians received a call from a lawyer who claimed that his client, the glass blower, was dangerously ill as a result of the investigation and threatened suit. All three, as Lohman recalled it, were concerned and thoroughly scared. They in turn consulted *their* clients, the two doctors, who accepted responsibility and committed the man to a hospital for treatment for burns. Whatever eventually happened to the patient is not known, but in return for medical attention and additional money he agreed to sign a release and the proposed suit was dropped. It was enough to discourage further experimentation in the field, although Cottrell did try seriously to interest a medically-minded friend at the university to make a study of the pathology of this new and unknown type of burn. Eventually, however, interest in the matter dwindled and the X-ray equipment was disposed of—the tube sold to one of the doctors who had underwritten the case, the transformer to Cornell University.

While Cottrell's brilliance as an original thinker and student was for the most part generally conceded, there were those, even among the faculty of the College of Chemistry of the university, who despaired of his method of applying himself. In the words of one professor, he "danced around all over the lot." When word of this got back to Cottrell he remarked without rancor to a friend, "You know, I think my dancing around may help to synthesize science." The extraordinary scope of his interests was, it is true, difficult for the pedestrian-minded to grasp. It did, on the surface, smack of superficiality and it is probably true that in some instances such criticisms were justified. But they were weaknesses and criticisms of which Cottrell was fully aware all during his life and which he recognized with complete acceptance as being as much a part of himself as his brown eyes or his urge to talk.

There was also some dissent among his students in Oakland High School regarding his abilities as a teacher. For those who could follow him he was a source of inspiration. There were, on the other hand, those who felt that his confidence in the capacity of the teenage mind to absorb even the elements of physics and chemistry leaned too heavily on the side of optimism. Still others report that by sheer enthusiasm for his subject he could make it interesting, and actually did raise the laboratory to a level of interest on a par with the baseball diamond even for boys prone to view the former with distaste. (According to one student, a girl, he "replaced patty-cake nonsense with the ardor of chemistry, so that even the most unscientific pupils sensed the difference.") Whatever the opinions held by his students, his approach to teaching had original touches. One of these was to place as little emphasis as possible on a strictly textbook diet, but whenever possible to awaken young interests through visits to chemical manufactories and industrial plants where applied chemistry was at work. He also encouraged the more talented to strike out on their own in however tentative a fashion and in this he must have felt he met with some success, for a former college friend wrote him: "It is gratifying to find that you have found such a good opinion of the capacity of your high school students, for I have so often thought the poor results so often shown in their work are more the cause of the teacher than of the pupils. Perhaps you will be giving a piece of original work yourself in pedagogy by demonstrating that original work can be done in high school."

In 1898, in his second year of high school teaching, Cottrell sniffed the scholastic air and scented danger. While he had not yet made up his mind just where abroad he planned to study, or even when his resources would enable him to go, he began to feel that the means were becoming confused with the end and his advanced work, conducted mainly over week ends at the university, was suffering. He felt he was settling much too readily into a teaching routine and found "the correcting of notebooks and examination papers quite on a par with cooking and housekeeping as far as trying one's patience" went.

To counteract this he threw himself with new resolution and zest into his postgraduate work on the heat of solution of liquid hydriodic acid and the solubility of manganous sulphate. Papers on both were published in the *Journal of Physical Chemistry,* then edited by Wilder Bancroft at Cornell University. In connection with these he entered into a voluminous and highly technical correspondence with Bancroft, who on one or two occasions had reasons to question Cottrell's findings. The letters shuttled back and forth, each making its points, but it was a field in which Cottrell could well hold his own, for finally, after one particular flurry, Bancroft wrote, "The sum total of this is that I am all wrong and you are all right."

In his work on manganous sulphate (which paper is credited by some as being the first really good one on the subject) the unorthodoxy of Cottrell's laboratory methods arched many an eyebrow on the Berkeley campus. In a general way the experiment involved solids placed in water, sealed up, and observed under a variety of temperatures. Control of the temperature usually necessitated the use of a thermostat, but for one phase of it Cottrell found what he believed to be an eminently satisfactory technique. Those who knew him readily understood that what he did was in no sense exhibitionism and that in all probability he was completely unaware of cutting any sort of ridiculous figure. At any rate he packed his apparatus in an improvised knapsack, insulating it in some manner on the outside. This he strapped to his back, the solution involved being nestled as closely to him as possible, and carried it around with him for several days, papoose fashion, so that it remained at constant body heat. Unfortunately there is no record of how he handled this part of the experiment during the few hours' sleep he felt constrained to allow himself most nights.

In a further effort to negate the "settling in" process of high school teaching Cottrell applied for and received permission to attend—as a special student—the Lick Observatory on Mount Hamilton, near San Jose, during the summer of 1898. This was in itself a small tribute, since observatories were regarded as essentially the province of bona fide astronomers, and dilatory graduate students were looked on as meddling nuisances. It was true that Cottrell came well recommended from the university. He had taken four astronomy courses in his third undergraduate year, receiving the highest grade in each of the four. He had impressed Professor A. O. Leuschner, director of the university observatory, as "brilliant and untiring," and had gone so far as to make an actual pioneering contribution to the department's observatory technique. Although visual spectroscopy was in use at the time (that is, a spectroscope was attached to the university's six-inch telescope), it had not, until Cottrell suggested and devised a means of doing so, occurred to anyone there to attach a camera to the spectroscope in order to interpret accurately the findings from a permanent photographic record. It was, Leuschner remembered, one of those intuitive ideas that came to Cottrell quite as a matter of course, and it was put into immediate practice without either consulting any literature on the subject or bothering to publish anything on it. Leuschner did in fact try to lure Cottrell away from physics and chemistry into stargazing, although without effect. Since in the pursuit of chemistry he reserved only a negligible portion of the night for sleep it is hard to conceive—in view of the nocturnal demands of astronomy—when he would ever have gotten any at all if he had decided in its favor as a life's work.

Even though he found that a Sunday in the laboratory was "the most restful way of spending a day that I know," Cottrell's was not entirely a lopsided existence. He still continued his hobby of photography although in a halfhearted fashion, never having achieved his father's finesse with a camera. He took to "tramping" (i.e., hiking) with enthusiasm, and in company with colleagues at the university made numerous trips into the Sierras, particularly Yosemite and King's Canyon. To this he brought the same indefatigability that he gave to the laboratory and was generally rated an excellent hiking companion. He was not able to discard completely the scientific point of view on such outings nor was it always easy to determine the direction his passion for the verities would take. Sometimes he became absorbed in geological formations or, as he did once, spent hours at a waterfall in an attempt to devise accurate means of determining the heat developed by friction through measuring the temperature of the water at the top and bottom of the falls.

Nevertheless, his effervescent geniality was an effective antidote to the ardors of an uphill climb, although his giant strides enabled him to maintain a pace not always popular with short-statured fellow hikers. He was, according to one, "like a mountain goat," but whatever inconvenience he caused in this respect was more than compensated for by his good humor and ingenuity around camp. On one trip he concocted a "Sierra sherbet," mixing the wild strawberries from the lower altitudes with the remaining snows of late spring at the higher levels. These were stirred together with sugar in a thoroughly cleansed lard bucket, sometimes using lemon and sugar to vary the recipe. Another—less popular but probably original—Cottrell creation was a stewed mixture of potatoes, onions, and a doubtful variety of cheese. Its name, "slum duck."

Cottrell was a good social mixer, if not in a country week-end sense, at least good enough to be in demand for turn-of-the-century group activities, although he sometimes seems to have entered into them with a reserved kind of zest. He could, in letters, describe them as having afforded him a "good time" but the feeling is that for the most part it was a good time in a detached way, a dutiful good time, perhaps best described as "jolly," as though one must make concessions to the light touch of social amenities just as one tried to master spelling. In reality, however, anything subtracting from time spent in what he then considered the more stimulating milieu of the laboratory was to be viewed warily. Since he presented an attractive masculine appearance there is no doubt that several young ladies, behind formally worded invitations to picnics and outings, were setting their caps for him, although there is doubt to what degree he recognized this. He shunned dancing wholeheartedly but did seem to take genuine pleasure in mixed campfire groups that would, on moonlight nights, climb 1700-foot Grizzly Peak in the Berkeley Hills directly behind the university. The climb up Grizzly, from which one could view San Francisco Bay in panoramic magnificence, was in fact to remain a favorite form of recreation (he made the hike the subject of a college English theme, aptly describing Alcatraz Island and its relation to the bay as "a miniature Malta in this Western Mediterranean"). To this sight he would return in a sentimental way again and again during later years whenever his travels brought him back to the West Coast.

Something of the spirit of a renaissance touched the university campus in the late nineties, although it was more of a first awakening than a revival. A "college spirit" was manifesting itself in rallies and bonfires; rivalry with Stanford was waxing; and the California football team was coming into its own as a focal point for new-found loyalties and enthusiasms. This fillip was not alone confined to rah-rahism. The financially well-equipped Mrs. Phoebe Apperson Hearst was endowing a building program with resources that stemmed from the Comstock Lode. The intellectuals resented the administration of President Kellogg, who to their mind was "narrow-gauge" and thought in terms of a small college rather than a university. Those who had gone East or abroad for their doctorates wrote back deploring the lack of research at California as well as the caliber of the faculty. One alumnus who had gone on to Johns Hopkins wrote Cottrell with a touch of bitterness, "It is not the most pleasant thing after one has been boasting about our great university out there, to be asked who we have on the faculty. It is always safe to mention Le Conte, but having done this it is always best to change the subject and talk about the weather."

A sounding board for this discontent was the California Union in which Cottrell, under the leadership of his old friend Harry Torrey, with whom he had once boiled and skeletonized a cat, was a moving spirit. For three years, or until its founders scattered in pursuit of higher degrees and its secretary fell in love, this organization served as a forum for those interested in the university's growth and development, striking so responsive a chord on the campus that they were deluged with applications for membership. They made studies of English and continental universities in the hope of adapting foreign methods to relieve California of its provincialism. The aging President Kellogg was resigning and the Union felt it should be heard in the choice of a successor. It did in all have a stimulating and salutary effect on campus thinking and in its brief life hastened the emergence of the university into post-adolescent maturity.

The other group to which Cottrell belonged with singular fitness consisted of a dozen or so students (mostly graduate) who dubbed themselves the "Kickers' Club." Its spirit was the essence of informality and its members each represented a different line in somewhat the same manner as a Rotary Club—Louderback the geologist, Cottrell the chemist, a physiologist, and so on. In addition to airing their grievances, major and minor, the Kickers served one another usefully by reporting the latest developments in the particular field of each. This, to Cottrell, was akin to the very breath of life, an outlet through which he could "dance all over the lot" in a sympathetic atmosphere. It, too, languished after several years and for almost the same reasons that contributed to the demise of the California Union, but it was so completely the environment in which Cottrell functioned harmoniously that he took the initiative in reviving the Kickers on his return from Europe with his Ph.D. several years later.

The Kickers also had their lighter moments in which Cottrell participated with an avidity almost equal to that shown during the club's weightier, or plenary, sessions. Frequently the meetings would be held in an Oakland restaurant whose menu favored sauerbraten, pig's knuckles, and good strong Pilsener. On such occasions the sterner demands of science had a tendency to recede into the background and give way to Good Ones about the drummer in the Pullman car, with college songs as a rousing obbligato. In this, too, Cottrell entered with conviviality of spirit for, regardless of his primary interests, he lacked the instincts of the prude and could adequately command a sizable fund of stories eminently suitable for stag affairs. He was, in those days, rated as a good storyteller of all types, being particularly adept at gestures to which his natural zestful enthusiasm lent authority. His appreciation of the risqué remained fitfully lively throughout his life.

During the three years he taught at Oakland High, Cottrell lived with the family at home in 1019 Filbert Street. It was an atmosphere solidly middle-class American of the period when thick leatherbound volumes rested in massive and undisturbed repose on the parlor's marble-topped tables; long, intricate lace curtains genteelly covered the bay windows; and chairs without antimacassars were seemingly regarded as nude. Suspended from the high ceilings were globed chandeliers, to which electricity was still alien, and the decorative value of large pictures was so highly prized that they not only hung from the walls but were propped up on corner tables around the room, and two—a Yosemite landscape and a religious group—shared an easel to the right of the marble fireplace which itself tolerated the portrait of a large, moodily depressed dog to mask the indelicacy of an unused grate.

It was neither a house nor a household to which comfort was indigenous. It held no warmth nor community of interests but was a staging area of conflict. What cohesion it possessed came from Aunt Mame, but the forces at work were centrifugal and even beyond her masterly efficiency. To it Henry Cottrell returned each evening from his work in San Francisco (as confidential secretary and chief lieutenant to a prominent ship broker) but he retired soon after the evening meal to the seclusion of the lower-floor study which he shared with Fred, and where he read and found escape in his passion for photography.

Harry Cottrell was achieving some local success with his authorship of skits and plays and in addition was playing heavies and character parts in a stock company at Oakland's Dewey Theater (he was the Marquis St. Evrémond in *A Tale of Two Cities* and La Farge in *Trilby*). It was not a calling of which Aunt Mame approved, although she dutifully attended a weekly performance to please Harry. In her thoughts, however, he remained "Poor Harry" and whatever impartiality she tried to maintain completely disappeared in one lament to Fred, when she wrote, "I am so thankful that *you* will not disappoint my desires and ambitions. I hope I will be permitted to see you take your higher degree and well started in your honored life work. I hope you will never be as unhappy as Harry is and I have no fear that you will for you have a cool and level head with sound reason to guide you." To Harry, however, Aunt Mame was still a minor goddess, regardless of her distaste for his professional activities. Because of his dependence on her, as well as for reasons of economy (the stock company paid him twenty dollars a week from which he furnished his own costumes), he remained, along with his bride, an active member in residence of the Filbert Street ménage.

It was Cynthia—the strange, the tempestuous, the impulsive—who industriously wove the pattern of discord in the eyes of the others in the household. Slowly but with a crushing inevitability, some time after the birth of Fred, doors in her own home began to close against her until the day came, with the arrival of Harry's wife, when the cleft was so deep that she could ask her new daughter-in-law, "Which side are you on?" There can be little doubt of her emotional imbalance, yet this must have been accentuated by the gradual ascendancy of her sister Mame in the affections of the children, as well as open recognition of the latter's firm hand in the guidance of household affairs. As she was gradually shut out Cynthia's rebellion took strange turns. There were pouting tantrums and wild rageful scenes. When the mild-mannered Henry would spend an evening playing cribbage with his daughter-in-law while Harry was at the theater, Cynthia would stalk into the room, slam her workbasket on the cribbage board and cards, and break into a tirade because of the conspiracy against her.

And conspiracy there was. Never one with a passionate regard for facts as such, which Fred so highly revered, she would give to the neighbors highly colored and garbled accounts of his accomplishments and activities at the university. Fred reacted with fury and disgust. He would tell her nothing, and if he were away all mail to Aunt Mame was sent to his father's office so that "she" couldn't "cabbage" his letters. Although Aunt Mame in her replies continued to refer to Cynthia as his "Mama," Fred simply relied on the pronoun. Cynthia became "she," or "Mrs. C." Harry was even less polite.

On his return from the summer on Mount Hamilton at the observatory Fred decided on a short vacation trip north of Oakland on which he arranged to take Aunt Mame. All preparations were made in such secrecy that Cynthia knew nothing of it until after their departure when Henry wrote Fred, "I did not say anything until I heard the gate shut that morning you left. Then I told your mother I guess you had prevailed on Auntie to go off with you for a trip. She got up at once, dressed herself and went out, came back in a few moments and wanted to know where you were."

Henry didn't tell, but there are times when the shutting of a gate can be an ominous thing.

Few but the most intimate of the Cottrell acquaintances knew of this family rupture. Some of Fred's fellow students who came to his home were aware of his dislike for his mother although, since he never discussed it, none of them understood. To outsiders her role was that of a charming woman graced with an air of presence and gentility. At home the battle lines were drawn, although in her mind not always sharply. She refused to recognize Fred's rebuffs. He remained her pride of whom she overenthusiastically boasted to relatives and friends. If, when he was away, he failed to write her, which he pointedly failed to do, she chose to ignore the slight but would regularly send him lighthearted and chatty letters, without chiding him for any neglect but expressing herself affectionately in the restrained way of one who wished not to be burdensome. This purblind correspondence continued during Fred's three years of study abroad. He kept the letters unread and unanswered. He never, in the course of his life, even opened them.

Cynthia's one acknowledged accomplishment was the piano. She played it skillfully and with grace, although it seems to be true that, once having achieved a level of proficiency, she confined it to a few pieces which, with repetition, gradually lost their charm for the rest of the family. It was the piano that ultimately shattered what few brittle ties remained between her and Fred. She would play it with headstrong defiance, sometimes in the dead of night. It must have been her challenge, her exultant compensation for the wrongs she felt done her, the affection denied her. She did this late one evening while Fred, still a student at Berkeley, tired and overworked, was preparing for exams. He asked her to stop. Cynthia, lost in her folly, taunted him further with her music. Again he asked her to stop, although now in his tone was a warning. What little self-discipline Cynthia ever could command surged wildly out of bonds in feverish release. Goaded beyond what his overwrought nerves could absorb, Fred lost control and acted. The music came to a painful, stunning halt, for he angrily flipped down the wooden keyboard cover on her still-playing fingers and stalked from the room. Cynthia stopped but it was years before Fred spoke to her again.

Several anticlimaxes followed the episode at the piano, but perhaps the most pathetic was this: both Aunt Mame and her dear friend Miss Horton, who still gloried in the progress of her old pupil, were invited by Fred to attend some function at the university in which he was to take part. It might very possibly have been his graduation exercises, although on this point there is some doubt. By devious means the two ladies kept word that they were attending from Cynthia. If this was not of their own choosing, they certainly did so at Fred's behest. By this time, however, Cynthia was wise in the ways of conspiracy and either guessed at, or was apprised of, their plans. By agreement, Aunt Mame, Miss Horton, and Fred went separately to a stop on the trolley line where they met and boarded the car. The wily Cynthia, by a circuitous route, took herself one stop farther on, where she surprised the trio by joining them with a decorous show of well-poised gaiety. The conductor approached her to collect her fare. Cynthia airily told him that the gentleman would pay. The conductor then turned to Cottrell.

"I never," said the son of Cynthia, "saw the lady before in my life."

The shutting of a gate can indeed be a terrible and final thing.

ITT WAS the June of a new and vastly promising century when Cottrell, at the age of twenty-three, set forth from Oakland bound for Germany, then the very Kaaba of the world of physics and chemistry. It was not a departure notable for dignity. The expressman failed to appear on time so Cottrell and trunk went galloping off to the train in a grocery wagon pressed into emergency service. Miss Horton, to whom he probably still remained a small boy, presented him at the last moment with a gift which he wedged into a pocket already bulging with camera and gloves. "It turned out," he reported back later, "to be some sort of sugar-coated oranges that squeezed out very easily. You can imagine the rest."

The journey had something of the nature of a pilgrimage with Cottrell as its dedicated Galahad. His boyhood had by-passed the stage of wanting to be a locomotive engineer. Organized sports held no interest for him and hence spawned no hero worship of physical prowess. He seems never to have been stricken by any doubts as to his aptitudes. The signs pointing to his ultimate career were unmistakable and he interpreted them accurately. The detour through Oakland High as a teacher was a matter of economic expediency and recognized as such. During this fretful interlude he watched others, one by one, go off to the great universities for further study and so he fought the harder against the "settling in" process.

There had been those of his friends who had succumbed to "Klondikitis," a byword of the day in California when Alaskan gold captured volatile imaginations. The Spanish-American War had come and gone. Cottrell's greatest expression of interest in this seems to have been a ferry trip to San Francisco to watch a fireworks display of the Battle of Manila. His unresponsiveness to such distractions lifted the Quaker heart of Aunt Mame into rejoicing: "I am thankful you have not the war spirit. I am glad your *larger* purpose in life controls you," she wrote him.

No, Aunt Mame rested easily on that June morning of 1900, for in her mind, too, the road ahead was a certain one. She could find comfort in knowing that she herself had packed his bags and trunk, taking full cognizance of the perils of treacherous foreign weather and exotic laundry marks. The ultimate note in reassurance was that he left with a fresh haircut.

What Aunt Mame did not know was that Cottrell had also left with an "understanding" between him and the Jessie May Fulton whom he had first met when both were students in a high school botany class. That early meeting had not been without its impact on young Cottrell. Many years later he told a niece that he was struck with the charming brightness of her appearance and the appeal of her short-cut curls. A vague reference in an early letter hints only at some Cottrell assistance in Jessie May's mastery of the bicycle. Whatever other contacts they had then are not on record, but by the time he was in college Miss Fulton had moved to San Luis Obispo and a punctual weekly exchange of chaste correspondence was passing between "Dear Friend Fred" and "Dear Friend Jess." Cottrell preserved the formal touch by signing himself "Fred G. C."

Jess, by this time, had grown to an attractive young lady with large shy eyes and a tentative smile—a smile made less sure by the fact that her girlhood had not been a happy one. Two years Cot-

trell's senior, she had been born in San Francisco of parents who had
originally come West in the gold rush to California. The spirit of
that adventure seems to have abided with her father throughout
his life. It kept the Fulton family in unstable financial condition
through his disheartening penchant for investing in dubious gold-
mining stocks and on his death left Mrs. Fulton and the dependent
Jess close to stranding in a fiscal low tide. Neither Jess's older sister
Frances, an elocutionist, nor her married brother Wallace, who was
rearing a family, were able to be of much help. Jess's inheritance,
therefore, somewhat a result of this unhappy economy, was a complex sense of insecurity reaching neurotic proportions—feelings
which her precarious health did little to alleviate. Indeed, her complete vulnerability may well have been part of her attraction for
young Cottrell, himself possessed of an optimism often so abundant
it must necessarily be shared. He was seldom able to take a deep
interest in either people or causes burdened with an aura of "normalcy" and success. A problem, on the other hand, exerted an endless fascination.

Jess wrote to Cottrell of her "uncertainty" and of her "battle with
doubt," telling him "it is something that has hung over me all my
life. From my earliest memory that feeling of no sure place to put
one's foot has followed me. There was an event that happened when
I was eight years old that stamped that fear upon my life. How I
hated the first of the month and the time for settlement, the anxiety
on my mother's face. They, mother and sister, used to try and hide it
from me, but I knew instinctively."

No knight-errant ever responded more quickly to distress than
Cottrell. He encouraged Jess to confide in him whenever she felt disturbed or discouraged. He put their relationship on a comradely
basis, then went one step further to foster the idea of their kinship
by adding, "Besides, what's the good of having a brother if you can't
make use of him in such a way?"

They were staunch shoulders, twenty-odd years in the broadening,
on which Jess leaned for comfort. On them she laid her timidity and
dejection, which sprang in part from the limitations of delicate
health. Her frailties robbed her of the energy necessary for the writing she hoped to do (a poem had been printed in the *Pacific Church-
man*), discouraged her from becoming a nurse during the Spanish-
American War, and rendered it inadvisable to continue her education

further than high school except as a special student. These frustrations she poured out to Cottrell in what they mutually referred to as "blue" letters. His ready sympathy answered with cheerful encouragement. She must make an effort, he told her, to get out in the sun and fresh air, to seek out more people and, above all, to learn to laugh.

"Sometimes when I'm feeling particularly out of sorts," he wrote, "and everything is going the wrong way or, on the other hand, when I've just got an ordinary periodic attack of the blues, I've just quietly got away by myself, well out of range of any possible interference of the lunacy commission, and started in to have a real good laugh—not at anything in particular but just abstractly. The very absurdity of the whole proposition soon supplies plenty of food for such merriment. To add to the force of the situation, you can sit in front of a mirror if you choose and laugh at yourself, baboon-fashion, and then the tendency is simply irresistible."

But Jess objected and in his next letter Cottrell admitted that perhaps in the light of her "nervousness" his prescription was a mite excessive. "Suppose," he counseled this time, "you cut down the dose to one or two minutes and repeat it oftener, say three times a day, just before meals as an appetizer." It cannot be said that Jess grasped the essence of such therapy.

The understanding between Jess and Cottrell (it could not be called a binding engagement) dated from a November Sunday afternoon in 1897. Cottrell was then teaching in Oakland High School and they had gone walking in the Berkeley Hills. As the shadows lengthened in the late afternoon sun a closeness of spirit enveloped them and Cottrell declared his love. Before Jess had time to bathe in the warming tenderness of this devotion he dismayed her by quickly adding, "But my work comes first."

With perfect male assurance that he was wholly understood, Cottrell went on to tell her of his plans and that it might take twenty years to reach his goal, while Jess thought with a tinge of bitterness, "Where will I be all that time?" And then another thought came to her: what right had she to ask such a question? To this, "No right" was the only answer she could find.

She fell silent then but all these thoughts she wrote him later in an attempt to resolve the conflict she found between his love and his work. At the time he left Oakland for Germany, however, this was their bond, their tacit tie—at some point, the misty future would be theirs for the sharing.

2

The trip East was Cottrell's first zestful step outside of California. Now the whole new and exciting world lay before him and he reacted with the gustful relish of a Lent-starved schoolboy tasting Easter sweets. He visited the University of Chicago, Cornell, Harvard, Massachusetts Institute of Technology, Yale, Columbia, Pennsylvania, Johns Hopkins, and the Smithsonian Institution, appraising the facilities and critically surveying the type of work done at each, deciding for himself where the spirit of research was progressive (Chicago) and where hidebound (Columbia). While Niagara's cynosure held much interest for him, including a trip on the *Maid of the Mist* and an inspection of the Cave of the Winds, they competed with an electroplating works, a paper mill, and power plants.

By the time he reached New York the unflagging pace had cost him fourteen pounds and the adjustment to the heat of the Eastern seaboard, of which he complained, caused an almost perceptible slackening of his eagerness to crowd one new experience on another. But later in Baltimore, which he declared to be the worst apology for a city he had yet seen, he was able to take a different view of the hot weather. He found he could like it because of the way it could "bring out the women in light dresses and without their hats. It makes them look very bright and cheerful."

At the end of June, Cottrell sailed from Baltimore on the *Waesland,* a small one-class German steamer of sparse luxury that ungallantly nosed a bosomy female figurehead, still attached to her clipper bow, into the seas before her. He embarked—an imposing young man of twenty-three—flexibly blended of firm convictions and open-mindedness. The convictions were of himself and what he must do; his receptivity and open-mindedness an invitation to knowledge not only of and for itself but as an indispensable tool as well—an intellectual bulldozer, as it were, which he could construct and make his own, to utilize in pushing back, as far as possible in his lifetime, the frontiers of science and technology.

This was the goal. Yet, desirable as it was, it was still not the most important tenet of his credo, as he once explained to Jess while still a graduate student at the university. "It's all right to work *toward* an end, but the people who work *for* an end only, miss most of the good of the way points. I am coming to feel more and more, as concerns us individually, results are only secondary and the ways and means to those results, with all that pertains to them, are really our own greatest reward and benefit. The ends are for others; the ways to them, for ourselves."

Again, somewhere about that time, he had reached the decision that his principal instrument for the achievement of these ends would be physical chemistry—an uncharted field which, newer than either physics or chemistry, frequently overlapped both. In America the broadest leaves on this branch of science were being unfolded almost imperceptibly in the pale light cast by an astrally aloof and hermitlike figure at Yale—Willard Gibbs—but he and his work were only beginning to be recognized. As yet no American universities could compete with the beckoning brilliance of the English and continental laboratories.

It was in many ways expressive of Cottrell's thinking that he chose this newer branch of science where the deeps had all to be plumbed, where relationships between separate fields had yet to be defined and integrated, and where the merging factors in contiguous areas held, for him, the greatest promise of discovery. This same tendency was later to be manifested in his constant attempts to achieve a kind of synthesis of the social sciences with technological advances where, again, it was a reaching for a unity, and for an adaptation of principles to apparently divergent fields. Perhaps the only clear reference to this he ever made in writing appeared in an undated, roughly penciled memorandum which he entitled *Random Notes on the Salvaging of Ideas and Personalities:* "Very possibly the fact that I grew up in the still pioneer atmosphere of the far west, unconsciously predisposed my natural interest and impulses into the borderline and less formally recognized fields of study and research. This soon forced upon my attention the relative lack of organization and support for just such work, for the larger and stronger an educational or research institution grows, the more conservative and rigidly classified its activities are pretty sure to become.

"The most fertile fields for really new fundamental developments are almost always to be found in between the edges of the orthodox ologies and professorships of the colleges (subjects recognized in our standard classifications of human knowledge). No one has had more striking proof of this in a single generation than the chemist in his own field. One needs but to cite the advent and recognition as new separate subjects, physical chemistry, electrochemistry, colloid and capillary (or surface) chemistry, to say nothing of the quantum theory and nuclear structure whether we consider the last as really chemistry or physics.

"Just as the prospector finds his best hunting grounds along the fissures and contact planes between different massive formations, so in the line of human thought and invention . . ."

Here the random notes ended.

3

It was as an untrammeled prospector from the raw American West that Cottrell strode the decks of the *Waesland,* made friends with the numerous other students aboard, and in his easily approachable manner joined in the sundry activities of shipboard life. This participation was not, however, unqualified. There was evidently something about him, an aura as marked as a clerical collar which clung to him and led people—on ships or trains or in hotels—to believe that he was of a strong religious turn. Since religion was a subject he left undiscussed, such could never have been inferred from his conversation.

The first night out on the *Waesland* a young Congregational clergyman began arranging services for the following day, a Sunday. He immediately saw in Cottrell (whose friends unanimously rated him as inept at carrying a tune) the man to lead the singing. Cottrell gently declined. The minister next asked him to lead in prayer. Cottrell guessed that all hands would feel closer to God if someone else were selected. The next day, after canvassing opinions on Cottrell's personality and habits among the other passengers, the young cleric tried to argue Cottrell into a stand on science versus religion. "I didn't bite," he wrote Jess, "so now we are the best of friends."

Jess's parting gift had been the Bible, which he promised he would read systematically. He did make the effort, but since he had once remarked, tongue in cheek, to a fellow student back in Berkeley that his only religion was "a Smith and Wesson .45," it is understandable why, for one who ordinarily read quickly, his progress was labored and slow. Once on board, however, he did find time to cultivate the acquaintance of a Boston nurse with whom he would promenade in privacy on the windward side of the deck, while the other passengers sought shelter. The artless Cottrell promptly wrote Jess that the nurse was "a very jolly little girl and we have a lot of fun together, much to the edification, I imagine, of the other passengers." Then as an afterthought, and by way of complete reassurance, the little girl aged with amazing rapidity and became "old enough to be pretty safe, however, so don't be alarmed." When he continued the acquaintance in London and Paris, informing Jess with his usual openness of every move, she was far from completely reassured. It was the first and very likely the only time she need have misgivings on the subject of other women, and when she expressed her apprehension Cottrell came close to a tone of righteous male indignation. "Really," he replied, "I think I find less temptation than perhaps you expect. And aside from this, I think you really know me well enough, if you stop to think, to quiet such fears."

This time Jess was convinced.

The *Waesland* landed Cottrell at Liverpool, which he circled briefly in sight-seeing, then with the unerring directness of a homing pigeon he wheeled and headed straight for Cambridge and the Cavendish Laboratory. There J. J. Thomson, who had taken up X rays and determination of the mass of the electron where Röntgen left off, greeted him cordially and assured him that he would be welcome to use the laboratories as a guest when he chose. It was Cottrell's first contact with one of the great names of science (Thomson had yet to be knighted), and while he undoubtedly found it stimulating, there was nothing in his letters back home to indicate that he was otherwise impressed. Whether out of courtesy or because he saw something of interest in this young man, Thomson invited Cottrell to dinner at Trinity College. Cottrell demurred on the grounds that his travel-stained clothing was not up to such elegance. When Thomson assured him that it was all very informal and that "morning dress would be quite the proper thing" Cottrell hurried off for a bottle of benzine, sponged his trousers, invested in a new pair of shirt cuffs, and enjoyed the meal.

While Germany remained the promised land, it had been Cottrell's intention on leaving Oakland to spend a brief novitiate at Bordeaux.

His plan, therefore, after visiting England, was to settle for a while in some economical corner of Paris and refurbish his French. "I don't want to appear too green when I strike [Bordeaux]," he told Jess, "because first impressions often go a good way." The path of the prospector, however, is anything but direct. There was Oxford to see ("crumbling away in quite a picturesque manner"). Then came London with its wondrous new electric underground (he counted 76 steps from the street to the platform level) and the London Monument (308 steps to a good view of the city). It was London at the end of an era with Victoria in the last year of her long reign— London of the Crystal Palace and of the grazing sheep in Hyde Park. He dutifully inspected all these conventional sights. But Cottrell's London included more—the old lecture rooms of Faraday and Davy at the Royal Institution along with relics of Tyndall and Cavendish; University College where he met his second scientific immortal—William Ramsay, with whom he had "a very pleasant visit" and where he saw Ramsay's work on liquid air as well as the new gases he had just separated from the air. Coincidentally, while it was Ramsay who succeeded in isolating helium from the atmosphere, it was Cottrell who, during World War I and just shortly after Ramsay's death, was to play an important role in America's significant contribution to the commercial production of helium.

Then came Paris. In order to convert Oakland French into Parisian he engaged a tutor. He even went so far as to become a member of the International Congress of Commercial and Economic Geography, attending their meetings to accustom his ears and tongue to Gallic sounds but the more he learned, the greater the number who failed to understand him. This discouraging discovery was accented by his talent for attracting everyone from lost Italians in search of directions to small children in the Jardin des Plantes asking the time—situations with which he struggled heroically but which all too often ended in defeat. After two earnest weeks in Paris the liquid language still congealed on his reluctant tongue.

Grudgingly he decided that he was never meant to be a linguist and the term he had planned at Bordeaux had better be abandoned. Besides—and there is room for belief that a certain amount of rationalization may have entered here—he came to the realization that "the style of the people and their institutions" might render a winter at Bordeaux dubiously profitable. In mid-August, therefore, he wrote van't Hoff in Berlin for permission to attend his laboratory the coming semester.

This partial retreat did not, however, prevent him from enjoying Paris and its Universal International Exposition, dominated by the Eiffel Tower. He went about sight-seeing, as in London, in a thorough and systematic manner. He observed student night life in the Boulevard St. Martin from a cautious distance and found it no more hectic than Berkeley football rallies. He pleased Jess by finishing Genesis, and his brother Harry by mailing back illustrated magazines that were as lewd as a wink and as daring as the cancan. Somehow these fell into Aunt Mame's hands and, since in her eyes Cottrell could do no wrong, she did not reprove him but thought them unsafe for the mails. "The French," she observed, "are so broad and take too much license in their publications." Aunt Mame had, in fact, begun to show distinct symptoms of Francophobia from the first moment Cottrell raised signals of distress with the language—a shame for which she was quite ready to call the entire French nation to account. "Are the American students," she asked indignantly, "expected to be more proficient in French, than the *French* are in the American language when they come to our country?"

After a month of Paris, Cottrell became surfeited of sight-seeing, wearied of the bedbugs that forced him from one hotel room, and of the "sporting-life crowd" which harassed his sleep in another. Even though van't Hoff had accepted him as a student in Berlin, the term would not start until the end of September and the feeling of time-wasting as well as the urge to "talk shop with someone" made Cottrell impatient. He hadn't, he wrote to Jess, realized how thoroughly a part of himself such a small thing as shoptalk had become and he was eager to surrender whatever charms he found in Paris for the atmosphere of the laboratory.

To fill in the time, as well as to see something of the country, he left Paris for South Germany early in September. Partly by train and partly afoot, he wandered down to Oberammergau to witness the Passion Play ("hard work to sit and listen so long on wooden seats"); then set his course for Berlin with a stopover in Leipzig for an inspection of Ostwald's laboratory, the fame of which, among physical chemists of the time, surpassed even that of van't Hoff's workshop. Perhaps Cottrell's most important discovery was that his study of German—which had been emphasized at the expense of

French throughout the years at Miss Horton's, as well as at high
school and the university—had equipped him adequately so that his
anguished wrestlings with this second strange tongue were somewhat alleviated.

Eager as Cottrell was to conquer scientific Berlin, he found the
veteran strategist, Aunt Mame, had already infiltrated that capital
of an ominously expanding German Empire. Armed by a copy of
In and About Berlin, by a Minerva Brace Norton, she timed a letter
to coincide with his arrival and in this gave a full and uncompromising picture of the city historically, politically, and meteorologically.
"There is so much to glean there," she promised him, "only don't
take to pipes and beer. Coffee and beer will soon upset your stomach
and dull your brain for study and work, for you are not German
and 'to the manner born.' It will seem strange to be in a city under
'court rule' where the soldiers are in evidence at all times in the
streets and everything is 'by order of the king.' You will need have
your passport in your pocket all the time, I reckon, keeping your
eyes and ears open and lips closed. They are so suspicious in these
times of foreigners." He would also need to keep an umbrella constantly at hand. There were, she pointed out, the fall rains.

Cottrell settled into a furnished room midway between the
suburbs of Charlottenburg and Wilmersdorf, the latter housing
van't Hoff's laboratory. He considered it a pleasant little room, with
its porcelain stove, iron bedstead, and boldly flowered wallpaper.
The touches he added were few—an American flag over the door
and photographs of family, friends, and the California campus
wedged in between glass and frame of the high, arched dressing-
table mirror. Twenty-two marks a month (about $5.25) covered
the rent and morning cocoa or coffee. For an additional mark and
a half all hell broke loose: rolls were added to the cocoa, the cocoa
was made with milk instead of water, his shoes were polished, his
clothes brushed and pressed. Cottrell elected the de luxe service.

The laboratory of Jacob Henry van't Hoff, although nominally
a part of the University of Berlin, was actually more in the nature
of a private laboratory. Born in Rotterdam, van't Hoff had accepted
the Berlin post the year of Cottrell's graduation at Berkeley, being
placed in a special and honorary category that exempted him from
the necessity of routine teaching. In 1900, at the height of his fame as
the most gifted of the world's physical chemists, he was in his late

forties, graying, yet youthfully fresh of manner, and still one year away from the Nobel Prize with the $50,000 it would bring him.

At Berlin, van't Hoff was engaged in the fourth and final phase of his lifework—investigation of the enormously valuable salt deposits at Stassfurt, Germany—deposits whose full potentialities were still unrealized. In the investigation of this he was the first to apply the theories of physical chemistry (and in particular the obscure Phase Rule of Willard Gibbs of Yale) to geological phenomena.

The laboratory itself, removed from the university, which was nearer the center of Berlin, was comparatively small and occupied the ground floor of an apartment building that was pleasantly fronted by a garden. Its few disciples were a carefully picked and polyglot mixture consisting of a Hungarian, an Austrian, an Italian, an Englishman, a German, and Cottrell. All worked on some phase of the Stassfurt salts problem, if not under the eye of the maestro himself, then under the supervision of Meyerhoffer, his brilliant lieutenant. Regarding a second assistant named Basch, Cottrell delivered himself of one of the few damning judgments he ever uttered. Basch was, he wrote Jess, a "consummate blockhead."

The routine of the laboratory was elastic. While it officially opened at nine o'clock and closed at seven o'clock, the spirit was one of laissez faire. This very mastery of one's own time was, Cottrell thought, one of the reasons Germans were so successful at turning out such a great volume of research work. The university lectures, in Berlin proper, began in the late afternoon with the majority of them scheduled between five o'clock and seven. To this schedule Cottrell added a physics colloquium—a small group of professors and advanced students who met once a week in the evening for informal discussions.

By early October, Cottrell could report that he had "gotten his teeth" well into the problem van't Hoff had assigned him. In some respects it did not differ greatly from his final work at Berkeley on manganous sulphate. If anything, it leaned more heavily on the side of routine inorganic chemistry rather than the holier grail of physical chemistry he had come in search of. It was essentially a study of some of the salts found in the Stassfurt deposits with particular reference to their composition and solubility. The whole project, he explained to Jess, was nothing really new and he scarcely expected to get anything of fresh interest out of it. At the most he would chiefly be confirming the results of others, possibly filling in a gap here and there and in so doing enriching his own knowledge and technique with a command of new methods.

While the problem in its initial stages did develop largely as he had anticipated, at the same time it began to reveal unsuspected discrepancies in the prior work. It even resulted in the extraction of another compound which, while not new, had escaped the previous worker in the field. None of this was of startling importance, but it did serve to bring Cottrell into closer contact with van't Hoff himself. Despite this, there were the inevitable disappointments of any researcher.

One of the particular regions under investigation was in the zero to minus 6 or 7 degrees centigrade range where Cottrell's solution froze to a solid mass. One night at closing time he became convinced from his thermometer observations that a type of crystal he was in search of was appearing in a test tube, there mixed with a mass of other materials into a thick paste. If it were kept in this state he could proceed at will the following morning. Since the weather in the area had been holding steadily for several days at close to zero Fahrenheit, Cottrell set the test tube on the outside window sill and proceeded downtown to his lecture at the university. That night the thaw set in and by morning the whole thing had returned to its liquid state. There was nothing to do but begin afresh. Since the crystallization in the particular form in which he thought he had found it, however, had been accidental to start with, a week of some thirty more attempts left him still as far from his goal as ever. It was irritating, tantalizing, like a forgotten name on the tip of the tongue. From his physical measurements he could almost *say* what kind of a compound it was and probably what it looked like, but the situation never did recur before he had completed his semester and was ready to go on to Leipzig. His only satisfaction was in having the results of his work published in two papers—one in collaboration with Meyerhoffer, the other with van't Hoff and Meyerhoffer.

In Cottrell's mind the work with van't Hoff, in addition to introducing him to different problems and new methods, had served another purpose: it had knocked some of the conceit out of him. This, he confided to Jess, was something he had felt a necessity for several years. Not that he looked on conceit as undesirable. It was simply a matter of degree and if indulged in to a moderate extent was useful as a firm stimulus *provided* "it is kept absolutely within the individual and doesn't make itself known to others by any outward means." His hope was that in Berlin an unnecessary surplus of conceit had been eliminated with the result that life would be pleasanter in a small measure for himself and those about him. In fact, since he was outwardly manifesting his views on the subject to Jess in violation of his own proviso, he felt it likely that there was still another layer in need of peeling off and perhaps Leipzig would furnish the opportunity for this.

For a time Cottrell had entertained the idea of continuing at Berlin for his Ph.D. There were, however, other considerations. His total capital at the beginning of the semester was $1442. Inexpensive as Berlin was, living in Leipzig would be still cheaper. More important, the work at Leipzig (which he had investigated on his earlier visit) would take him into the very heart of that phase of physical chemistry about which he knew least. A third consideration, not to be overlooked, was that in Cottrell's opinion a Leipzig science degree, circa 1900, carried with it more prestige—a cut, perhaps, above that of Berlin. Testimonial of this was the fact that over half of the recognized men in the field had at one time or another been students at Ostwald's laboratory.

The fame of Wilhelm Ostwald rivaled but did not eclipse that of van't Hoff. Together with Svante Arrhenius of Sweden, they formed a kind of Holy Trinity of physical chemistry, although the property of indivisibility was conspicuously lacking especially after Ostwald propounded his disbelief in the existence of atoms and molecules. To physical chemistry Ostwald had made (and was still to make) numerous great contributions, among the most notable of which was the forging of early loose principles into the sharp edge of an exact science. His laboratory at Leipzig was larger and more sought after than that of van't Hoff, and while it could accommodate fifty or more students, the number of applicants far exceeded its capacities.

In his fourth month at Berlin, Cottrell wrote Ostwald but it was not until February of the next year, 1901, that the latter could confirm the fact of an opening for him. About this same time, an ocean and a continent away in Berkeley, events were taking shape that were to have a profound effect on Cottrell's future. Benjamin Ide Wheeler, already in the presidency of the University of California, was in various and vigorous ways "promoting" the place, introducing new courses and attracting more luminous names to its faculty. In his report to the regents in January 1901, Wheeler, a classicist at heart, pleased the science faculty by recommending that physical chemistry be recognized and an assistant professorship in the field be established. Almost immediately W. B. Rising, head of the College of Chemistry, wrote Cottrell asking his opinions and soliciting the names of any good young men in Europe who might be suitable. "I think," Rising ended, "you know what I mean."

Whether Cottrell did know what he meant or whether the remark was an open invitation for Cottrell to advance his own cause is open to question. Cottrell at the moment was undergoing what, for him, was a strange change of heart in the matter of a Ph.D. Presumably the degree was what he had come to Europe for, and while still at Berlin, he mentioned his preference for getting it at Leipzig. It is possible that he rebelled at spending all the time his money would allow in Leipzig, while he yet hoped to get in some work with Thomson or Ramsay in England, as well as at Harvard or Chicago when he returned to America.

Shortly after his arrival in Leipzig in March 1901, Cottrell decided that since his resources might not be sufficient to last him the four to six semesters most students found necessary for a thesis he would avoid deliberately aiming for a degree. Rather he would concentrate on those problems best adapted to Ostwald's laboratory and from which he could derive the most broadening benefits. What makes this decision the more difficult to understand is that his reputation was such that any number of Californians would have been willing to lend him the necessary money. It is possible that he had arrived at the stage that comes to every thinking student during his academic life when overemphasis on a degree seems a confusion of the end with the means.

Degree or no degree, Cottrell was soon adapting his usual strenuous pace to the Leipzig routine. A month after his arrival he wrote Jess, "My old-time enthusiasm, which during my Berlin stay may sometimes have waned a little, is coming back in full force and I find I have about twice to four times as many schemes to try as there is possibly time for. The change is mainly due, I think, to my being turned loose once more on my own work and being thrown in contact with a large number of men with diverse ideas."

One of these men, Arthur A. Blanchard (later professor of inorganic chemistry at Massachusetts Institute of Technology), had the following recollections fifty years later of Cottrell's arrival at Leipzig: "There quietly appeared one day this man of large stature in a serviceable but not carefully pressed brown suit that I can picture to this day when I shut my eyes. He was a very friendly man but far from aggressively so. . . . He determined he would have a try to see if he could measure up to the real scientists of the day. He was such a modest man with all his ambition, his only feeling of confidence was in his determination to work. He did not know that he would not fail, but he did know that if hard work would gain success, he would be successful. He had a naturally powerful physique but he drained that unmercifully and at times he had a haggard appearance. He habitually worked through the night well along towards morning. He went on the theory that along about two o'clock in the morning when one's physical powers are at the lowest ebb, one's mental powers were most acute.

"In spite of his steadfast devotion to work, there was one activity which he considered more important, that was conversation with his fellowmen. He was always ready to break off work if any opportunity arose to discuss anything whatever with anyone who happened by. I remember one time I was exasperated with him for wasting his time with a particularly footless bore, and I tried to reprove him. He replied that discussions were one of the most important ways of getting new ideas and one could never tell when the most unlikely discussion would bring out most valuable ideas."

It was Ostwald's habit, as Blanchard recalled, to offer each new student, as a subject for research, a theoretical study of the effect of counterflow of an electrolyte in minimizing the back migration of hydroxide ions through the diaphragm in an electrolytic cell. As of 1900, when Blanchard entered the laboratory, Ostwald had yet to find a taker. Blanchard himself, already wise in the ways of ions, had previously worked on the theoretical treatment of the problem as assistant to the great A. A. Noyes, a former Leipzig Ph.D., then professor of theoretical chemistry at M.I.T. It had left both completely baffled, so that Blanchard sniffed Ostwald's bait and declined to be trapped. Then, as Blanchard remembered it, "Cottrell appeared on the scene, as innocent of suspicion of his fellow man as anyone who ever went abroad to study, and when Ostwald offered him this subject, he unhesitatingly accepted it. Moreover, he carried it through to a brilliant success!"

In whatever manner Cottrell did come in touch with his problem—and his doctor's thesis ultimately dealt with the subject of diffusion—he worked it out so brilliantly and successfully that as late as 1939 a paper on the study of micro-electrodes cited Cottrell's work (in which he adapted the general theory of diffusion in such a way that this phenomenon could be studied in electrolytic cells) as an original reference. Very possibly this field was suggested to him by Ostwald, although three months after his arrival in Leipzig, Cottrell wrote Jess, "I have been more than once surprised at the lack of independence of the men here as students. Out of the fifty here doing research work, at least half of whom are here as prize scholars of one sort or another, there are only two of us as far as I have found out so far, that have brought our own work and plans with us and we are looked on as rather odd phenomena." As a result, Cottrell concluded, he now felt more certain that he had chosen wisely in a university career as his life's work.

This self-confidence, while warranted, was not as abiding as Cottrell made it sound. One reason for its occasional systole was his deliberate choice of the most difficult method of approaching work that could lead to a degree. He could have accepted, as did most of the others, a more or less routine problem based on well-known principles, developing it further through dull but painstaking measurements. This route to a Ph.D. led the conservative traveler along the better-lighted boulevards and provided a minimum of exciting new wayside scenery. Such, however, were not for Cottrell. He chose instead to try a variety of new problems, all of which could easily return negative results useless for thesis material. He chose, indeed, to play for high stakes—to search for new phenomena based on principles never before observed or measured; to apply new methods to old fields and old methods to new. The less one had of money (and hence time), the greater the chance of failure. Thus Cottrell gambled.

He had arrived at Ostwald's laboratory in March. By June he was telling Jess of some of his short-lived triumphs and moments of despair:

"It's wonderful," he wrote, "if you make an appointment with yourself in a different mood at a certain time and thoroughly trust in it, how naturally you get there on time. I had a good illustration of it today myself. I had been planning and arranging for a certain experiment off and on for the last two months and it had come to seem the most interesting and promising of the many schemes I have had in hand. It had taken a good deal of preparation and thought to get things ready and today I did the decisive work on it and it turned out absolutely negative results, as far as I can see, which simply means that the whole idea or hypothesis on which the work was carried out simply disappeared as a wild vagary and I have turned my attention to something else.

"I must confess that though, from the first, I had clearly realized that the chances were much greater against than for it, its utter failure did have a depressing effect and I felt very little inclination to do any other serious work this afternoon. It was as if I had lost interest in my work and almost wondered whether it was worthwhile. I at once realized that I must be in one of those temporarily abnormal moods and made an appointment with myself for tomorrow morning to take up matters scientific in normal condition once more and dismissed the whole matter from my mind, got lunch, came home, stretched out on the sofa and started to read the papers from home which had accumulated, as if I had no other care in the world.

"All of a sudden a band of music out the window attracted my attention and I found there was a long procession of children marching out to some sort of a Sunday School picnic. So I put on my hat and went out to investigate, and before I got through with this, found myself almost unconsciously getting ahead of my 'appointment,' and in abstracted moments here and there, planning away as hard as ever on new work with as much enthusiasm as ever and having the impudence to go poking around the tumbled down ruins of my shattered 'pet scheme' to see if there couldn't be enough found still intact to build a new structure."

The problem that gave him worry was an attempt at clarification, by experiment, of the confusion then existing in the method of determining single potential differences between metals and electrolytes in solution as measured by a Lippmann electrometer. It was Cottrell's hope to show one promising point in the theory of the phenomena which had, it appeared to him, been overlooked. He hoped also, in a wider field, to clear up some of the discrepancies between theory and experiment in the phenomena of galvanic polarization in general.

Here was something to tax even Cottrell's endurance. There were nights when he studied until 3 A.M., then lay down until five when he would be up and working until breakfast. There were days when his diary noted he was "decidedly off, breaking everything I laid hands on." But by mid-August he felt he had developed it sufficiently to prepare a "Preliminary Note on the Theory of the Lippmann Electrometer and Related Phenomena" for submission to the August meeting of the British Association for the Advancement of Science in Glasgow. Because of his finances his decision to attend was not easily made, but so engrossing did he find his problem that he was able to acknowledge, "I don't feel at all ashamed to admit the keen interest I feel in the question of bagging this particular bird myself. Some of the biggest men in the field are turning a good deal of their attention on the problem and have been for several years past, and when I see how near they have come to the clue I believe I have found, I must confess it makes me feel a little nervous."

Spurred on by his father, who promised a loan if he ran short, by Aunt Mame, who foresaw it as a "rich experience," and by the opportunity of spending a month in Thomson's laboratory at Cambridge, Cottrell decided to disregard the cost and spend the summer recess in England. But the urge to strictest economy was beset by temptations before which the strong-willed Cottrell was all but powerless. By covering en route all quadrants of the compass except East, he managed to take in laboratories at Göttingen, Giessen, Bonn, Amsterdam, Leiden, and the Hague. For this, a kind of fiscal compensation was achieved by abjuring a berth in favor of sitting up all night on the deck of the Rotterdam–Harwich steamer.

This matter of money brought into bold relief one of Cottrell's subtler scruples. His father had already offered to advance him forty dollars a month but Cottrell had refused. The truth was that Cottrell, before leaving for Europe, had given some money to Jess's ailing mother, whose bouts with an unpromising heart caused Jess as much uneasiness as their inability to quite meet the mounting medical fees. The loan was a private matter known only to the Fultons—mother and daughter—and Cottrell. Such being the case, Cottrell reasoned that to put his father to an expense he could not easily afford while he, himself, spent his money for other than educational purposes was "sailing under false colors," and in refusing the elder Cottrell's offer, he explained to Jess that he wanted to be able to think of his money as his own and thus be utterly free from any hesitant qualms in spending it as he saw fit. Not all college students, graduate or undergraduate, have always entertained such inhibiting thoughts about money, but once Cottrell handed down an opinion, his family, as always, accepted it as final.

The trip to England that summer was something of a disappointment. The Cavendish Laboratory closed two weeks earlier than Cottrell had anticipated, leaving him with an appalling and unplanned hiatus. Cambridge was "beautiful and picturesque" but the easygoing living for its own sake that, along with the obtrusiveness of wealth, saturated the collegiate atmosphere was too stultifying a hothouse for Cottrell to endure in idleness. His final judgment was that it was an excellent breeding ground for snobs, where "everything is apparently adjusted for the wealthy and the rest hang on to the edge and do their best to keep up appearances as they may be able. The luxury and general cumbersomeness of the methods is oppressive to me."

He wrote to University College, London, only to find that Ramsay's laboratory was closed, then went on to Manchester to visit Norman Smith, with whom he had struck up a warm friendship in van't Hoff's laboratory. It was while here that he permitted himself one of the few expressions of bitterness over the frictions and tensions that had characterized his own home life in Oakland. By contrast, the halcyon qualities of the Smiths' home, the convivial warmth and sympathetic air pleased him greatly. The contrast was, in fact, too disparate to go unnoticed and he wrote Jess of the visit, "I have thoroughly enjoyed and feel better for it though I must confess that it brought up more than one old recollection and opened old sores."

4

It was almost October when Cottrell returned to Leipzig, where the brisk hands of autumn were tirelessly busy with a prodigal scattering of leaves. It was almost like a home-coming and Berkeley itself, he said, could scarcely have given him more pleasure. While the stay in England had not been up to his expectations, his spirits had revived somewhat at the meeting of the British Association for the Advancement of Science where he had read his paper on the capillary electrometer before Section A. It was not the type of report that would inflame even scientific imaginations, and if it was received without enthusiasm Cottrell was pleased that at least it had the value of establishing his priority to the method employed. What really had stirred Glasgow while he was there was the shocking news of President McKinley's assassination; every flag in the city flew at half-mast.

Once back in the familiar routine of Leipzig, Cottrell resumed his work with fresh intensity, no longer uncertain as to his own intentions in the matter of obtaining a degree. Something had happened that moved him, had penetrated the stout bulwarks that ordinarily made him so impervious to the opinions of others, and caused him to reconsider. About this time he received a letter from Edmund O'Neill, associate professor of California's College of Chemistry, who, during Cottrell's graduate days in Berkeley, had come to regard him as more friend than pupil. O'Neill told him of the whole new spirit which President Wheeler had injected into the university, of the push, the rush, and the advertising. All this he mentioned as a prelude to the fact that he had spoken to Wheeler about the prospects of Cottrell's returning there to teach. Wheeler's contact with Cottrell had been anything but close during the latter's loose affiliation with the university while still teaching at high school. Cottrell, it is true, had interviewed him before leaving, sounded him out on one or two opinions, then told Wheeler that, while he valued his advice, he, Cottrell, must in the final analysis rely on his own judgment of educational aims and methods. Wheeler, therefore, had ample opportunity to form his own ideas of Cottrell, two of which were cardinal. To be considered for an appointment Cottrell must first have a degree. But even with this won it was still Wheeler's belief, according to O'Neill, that Cottrell was "not steady enough and that you spread your efforts over too large a field" (Wheeler may possibly have been advised by the man who thought Cottrell "danced all over the lot"). In order to receive any consideration Cottrell must not only have his academic knighthood but also give some evidence of what Wheeler termed "staying power."

One of Cottrell's reactions to this he wrote to Jess: "I only think the more of him for taking the stand he has. They have been too

easy-going about filling positions at Berkeley for a good time past
and Wheeler is starting to break it up. The policy is a good one and
will eventually make the competition keener and build up a better
spirit of work in the department."

Had any inkling of Wheeler's stand ever been communicated to
Aunt Mame it is conceivable that McKinley's would not have been
the only newsy assassination of 1901. Instead, she sang his praises in
eulogistic letters to Cottrell that caused him to write Jess with
tolerant amusement, "I can see she feels sure that the president is
just as well satisfied with my general make-up as she is. I can
imagine what a mix-up it would make of her feelings if she knew
how things really stood. I think we must admit that old folks have
more excuse for having whims than those of us who haven't so
much of life behind us and it behooves us to be charitable and
overlook good-naturedly much that seems unjustifiable when tested
by strict reason."

A further reaction to Wheeler's insistence on a Ph.D. was Cottrell's
new determination to get his degree if at all possible without
sacrificing any of his rigid principles of freedom of research that had
led him into scientific terra incognita in the first place. As a result
there were times when his efforts made the routine of a Trappist
seem sheer lotus-eating by comparison. Jess, already aware of his
conviction that health could be sacrificed if the goal warranted it,
expressed her alarm and in reply received a rather singular essay on
the subject.

"I look on health," Cottrell wrote her, "not only as a thing for itself
but, even more, as a means to an end. It is a sort of capital that one
must set out with on new enterprises and use with discretion and
care, never wasting it if it can be helped. Yet, I believe there are
times when one is justified in taxing it to the limit in the discharge
of what he considers his duties, be that the care of those immediately
about him or in less clearly defined fields of professional activity.

"I don't believe in being afraid to work under any pressure that
the case seems to demand and you are able to keep up. There certainly is, as you say, a limit to which it pays to stretch one's strength
but I don't think there are many people in full possession of good
health that often reach it. Nor do I think it necessarily corresponds
with the point where the first perceptible harmful effects can be
perceived. I believe it is better, if necessary, to sacrifice one or two of

the late years of life if by it one can accomplish as much more of lasting value as many do in a whole lifetime. In fact, I have of late had to take myself to task more than once for positive laziness, and I have even been guilty of indulging in a German siesta of a Saturday afternoon."

There was another phase of his philosophy of work on which he held equally positive ideas. This he referred to as the "rapidity and intensity factors" whose absolute importance to his work he also explained to Jess:

"Since I have started this trip, I have kept my eyes open particularly to see if I could discover in the men I met just how big a part the rapidity and intensity factors played and I must frankly say that I have been led to give it even more weight than before. In fact, it seems *the one* factor which you find in the top layer of men which distinguishes them from those just beneath the crust. They both have ability, industry and clear headedness in common, but that very intensity (rapidity which seems linked inseparably with it, though not perhaps *the* thing itself) keeps them just far enough ahead of this second layer to always leave the pickings of the bone to them.

"Ostwald is an excellent type of the very best of the second class and van't Hoff of the first, and I have been much interested in comparing them. If you will run over whatever list of men you may have in mind (men that came to the top in moments of crisis) I feel sure you will admit that they were every one 'men of intensity' in whatever they did long before they took the helm. It isn't that by working more rapidly or intensely a man gets more done in the gross sense— often quite the reverse. But there is a certain kind of work for the accomplishment of which that habit of mine which is acquired by intense work seems absolutely necessary. In modern scientific work, the question takes beside, a more special aspect. The means and methods which are the very tools of research are being advanced so fast that it takes more than ordinary energy simply to keep abreast of the times. A good example of how problems do not wait for a man in science today, you can see in the fact that since I left home, at least three of the pieces of work I was then busy with have been more or less taken up by others and the results have already been published."

The astringent application of Cottrell's logic to Jess's doubts and fears was seldom of lasting value. Treat them as he might symptomatically, her apprehensions were a many-headed hydra against which his only weapon—reason applied by slow mail—was not always effective. It is possible that the ordinarily perceptive Cottrell made the grave error of considering an understanding of the female ego amenable to laboratory technique. He and Jess had parted with a mutual declaration of love and what was tantamount to an engagement. To these Cottrell had added an audibly verbal codicil, ". . . but my work comes first." By the time Jess had felt the full impact of these five words Cottrell was already in Berlin and Jess could only counter by writing, "To me, my love has meant the biggest and best there is in life and the feeling that anything is more dear to you has meant much pain to me." And again, "I know, and you know, that when you first told me of your love that you would have crushed out every bit of it if it had stood as an impassable barricade to your ambition. It is there where [my] dislike for your work has come in."

This, then, was the unyielding essence of a conflict that pursued them—although not always unhappily—through life. It resolved itself occasionally by compromise, often by being ignored, and once by a particularly brilliant piece of Cottrellian dialectics that somehow failed in practice.

Not long after his arrival in Berlin, Cottrell made his first attempt to correct what he conceived to be certain basic errors in Jess's point of view. Love and work, he said, lay in two entirely separate fields. Love was purely personal and concerned feelings which bore no particular relationship to anyone or anything about them. His work, on the other hand, was something entirely different. It had "little or no meaning in so far as it applies only to myself, but is, on the contrary, interlaced in every direction with my duty to the world about me." It was his first written use of the phrase "duty to the world." He used it sparingly, for duty, like conceit—or a heart—was not a chevron on a sleeve. But the idea of it was to pervade his acts as compulsively as another man's lust. Nor was it the messianic concept it might at first appear, for he believed that every man had such a duty to be discharged in accordance with his talents and abilities—to give of himself as much as he was able for the welfare of all.

In the same letter to Jess in which he first spoke of "his duty" he immediately amended it to "our duty" and begged her not to "always put these two matters [love and duty] as if they were in eternal conflict with each other.

"We have," he continued, "two distinct things to look at. Our own personal comfort, including all the ordinary pleasures and cares which make up a home, and, on the other hand, our duty to the world over and above the mere matter of 'living and let live.' And here, of course, comes the pleasure derived from accomplishing something. This last is the selfish part, undoubtedly, and the worst of it is that I defy any man to say even to himself, just what part of the whole this last motive is. I freely confess that I have never been able to satisfy myself just what part it has and does play with me. All I can do is to hope it's small and growing less."

This rigidity of Cottrell's devotion to work and to duty led Jess, rightly or wrongly, to the conclusion that he was beset by ambition. She said she didn't blame him for it, but said it in a way that gave a fair indication that she did blame him for it. "Life wouldn't be much without it, but it has been the strange, cold way you have put it. Before you spoke [of your love] your plans were all laid and if I was willing to bow to them, all right; if not, the matter might end."

Cottrell said Jess misunderstood him. Jess replied that Cottrell misunderstood her, but conceded, "I have always been willing to admit that your ambition in point of time should come first. But never, from the very first, have I been willing to divide your love in any way. Perhaps you can understand why the tears would come so often when you would speak of your work and you would fail to understand me."

It was a cry as old as man and, conceding the primacy of Adam, older than women, but before the confusion could be further compounded Cottrell, in a masterly stroke, pointed the way out of the dilemma.

"You insist," he wrote, "on considering love and home as the highest aim in life and making everything else simply a means to this end. How does this way of looking at it strike you? If love and home are to mean anything worth the name and ideal, they must mean the formation of a single individuality which shall absorb the two distinct individualities existing before. Don't mistake me as meaning a sudden cataclysm of any kind, but on the other hand, the safety and stability of the result comes from the slow steady change which brings it about. This is the change and the result, I take it, which are so dear to you and which you insist on being considered the aim and end of life and to which all other things must be only the means. I think I am safe in saying that this is as dear to me as to you and means as high an ideal as regards its accomplishment. But if everything were simply to be a means to this end, when this is once accomplished, then what? Is the only object then to preserve it, and beyond this, are we to simply lay back and enjoy it?

"It's a pleasant picture, I grant, but I can't consider it the highest ideal for this 'new individuality' to hold. If, from this point onward, we consider ourselves (and I think we ought) simply as a single individual, this would seem to me to be a little selfish and like every selfish thing have some tendency to react badly on itself. In other words, what can we do for the world about us, once we have accomplished and established the first?

"The assumption of such a second ideal by this composite individual (i.e. us together), even placing it apparently before the one already accomplished, is, I believe, the truer and nobler way and the very safest way of protecting and guaranteeing the former. If you will stop and think a minute, you will see that I have had thrust upon me some good samples of the disastrous working of the other method and perhaps that is one thing which has emphasized the matter to me. It is just this feature in my work which I have tried to cling to so tenaciously and which has so often discouraged you. You say, 'I have always been willing to grant that your work should come first in *point of time*,' i.e., only a means to the other end. This second ideal of *our* contribution to the world's good, however, reverses the order of the matter largely and becomes the end to which the other is, in great measure, the means.

"Certainly, I don't mean to hold up my present line of work as our only contribution to this end but it seems, under the circumstances, as the most natural nucleus around which to group the rest, which is probably the greater part. It's the old story, Jess, the person who pursues personal happiness as an end in itself is taking the greatest chance of all of losing it (I've been interested in studying the 'professional tourist' of late from this standpoint).

"To sum up in a measure: if we can work *together* for some such high ideal over and beyond ourselves and our own direct personal pleasure and keep this ideal steadily before us as the end, it seems to me that it will be the safest and best of all possible ways, not only of accomplishing this, but the other as well. It strikes me more and more that the things we look ahead to as ends, when accomplished, often disappoint us from the very prominence which we have been so long used to giving them in our mental views, while the steps by the way, which we have made use of, stand out in refreshing contrast as real points of satisfaction. I can't consider it as any degradation of an ideal to place it in the position of one of these steps. The steps should be something that permit of practically complete fulfillment while the end should be far enough ahead of possibilities never to be really reached, that is, it should be to a certain extent vague, though clear enough in direction to be rationally worked toward.

"This chasing the will o' the wisp and purposely pinning your faith to a phantom, almost which you never expect to catch, simply to keep yourself at highest working pressure, takes nerve and courage and backbone, and I have always hesitated from asking you to take hold in this way with me, for it always seemed when I spoke of anything of the kind to be such an incomprehensible idea to you, and you clung so to the other ideal for strength that I was afraid it was expecting too much of your nerves and strength. But I'm taking courage from your late letter in this regard and hope you are building physical foundations now which will stand that sort of test.

"Then, too, although I can't say I'm conscious of any material change of view, I don't believe I could have put this matter in just this form six months ago. Perhaps I didn't understand my ideas sufficiently clearly to explain them to anyone. I clearly realize that at the outset, years ago, personal ambition—desire for recognition in the special field of work—was practically the only driving motive and unquestionably, today, there is a good deal of the same unconsciously or consciously mixed up with the driving force. But I owe it chiefly to you, I feel, as these self-questionings which have resulted from our companionship, that a determined effort has come in the last few years to put aside as far as human nature (or at least as far as my nature) will permit, the personal ambition and substitute for it the ambition to accomplish the maximum good without regard to what recognition it may receive, except in so far as this may serve to help the work itself. I give you full leave to do all you can, as heretofore, to down the personal ambition, but please don't throw any cold water on the other part, for it's the part we can fully share in common."

Thus, Cottrell's testament to life, to love, and to duty.

5

It would be pleasant to record that with Cottrell's declaration of unity, his admission of Jess to a part in his life's work, the formation of a concert of ideals resolved forever the discordant themes. Analytically unimpassioned as was Cottrell's rhetoric, to Jess his words held all the warmth of a high hot sun under which her starched defenses quickly wilted. She eagerly acknowledged her understanding of this new concept of togetherness, saying, "You were afraid to fully trust your love and let me in. You had the idea that it would take the working ability, to a great extent, out of you. You couldn't understand how a greater force would give you the nobler determination to give your best to the world. Fred, you have at last made me truly happy—something that I have never known and I thank God for it!" Hungering for more, she urged him to "let your heart beat, and not your reason altogether." Shorn of her doubts, she conjured up a detailed picture of their future home and life together—he the teacher, she the homemaker, together the force for good they could exert through culturally enlightening entertaining in an academic atmosphere of charm and intellectual grace ("a home so established cannot help but be a true resting place for us and all the friends we can gather around us").

It was not an unreasonable, if wholly feminine, picture that Jess painted, but when read in the chill austerity of Cottrell's Leipzig surroundings, he took fright. In answer he expressed agreement with the broad general spirit of her letter but bluntly tempered her enthusiasm by saying, "[I] feel you don't yet realize the character of the work I shall probably have in hand and what severe demands it makes upon the patience and forbearance of those about me if it is really to be conscientiously carried out."

Jess, in truth, could not know, but she was to learn. Before any more details of their newly found relationship could be further discussed Mrs. Fulton's tired heart gave out, throwing Jess into fresh states of uncertainties and leaving her dependent on her firm, spinsterish sister Frances—an elocutionist of sporadic popularity.

6

Abetted by some of the world's finest beers, the social life of German universities tended toward a boisterous camaraderie which sometimes even penetrated the graduate student stratum and cast an unusually pervasive sentimental glow, beloved of alumni, on those who responded. Work, study, and correspondence reduced the gregarious Cottrell's susceptibility to such conviviality to a minimum. There was at Leipzig an American students' club for which he was automatically eligible and while he attended a few of its gatherings, including a Fourth of July picnic complete with fireworks, he found them enjoyable but time-consuming. He considered the companionship derived from each such affair well worth the while, but by the time the next meeting arrived his enthusiasm had been dissipated and lost in his preoccupation with work in the interim, so that his attendance, at best, was spotty. Nor did his absence of contact outside of the laboratory and lecture room ever seem to cause him feelings of lonesomeness. To a remarkable degree his scientific mind was self-sustaining and could, on occasion, relax itself in whimsey. Late one night he cleaned out the cupboard in his room and discovered a collection of four kinds of bread and innumerable varieties of German sausages and European cheeses with which he nursed his late-hour hunger. The next hour he passed in determining how many possible combinations involving one of each could be formed. He then decided, as he wrote his father, "when I have the time, I must figure the problem out from a purely theoretical and mathematical standpoint and then see how near I came to exhausting the field experimentally."

But even Cottrell did not live by bread, cheese, and physical chemistry alone. He found he had a taste for Wagnerian opera, and since standing room was to be had for a single mark he frequently attended. He made side trips to Dresden and Cassel to take in the art galleries and if his own admiration was tepid he at least pleased Aunt Mame, who praised him for leaving no cultural stones unturned. He even made a valiant attempt at sport and took up ice skating. Before he could attain anything in the way of proficiency summer arrived and by the time ice formed again he was too absorbed in other things to resume the attempt.

Cottrell's closest approach to friendship at Leipzig was with Harry W. Morse, a Stanford graduate whose brilliance approximated that of Cottrell, and who was later to be identified for several years with the method of electrical precipitation which Cottrell had yet to devise. Together, during the Christmas recess of 1901, they visited Göttingen, where they had a mutual acquaintance in P. G. Nutting (later of the United States Geological Survey) who shared their Stanford-University of California backgrounds. It was Cottrell's hope to get in a few days' work at the Göttingen laboratories just by way of a busman's holiday. He was disgruntled to find the social life there so intense that he, as a guest of Nutting, could not escape it. He settled for what scientific shoptalk was available, then wound up the year in a rousing student celebration at the Café Nacional—a night heavily laden with Scotch and auld lang syne, beer and *Gemütlichkeit*. In search of fresh air he, Nutting, and another student, leaving Göttingen at 3 A.M., started the year 1902 with a walk which, after taking in a sizable arc of the countryside, returned them to their rooms at ten o'clock in the morning. "After breakfast," he noted in his diary, "the boys turned in and I went at Nernst's latest paper, taking a nap of a half hour in the middle of it. Day passed quietly and pleasantly."

It was Ostwald's conviction (which Jess would have understood and appreciated) that science had its social side, and with Mrs. Ostwald taking an active part in the affairs of the laboratory, the life there was not without homelike touches. Mrs. Ostwald managed the "student Sundays" at which, about once a month, the students shared, in so far as she could make it possible, the Ostwalds' home life. No invitations were issued or needed. The fame of her coffeecake, the caliber of the conversation, the brilliance of occasional visitors (van't Hoff, Arrhenius, Landolt of Berlin, Ramsay, Boltzmann), the impromptu entertainment of piano or string quartet, all suffused with an air of warmth and good living, would crowd the three large rooms and garden with as many as a hundred guests. Some of these affairs Cottrell attended and it was at one of them, early in 1902, as he noted in his diary, that discussion centered around "the new international language." Since no other references follow, what was probably Esperanto seems to have had a very limited appeal for him, and almost two decades were to elapse before he was to espouse the idea of an international language with a persistence and fervor that sometimes jeopardized his reputation as a scientist. At the moment, however, his German was proving adequate, although one fellow student (William Gabb Smeaton, later of the University of Michigan) recalled that in making a report on his work before the laboratory colloquium the brand of German Cottrell exhibited completely dispensed with the problem of assigning nouns their proper gender in favor of the simpler system of rendering them all as feminine.

The fall and winter semester of 1901, after his return from the Glasgow meeting, was a dispiriting one for Cottrell. The better part of two years had elapsed since that bright morning of promise when he had left Oakland. His initial fund of money was running low and he was not much nearer the degree he had now decided on than he had been then. What contributed to the uncertainty was his insistence on following his own lead in the laboratory with an independence that at times seemed almost a defiance, not only of Ostwald but of Luther (the acting head of the laboratory) as well. There were no co-ordinates, few beclouded fixed stars, and many conflicting signposts on a pathless trail over flinty ground to mark his progress. Worse still, after returning to the laboratory, he found some discouraging errors in the paper he had presented at Glasgow and he more than once had to stop and ask himself: "Am I floundering? Am I giving all the symptoms of the typical freak who doesn't fit in anywhere? Am I just a hopeless dreamer? Or am I climbing over the heads of the others to something better?" One thing he knew for a certainty: "If a man is mediocre, he will accomplish the maximum he is capable of by following the beaten path and in no other way. If a man can break out new paths for himself and others which really reach new fields, then he would waste his very best and most valuable efforts by staying in the old beaten paths." Cottrell, in spite of his doubts, knew he was gifted beyond mediocrity. He was concerned only with the question of how far he might have overestimated that margin.

He continued his practice of working on several problems at once because he found that when he came to a certain point in an experiment that necessitated a wait—perhaps for new apparatus—the interval was unendurable unless he had something else to turn to. His impatience was aggravated by "the slow German method" and he once testily complained to Jess, "I never saw such a procrastinating race in my life." His main problem, however, was to find a new and accurate method of determining rates of diffusion of salts in solution by use of electrolytic cells. This subject, he declared, surpassed all others in physical chemistry in the amount of time spent on it with completely unrewarding results. While both Ostwald and Luther offered him all the help they could, both recognized their limitations in this special field and, though sympathetic, could not be expected to sidetrack their own interests to any appreciable extent for an unorthodox student from an obscure university in the American Far West.

Some of Cottrell's own tortured wrestlings with the work he described to Jess: "It has been in many ways very amusing to see how the problem has changed its whole appearance from time to time. Now it begins to look as if in the very outset I came very near the correct end result by an entirely wrong method and when I convinced myself that the method wouldn't hold water, I naturally expected the result to be wrong itself and the experiments I made seem to agree with this. Now, it begins again to look as if the result was right in itself and could be proved so by a different, and this time, correct mathematical analysis but at the same time the mathematical analysis shows why the experiments didn't show what I was after as there was still another set of conditions outside of any I had yet taken into account in the theory, which in this particular case were the all important part."

It is unlikely that Cottrell could have given any clearer indication than this of why both Ostwald and Luther had advised him against the subject and why the only other student at the laboratory working in the field had given it up in hopeless discouragement after two semesters. It is possible, too, that Cottrell, acting on the advice of both mentors, might also have succumbed but Wheeler's slurring reference to "staying power" still rankled, and while Cottrell was far from hypersensitive, a wound that penetrated did so deeply.

Despite frequent differences of scientific opinion between Luther and Cottrell, the two held each other in high esteem. The latter, if not already aware of Luther's regard, was made so one day by Morse as the two of them walked down the street from the laboratory. The usually talkative Cottrell was silent, thinking over a theoretical point on which he and Luther held divergent views and which they had discussed that morning. Suddenly Morse, as though aware of his companion's thoughts, looked up at him with an odd smile and said: "You know, Luther thinks a lot of you."

"Is that so?" asked Cottrell noncommittally.

"Yes," replied Morse. "He told me the other day he considers you now the best man in the laboratory. As long as Heathcote was here he never could decide which was the better, but since he left, he says there is no further competition." Even the iconoclast has occasional need for the respect of his peers and Luther's approval, reported though it was at secondhand, went far toward bolstering Cottrell's confidence that he was, in spite of his own doubts, pursuing the right course.

During the early part of February 1902 dogged perseverance showed its first faint sign of reward when Cottrell seemed to grasp an idea of the method he sought. It was clearly enough conceived so that both Ostwald and Luther could approve and encourage him. Only the day before Luther, with blunt frankness, had told Cottrell that the problem until then had seemed to him insurmountable but now he, too, was filled with enthusiasm. With great jubilance Cottrell wrote Jess of his high spirits. He was, he said, like a kid with a new toy. This at last made the doctorate seem possible. The prospector had struck signs of pay dirt, the gambler saw his luck turn.

There was still much to be done. It must be developed both experimentally in the laboratory and on paper in the realm of mathematics. The former required measurements of a most delicate nature, skill, energy, and new apparatus. In order that he might work undisturbed Luther furnished him with his own room in the basement of the laboratory. Once that was organized, Cottrell turned to some of the theoretical phases. "I had a couple of tries," he wrote Jess, "at calculating out some of the 'absolute' values from my measurements but got hopelessly mixed up in my arithmetic and thoroughly disgusted with myself. Last night I settled down to it in earnest and cut the American Club meeting in order to pursue it up. I worked until 1:30 and things were getting worse and worse till I turned in. I woke up early with the wheels still going round on the same problem and began to calculate the thing out in my head and before I got up had the thing all straightened out and half an hour more with pencil and paper tied it down and I was simply amazed to see how well the numerical values I had measured agreed with theory."

By mid-March he had run into no important obstacles and when the summer term opened on April 20 he was well enough along so that he not only felt certain of finishing that semester but was relaxing sufficiently to take in more Wagnerian operas and, mindful of his promise to Jess, to reach Luke in the New Testament. A month later he was sure enough of his results to begin writing up his thesis, which when translated into German under the title of *"Der Reststrom bei galvanischer Polarisation betrachtet als ein Diffusionsproblem"* was bound and ready for presentation by mid-July.

In the meantime several things had happened, one of which gave him an opportunity to test his commodity theory of health. A severe case of grippe during the winter had sent him to a Leipzig physician who interested himself in Cottrell's heart. This he pronounced half again as large as it should be, the heart muscles weak and the pulse high and feeble. With rest and proper care, the doctor said, these would return to normal over a period of time, and he recommended a quiet month taking the baths at Mannheim. The good man could, with equal hope of results, have advised a winning horse coming into the stretch to slow to a trot for that shortness of breath. Cottrell found the idea of a sanitarium "amusing," removed his heart from the doctor's office, and returned it to the laboratory where it belonged.

As his work progressed Cottrell had kept his old friend Professor O'Neill back in Berkeley advised of his prospective success. O'Neill, with the backing of Rising, dean of the College of Chemistry, continued his forceful advocacy of Cottrell with the president. Wheeler was apparently at last impressed with some evidence of "staying power," as well as with the possible degree, and began to think of Cottrell in a more sympathetic light.

The story has been told and printed that Wheeler, in search of the best possible man to fill the newly created post in physical chemistry, cabled the scientific capitals of England and the Continent for recommendations. The replies—again according to the story—uniformly read "Cottrell, University of California."

Actually Rising did query van't Hoff, Ostwald, and Nernst (Göttingen) for suggestions. Nernst had no English-speaking candidates, Ostwald endorsed his assistant, Ernst (with the qualification that Cottrell would be the better man after a few years of teaching experience), while van't Hoff, after due reflection, thought "Mr. F. G.

Cottrell from San Francisco who just now is working with Ostwald is the one to mention as first in line."

In May, Wheeler wrote him a formal offer of appointment at a starting salary of $1000 a year, his duties to begin in August. The University of Missouri made what was tantamount to a similar bid, while Harvard (on Cottrell's solicitation) appointed him to a Thayer scholarship of $300 for further study. Cottrell at last felt his judgment justified, his prospector's course vindicated.

The fateful day of examination for the degree was set for July 25 and his inquisitors were to be Ostwald, Boltzmann, and Zirkel, three of Leipzig's first-magnitude men of science. Cottrell wasn't nervous but did complain of a "peculiar vague feeling" to which he certainly was entitled. The exam was set for three in the afternoon and the account of what went on before he could make his appearance leaves his Oakland departure in the grocery wagon a marvel of stiff-necked dignity by comparison. He described it thus to Jess: "Pickard (who had his degree before me) and I went around together Wednesday and made our formal calls on the professors. These, you know, are made about noon with full evening outfit—dress suit, high hat, white kids and all. It was a warm, showery day, so after getting along over here on my whole trip for over two years without an umbrella, I had to get one that day to protect Morse's silk hat which I had borrowed for the occasion. We had to make a flying rush around through the heat and rain to catch all three professors on time and when I got through, I found my dress shirt and collar in a sadly collapsed condition and the left glove split on the seam of the thumb for about an inch. [His landlady] took the latter in hand and made a very fair job of it which lasted through the exam O.K. Overhauling my wardrobe, I found there was but one other dress shirt to be found and that had Glasgow tea stains on it that were pretty bad in daylight, though invisible at night, so I took the collapsed one around to a little laundry on the corner and they promised it to me by noon Friday.

"Friday . . . kept me busy chasing steamer accommodations until about 2 P.M. Then I made a flying jump to that laundry and you ought to have seen what I was presented with. It looked as if it had been put through the wringer after ironing instead of before. It was a perfect sight. Well, I took it under my arm and broke for the nearest furnishing store, but this is fairly well out in the suburbs and the stores are mainly of the small shop type. So next came a revelation in the line of German taste in linen. After ten minutes of pawing over the fellow's stock, I decided that there was nothing there that a man could safely be found dead in and as it was then after 2:20, I gave it up as a bad job and made up my mind to fall back on my own resources. It was half-past when I got to my room and the exam was at the other end of town. I resurrected the Glasgow wreck once more and remembered that white powder might do good service in such an emergency. I did a little artistic work on the one side with toothpaste; dexterously sewed my silk handkerchief so as to cover the rest; tumbled headlong into the remainder of my clothes including Morse's hat; climbed into my overcoat (although a linen duster and a fan would have been more in keeping with the weather) and caught the car to the trysting place. The clock was just striking three as I got there."

He passed, did Cottrell, *summa cum laude*. His father's pride was great but contained. Aunt Mame rushed congratulations in a letter addressed to *Dr. F. G. Cottrell*. Miss Horton said, "We had you marked for some such course of attainment and service when you were a little (?) ten year old boy." Wrote President Wheeler, "A magnificent success." Van't Hoff commended the thesis as remarkable for its "originality and vigor." The Berkeley correspondent of the San Francisco *Examiner*, however, must surely have interviewed Cottrell's mother, the fact-fuddled Cynthia, for in that paper Cottrell was referred to as a Leipzig instructor (his middle initial wavering between "C" and "S"). He had, said the story, been placed in this post by Professor Ostwald, one of the greatest chemists in the world, who had heard of his work as an Oakland High School teacher and sent for him. The Miss Wetherells and the Miss Hardys who, in those far-off days, had despaired of Cottrell as a speller and linguist could, with pursed lips, have nodded sagely had they known how he faltered in reporting his moment of triumph to Jess: "I got through and even came off with the highest grade they give—'sumun cum laude' (if that Latin isn't spelled right it only goes to show that a doctorate doesn't cover all sins)."

On the day following his exams he overslept and to the incredulity of his German fellow students decided to put in most of the day in the laboratory. This, in a way, gives an added clarity to an episode that took place three years later in 1905. A colleague of Cottrell's at

Berkeley, Professor W. C. Blasdale, was then making a European tour in the course of which he visited the Ostwald laboratory. There he inquired if any of the men had known Cottrell.

"He is not here now," said the instructor who replied and then added thoughtfully, "but his spirit is."

HE WAS tired. He was tired in a way that was unfamiliar and disturbing and rest was not what he wanted. The old intensity on which he had always confidently counted to brand his work as boldly as a trademark seemed to have dissolved along with the solute particles whose rate of ionic diffusion he had sought to measure in Leipzig. Yet the formula he had adapted for those was a worthless equation for an understanding of the dimensions of his own weary exhaustion wherein his mind seemed distracted by its perpetual yawning. Certainly a young man of twenty-six whose reputation for vigor was already something of a minor legend had cause for concern.

And concerned he was. For six months now Cottrell had been back in Berkeley and for one who had always found a certain satisfaction in feeling appreciably tired ("It's a sort of assurance that something has been accomplished, whether there are any other visible evidences of it or not") this odd prolonged lassitude was causing him acute anxiety. He had wound up his affairs at Leipzig in an aimless fashion, puttering the meanwhile about the laboratory in a desultory way, but the feeling of anticlimax was too strong to make the interval before sailing seem anything but pointless. He could only conclude to Jess that he "was never built for a gentleman of leisure." Thus, although he sat for his examinations in July, it was not until mid-September that he sailed from Antwerp on a slow replica of the dowdy old *Waesland* that had brought him over.

His arrival in New York at the end of September had nothing of the high sharp spirit of adventure that had marked his departure from Baltimore a little over two years earlier. After tipping the stewards, he was left with a working capital of fifteen cents so that his first urgent move was to draw on his slender letter of credit. From President Wheeler he had already obtained a leave of absence for the balance of the year, leaving him free, or as free as Jess's strenuous objections would allow him to feel, to take immediate advantage of the Harvard fellowship.

It had been Cottrell's hope that the easy relaxation of shipboard life would furnish him with a void during which the wells of energy he had drawn on so deeply would, by a slow process of natural seepage, fill once more to their normal brimming state. When that failed to happen he felt sure that what was needed was not so much a fallow period of vacuity but to lose himself in a burden of new work, fresh problems, and unfamiliar methods. It was with this thought in mind that he hurried through New York and, after an overnight visit with the Newport Cottrells (who again found it fitting to remark on his likeness to his Uncle Gard), continued on to Boston.

The little awkward touches that seemed to have a strange magnetic attendance on his departures and arrivals did not desert him in Boston. On awakening in a hotel the first morning, he found he had checked the wrong suitcase at the railroad station and so had to fall back on parting his hair with a jackknife and brushing it with a handkerchief. This much he noted in his diary although he failed to mention how he treated his beard, which "to save a lot of time and bother" he had grown during his last Leipzig semester.

The beard, together with his dark, deep-set eyes, his strong prominent nose, and the embedded lines that already flared and curved from nostril to lip, gave him a deceptively old appearance. It was this young-old man, looking not unlike Lincoln, who was greeted with warm cordiality by Theodore Richards at Harvard. Both Ostwald and van't Hoff considered Richards the best man in America under whom Cottrell next could study. Harvard, too, had but recently recognized his importance by raising him to a full professorship of chemistry rather than lose him to Göttingen, and Richards, in a 1901 issue of an American chemical journal, had already publicly commended Cottrell's work on manganous sulphate. So sympathetic was Richards and so closely allied were their interests that Cottrell could say he found himself being treated more like an old friend than a student.

In spite of this harmony, things went badly. It was irritating to find Harvard, which Cottrell considered the very center of American university life, "terribly conservative" and its research bedeviled by red tape. American though it was, he felt even less comfortable there than in the plush British atmosphere of Cambridge. Too, there may have been a touch of homesickness in a resurgence of enthusiasm for Berkeley and a renewed conviction that, after all, "the West is still the place of opportunity for young people." But he was honest enough to recognize that some of the background of his criticism might well lie within himself. He felt himself to be unsettled and adrift in currents he was helpless to control. He worried that he was losing the firm grip and the confident approach that had always characterized his handling of any problem. He complained of a complete inability to make any headway and a chronic state of indecision came over him such as he had not known, he wrote to Jess, since he was twelve years old.

The result was that he took his troubles to Richards. He confessed his shame at his condition, of the horror with which he looked ahead to two more months of such uselessness, of the guilt he felt in wasting scholarship money which might better be used on a more deserving man with a solider course of research to pursue. This *mea culpa* he climaxed by offering to resign the scholarship. Richards laughed and reassured him. It was, said Richards, the usual state in which men returning from abroad found themselves before they could get reacclimated and again settled down. As for the scholarship, Richards thought that had better be left to the judgment of the committee of which he was a member.

But the "bluff" and "parody" of fainthearted laboratory work proved too much for Cottrell. As his sense of futility deepened, the brighter loomed the horizon over Berkeley. There he thought a fresh start could be made and his interest in work revivified. Jess was anxious that he return West and O'Neill wrote coaxingly of the remodeling of the chemistry building that would give ample room for Cottrell's new department. Moreover, a substantial sum had been set aside for equipment and special library facilities, all of which Cottrell could have the satisfaction of ordering for himself.

And so in October he withdrew all claims to the fellowship and by early November was headed homewards. It would seem that, considering his mood of depression, he would have lost no time en route. There is even room for a fleeting suspicion that perhaps he wasn't as anxious to return as he thought he ought to be and that this guilty knowledge contributed to his dawdling indecision. In any case his homing trajectory was not exactly arrowlike. He first must visit Schenectady and the General Electric Research Laboratory which, under the directorship of W. R. Whitney, was beginning its distinguished career as a potent center of industrial and scientific research. This was followed by a stopover at Cornell and then in turn the Universities of Chicago, Wisconsin, and Minnesota.

Jess at this point had come to a brief rest in company with her sister Frances, the itinerant elocutionist, at Walla Walla, Washington. There Cottrell arranged to meet her and stay for two weeks. When they met they talked of marriage. They dwelt on such intricate imponderables as a man's duty to his work and how far it was just for him to ask a woman to let him risk his health and life in the discharge of that duty. He held her in his arms and Jess cried but never was courtship more blessed with logic or so completely free of the errors of impulsiveness.

As with all horizons, the bright one of Berkeley receded at his approach. At first it was good to be back and to be master of his own laboratory but this was quickly offset by the gloom with which he returned each day to Oakland and the warping strain of the Filbert Street household. But if the evenings were bad the Sundays were worse. He came to dread Sunday dinner. So at odds were they from his dream of a home life, so disconcerting was Cynthia's witless dinner-table conversation that each occasion struck him as a "perfect parody" of what it should be. Despite his hopes of first becoming settled in his new work and saving some money before risking marriage, only the thought of a home of his own could ease the discomfiture to which he found himself constantly subjected in the heaving bosom of his family.

Then another mood of indecision gripped him. No sooner had he arrived home than he received a letter from Whitney with a flattering proposal. Ever since establishing the General Electric laboratory, Whitney had been on the lookout for an assistant director who could measure up to his exacting standards. In Cottrell he thought he had found his man. Would Cottrell telegraph terms, salary, etc., etc.? He showed the letter to O'Neill, who saw in it a useful lever to get a promotion and salary increase for Cottrell as soon as the opportunity might arise and who rushed the news to Wheeler. Obviously impressed, Wheeler felt Cottrell "ought not for a moment consider any such thing as this offer represents" and so Cottrell declined yet left the door ajar by saying that for a year at least he was too firmly committed to consider a change. Strangely enough, it was Jess who took the more positive stand, for when Cottrell argued that here was a chance to solve his financial worries and enable them to marry and start off on a healthier footing, it was she who replied, "We've sacrificed considerable for the university work and now we're not going to get cheated out of it." Luxury, she urged, could wait, for—under the circumstances—"you ought to know me well enough to know how miserable such comforts would make me."

This mere suggestion that he might be sacrificing Science to Mammon shocked Cottrell, and he took Jess severely to task. "There are," he told her, "one or two points in this last letter of yours which show that you don't fully understand the Schenectady matter yet. You speak of it as merely a mercenary matter on my part and attribute it to a desire to make you more comfortable and surround you with luxuries. I hope it might do that to be sure, but it was not the real motive which has forced the matter to the foreground. I doubt whether, with the conditions we would have to look forward to in Berkeley if we made such a start, I should be in as good a position to carry out my work as I should even in Schenectady where we should be relieved of many of our heaviest drags and we would be far enough away from the scene where we had planned to really accomplish something so that the future in this clime would not throw such a gloom over our home."

Gloom there was as the months wore on. After the hermitlike solitude of Leipzig the chafing proximity of others in his home rubbed his nerves raw, left them smarting under deepening doubts. He wrote Jess: "You know how dissatisfied I have been with my own performance this past term and how much I have missed the old energy and enthusiasm on which I had based hope of success. I don't think I have been in a better mood to be discouraged from without and convinced that after all I have overestimated my own powers and been more ambitious than my ability warrants. I don't think there has ever been a time when you could probably urge your old complaints against my work with so much chance of carrying your point as now. Whether you care to take advantage of the opportunity must lie with you. There is nothing so depressing as a swarm of old debts hovering over one's head."

What he had overestimated was his resistance to the utter exhaustion which the punishing strain of Leipzig had induced. He had returned to Berkeley in December 1902. By the following May he was not far from collapse, a fact of which only Jess was fully aware. "I've been trying to work this afternoon," he confessed to her, "but it's no use. My nerves are simply all gone for the time being and it's a long time since I've felt such an absurd desire to burst out shouting or crying or almost any old thing simply to relieve my feelings. I've tried nearly every scheme I ever thought of to awaken my old-time interest once more.

"I got this far down in my office and then had to simply get up and 'break for the woods' so here I am working on the hillside above the old tank where we used to watch the sunset from. The clock has just struck five. . . ."

He was still "fighting this nightmare" as he walked down the hill and back to the laboratory when another mood seized him. "I went in a minute to get my mail and I never had anything strike me more suddenly than as I came onto the step and opened the door. Why it was I don't know, but just at that moment all the worry and care seemed to leave me and all the old enthusiasm and even the old associations of the building rushed in on me. I was strongly tempted to take off my coat and go to work again but thought better of it and came home to dinner on time for once and my good spirits lasted me through. Now isn't that a triumph of optimism?

"But yet I know too well from the experience of the last few months that if I went to work in the lab, the other blank, stupid feeling might come over me at any moment. . . . I wouldn't mind so much but I'm simply useless at such time, my memory and all seem simply stunned. . . . My feelings seemed as if balanced on the point of a cambric needle and the equilibrium placed almost as good as wholly out of my control."

To sleep out under the trees, to fill his lungs once more with great calming drafts of High Sierra air, to command again serene and lofty vistas from the mountains—these, he thought, would return him to a functioning whole. He would do it, he decided, come summer vacation. Instead, when June arrived, he went up to visit Jess, now living in Santa Rosa. She had, of course, long since seen to it that he had shorn himself of the Leipzig beard.

2

In Filbert Street that December day in 1902 there must have been strange little drafts of eddying air raised into small swirling vortices by the sweep of long skirts hurrying with unladylike speed back to the house at 1019. Aunt Mame, on a visit to her friends the Engs, first heard the news and fluttered into a tizzy. Never in all her life had she been more surprised. Yet there it was in black and white in the Engs' copy of the San Francisco *Bulletin*. Although age was beginning to tell on her, she left for home in great haste and there, as providential luck would have it, met Cottrell at the gate on his return from Berkeley.

"Say, did you know?" she burst out excitedly. "Your engagement was announced in that paper you sent Jessie." Only that afternoon Cottrell had mailed Jess an assortment of local papers along with his regular letter—a matter of routine of which Aunt Mame was aware.

The news reached Cynthia in a different way. She, too, had been out that afternoon and met friends who stopped to offer their congratulations. A scant three weeks had passed since her Fred had been back from Germany and she took it to be this return to which her well-wishers were referring.

"Oh yes!" she exclaimed, pleased to have her motherhood recognized. "I've been receiving congratulations all around and we are all simply delighted at home."

In the prattle of conversation that followed, Cynthia carried on blindly until, with a resounding thud, someone dropped the clue, "your new daughter." Allowing for Aunt Mame's age handicap of seven years, it is likely that Cynthia's homeward rate of speed surpassed that of her sister. She could and probably did assume, almost as a matter of reflex, that the engagement was common knowledge to the rest of the family and withheld, in a manner to which she was used, from her. She arrived home to find Aunt Mame already there, and it took all of her sister's appeasing stratagems to convince Cynthia that, tactically, the surprise was complete. Then Cynthia must know was Jess light or brunette; tall or short; where she and Fred had met; was Jess at all musical? These and other questions Aunt Mame answered where she could and where she couldn't countered with the fact that Jess was quite active in the Episcopal Church.

"Oh, then I'm sure she's all right," Cynthia burst out delightedly, "*must* be all right." Mysteriously she added, "All the Episcopalians are saints. Well, when we get a little acquainted I can make her a nice shawl."

Cynthia's shawls—if they ever got made—had apparently long been a part of the family legend, for in reporting this conversation (supplied him by Aunt Mame) to Jess, Cottrell wrote, "My aunt said she had the hardest time keeping a straight face."

The fact was that the miniature journalistic scoop served up by the *Bulletin* was also news to Cottrell. Interesting, too, was the paper's promise that the wedding would take place in early summer. He puzzled over the source of the information and could only conclude that loose tongues at the university had been at work, then resigned himself to the inevitable. "On the whole," he wrote Jess that night, "perhaps it is about as convenient a way of having the thing settled for us as to be put to the bother of starting the ball rolling ourselves." With the matter thus precipitated, he set about looking for an engagement ring.

Jess accepted the situation calmly but not because it rid her of all her apprehensions of Cottrell's family. For years she had tried to soften the rigidity of his hate for his mother. In this she had been noticeably unsuccessful. She was suspicious, too, of Aunt Mame and for this she had reason. It had long been Aunt Mame's thesis, and one she never tired of propounding to Cottrell, that a marriage before he was well started on his career held dark, inherent dangers. By way of example she pointed to his brother Harry. Harry was by now writing plays that were achieving state-wide success, but a Western reputation had little export value outside the boundaries of California. For the sake of immediate cash he sold his dramas outright and thus deprived himself of royalties that might have financed him for a period on Broadway. His inability to break this cycle, Aunt Mame reasoned, was all the fault of his early marriage with its attendant responsibilities. And so Cottrell must beware lest he, too, become similarly trapped. Presumably this doctrine had not been without its effects on Cottrell, for he once wrote Jess from Berlin, "Before taking such a step, I feel a person should have a steady and regular income with his debts paid up and be in a position which leads to the direct line of promotion which he hopes to follow." Besides, even if all this weren't sound enough logic, there was Aunt Mame's motherly instinct that quite probably made her wonder where was the woman worthy of this boy she had raised —this man she had counseled.

Jess was a woman, so all this Jess knew and the knowing made her uneasy. While Cottrell was still abroad she wrote him, "I presume you have guessed that there is no true affection between your aunt and I. I can't say there has been anything but courtesy and kindness between us, but I have felt it was to please you. I felt sorry for your aunt, for you are her one treasure and hobby and it seems a pity we could not meet on the same footing. I have more than once said it was a blessing that I knew you before I met your aunt as I should never have cared to meet so perfect a person. . . . In all my life I have never met anyone who has the depressing effect on me that [she] has."

Cottrell, in reply, met the issue head on: "The hardest thing anyone has to do is to control one's own feelings towards others and especially to keep them free of the influences of what one thinks or feels the other's feelings toward them may be. Don't misunderstand me as really expecting this of you, Jess, for I know enough of women's nature to realize that that would be expecting something which is very unusual. From the average man of moderate strength of character, I think we can thoroughly require a good proportion of this. His rubbing up against the world serves as good training ground in this, among other things, and we find many men able to take a stand. Here, then, we can thoroughly set this standard and censure a man in proportion as he falls below it.

"With women it's different. It seems to be far more difficult for them to do it and requires a relatively stronger force of character to accomplish it. I've come to feel that here it's hardly fair to set it as a standard or normal—that's, perhaps, asking too much. But when, nevertheless, we do find it, it marks the exceptional character and we appreciate and honor it all the more and it certainly brings its own reward in many ways, not the least of which is peace of mind and independence of surroundings. All I may say is that I feel sure whatever you can accomplish by way of self-control in this direction will repay you and you can feel sure that it will not go unappreciated as far as I am concerned."

With the appearance of the *Bulletin* item, Aunt Mame was prepared to accept the fait accompli with such good grace and enthusiasm that Cottrell surprised Jess by saying, "She certainly does think a lot of you."

Jess was dubious.

This was the state of affairs at the time Cottrell made his visit to Jess in Santa Rosa between the end of the spring term and the beginning of summer school in 1903. They talked of an immediate marriage and then decided with finality that the Christmas holidays would be better. Whether or not as a result of this sweeping away of irresolution, Cottrell's spirits almost immediately began an upsurge. Somewhat buoying, too, was the fact that Whitney had again tried to lure him to General Electric and the assistant directorship of research at $150 a month "just for the summer." Cottrell was relieved that it hadn't been more and thus had proved a serious temptation, for once again the "old spirit" was upon him all during that summer and elatedly he and Jess ticked off to each other the fast-flying weeks until their marriage. And so he started the fall term at the university, his fervor and confidence fully restored, when Henry, his father, fell seriously ill.

It was soon apparent to all, including Henry himself, that his condition was hopeless. Between late September and mid-November he lay abed, bloated and swollen from what was diagnosed as a kidney ailment. With the aid of a professional nurse the family took turns at a bedside watch, administering what comforts they could, the wedding plans being indefinitely postponed. Even if death were to come quickly there was still a hazard of which Aunt Mame warned

Fred. After the death of her second son, Paul, Cynthia's grief had amounted to a hysteria that had prolonged itself for months. So fearful had this been, as Aunt Mame described it, that Cottrell foresaw the possibility that Cynthia might "have to be taken care of for some weeks with as much attention of a different kind, as my father's case demands at present." This, surely, would be no atmosphere in which to induct a sensitive bride.

Then shortly after eight o'clock on the morning of November 13 the nurse summoned Cottrell to help fix his father's pillows and relieve a choking spell. Cottrell raised the stricken man slightly to ease the paroxysm and, with an arm about him for support, held him thus as Henry Cottrell died.

3

By an odd coincidence the wedding took place in the little town of Nevada City, California, in the foothills of the Sierras. The Nevada City *Mirror* for January 1, 1904, forecast the event thus: "There will be a quiet New Year wedding in this city this morning when Frederick G. Cottrell of Berkeley and Miss Jessie M. Fulton will be married. The event will take place in the young lady's home in the Hamilton House on Main Street, and the nuptial knot will be tied by Rev. W. A. Rimer of Trinity Episcopal Church, only relatives and a few intimate friends of the contracting parties will be in attendance.

"After partaking of a sumptuous wedding breakfast, the couple will leave on the 9:00 o'clock train for Berkeley where they will make their future home. Mr. Cottrell is a professor of chemistry at the State University and is a learned gentleman, while the bride-to-be has made her home here with her sister, Miss Frances G. Fulton, elocutionist, for several months past. During her stay she had made many friends who will join in wishing them much happiness and prosperity."

In spite of Aunt Mame's fears, Cynthia's raving megrims had not materialized and so the original wedding plans were adhered to. In spite of the *Mirror* prophecy, the terms "relatives" and "friends" might well have remained singular. There was Jess's sister Frances and Cottrell's friend of boyhood days, Edwin Letts Oliver, who with his brother had published the *Penny Whistle* in competition with Cottrell's *Boys' Workshop*. It was Oliver who was responsible for Cottrell's presence in the Nevada City area.

After his father's death Fred had taken stock and found, as he had suspected, that Henry had no source of income other than a salary. This was no surprise but the fact that such a matter was never discussed by father and son is indicative of the level of intimacy existing between the two. With the onset of Henry's illness, fiscal outgo had exceeded income to the extent of some $700. Medical fees came to over $200 more but this was offset by the estate's residual cash. It was possible, although far from a certainty, that Harry would be able to relieve his brother of some of this debt, but failing that, it was up to Fred to assume liability. This was, of course, in addition to providing for a new bride, a mother, an aunt, and to a certain extent subsidizing the not quite self-sustaining elocutionary work of his new sister-in-law, Frances.

All in all it was enough to make a man with a $1200 yearly income (he had been raised) cast a net that might bring in more fish to fry. Cottrell thought he saw one such opportunity in a forty-five-year-old English mining engineer who had come up from Mexico and enrolled in the university as a special student. In an attempt to work out the details of a new refining process, the Englishman solicited Cottrell for ideas with the understanding that if there were any worth-while developments Cottrell would share in them. Then it was regrettably discovered that the Englishman was suffering from a case of paresis and this possibility came to naught.

Cottrell cast the net again. "Of all fool things, what do you suppose I'm working on now?" he asked Jess. "Well, don't tell anyone. I'm having a shot at artificially forming real diamonds. [It is a] scheme I've had in mind to try for a long time and just got some new suggestions on it the other day by accident." He readily agreed that this would probably bring him nothing more than a new and stimulating experience. It proved to be just that but it was an idea he entertained with varying degrees of enthusiasm for the rest of his life.

Then in November he was sought out by Oliver, who had just come down from Grass Valley in search of advice on some problems connected with the North Star mines. Oliver (who later founded Oliver United Filters, a firm that became internationally famous in the world of mining machinery) was attempting to work out a method of precipitation of gold and silver from cyanide solutions that were not proving filterable. Cottrell was eager to, help and within a month had offered enough valuable suggestions so that North Star voluntarily raised his $50 fee to $100. With the advent of the Christmas holidays he took this work into the field and joined Oliver in Grass Valley ostensibly for the sole purpose of furthering the precipitation of gold and silver.

A scant four miles separated Nevada City from Grass Valley where Cottrell spent his days at the North Star mines. Each evening after work Oliver would invite Cottrell to join him for dinner and each evening Cottrell declined with courtesy but without giving reasons. To Oliver's increasing wonder, this odd circumstance continued through a week of the Christmas season until the last day of the year when Cottrell, in a burst of confidence, told Oliver of his plans for the next morning's wedding. He invited Oliver to attend and together they set off in darkness on the first trolley out of Grass Valley in the predawn of New Year's Day. The tying of the nuptial knot and the sumptuous wedding breakfast must be over in time for bride and groom to catch the first train to Berkeley and home.

Whatever Oliver expected of a bride at an hour more fit for the rites of Druids than good Christian sacrament, he was not prepared to meet anyone as shy and reticent as Jess—a woman obviously destined to play South Pole to Cottrell's magnetic North. When he had recovered from that surprise he was thrust into another by Cottrell, who placed a ring in his companion's hand and asked him to be best man. The wedding breakfast, as did the ceremony itself, took place at the Hamilton boardinghouse where Jess and Frances were staying, but it was not a leisurely thing of champagne and innuendo, for daybreak had come and there was a train to think of. The food was rushed through and this might have been an omen for Jess, for it later became one of Cottrell's few known boasts that he never caught any of the uncountable trains he was to catch with more than a minute to spare.

Oakland now was no longer home. Even before Henry's burial it had been decided almost as a matter of course that the Filbert Street house would be abandoned in favor of something smaller and cheaper, nearer the university. The proposed change brought in its wake a problem of some delicacy, the handling of which, by tacit consent, fell to Cottrell. Harry and his wife Min preferred to move to San Francisco. Aunt Mame would live with Cottrell and Jess as a kind of Elder Housekeeper and guest. That left Cynthia, the perennial enigma. The relationship of Cottrell and his mother was still only dimly, if at all, understood by friends and other outsiders. How then, in a small university town where lively faculty gossip was a factor to be reckoned with, could one explain why a healthy aunt was brought into the family while a less robust-looking mother was put out to board?

In the end there was no solution to this question except the one pointed to by the implacable fact that under no circumstances could Cynthia live with them. Jess, as well as Cottrell, had had her fears on this score which he had sought to allay before their marriage by writing, "She has ruined one home and is not to have a chance to get a start on ours." To prevent this meant that Cottrell must, for the first time since the night at the piano, speak in something besides monosyllables to his mother. This he did—plainly, coldly, and with no qualifications. His father's illness and death, he told her, had in no way mellowed his feeling. Since she had either shirked or proved unreliable for nurse duty he did, in fact, think his resentment had deepened. She must find a room of her own where she could board and for this he would give her $25 a month, which under no circumstances was she to exceed. Cynthia asked if she were to be allowed to visit them. He told her that if Jess would consent to receive her socially he would not interfere. However, this must be at a prearranged time and he would see to it that he would then be away from the house. Only one concession was to be made to appearances. Until he returned from Nevada City with his bride she and Aunt Mame would be allowed to share a room in the new home. On their return Cynthia must go while Aunt Mame would discreetly find other quarters for a few weeks until the couple adjusted themselves to their new quarters, and after that take up residence with them. Cynthia, without a scene, bowed before the icy blast of the inevitable.

It was, then, to a five-room cottage on Spring Street in Berkeley that Fred brought Jess to start a new year and a new life. The rent was only $18.50 a month and the view from the 400-foot elevation was excellent. Here they could begin to realize the things of which they had written during Cottrell's long months abroad. Here they could start his university career, raise their children, and round out a quietly good and useful life. Here they could discharge, through Cottrell's teaching and contributions to science—made with Jess's patient help—their preconceived duties to their fellow men. Had they not been so badly in need of money there is even a chance that it might almost have turned out that way.

4

To the scientist and the inventor has fallen the lot of closing the gaps in man's technical progress toward dimly perceived ends. In the pursuit of this he has one distinct disadvantage as compared to the closers of other gaps—those who would span chasms, bridge rivers, or dam canyons—for, once the work of the latter has begun, the end is always in sight. The concept of a new technical idea, however, is in the beginning often a one-sided abyss, and if its other rim be successful commercial application the crossing is only for those possessed of many things. Among these are courage, health, perseverance, money, intelligence, and devotion to an idea, all in a combination sufficiently tensile to withstand false leads, compromise, changing goals, delay, discouragement, and temporary failure. There are other necessary ingredients to such success (for example: a need must exist) but the patent offices of the world are congested with ideas now moribund—relicts of those who lacked one or more of the essentials in the process of transforming the thing-in-mind into successful application.

Sometime during 1905, Cottrell, in his continuing search for ways to bring his income up to the subsistence level, had the genesis of an idea. Like many such, it was not entirely new nor did it spring full-blown from his scientifically intuitive consciousness. Indeed, what he later developed was not what he originally sought. The fact that his thought may have been derivative he quite cheerfully acknowledged, and this debt to the past he was later to recognize in a magnificent gesture that was in itself a tribute to the innately creative nature of his thought processes. That, however, was some years yet in the offing and, as of 1905, he had only reached the brink of the chasm.

At this time his work at the university had hit full stride and he was, at last, measuring up to his own expectations. For one thing, he was doing extensive work with a new liquid air machine (the first on the Pacific Coast) which he had ordered and installed in the base-ment of the chemistry building—work which was to form the basis for his intensive interest in and wide knowledge of gas liquefaction. These in turn were to lead him into his important role in the produc-tion of helium during World War I. He was, in so far as any teacher ever is, satisfied with the progress of his students, and the technique he relied on to teach them he described to Professor Miles Sherrill of M.I.T.: "I use the pretty well worn standard experiments . . . to start the men off on and if they show any stimulation under that at all, encourage them to follow up such leads as they find. I don't try to lay out a definite set of experiments for each to cover. In fact, it often happens that a man will spend nearly a whole term on one experiment and its ramifications but I hold everyone in the course responsible for a fair first-hand knowledge of what has been done by all the members during the term. They then have to watch each other's work and get all they can from it."

Yet his students found him alternately a source of buoyant in-spiration and black despair. He took a deep interest in the work of each with singular freedom from favoritism, helping and sug-gesting whenever possible, throwing all his energies into any experi-ment if, in so doing, he could increase its chance of success. It was a gifted student who could respond to the full, and one of them one day went almost tearfully to Cottrell's colleague, Louderback, in search of advice. He could not see, said the student, how he could ever finish his work for the term in Cottrell's course. Time was running out and there was no relief in sight, for no sooner did he get his apparatus set up to start on his experiment than Cottrell would come along and in a five-minute chat suggest a half-dozen new and different ways in which the thing could be carried out with the possibility of better results. It was a trait that in years to come was to haunt many a hardened researcher who could choose and reject such ideas as he saw fit. To an impressionable student, however, it sometimes appeared to be an open door to chaos.

About this time, too, Whitney made what had seemingly be-come his biennial bid, this time extended personally. The visit took place in Cottrell's own laboratory, both men seated with feet propped comfortably on a desk, when at a crucial point their con-versation was interrupted by the clatter of crashing glass. A student assistant, busily engaged in the background washing laboratory dishes, had dropped a large beaker at the moment he thought he heard Whitney make the unlikely offer of $10,000 a year. In confusion the young man hurriedly picked up the pieces and left the laboratory. Whether or not this was the amount, word got around the campus that all manner of fabulous sums were being pressed on Cottrell to transfer his talents to Schenectady. Another student at the time remembered having heard of $25,000—a distinctly tidy salary circa 1905. Whatever the fact (it was probably closer to the lean side of $5000), it also set tongues wagging that Cottrell had refused and so it was probably here that the legend of his fine disregard for money was a-borning.

Whitney's, however, was not the only offer Cottrell rejected. Between 1905 and 1906 he published four articles in various scientific journals. These ("A Review of Physical Chemistry for the Year 1904"; "The Liquid Air Plant of the Chemistry Department of the University of California"; "On Crystalline Habit"; "On Air Liquifiers"), aided by favorable reports disseminated via the collegiate grapevine, were heightening his academic stature to a point where Western graduate students were applying for work in his laboratory in much the same manner as he had once sought to study in those abroad. His reputation even crept southward, which, of itself, spoke well for one holding only the junior commission of instructor, so that when, in May 1906, Texas Agricultural and Mechanical College was looking for a man to head their chemistry department, they offered Cottrell the chair at approximately double his California salary and a house, rent-free. Cottrell was inclined to accept.

How he appeared at this time in the eyes of those colleagues who admired him is best exemplified by a letter of Professor O'Neill to the president of Texas A and M in support of Cottrell's candidacy: "All the men with whom [Cottrell] came in contact [during his graduate years] regarded him as the most promising young man they had never met. Among the men who have expressed this very same opinion to me personally are Professor Ostwald of Leipzig; Professor van't Hoff of Berlin; Professor J. J. Thomson of London; Professor Jacques Loeb of this University; Professor Whitney of the Massachusetts Institute of Technology; Professor Campbell, Director of the Lick Observatory, and many others not as prominent as those I mention. In fact, everyone who has come in contact with him has only words of the highest praise. He is the best student we ever had in our department. He is the most industrious man that I have ever come in contact with. He is wedded to his subject and spends about eighteen hours of the twenty-four in his laboratory. His work is of the highest order, both in the higher scientific aspect and in the applications of science. He is one of the very few men whom I have met who have a thorough knowledge of the theoretical side and who, at the same time, are most apt with their hands. He is a very dexterous manipulator and is one of the few men who make their own apparatus and repair anything that goes wrong. With that he has the power to enthuse his students and make them work almost as hard as he does. He is interested in all phases of the subject and has a most remarkable knowledge of them. He is the best man in our department and we all expect great things of him.

"Personally he is a very large man, very good looking, has a genial manner and much personal magnetism. He makes friends everywhere and has a host of them in this university. . . ."

Later in this panegyric O'Neill drew a breath and paused to pat Jess on the head as "a very agreeable lady," but down in Texas, a state never noted for restraint, they might well have wondered what manner of man was this intellectual *Sequoia gigantea;* what breed was this that California now lay claim to producing?

Aside from the salary, what moved Cottrell most to consider deserting Berkeley was a direct result of San Francisco's earthquake and gutting fire which in 1906 threatened to drain off half the university's annual appropriation, thus seriously crippling the research to which Cottrell's teaching theories were pegged. The fire had dealt him still another blow. Experimental work on the idea he had conceived the year before was being carried out in a small laboratory in San Francisco, all data and apparatus having been lost in the holocaust. While this was in no wise irreparable, it was on the fruits of this that he had counted to bolster his income and for which the higher Texas salary might well serve instead. However, before he committed himself definitely to accept, three things led him to decline the opening. One of these was that the university funds were not as badly curtailed as he had feared. Next, in view of the Texas offer, Berkeley officials saw the light, raising him to an assistant professorship and increasing his salary to $1400. The third, and very possibly the deciding factor, was that the idea on which he had been working suddenly took a whole new turn and he became surcharged with enthusiasm over the expansive vistas which now seemingly lay open before him.

During Cottrell's stay abroad the Du Ponts had constructed a plant for the manufacture of explosives and acids near Pinole, California, some twelve miles north of Berkeley on San Pablo Bay. In the production of sulphuric acid the Mannheim process was employed—one of the first of the country's few plants then using the new "contact" method which was replacing the slower, more cumbersome and costly "chamber" process. In the contact process sulphur dioxide and oxygen were passed through an iron oxide catalyst and from the sulphur trioxide that was formed a strong pure sulphuric acid was made. At Pinole, however, they found they had a problem in removing arsenic, which was forming and "poisoning" the catalyst. Could Cottrell, they asked, remove the arsenic?

Cottrell thought he could and devised a centrifuge machine out of a glass tube thirty inches long and one and one-half inches in diameter which he rotated at high speed. The arsenic-contaminated acid was introduced into the cylinder in the form of a mist, and in the process of spinning, the respective particles separated and condensed. This in turn gave rise to an idea which automatically followed: it was a final step in the contact process to bubble the sulphur trioxide gas through water or dilute sulphuric acid in order to get the end result of relatively pure sulphuric acid. In so doing, however, a dense white cloud was formed, making the acid difficult to collect by the ordinary methods of gas "scrubbing." The formation of this dense mist therefore was considered a thing to be avoided. But, said Cottrell, far from avoiding such a step, instead let such a vapor form as often as possible and collect the acid by the centrifugal action of his device.

The laboratory results stirred a cautious enthusiasm in the Du Pont officials, and while they showed no eagerness to back further experiments financially, they were quite willing to offer all the plant's facilities plus unlimited amounts of sulphuric acid to test the plan out. It was here that Professor O'Neill once again proved the valuable friend. One of his former students was Harry East Miller, a consulting chemist fifteen years Cottrell's senior and a member of one of Oakland's solidly established families. Miller provided the money for apparatus as well as laboratory space in his San Francisco office. Here, in rooms above the old San Francisco

Stock Exchange, they whirled their centrifuge machine so zealously that on more than one occasion a note came up from the Exchange below with the request that experiments be stopped so that the business of stock transactions could go on. It was here, too, that they drew up Cottrell's first and second patents covering the process. Here on a larger scale they designed a pilot plant which was tried at Pinole and, perversely, didn't work. It was the models and data for this equipment which were lost in the San Francisco fire, but neither Miller nor Cottrell was daunted by these two setbacks, for Cottrell had yet another idea.

5

When, in 1890, Cottrell the editor briefed the readers of his *Boys' Workshop* on the current state of things electrical he mentioned the "deposition of smoke and dust by electrical aid." How this buried little gem of information next came to his attention is impossible to say. There are those who believe that, while still a student at Berkeley, Cottrell saw E. P. Lewis, professor of physics, perform an experiment based on an early (1824) suggestion made by Hohlfeld in Germany indicating that ordinary smoke could be dispelled by use of electricity. By another account it was much later and in a discussion of his centrifuge work with Dr. James G. Davidson (also of the physics department) that together they looked up the work of Sir Oliver Lodge in electrical precipitation. Possibly the precipitation work he had done with Edwin Letts Oliver at the North Star mines suggested something. Cottrell himself seems to have no clear-cut recollection of how the idea occurred to him. In 1913 he wrote, "Some eight years ago, while studying various methods for the removal of acid mists in the contact sulphuric-acid process at the University, the author had occasion to repeat the early experiments of Lodge and became convinced of the possibility of developing them into commercial realities." In 1948 he said that in 1907, at the time of filing his first application for a patent on the electrical method, "no precipitation classification existed in the Patent Office so in looking ours up we had never run across that of Sir Oliver Lodge. When it came to my attention, about the time we were making the installation at the [Du Pont] powder works [near Pinole] I wrote to Lodge, expressing my admiration for his work and told him what we were doing. I assured him that we were not trying to steal his show and recognized his intellectual priority." Whatever the case, sometime early in 1906 Cottrell applied electricity to the problem of collecting sulphuric acid mists and in the process a new industry was born.

It was a new industry but an ancient problem to which it was applied. The twentieth-century complainers of smog had their counterparts as far back as 1306 when the use of "sea coales"—presumably by such troublemakers as armorers—was prohibited by royal proclamation in England. One or two cities in Germany, or rather its Holy Roman predecessor, had occasion about the same time to ban the use of coal as fuel for metallurgical purposes. Later, members of the English Parliament found coal smoke so offensive that Queen Elizabeth obligingly forbade the burning of coal in London while the delicate nostrils of that body were collectively assembled.

While the problem at that time—if problem it were—could largely be considered an aesthetic one, with the advent of the Industrial Revolution it became quite a serious matter indeed. England, with her high humidity and dense fogs, began to suffer acutely. It was only natural, therefore, that the most ambitious attempts to cure the evil should have originated there with Lodge, although, in the years between Hohlfeld and Lodge, Guitard in England attacked the subject while at least four others of assorted nationalities unsuccessfully investigated the field between the work of Lodge and that of Cottrell. Lodge had, in fact, gone so far as to try to dissipate the Liverpool fogs. Then, in collaboration with a colleague named Walker, he devised a precipitation plant for the collection of the lead fumes at the Dee Bank Lead Works in Wales.

At the time this experimental installation was taking place the seven-year-old Cottrell had just come to grips with the alphabet and the word "precipitation" was not on Miss Horton's elementary spelling list. He could not know then of the chagrin of those who witnessed its failure. Yet the works manager of the lead plant (a Mr. W. M. Hutchings of Willington Quay-on-Tyne) who assisted Lodge with that early Welsh work wrote Cottrell in 1916: "It is, perhaps, not inappropriate that [I] who in 1884 conducted the first industrial experiments in the direction, in Wales—and failed—should salute and very heartily congratulate the man who has, some thirty years later, made so brilliant a success.

"Our failure was a very great disappointment at the time and I have sometimes thought that we were not clever enough, or gave up our attempts too soon; but there is a good deal in what you say as to the inadequacy of the electrical appliances then at our command. . . ."

What Hutchings said was true. All attempts previous to Cottrell's had failed because of an inadequate source of electrical power. All had, in the laboratory, been able to demonstrate that if a charged wire were introduced into a smoke-filled jar the smoke would disappear. Once in a flue, smoke particles had a baffling way of continuing unabated past any electrical traps and on out the chimney.

Cottrell's contribution to the problem is perhaps best told by Walter A. Schmidt, a Cottrell pupil, who later became one of the foremost authorities on and contributors to the art of electrical precipitation: "Cottrell made the first big advance when he took hold of the weapon which was given to him through the development of alternating current and the transformer. He rectified this high-tension alternating current and at last had a positive source of power with which to work. His first little outfit gave him only a few thousand volts, but with this he made an accidental discovery one evening while working in his laboratory with the lights turned out. He observed that cotton-covered wires, which were strung across the room and which served as conductors, were luminous in the dark. Here was the answer to the question of how to produce proper discharge —namely, cover the electrodes with innumerable fine hairy points from which the charge could leak away. A small laboratory apparatus was built and tried out on sulphuric acid fume. It worked. . . ."

The cotton-covered wire which glowed in the dark was immediately dubbed—either by Cottrell or by his patent lawyer—a "pubescent" electrode. Of this, Cottrell later wrote, "I had really considered the pubescent electrode idea and [patent] claim as my own important and distinct contribution to the art and without it should very likely never have ventured into practical exploitation of the process." Such is the nature of invention, however, that even the discoverer cannot always properly assess the merits of his discovery. This idea of the pubescent electrode to which Cottrell stubbornly clung for several years, through both successes and failures, eventually turned out to be all but worthless for the weightier work electrical precipitation was soon called upon to do.

Elizabethan distaste of the burning of "sea coales" had by 1900 grown into a behemoth of resentment, especially in the mining areas of the western United States, where smelters were charged with killing forests, poisoning cattle, ruining the soil, ulcerating sheep, searing crops, turning good horses into "roarers," devastating orchards, and bringing all manner of harm to man's good health and prosperity. For once, in some sections of the country, both sin and the locust had competition in rural public opinion. The fumes of arsenic and lead, as well as the true gas, sulphur dioxide, were among the chief offenders and the smelters found themselves in a welter of claims and litigation and, occasionally, even with the threat of closure. In some cases the dust and fume could be controlled by ante-Cottrell devices—by newer, more efficient smelting methods and by taller smokestacks—but the nature of the gases and fumes had never been thoroughly studied nor were the factors that affected their control (such as temperature and humidity) fully understood. Strangely, too, the problem was largely considered from the standpoint of being a nuisance and little thought was given to the loss of "values"—the thousands upon thousands of tons of recoverable material that was daily pouring out of the nation's industrial smokestacks to be dissipated and lost in the winds that carried them away. The question of damage was often further complicated by the absence of any scientific study by which the smelter could establish its innocence in a specific case and so in many instances of small claims—for a horse or a crop—a policy of appeasement was followed, a compromise reached, and the farmer or grower paid off.

In the first decade of the century there were three well-publicized and classic examples of smelter smoke injury in the United States—at Ducktown, Tennessee, at Salt Lake City, and at Anaconda, Montana. Some indication of the scope of the problem can be seen from a study that was eventually made at the latter and which revealed some startling figures. In a normal day's operation, up and out the stack of that copper smelter went the amazing total of 3200 tons of sulphur dioxide, 200 tons of sulphur trioxide, 30 tons of arsenic trioxide, 3 tons of zinc, and over 2 tons each of copper, lead, and antimony trioxide. The marvel is that anything remained, but nothing could more clearly demonstrate that here in full bloom was a cardinal essence of successful invention: a need existed.

Professor Robert E. Swain of Stanford University, in a (1949) historical review of smoke and fume investigation, wondered "what would have been the outcome at Anaconda if Frederick Cottrell had not been curious enough to try out the experiment of Sir Oliver Lodge. . . . The emissions from the low stacks of an old plant operated at a neighboring location had killed all vegetation, and losses of livestock by arsenical poisoning had been heavy over the near-lying area. Years after the plant was dismantled, the topsoil of a large area centering at the old site was stripped off, sent through concentrators, and smelted at the new plant with a reported recovery of over $1,000,000 in copper and other metals.

"Then the new smelter was erected, the largest of its kind in the world, and a marvel of engineering skill in design and operation. When its four 200-foot stacks failed to abate losses in livestock, a new stack, 30 feet in diameter, 300 feet tall, and located on a spur of the Rocky Mountains 700 feet above the roasting furnaces and 1,100 feet above the floor of the Deer Lodge Valley, was erected as a common outlet. Its great height, the buoyancy of its hot gases, and the 6,000,000 cubic feet of settling chamber and flue space were the reply to the challenge. But it failed."

Thus it could not be said that some smelters did not try to solve the problem in the light of what knowledge they had. Nor was electrical precipitation alone to prove the single final answer in all cases; but before Cottrell was ready to test his method on the Anaconda leviathan there was many a slip and several discomfiting failures.

While 3,000,000,000 cubic feet of gases were pouring daily out of the 300-foot stack at Anaconda, the same student assistant who had dropped the glass beaker during the Cottrell-Whitney conference was learning to smoke a pipe. The responsibility for this probably rested lightly on the shoulders of Cottrell, a non-smoker, for the results were too exciting. As it was blown into a glass jar containing a charged pubescent electrode the smoke disappeared. This was taking place in a glass-covered areaway in the chemistry building at the university where Cottrell had resumed his experimenting after the San Francisco fire. Next he rigged up a miniature contact sulphuric acid plant using odds and ends of laboratory equipment and passed the resultant sulphuric acid mist into the round glass jar which was about the height of an ordinary table-lamp stand.

With the current turned on, these fumes disappeared and acid collected.

What was happening was this: inside the jar was a cylinder of wire screen around which were wrapped several turns of asbestos sewing twine (asbestos had supplanted the original and fragile cotton wrapping) and which served as the discharge electrode. The walls of the jar, wetted by mist, became the collecting electrode. Although it mattered not, for purposes of simple experimental precipitation, which electrode was positive and which negative, it was later found in commercial practice that if the discharge electrode were negative a more stable and efficient operation resulted. This Cottrell considered his second important discovery. The electric field between the two electrodes then represented the passage of a constant stream of ions from one pole to the other. The mist consisted of an agglomeration of minute sulphuric acid particles which, when introduced into the jar, underwent a bombardment of ions which gave up their charges to the particles. These in turn, under the influence of the electrical field, migrated to the collecting electrode (in this case, the walls of the jar), where they collected and flowed from force of gravity into a suitable container. The laboratory simplicity of that, however, was not to prove equally effective in practice for a variety of reasons.

The discovery of the pubescent electrode and the utilization of negative polarity were not the only two factors contributing to the ultimate success of Cottrell's experiment. The third, and most important, was his use of rectified alternating current in connection with electrical precipitation, although he was not the first to use rectified alternating current. The early Lodge-Walker method depended for its electrical power on the then new Wimshurst machine driven by a one-horsepower steam engine. Cottrell had had some experience in rectification in his X-ray work with Little Joe Le Conte and with his partners at the Oakland exhibition, Lohman and Dyer. It is possible that it was on this that he partially drew for his precipitation work. He found in the course of his experimenting that alternating current could be successfully applied under some circumstances (this was later to play an important part in his next inspired application of the precipitation principle) but for large volumes of swift-moving gases in smelter flues a unidirectional current was vital. There were, however, too many insulating obstacles to building a direct current generator. In the laboratory, therefore (again utilizing as much homemade equipment as possible—a synchronous motor improvised by substituting a plain iron cross for the squirrel-cage armature in an ordinary electric fan motor), he transformed the alternating current from the chemistry building's regular lighting circuit up to as high as 10,000 volts. This then, through a special rotating contact maker, was commutated into a suitable intermittent-direct current. It was the belief of at least one student of Cottrell's work that in setting up this electrical apparatus Cottrell independently had invented a mechanical rectifier, entirely unaware that it had already been devised and covered by the Lemp patents of the General Electric Company. Whether or not this was the case, he now, of his own contriving, had a type and source of effective power unknown and unavailable to the earlier experimenters.

As with all prototypes, Cottrell's laboratory apparatus was crude but workable. If it were to solve nothing else, it at least drew the sting from his problem of nagging finances, for the day came when his tentative backer, Harry East Miller, was convinced that they "had something"—a something that was a far cry indeed from the first simple centrifuge.

"I'll make you a proposition," then said Miller. "I'll give you $500 for half interest and put up $2000 more for lab and patent work."

The problem of Cottrell's debts was thus momentarily solved, it is true, but he had in the process created something of a paradox. The ends it was to serve would be largely for others. For himself in the immediate years that followed, it turned out to be more of a Frankenstein, which, from his own indefatigable effort to control it, almost destroyed him.

6

The year now was 1907, the century still in its springtime, and in many ways the signs were auspicious for Cottrell. In January he turned thirty. Sometime during the early summer the certainty of Jess's pregnancy was established. In July the first commercial installation of electrical precipitation was begun at the Selby Smelting and Lead Company. On September 28 the articles of incorporation of the International Precipitation Company and the Western Precipitation Company were signed. Of these two firms, the quondam Prop.

of the *Boys' Workshop* Publishing Company, of Cottrell's Electrical Works, of the job printing establishment, and sundry other units of the Filbert Street syndicate, was named vice-president and one of three directors.

When it became evident that additional help would be necessary in order that Cottrell and Miller might do justice to the possibilities inherent in the success of the laboratory experiment, the latter interested E. S. Heller, a well-known San Francisco attorney of wealth and conservative persuasions. A fourth partner was Professor Edmund O'Neill, whose faith in Cottrell was by now of over a decade's standing. Together they decided that the time was ripe for a business organization. It was to be the function of International to take out and own all the patents on the process, foreign and domestic. Western was to be an operating unit, owned by International and licensed under those patents. At the moment of signing the articles of incorporation neither organization could have been considered Big Business, for between them they commanded a balance on hand of $95. Patent costs and miscellaneous expenses had eaten up the $1500 which Miller, Heller, and O'Neill had contributed in equal parts for the expenses of corporate midwifery.

The capital of International was divided into 10,000 shares of preferred and an equal number of shares of common stock—par value one dollar each. These were apportioned as follows: Heller, the president, held 1500 shares of both; Cottrell (vice-president) and Miller (secretary-treasurer) each held 3000 shares of both; O'Neill, neither an officer nor a director, received 500 of both. The balance remained in the company treasury. Once established, a personal loan of $3000 from Heller plus an additional loan of $1500 from the Wells Fargo Nevada National Bank in San Francisco put the companies on a reasonably sound operating basis.

It was with equipment capable of operating on a scale some two hundredfold larger than his laboratory apparatus that Cottrell turned to the powder works at Pinole to redeem the failure of the centrifuge device with which he had tried before to correct the difficulties in the contact process of sulphuric acid manufacture. This time, with his electrical apparatus, he found that he could successfully treat between 100 and 200 cubic feet of gas per minute, and in a few months things were operating so smoothly that he could jubilantly write, "Once again the results have exceeded our expectations. We have actually handled a gas current representing about three tons per day of real [sulphuric acid] with a power consumption of less than one third kilowatt including all losses and had no difficulty in collecting every bit of the acid in the gas. The whole apparatus, beyond the catalyzing chamber and cooling flue, cost less than $200."

All this was done at the expense of the new corporation as a demonstration test—it was no longer an experiment—of a new manufacturing process. Here at Pinole there was no question of fume or dust control, and it was simply the hope of the precipitating quartet that the powder people would take a license from International in the interests of more profitable operation. But before its unquestioned efficiency could be established here, negotiations were agreeably interrupted. At Selby, less than a dozen miles to the east of Pinole, where San Pablo Bay becomes pinched into Carquinez Straits, the Selby Smelting and Lead Company was chimney-deep in trouble.

In 1905 the indignant citizens of Solano County, directly across the straits, rose in protest against the Selby smelter in adjacent Contra Costa County, claiming that for eight months of the year the prevailing winds from the Pacific were carrying the smelter smoke across the county line and thereby causing manifold nuisances. Some objected to the odor, which they likened to the burning of sulphur matches. Old-timers declared that in years gone by Solano County had once produced the largest grain crops and the finest fruits in all of California, but with the coming of the smelter and its pervasive fumes the produce of the area had sadly deteriorated. Householders complained of corroded window screens and exposed metal surfaces; cattlemen of the damage to wire fences. That some sort of an evil existed, even the smelter people were willing to recognize, but like an old wives' tale the results credited to it grew and multiplied till life itself, as well as liberty and the pursuit of happiness in Solano County, seemed threatened. The result was a petition for an injunction to prohibit the smelter from permitting this offending condition.

The trial began in August 1906 but so lengthy and involved was the testimony that it was not until April 1907 that the findings of fact and conclusions of law were filed by the court. Even at that point the case did not look too hopeful for the defending smelter.

When, therefore, the smelter officials heard that summer that some successful precipitation work with sulphuric acid mists was being carried on almost within hailing distance, Western Precipitation Company had the figurative thrill of hearing the first paying customer knock on the door, or in Cottrell's own words: "When the Selby people saw this demonstration set-up work, they insisted they were much more in need of it to avoid damage suits than Du Pont merely for manufacturing economies and were consequently better clients for us to accept."

Western Precipitation Company delightedly accepted to the point of dropping the work at Pinole for the time being in order to concentrate on the greater need which pointed with almost compelling certainty to their future.

The problem at Selby was threefold, each phase of it being represented by a tall fuming stack. The most serious offender of these three was the stack carrying off several tons of lead fume daily from the lead blast furnaces. This nuisance was solved, about the same time Cottrell installed his precipitating equipment, by a pre-Cottrell device of known efficacy called a baghouse. The baghouse operated on the simple principle of filtration. In the case of Selby the dust-laden gases were blown through a filter structure consisting of almost 2000 woolen bags, each thirty feet long, from which the fine particles were deposited by a mechanical shaker. However satisfactory, a baghouse has its drawbacks. Wool bags are expensive (cotton can be used if the gases are cool and acid-free), they corrode, and their pores tend to choke up with dust. There are other disadvantages, but in some cases—as at Selby on the lead blast furnaces—they can and do work.

A second stack at Selby symbolized another smelting affliction. From this were given off mists from the refinery wherein sulphuric acid was used to dissolve the silver out of the gold and silver alloy extracted from the lead. It was here that electrical precipitation was first applied to a nuisance problem, its burden now that of a man and no longer merely an interesting exercise in dispelling tobacco smoke blown from a student's pipe into a glass jar. Nor was a simple piece of fuzzy cotton fiber equal to the task of serving as an electrode, for almost 5000 cubic feet of dense white sulphur trioxide fumes or sulphuric acid mist passed up the stack per minute.

Nearly the whole of Cottrell's summer vacation period in 1907 was spent in devising the actual form the precipitating equipment was to take and he attacked it with the wholeheartedness that had characterized his work for the Leipzig degree. What finally emerged, about the time he was ready to resume teaching in the fall, was a piece of equipment whose dimensions, by an odd circumstance, were heavily dependent on the figure 4. In a 4-foot-by-4-foot lead flue were suspended several rows of vertical lead plates, each 4 inches wide and 4 feet in length. These—the collecting electrodes—were spaced 4 inches from each other. In between each plate was a lead-covered iron bar that bore a striking resemblance to a swordfish's sword, each "tooth" serving as a point of discharge. After much experimenting, mica was considered to be the best material for these discharge electrodes—a conclusion arrived at only after months of sometimes heartbreaking trial and error. It was here that Cottrell discovered that negative polarity of the discharging electrode (since it permitted the difference in potential between the two electrodes to be increased without setting up sparking arcs) was by far the most effective for commercial precipitation work.

Such new discoveries, as well as constant changes in technique as the work progressed, brought home to Cottrell the necessity of maintaining some sort of record if only for use in drawing up patent claims and specifications. During his trip abroad, and with reasonable consistency, he had kept brief diary notes—a practice abandoned on his return to Berkeley. Then on July 1, 1907, he resumed and continued the diary (with only infrequent interruptions) for the next forty years. The entries were from the head and not the heart, and sometimes their brevity left Cottrell himself hard put later to recall meaning and intent. Then again, he alone was unbaffled by his handwriting, which amazingly combined the worst features of a cramp and a scrawl, as if he found a pen point a tardy, inefficient electrode for the discharge of ideas. It was chirography of an order that could set his correspondents to twitching and led several of them to the conclusion that it alone could stand as a mark of Cottrell's genius.

From this diary it is possible to trace some of the progress at Selby. In August the apparatus was working and the mist fairly well held down although "an appreciable amount escaped." Later that month they got a "pretty fair test which was moderately satisfactory." It was not until October that he could write of relatively continuous success, which he described in a letter to a friend: "The apparatus takes about a kilowatt and is simply started up and left to itself all night with nobody there to look out for it and, although it has now been in steady use almost two weeks, no trouble has occurred and the dense acid fumes which used to pour out of this mess have entirely disappeared to the eye." There were, moreover, pictures to prove it. Using the "before" and "after" technique common to hair-restorer advertisements, Cottrell took photographs of the refinery stack with the current turned off. Heavy white fume poured from it, streaming off in the direction of irate Solano County. The next photograph, taken a few minutes later with the current turned on, showed off the work of the Western Precipitation Company to decided advantage. From a distance of perhaps two hundred feet only the faintest of thin white puffs was noticeable. From across Carquinez Straits in Solano County that part of the smelter might well appear to be shut down.

In some respects good fortune attended Cottrell that summer. Had his first real installation been made at another smelter with a different set of conditions, it is possible that effective precipitation might have been considerably more elusive. It was indeed soon to prove itself so. Instead, success at the moment was so complete that this first (and substantially the same) precipitator was to remain in good working condition at Selby for almost the next four decades. After it had been in daily operation for seven years Cottrell was able to report that its cost for labor and repairs was less than $20 a month. Moreover, by applying the recovered acid to the making of bluestone (used in dyeing, pigments, etc.) the smelter was spared the cost of buying it, so that by 1913 the savings thus made had repaid the entire cost of operating five times over.

But Selby had still a third stack, on whose conquest Cottrell next set out. This discharged gases from the roasters—over 50,000 cubic feet per minute of invisible sulphur dioxide mixed up with a dense white cloud of sulphuric acid, arsenic, and lead salts. Here the early Cottrell process met its match and with this came the first revelation that precipitation apparatus was not amenable to a standard assembly-line technique. Henceforth each installation must be considered as a separate problem, each apparatus a custom-tailored job to satisfy the variables involved—the type of fume or dust or smoke to be treated, the temperature of the gases, their velocity, degree of humidity, temperature—not to mention the limitations imposed by the physical structure of the plant to which the equipment was to be adapted.

The process of such discovery at the Selby roaster was both lengthy and nerve-racking. Had not the initial success been achieved at the second stack, it is possible that electrical precipitation might once again have been abandoned until the next courageous investigator put it to the test. As it was, work on the roasters started in the fall of 1907. Yet in August 1908 (after uncountable trips to Selby) the diary was still a terse record of trial and error: "Planned out scheme for 8″ tube in roaster flue set through cast iron floor plates with 3″ tubes carrying asbestos etc. supported from beneath. Submitted plan to Braden and Englehart [smelter officials] who said go ahead 'as we must do something.'" *August 12:* "Got scheme of blowing air through bag electrode from within to prevent foulings. Also in p.m., idea of abandoning series treatment on account of fouling of high-tension electrodes and going back to idea of enough tubes in parallel to handle whole gases at one treatment and keep electrodes clean." That was 1908. By Christmas 1909 the recalcitrant third stack was still resisting him—a fact which held more meaning for the dogged Cottrell than any Yuletide sentiment. He arose at dawn on December 25 and took the seven-forty-five morning train to Selby. Then, on the last day of that year, they "started up roaster flue on first 24-hour service at 2 p.m."

It worked—but only after a fashion. In the end the smelter changed the furnace equipment, installing new roasters, which disposed of the main fume problem, and the permanent installation which Western Precipitation proposed at that third stack was never carried out.

7

The $500 which Harry East Miller had paid for half interest in the precipitation process before the organization of the two companies afforded Cottrell but the briefest of respites from money worries. It had, it is true, enabled him to pay off those debts remaining from his father's illness and death but the expenses of launching the new venture were too great (and the four partners equally scrupulous about insuring satisfactory development) to expect immediate returns in the form of dividends. Electrical precipitation, moreover, was voracious not only in its financial appetites. It also consumed inordinate quantities of time—the burden of which, from the technical end, fell mainly on Cottrell. Miller was of great assistance as a consultant, and a technician in residence named Harry A. Burns was installed at Selby to relieve some of the strain from Cottrell, but the almost daily trips to the smelter during 1907, the frustrations of the roaster installation at the third stack, which steadfastly refused to precipitate for longer than test periods, the classes at the university which Cottrell's conscientiousness would never allow him to neglect, meant that time must be borrowed from somewhere. As Jess had foreseen and feared long before their marriage, the hours were necessarily subtracted from those of relaxation at home.

To ease some of this pressure Cottrell, in December of that year, wrote Charles A. Kraus, a former California colleague and assistant professor of physics at Massachusetts Institute of Technology (later director of the Metcalf Research Laboratory at Brown University), in the hope that Kraus would consent to replace him during a leave of absence: "I have been spending some of my spare time in the past on some technical matters which have just come to a head and promise now to command more attention than I like to devote to them while having regular University classes on my hands. I have been expecting to give this whole winter vacation to this work and get it off my hands but it now looks as if a severe sickness of my wife will prevent my getting away much before the beginning of the term and that in itself makes the prosecution of this technical work more necessary than ever from a financial standpoint, besides presenting the further possibility that I may have to take her away from here for a portion of the term."

Jess, indeed, had been ill the entire summer and fall of an unspecified complaint rendered the more dangerous by her pregnancy. She herself did not expect to survive it, for, brooding in confinement, she wrote of her apprehensions to Cottrell: "I have often thought as I have lain here these last few months of the possibility of my being taken at any time as one that might happen. . . . Don't grieve for me, dear, I have been spared far longer than I ever thought I would. These years together have been happy ones to me. We have had our trials but they always seemed to grow so small. . . ."

So foreboding a thing was it that the blow, when it came, could not have been entirely unexpected. What happened is told in only the most tight-lipped of diary entries:

"*Dec. 10:* Called at 2:00 A.M. to take Jess to the hospital and spent the whole day there. Birth at 4:22 A.M.

"*Dec. 12:* Found phone from [Dr.] Burnham on return home that baby was failing.

"*Dec. 13:* Phone from Mrs. Burnham that baby died at 1:00 A.M."

For a year that had started out with such happy expectation, Christmas 1907 was one of no rejoicing. Yet neither was it one of despair. Badly as he—and Jess—had wanted a child, Cottrell's self-discipline (he had written her from Leipzig on the futility of regret) was equal to the realization that mourning for this lost son would help nothing. And so, between visiting hours at the hospital, he spent that Christmas Day with Miller examining sites in Oakland and Berkeley which Western Precipitation Company might use for the laboratory and shop which at this point they considered setting up.

Surprisingly, though, once the shock wore off, Jess rallied quickly even to the point of leaving the hospital early in January. By the fifth of that month Cottrell could report her as "picking up rapidly" and three weeks later she was well enough along so that he felt justified in leaving her in Aunt Mame's care while he made a trip to Montana. His leave from the university had been granted and now in the unfamiliar role of a sergeant of industry he was off to investigate a promising opportunity which the infant precipitation company would show either high courage or extreme presumption in tackling—the world's largest copper smelter, the giant at Anaconda.

It was eight years now since he had crossed the Sierras eastward yet something of the same feeling of conquest was still present. Now, to be sure, he stepped out on the platform for a look at the stacks as the train passed Selby, but for the most part, he wrote Jess, he relaxed in his seat and so enjoyed being waited on in the diner that a mood of expansiveness came over him. As on that first trip a challenge lay before him and it was with high good humor that he now saw himself as "gradually swelling up so that by the time I reach Montana I will feel bigger than the whole Amalgamated [Smelting and Refining Company] push and be in a position to be condescending to them as befits the representative of a great corporation like the International Precipitation Co."

It was just before starting on this trip that Cottrell, giver of ideas, first came into conflict with Cottrell, man of business and representative of a great corporation. The chief chemist at Anaconda was Frederick Laist (California '01), who was later to become a prominent figure in the mining industry and the two had met in earlier days at the university. During 1907 they discussed electrical precipitation equipment in a general way by correspondence, Laist urging that Cottrell sell the Anaconda people on the feasibility of installing the process there. On a trip to Berkeley, Laist went into the matter further with Cottrell, studied blueprints with him, and left with the understanding that, from the information and specifications thus gathered, he was free to investigate the possibility on his own for the sole purpose of determining whether or not the process was applicable to Anaconda. All in good faith and with respect for the fact that Cottrell might wish to keep the matter confidential, Laist built his own model precipitator and, on finding that it did not work, wrote Cottrell the details, wondering where he had gone wrong.

At this time the patent on the electrical process had been applied for but there was still no knowing which claims would be allowed. When word of the Anaconda experiment reached Western Precipitation Company, therefore, Cottrell must have been called to order by the partners, for he wrote hastily to Laist in tones of un-Cottrell-like severity. The letter was, in fact, a cease and desist order, for it had, he said, put him in "a very awkward position both in regard to my associates and touching other negotiations we have under way. . . . Under the circumstances, the failure of the experiment you describe was perhaps the best thing that could have happened." Laist could only reply in a tone of hurt bewilderment: "I must say I fail to see in what respects I have placed you in an awkward position or in what particulars I have acted other than in accordance with our conversation at Berkeley. . . . I have no intention of intruding into this business of yours against your wishes. . . ."

Cottrell relented with "kindest regards," good feeling was restored, and he decided to make the trip to Montana as soon as his affairs in Berkeley permitted.

The situation at the Anaconda smelter was not as legally threatening as that at Selby. Although quantitatively the emission of gases, dust, and fumes from the former was vastly greater, the nearby Deer Lodge Valley farmers were regarded with less sympathy than those of Solano County by a Master in Chancery who found (with considerable inaccuracy) that the damages claimed were due not to sulphur but rather to arsenic. These findings concluded that the farmers would suffer greater economic losses if the smelter were to cease operating, and hence shut off their market, than if the smelter were to continue as it was—pouring out smoke but paying out damages when forced to do so.

In spite of the verdict of the Master in Chancery, Anaconda officials considered it advisable to take what steps they judiciously could from an economic standpoint to forestall future damage claims, or, as Laist wrote Cottrell, the management would consider installing the Cottrell system for "sentimental reasons" even though the farmers would "have a hard time collecting" damage claims.

An installation of electrical precipitation at Anaconda, however, promised to bring about a curious situation arising from an old, old dilemma—sometimes in solving one problem, others are automatically created. The principle involved is one of many facets: politics —in the process of destroying one enemy, new ones are made; philosophy—in devising the machine to ease human toil, the cry has been raised that man's soul is somehow damaged; nature—in ridding Hawaii of snakes you introduce a plethora of mongooses. One of the ramifications of this very elastic doctrine immediately became apparent at Anaconda.

At the time of Cottrell's visit it was roughly estimated that 20 per cent of the sulphur burned there went out the stack as sulphur trioxide. Collected by precipitation, this would amount to about 500 tons of sulphuric acid a day, which the smelter would then have on its hands to dispose of rather than simply letting the old order take its course wherein the acid drifted in its gaseous state out on the Montana winds. Here was a splendid example of how embarrassingly indestructible matter can sometimes be. Anaconda had no use for acid in such prodigal amounts. To store it for unknown purposes was obviously impractical; to dump it into rivers was to create a worse nuisance than that they sought to correct; to market it elsewhere was poor economy in the face of prohibitive freight rates from remote Montana. These facts, of themselves, stood as an economic inhibition to the Cottrell process at Anaconda, and it was only later that the general problem of utilization of sulphur dioxide and sulphur trioxide was to be attacked and solved, sometimes wholly, sometimes in part, in a variety of complex and ingenious ways. Strangely, and as a matter of hindsight, the potentials of a solution at Anaconda were already there at hand. The greatest single use for sulphuric acid being phosphate fertilizer (one ton of sulphur made three tons of concentrated sulphuric acid which made six tons of superphosphate fertilizer), economically successful production of that commodity required the proximity of phosphate rock. That there were large deposits of this in Idaho, Utah, and Wyoming was only coming to be realized but even turning excess sulphuric acid into fertilizer would not solve Anaconda's dilemma, for in some cases Western soil was still virginal enough to produce highly satisfactory crops, and where there were signs of exhaustion the chances were that the farmers had not yet been educated to the necessity of replenishing the soil. Thus no sizable local market for fertilizer yet existed in the West.

But this was only a minor reason why Cottrell's Montana trip brought no immediate results. The chief stumbling block was the amount of royalties Western Precipitation was to receive. It was the theory of the Anaconda management that, since theirs was the world's largest copper smelter and, as such, a point of focus for metallurgical eyes, Western Precipitation should consider the advertising value of an installation there and moderate their fees accordingly. Cottrell had an answer to this as well as to another concept: "The advertising side of the present installation," he wrote Laist, "does not appeal very strongly to us just at present, at least not as part payment, for we find we are constantly getting more advertising than we know what to do with. Everyone that approaches us tries to work the advertising idea. Neither are we altogether willing to base our estimates of royalties entirely on the 'sentimental reasons' of the Amalgamated Copper Co. for wanting our process. Sentiment isn't ordinarily reckoned as one of the chief assets of a corporation of this size and would, at best, be difficult to put a dollar and cents value on."

The trip did prove one thing. If Cottrell the idea man constantly erred (in the eyes of the others) on the side of openhandedness, Cottrell the businessman could on occasion be a man of business. Anaconda made a tempting offer which, according to the diary, was "$5,000 a month up to $200,000 for metallurgical side. Ten cents per ton H_2SO_4 up to $100,000," but even these fat round figures fell short of Western's terms. Cottrell declined. There was, Anaconda officials then pointed out, a man named Richards whose invention they were considering installing and his eager terms made those of Western Precipitation "look like a hold-up." Matthewson of Anaconda ventured to say that the difference lay in the fact that Western Precipitation had a lawyer behind it. "I called attention," Cottrell wrote Jess, "to the fact that his company usually had lawyers behind it." Then he added, "I made the remark yesterday morning that I didn't pose as a businessman myself and wanted to leave this to abler hands. Matthewson looked very funny and said almost testily, 'Well, I think you have showed yourself a pretty good businessman *this* morning.'"

There was no immediate compromise and so Cottrell returned to Berkeley and the grinding Selby routine. The trip did give him an excellent grasp of some Western smelter problems, for he visited not only the smelters at Anaconda and Great Falls but also several in the vicinity of Salt Lake City. Here the new Garfield plant of the American Smelting and Refining Company was undergoing tribulations as great as those at Selby and Anaconda. In a good-sized arc, this smelter had bought up land for a distance of ten miles along the general course of the prevailing winds. They found, however, that complaints and damage suits came from fifteen miles in the opposite direction. It was only a matter of time, therefore, before Garfield was to become a precipitation customer.

Although the leave of absence had freed him from his university classes, the liberated time—and more—was given to the Selby roaster. Sometimes the precipitator would work and again it would not. This was particularly and exasperatingly true when it would be readied for a test, then started up, and for a brief encouraging period all fumes would be completely held down just as they were at the second stack. Gradually, however, visible smoke would begin to appear, it would increase to embarrassing proportions, and the current would have to be shut off to try again. The chief, and recognized, fault was the discharge electrode, which functioned efficiently when clean but which matted and fouled during prolonged use. Experimenting with a variety of materials, Cottrell still clung to the pubescent idea, but the worry and strain of trying to prove its efficacy were beginning to tell on him. His hours were long, his eating habits (which were really more an absence of habit) were irregular.

What with Jess's illness, expenses had mounted and since his university salary had been cut off during his leave he was dependent solely on an income as a paid employee of a Western Precipitation Company which had still to show dividends. Set against these pressures was his tenet that a man had a right to tax his endurance and health even beyond the point where it first gave evidence of deteriorating.

Such signs there must have been. In all probability he ignored them, for the first indication of near disaster appeared in the diary on May 26, 1908. On that day he noted that he had an attack of indigestion after lunch. This he apparently did not let interfere with his day, for it was eleven that night before he was on the way home. Then even Cottrell could no longer overlook the fact that he was a very sick man, although it was not until two-thirty in the morning that he let Jess call the doctor.

They operated for appendicitis. It turned out to be that and more —strangulation of the bowel and what was then called ptomaine poisoning. After three hours of surgery Dr. Burnham closed the incision and set about preparing Jess for the very likely possibility that Cottrell would not live.

8

For three days after the operation death was a shuttlecock. Then, slowly, Cottrell's resilience asserted itself until he had gained enough strength to return home after four weeks in the hospital. From that point on recovery was rapid and early in July he went north to Upper Soda Springs for a change of scene and to complete the recuperative process. It cannot be said that there Cottrell rested.

The crisis had necessitated still another leave—this time from Western Precipitation Company, which paid him a salary of $125 a month during his absence. If this was not enough money to meet all obligations it at least took care of the immediate necessities, for those obligations had by this time been compounded. Since his father's death there had been Aunt Mame and Cynthia to care for, as well as occasional help to his sister-in-law, Frances. Lately, however, another circumstance had come to the fore. Jess's brother Wallace had met an untimely death in 1902 at the age of thirty-four, leaving a widow and four children in less than comfortable circumstances. This growing family required more for clothes and schooling than their mother's slender income could now supply. There was no one to turn to but Cottrell, who as always could be counted on for uncomplaining aid.

These, however, were not the only worrisome things. Dr. Burnham and Professor O'Neill both urged him, in the name of his health, to take an additional leave from the university beginning with the fall term, but over this Cottrell fretted: "I don't want," he again wrote Kraus at M.I.T., "to drift out of the academic work into business life as so many have and I realize that the more time I take off from college just now, the harder it will be to settle down in the old traces once more." With this point he overruled the advice of Burnham and O'Neill and decided to return to his classes after the summer vacation.

Upper Soda Springs proved much too accessible by mail to keep Cottrell untroubled by still other nagging affairs. Miller had taken over the Selby work during his absence but had no better luck than Cottrell with the electrodes. "I'm afraid," Miller wrote, "that we must find some substitute for the asbestos. Its life is too short and I cannot for the life of me think of a proper substitute. I am beginning to doubt the lasting qualities of any pubescent electrode in roaster gases. These gases are too hot to keep the carbonized cotton moist and when once dry it soon burns, touching fire from an occasional arc. But even if we could find a resistant substance, the dust collecting on the fiber mats the same and defeats the very purpose and the asbestos becomes brittle and also mats." And if these difficulties were not enough a sense of urgency was added when in July the Superior Court of Solano County found that a nuisance existed at Selby during the windy part of the year from mid-March to mid-November and enjoined the smelter there from operating during that period unless the fumes were abated. In the case of the first and second stacks this had already been accomplished with the baghouse and Cottrell apparatus respectively, leaving the roaster gases the only villains. (So deeply rooted was their depravity in the minds of Solano County residents that on one Sunday large numbers of people complained bitterly that the fumes were stronger and more nauseating than ever. On this particular date the roasters and blast furnaces had already been completely shut down for three full days.) Then the urgency increased almost to desperation when it was found that the court would not allow the roasters to be run even for experimental tests on the precipitating equipment at that stack. It is more than unlikely that Cottrell, presumably vegetating in sight of Mount Shasta, was unmoved by these troubles. But if they bothered him it was not to the extent of rendering him immobile, for a letter to Norman Smith, his British friend of Berlin days, indicates how devoutly he was following (by the end of the second week there and a month after his discharge from the hospital) the doctor's orders of a complete rest: "I took a 30 mile tramp including some 6,000 foot climb over to Castle Lake, sleeping out one night a few hundred feet from a snowdrift without blankets, so I feel that I am no longer sickly and in the invalid class. Although my physical health is now as good or better than when I was taken sick, my weight and nerves are not quite back to par."

His nerves were, rather, in open rebellion. Though he adopted a quiet and unstrenuous routine after his return to Berkeley in August, they continued to plague him. Possibly as a result of this, as well as Jess's own tenuous health, he and Jess moved across the campus to another cottage, leaving room for Cynthia to move in with Aunt Mame in the old one. Yet week by week through September and October he grew worse, his weight now (normally around 215) down to 187 pounds; grew worse until one day early in November he made this diary entry: "Very nervous. Aunt Mame over to lunch at which my nerves broke badly."

Whatever happened at lunch upset him enough to send him back to Dr. Burnham, who recommended "giving up *all* work and getting out." This suggestion led him seriously to consider forsaking both teaching and the precipitation business, going instead into some such technical work as General Electric had offered until he was financially independent. In the meantime, while considering such a move, he took up water colors for relaxation. Frequently of an afternoon on which he had no classes he would wander, with sketch pad and a book, back into the Berkeley Hills he loved in an effort to shake himself of his overwrought state. It was on one of these jaunts, after two weeks of irresolution, that he came to a decision. On the following day he notified O'Neill of his plans and arranged to be relieved of his classes. Then he and Jess packed—including fresh supplies of water colors—and on November 22 boarded a coastwise ship for an indefinite stay in Southern California.

In leaving, he turned his back for the time being not only on the university and the vexations of electrical precipitation in the smelter industry but also on something else: a new adaptation of the electrical precipitation principle which, in conjunction with one of his former special students, an engineer named Buckner Speed, he had roughly worked out in the three months between his return from Shasta County and his embarkation for San Diego. It, too, was to create a new industry—this time in the salvation of potentially valuable oil wells on the brink of abandonment.

9

The old shibboleth, "ask Cot," had lost none of its potency in the years that had ripened the questing undergraduate into an assured assistant professor. As his reputation in the field of physical chemistry grew Cottrell's advice and suggestions were sought on all manner of questions scientific; the queries were not restricted to the California campus alone but came by mail from strangers as well as acquaintances in an ever-widening radius. To all Cottrell replied unfailingly—helpful in spirit where he could not be in fact. Neither the state of his health, the demands of his university work, nor the time-devouring precipitation business seemed to have deterred him from the obligation he felt to disseminate knowledge in spite of the irksome correspondence this often involved. It is doubtful if by this time he even found it flattering.

On his return from Upper Soda Springs, Buckner Speed came to him with a question. Speed's problem was an interesting one and dated back to 1904 when, as engineering trouble-shooter for the Southern Pacific Railroad, he had become involved in the transportation of oil. Southern Pacific then had a subsidiary oil company in the Kern River basin in California from which the crude petroleum was transported 350 miles in tank cars to San Francisco Bay. The question naturally arose as to the practicability of a pipe line but this oil was deemed to be so viscid that to pump it in this manner would require too many stations for heating as well as pumping. To reduce the friction of the heavy oil against the inside of the line, Speed, a clever engineer, invented a kind of pipe, rifled much in the manner that a gun barrel is rifled. To this idea he added that of a thin sheath of water between oil and pipe. Thus "wrapped" in a coating of low-friction water, the column of oil advanced along the center of the pipe line while the spiraling action of the rifling forced the water to continue in the outside position. Speed demonstrated this in his own back yard, applied for a patent, sold Associated Oil Company the idea, and eventually an eight-inch pipe line was built from Bakersfield to San Francisco Bay for $4,000,000.

It was a beautifully conceived approach but a serious hitch developed. In spite of the ease with which the water carried the oil, twenty-eight pumping stations were required en route, and the action of these destroyed the protecting sheath of water so that by the time the oil reached its destination it did so in the form of an emulsion—water and oil inextricably mixed. This was the problem Speed brought to the recuperating Cottrell in the fall of 1908, and twelve years later Speed recalled that these things had happened: "Instantly [Cottrell's] mind worked with a snap. 'Why,' he said, 'it's the same problem. For air put oil; for smoke particles, the minute water particles,' and then his favorite form of expression: 'What will happen if we put a high electrostatic stress on the oil?' Then in his characteristic quick manner, in a few minutes there were thrown together a beaker of oil, a spark coil, and two pieces of copper, and lo! the de-emulsification of the California oils had been solved.

"Within a few minutes on a block of paraffin under the microscope there was spread out a drop of the emulsified oil with two electric wires touching its edges. When the spark coil was put in operation, the water drops were seen to arrange themselves in the field of the microscope like the iron filing between the poles of the magnet, to dance about and jiggle themselves into larger drops; and in these few minutes of experimentation the problem was solved by which millions of barrels of unmerchantable California oil were rendered fit both for refining and for fuel purposes.

"It was a familiar phrase to be heard in the University of California, anywhere from the botany to the physiology departments, when any question of any description came up: 'Oh, go over and talk to Cot about it. He doesn't know anything about the subject, but he will put some idea in your head before you have talked with him ten minutes.'"

The ideas put in Speed's head proved abundantly fruitful, nor was Speed's recollection greatly sentimentalized. According to the diary, it was on November 3 (the day following the lunch with Aunt

Mame at which his nerves gave way) that Cottrell and Speed first discussed oil and water separation. Six days later, on November 9 ("nerves bad"), Cottrell drew up the first draft of a patent, naming Speed as co-patentee. In that short week much of the California oil industry had, without its knowledge, gained a new lease on life.

After almost two months of Southern California, Cottrell had decided that the change had accomplished its purpose, so he and Jess returned to Berkeley. Speed, meanwhile, through his contacts with the oil industry, had found a market for the new apparatus eager and waiting. The Lucile Oil Company, operating in the Coalinga field, approximately halfway between Oakland and Los Angeles, was faced with a prospect as grim in its way as the outlook of the Selby roasters was in the abatement of fume. The chief market for Lucile's petroleum was Associated Oil, whose specification of no greater than a 2 per cent water content conformed generally to that of the rest of the industry. The Lucile wells, however, were averaging closer to 15 per cent, which Associated was willing to accept when oil was scarce but oil, at the moment, was plentiful. The result was that Lucile tanks overflowed, and the operators were feverishly throwing up mud banks to contain a lake of the rejected and watery oil. What did not soak back into the ground or evaporate from this pool was an open invitation to fire. Bankruptcy loomed.

The arc between Speed's question and Cottrell's reply had first jumped into spark in November 1908. By mid-April 1909 a contract was signed with Lucile Oil, and in early July, Cottrell wrote Heller that this first plant, hastily erected, was a thorough success. The apparatus was treating 600 barrels a day and reducing the water content to 1½ per cent. Had it been necessary, this figure could have been brought even lower but the oil was now marketable, the Lucile Oil Company saved, and, as a gesture toward the experimental nature of the device, International Precipitation was content to accept only half a cent a barrel royalty. They had, however, already determined as a matter of policy that their next oil customer would be charged more in keeping with what the traffic would bear.

As in the case of Selby's second stack, Cottrell had once again been blessed with a measure of luck. With even greater individuality than stack gases, emulsions have personalities of their own. Along with the water usually come mineral salts to complicate the emulsion, and electrical precipitation is not always effective—a fact of which they soon became aware in their next installation at the Santa Maria fields, which ended in failure. This uncatholicity of application was later found to be particularly true in the geologically older oils of the mid-Continent field, although those of California and the Gulf were more often susceptible to electrostatic treatment. It later also proved to be true that most crude oils could be de-emulsified in the field more efficiently with chemicals than by the Cottrell-Speed process. As of 1948, however, the electrical process which grew out of the Cottrell-Speed patent was still a potent challenger to the chemical process in the desalting operation and in this accounted for about 500,000 barrels daily in the United States.

It was Cottrell's luck, therefore, that the first attempt at commercial dehydration took place at the Coalinga field with an emulsion admirably suited to the process. The next attempt, at Santa Maria, was as harassing as the third stack at Selby, but compared to the precipitation of particles in gases, the success first scored in de-emulsification was relatively cheap and easy. For the moment the success at Coalinga made it appear that the chief obstacle to the general adoption of the process was only the lack of electrical power and transmission lines at many of the oil fields, which often made it necessary to install a complete electrical power plant before operations could begin.

Despite the fact that the problem of the Selby roasters had still not been solved, the four partners now felt there were reasons aplenty to expect great things of their precipitation companies, Western and International. For Cottrell, under strict injunction to ease the burden of his work, this oil development only added new terminals to his Selby-Berkeley circuit. Speed, it is true, at first attended to most of the field work of the new process. In Cottrell's eyes he was "one of the most brilliant fellows I have ever met but impatient to the last degree," to which traits were added a "contempt for ordinary business methods." Speed, too, had personal debts of which he wished to rid himself and eagerly sold his half interest in the patent to the International Precipitation Company for $5800. The resulting situation in which Cottrell then found himself with regard to his own half of the patent he explained in a letter to Heller, who was then combining business and pleasure in Europe: "I received no part whatever of the $5,800 nor has the International paid me anything for the assignment made with Speed of our patent rights nor have they obligated themselves to do so in any way. If the company had had plenty of money in hand, I shouldn't have hesitated to have asked for something myself on these patents as I think you will see that the deal is really outside of our original agreement and I shall have to raise a few hundred dollars from some source within the next month or so to take care of personal matters here."

Aunt Mame, as well as Cottrell, realized the magnitude of what he had lightly passed over as "personal matters." In so doing she chafed at the impotence her own lack of money engendered: "If I could only turn my doing to some account that would relieve and help you I would be very happy. That is all I care to live for."

The fact was, Jess was pregnant again, and as the summer wore on her strength steadily failed her. In September she entered the hospital. Here again was a grim period of waiting for what, in view of her frailty, could only be regarded as inevitable. After an operation the baby was delivered on the afternoon of October 11 and died early the following morning. Once more Cottrell, accompanied only by Aunt Mame, followed a hearse with the smallest of coffins to the cemetery. They might well have dug this grave deeper, for now, with his daughter, he buried in addition all their dreams of a family.

10

The turning point for the precipitation companies arrived in 1911, when for the first time they found themselves out of debt and the techniques of the art in a post-adolescent stage. It had come about in this way: Although electrical dehydration of petroleum had worked at Coalinga, it failed at Santa Maria. With Speed's departure from the field after the Coalinga installation two new men were brought in, both former Cottrell pupils. One of these was Walter Schmidt, whom Cottrell characterized as an "excellent student" and who had been in the laboratory during some of the early precipitation-by-centrifuge experiments. After the success at Coalinga, Cottrell bethought himself of Schmidt, a Los Angeles resident, who might prove valuable as a representative of the new process in that capital of the California oil industry. Although this opportunity did not materialize, Schmidt entered the technical end of the work at Santa Maria. Cottrell next brought in another former pupil and instructor of mechanical engineering at the university, Allen Wright.

Wright was thought of as a "go-getter" and, as Cottrell described him to Heller, "he can drive twice as hard a bargain as either Miller or I."

Together Schmidt and Wright struggled for a year with the rebellious Santa Maria oil—tanks of which had sat on the Western Union Oil lease for two years in a worthless state. In that year it cost International-Western $10,000 to find out how stubborn were emulsions and why their process was not always workable. Most of this money was borrowed against Heller's signature, for royalties from the Lucile Oil works were bringing in only $200 a month. It had been Cottrell's idea to finance the work by selling some International stock, but Heller demurred against "enrolling upon our little tablet any persons who could in any way disturb our harmonious adjustment. I want to be in safe hands myself for all times," he wrote Miller from Europe, "that is, in your hands and in the hands of Cottrell, to say nothing of O'Neill, and I have no doubt that the rest of you feel toward me as I feel toward you.*

But Heller had reckoned without Cottrell who, in seeking to avoid placing all the financial strain on Heller, had, with Miller's consent, agreed to the sale of 1500 shares for $10,000 to three takers including Wright. Heller, when he heard of this, favored Wright but objected to the other two. Nevertheless, the harmonious adjustment which Heller prized received its first perceptible nudge. Then the Santa Maria venture stumbled, and some believe that friction developed between Miller and the more aggressive Wright. The loss of $10,000 certainly jolted both Heller and Miller and the question arose, weren't they after all taking their eye off the main chance— smelter fumes—in the pursuit of this diversionary oil business?

This issue was still unsettled when the emphasis again shifted to fume and dust. North of Berkeley, in Shasta County and in an area that was eventually destined to be covered by the man-trapped waters of Shasta Lake, were copper smelters facing the old familiar injunctions and lawsuits. Here, however, they had a new enemy in the U. S. Forestry Service, for what had once been heavily wooded mountains in the vicinity were now denuded for miles around; were now obscene mounds of raw red earth, bare and eroding. One of the transgressors was the Balaklala smelter at Coram. For electrical precipitation to tame the main flue here represented a step over Selby (50,000 cubic feet of gas per minute at the third stack) as

Selby had over Pinole (200 cubic feet), for the Balaklala stack handled up to 500,000 cubic feet of gas per minute.

After building a test apparatus, the main precipitator was begun
in the spring of 1910. This was no makeshift gadgetry, for when
completed at a cost of $125,000 it had the appearance of a small
smelter in its own right. The Balaklala management spared no cost
that the precipitator might be a success, and in testament of this
Cottrell himself wrote back to his partners glowing reports of the
co-operation he was getting. Yet in the process of erecting it (an
electrical engineer from the nearby power company remembered
many years later) Cottrell had need of an oscillograph. The type
required was then on the market for several hundred dollars. Such
luxuries were not for Cottrell. He decided to make his own which,
according to the electrical engineer, he did at a cost of less than five
dollars—not including an alarm clock for which he found use as an
auxiliary piece of apparatus.

For several months after its completion the precipitator did a
creditable job, but it failed to solve all of Balaklala's problems. It
could, as was claimed for it, collect most of the suspended particles
of metallic oxides but could not, as was understood before its installation, halt the true gas, sulphur dioxide. When the price of copper fell and damage complaints continued, the smelter closed. But
here again the problem of discharge electrodes had caused endless
difficulties. Here Cottrell returned to the pubescent idea on a large
scale, using asbestos fibers, trying mica also with more success. And
it was here, finally, that the idea he had once thought of as his most
significant contribution to the art—the pubescent electrode—was ultimately discarded.

This problem of the recalcitrant electrodes was solved in an unexpected way when in 1910 the precipitation business entered another new field—the Portland cement industry—whose distress was
no less acute than that agitating the smelters.

Down in Riverside, almost due east of Los Angeles, the hot sun
of Southern California, instead of ripening the fruit in the immensely
valuable nearby orange groves, was baking a substantial incrustation
of lime and clay on leaves and fruit alike. This came at the rate of
about 100 tons a day from the kilns of the Riverside Portland Cement Company, and the calcined lime, in settling on the trees, drew
moisture from the foliage and cooked itself on to a point where even

the winter rains had no cleansing effect. The cement company had tried to buy up the surrounding land but so costly was this process that after spending $1,000,000 for the purpose the dust was still within easy sifting distance of numerous groves. The result was the usual injunction within only three years after the plant had opened.

This situation was behind the query contained in a letter that Western Precipitation Company received from the cement company in February 1910: "Do you believe that your process could remedy the evil?" Although new problems were involved, Cottrell thought it could. The new factors included over 1,000,000 cubic feet of gas per minute which must be treated (double that of Balaklala) and, more serious still, the temperatures of the gases to be handled were extremely high—400 to 500 degrees centigrade.

Cottrell, at first, was none too eager to assume this fresh burden of responsibilities. Balaklala was taking up his week ends and vacation periods from the university, but now, too, he was at last giving belated recognition to the simple limitations inherent in being mortal man. Yet the plight of the cement company was desperate, and their insistence led him to propose that the installation be carried out by Walter Schmidt, operating independently under a license from Western Precipitation Company. Aside from thus relieving himself of any additional strain, Cottrell hoped in some measure to compensate Schmidt for the year of unsuccessful oil work in the Santa Maria field.

Though Schmidt's experience was limited, his selection proved to be a wise choice. Here the extremely high temperatures made the problem of electrodes all the more baffling—a problem that was solved only after a year of developmental work. Schmidt, after trying and discarding all previous types, came up with the "fine wire"— simply a bare wire of moderate diameter—which, in conjunction with the high voltages unavailable during Cottrell's early experiments, rendered unnecessary a pubescent type of discharge. This development, together with Cottrell's negative polarity and the use of rectified alternating current, then brought electrical precipitation out of its adolescence and the three ideas together formed the basic principles which held the art together for the next twenty years.

(The fine wire electrode also came into its own in the smelting industry about this same time and quite independently at the Garfield, Utah, copper smelter which had bought up land ten miles to leeward of its stacks only to find complaints and lawsuits coming from the upwind direction. Here R. B. Rathbun, an engineer who had been inducted into the art at Balaklala, made the first completely successful application of electrical precipitation to the metallurgical field.)

It was 1912 before the Riverside precipitator was completed but its cost proved to be a $200,000 bargain. Before World War I the United States had relied on the 1,000,000 tons of potash salts imported yearly from Germany as almost the sole source of this valuable fertilizer. Germany embargoed such exportation in 1915—a year in which the United States was barely able to produce 1000 tons of actual potash from its own resources. While an American potash industry was being developed to fill the void, it was found that the potash in cement dust, collected by electrical precipitation and processed, was—under these circumstances of scarcity—actually more valuable than the cement itself produced by the mills. Moreover, by one of those curious ironies that often and disconcertingly creep into human affairs, the potash thus collected at Riverside was sometimes sold back to the very farmers who had been instrumental in obtaining the original injunction. The dust was bountiful in another way: it could be used, to some extent, in making cement again—a not inconsiderable item since the compilers of figures on cement mix estimated that the Riverside precipitator, in the years of its operation up to 1950, had collected well over 1,000,000 tons of dust.

At last Cottrell and his co-workers had succeeded in devising an effective tool that could reap strange harvests.

THERE WAS, of course, no way that readers of the Washington (D.C.) *Herald*, thumbing their copies on December 30, 1911, could know that the man named in the lead paragraph of a story had once, as a thirteen-year-old boy, dedicated his weekly pamphlet to the public in general; had once, as a student, been fired by the ideal of a duty to the world; was now a man of thirty-four who, but two years earlier, had all but broken under the strain of achieving an ideal that had refused to die with youth. For readers who paused, the story ran:

"F. G. Cottrell . . . announced last night at the convention of the American Chemical Society that he and several Californians associated with him have turned over their patent rights for a device for the suppression of smelter fumes to the Smithsonian Institution and that the gift had been accepted by the Regents in behalf of Secretary Walcott. The profits which may come to the Smithsonian Institution through royalties are meant not only to increase the revenue of the Institution but also as a direct opportunity to guide industrial developments in new and useful paths."

The New York *Sun* of the same date caught more of the spirit of the thing when it added: "Mr. Cottrell and his associates, mindful of the struggle they had to carry their experiments beyond theoretical demonstration, decided to assign their right in the patent to the Smithsonian so that the royalties in the future might go to aid other investigators to bring their ideas to practical accomplishment."

It was a tangible, news-making gift, however understandably difficult it might be for the casual reader to assess. More easily grasped, for instance, were the announcements made earlier that year that Andrew Carnegie had given $10,000,000 more to the Carnegie Foundation as well as $25,000,000 for the promotion of education. To those who enjoyed toying with imponderables, it might have seemed that here at work was some ill-understood law of progression by which mankind might stand to become further enriched through Cottrell's suppression of some of Mr. Carnegie's smoke and fumes.

With this renunciation of potential wealth which seemed likely to derive from the Cottrell process, Heller, Miller, and O'Neill, led by the pace-setting Cottrell, were in distinguished company.

At the time the offer was made to the Smithsonian, and ever thereafter when he had occasion to refer to it, Cottrell carefully linked Heller, Miller, and O'Neill to the gift either by name or collectively as his "associates." He often implied that this group, from the start, had had some such purpose in mind. There are several indications that such may not exactly have been the case, although Heller, Miller, and O'Neill seem to have been public-spirited beyond the ordinary run of men, and that Cottrell called the turn.

Even before the precipitation companies were formed in 1907, Cottrell, in one of his several efforts to supplement his income, had been involved with a mining and metallurgical promoter with whom he had worked out a potentially patentable process for making a molybdenum steel. In a letter to this entrepreneur defining their relationship Cottrell wrote, "As you will doubtless remember, when this matter first came up I told you that I wanted nothing in the way of financial profit from it myself but did want a fair share of any profits which resulted from the invention to come directly to the University." Other correspondence implies that he would have been willing to accept some compensation for acting as consultant to any company that was formed but, at the time, electrical precipitation was making such stirring progress that it absorbed nearly all of Cottrell's vast aptitude for attention. Although nothing seems to have come of the molybdenum process, the gesture toward the university's welfare was, nevertheless, still there.

The first entry in the diary showing this trend of Cottrell's thinking was in 1909, two years later, when he noted that he had discussed with O'Neill "the possibility of eventually turning International Precipitation Co. into an endowment for scientific work." He later spoke of it more often and of "Miller's growing interest," although the latter put it in a different light to Heller. "Cottrell," wrote Miller, "has some great ideas about endowing some sort of research laboratory with the extra abundance of funds and I would not be loath, but I feel charity must first commence at home and while any of my kinfolks or any of those of my wife are in need, they should have first call. I don't do much castle building but have great faith in our ultimate success and even if we do not become millionaires, we should receive a handsome competency."

In the end, however, Cottrell's idea prevailed. For one thing, when moved by a conviction, he was not an easy man to resist, but there were other factors that may have motivated his associates as well. One of these was the discouraging amount of money lost in the Santa Maria oil dehydration venture which resulted in International Precipitation selling out the oil rights to Allen Wright, who had taken charge of the work in that field. Another may have been that the results at Coram, before the Balaklala smelter closed down, while satisfactory, were still inconclusive. Aside from these, all three—Heller, Miller, and O'Neill—having professional interests of their own, had never really established themselves as other than precipitation dilettantes. Finally, as Heller had once pointed out, the group had a certain esprit de corps and did not care to go on without Cottrell. When, therefore, Walter Schmidt, who was so successfully handling the Riverside cement work-in-progress, offered to buy out such rights as the four wished to dispose of, negotiations were begun. Heller and Miller had one reasonable proviso: any deal must allow them the return of their original investment plus 5 per cent. To this Cottrell had no objection, although it meant that once more his opportunity to lay hands on some ready cash was thwarted. His share of the sale of the oil dehydration rights to Wright amounted to around $5000. Now (as Cottrell wrote a friend) "the necessity of paying back the whole working capital of our company just at this time, which is one of the conditions of my associates' turning over the future business into the research endowment, will mean cutting off the bulk of the cash return I might otherwise have expected out of the recent sale of our oil purifying patent. This will necessitate my looking practically entirely to my salary to meet current needs for some time to come."

It was first decided that Schmidt should have the precipitation rights to the Portland cement industry throughout the United States. To this were added smelter rights in California—a concession which finally included smelter rights in Oregon, Washington, Idaho, Nevada, and Arizona as well. This left the electrical precipitation industry, in the plump balance of the United States, with the exception of these reservations and the oil dehydration business, open to someone as a gift. For the time being foreign rights, protected by patents which International had carefully taken out in the most likely countries, would be disposed of as the occasion arose. In addition to this, Schmidt agreed to grant the use of his fine wire and other patents to Cottrell's endowment project, which would then reciprocate by allowing Schmidt's Western and International companies the use of any further technical discoveries that might be developed by whatever organization Cottrell established.

All this was well enough, but the question remained: To whom does one give patents? The Cottrell group was not by any means the first to think of placing the public weal above personal profit in the matter of invention or scientific discovery. There were, in America at least, several distinguished precedents, not to mention the Curies, the Pasteurs, and others abroad. When the governor of Pennsylvania offered Benjamin Franklin a patent on the stove which still finds uses, he declined with memorable polish, saying, "That as we enjoy great advantages from the inventions of others, we should be glad of an opportunity to serve others by any invention of ours." There were others later who felt the same although none who are on record with such a pediment-gracing quotation. There were, to mention but two, Professor Charles E. Munroe, who at considerable cost to himself gave his invention of smokeless powder to the government; and Dr. Marion Dorset, who as a Department of Agriculture scientist chose to derive no profit from his hog cholera serum—a gift of incalculable value to animal husbandry.

It seems to have been Cottrell's peculiar idea, nonetheless, to have invention and discovery feed back upon itself, for he was astute enough to see that he himself was a component of the wave of technicological advance by which the twentieth century was, among other ways, to distinguish itself. He was acutely aware of the courtship of science by industry wherein the latter was now generally awakening to the commercial value of research. Of this the General Electric laboratory which had so persistently tried to lure him to Schenectady was a good example. Scientifically trained college graduates were coming to be in greater demand in industry to replace older rule-of-thumb technicians. The laboratory was moving to the factory and the industrialist beginning to call on the university for knowledge and advice—Cottrell himself was a palpable example of this, for industry, too, had found it useful to "ask Cot." In this perceptible merging he saw both benefits and dangers for each side. For the dangerous reasons, he and his associates rejected their first impulse to give the patents to the University of California, which had in a way been so intimately connected with their formulation. They believed industry should not control academic research, and universities with successful patents should not compete but, rather, co-operate with each other.

Cottrell and his friends next thought of the American Chemical Society as a possible recipient, but this idea, too, was discarded because ACS was not yet solidly enough established to administer the patents effectively. They discussed alternatives among themselves, and Cottrell talked of the endowment plan freely with others. He talked with "a number of people . . . who have had experience of handling new processes and other large technical ventures in a business way and nearly without exception they looked upon the successful handling of such developments by any public institution as out of the question and merely the dream of an enthusiast. My discussions with them have had quite the reverse effect of discouraging me, however, but have impressed on me the truth of their common fundamental premise, that is, that no new thing no matter how good will develop itself even after its broad foundations are securely laid unless there is someone with ability and enthusiasm behind it continually.

"Their second premise is the one I am not ready to accept as inevitable, namely, that it is impossible to secure the necessary combination of ability and enthusiasm on any other basis than that of a purely private interest from a strict dollars and cents standpoint."

Cottrell, Heller, Miller, and O'Neill were still hunting for ways to bestow their largess when Cottrell met a man who was to deflect sharply the course of his life—the director of the newly created U. S. Bureau of Mines, Dr. Joseph A. Holmes.

2

About the same time the Western states were becoming aroused over the problem of smelter smoke considerable concern was being expressed east of the Mississippi in regard to disastrous coal mine explosions. The cost of these in lives was so alarming that Congress, in 1908, voted funds for an investigation to be undertaken by the U. S. Geological Survey, and out of this, by a process of natural governmental fission, grew the Bureau of Mines two years later. Holmes, its first (and sometimes acclaimed its greatest) director, was a forceful, effective, and indefatigable idealist; was, in many respects, an elder Cottrell—temperamentally and imaginatively. When they met at a San Francisco meeting of the Mining and Metallurgical Society in the fall of 1910 there was immediately established between them a deep bond of regard and respect—perhaps the most harmonious contact of mind and personality that Cottrell was ever to experience.

That was in October, but it is more than likely that Holmes's attention was earlier called to Cottrell in July of that year when the American Chemical Society came of age by holding its first annual meeting, which, fortunately for Cottrell, also took place in San Francisco. At this gathering Cottrell delivered, from notes, a rambling address on electrical precipitation and its application to the smelter-fume problem. It was his first major public discussion of the work and the resounding effect was instantaneous on an international scale. A variety of industries all over the United States queried the International Precipitation Company to find out if the new process might solve their smoke and fume problems. Metallurgische Gesellschaft of Frankfurt, Germany, wrote asking to take over the rights for Europe and Australia. Civic organizations were curious as to how electrical precipitation might end the nuisance of ordinary coal and oil smoke. To the latter question (still being asked) Cottrell always replied that the electrostatic method would work but that the problem there was rather to get more perfect combustion from a coal- or oil-burning furnace than to undergo the expense of trying to collect the products of imperfect combustion. Besides, like the sulphuric acid at Anaconda, catching ordinary household or office building smoke particles meant that large amounts of soot would have to be disposed of and, while the sulphuric acid was of potential value, soot was considered nobody's friend.

As a further result of his speech, almost every scientific and technical journal in the country, to which electrical precipitation could be considered a pertinent subject, wrote Cottrell asking for a paper on the process. To each he explained that he had spoken only from notes, that he was too fully occupied to prepare an article at the moment, and ended with a vague promise to comply at a nebulously future date. Then came offers of employment. There was, almost inevitably, one from Whitney, who saw in electrical precipitation a promising field for General Electric. Another was tendered by Robert Kennedy Duncan, whose academic distinctions included simultaneous positions at both Kansas and Pittsburgh Universities. Duncan's plan of industrial fellowships (industry endowing university research for specific problems) had but recently won the backing of the Mellons in Pittsburgh and he was there concerned with ridding that obfuscated city of some of its depressingly polluted atmosphere. "I hope you understand," Duncan wrote him, "that we mean the largest kind of business in this work and that we shall see to it that you are provided with a perfectly comfortable stipend for living expenses, together with every consideration in the disposal of the ultimate method." Cottrell said he would remain in California but co-operate with Pittsburgh. Duncan proposed his living in Pittsburgh and co-operating with California. Cottrell declined, although the matter did not end there.

There are no indications as to how this first pointed touch of fame reacted on Cottrell. If it moved him at all it probably did so as a means of gaining more effective recognition of his idea for endowing someone or something with the patent rights remaining. The answer was soon to come, for Cottrell had called attention to himself at the ACS meeting in still another way. Out of that convention came strong but organized sentiment for the establishment of "a committee or board constituted under the auspices of the Society to collect and distribute information and otherwise encourage and stimulate cooperative investigation aimed at the fume problem and particularly with reference to sulphur dioxide." Subsequent correspondence to Cottrell refers to this as "your suggestion" as, very likely, it was. When, then, the local section of mining and metallurgical engineers met in San Francisco in October the idea of such a committee was again broached, capturing the interest of Holmes, whose attendance highlighted the meeting. To Holmes it seemed naturally a matter falling within the province of his new Bureau of Mines.

Although the bureau, on its establishment, had been primarily concerned with coal mining, Holmes envisioned a wider metallurgical scope for its investigations centering around an office and laboratory to be located in San Francisco. He was looking for a man to take charge of such work when the October meeting brought him together with Cottrell. As a result Holmes wrote an acquaintance, "No one impressed me so favorably as did Prof. Cottrell." Nor was he disappointed when he sought other opinions of Cottrell, for one such reply (from Professor E. C. Franklin of Stanford) read: "I can say, freely and with enthusiasm, that I consider Cottrell, without exception, the ablest chemist on the Pacific Coast and a man that has few equa. and fewer superiors anywhere."

Holmes searched no farther.

Cottrell, at first, volunteered to serve without pay (while retaining his university affiliation) in setting up such a sub-bureau, but the complications involved in giving one's services to the government seemed to strike too deeply at the very foundations of the Constitution as interpreted by Washington auditors so that idea died haplessly. He next decided to give up teaching, and what followed later became part of the folklore of the Bureau. When asked what salary he would accept, Cottrell is said to have replied that he would leave it to Holmes. Holmes was firm.

"No, Dr. Cottrell. Tell me what your services are worth."

"Would $200 a month be too much?" asked Cottrell, whose university salary was then $2000 yearly.

"Dr. Cottrell," Holmes replied, "I don't like your idea of pay. We will start you at $4000."

The salary was $4000.

The prospect of being a government servant connected with the efficiency of mining operations and the possible investigation of smelter smoke rendered it all the more imperative that Cottrell divest himself of any United States interest in his process. He discussed the matter with Holmes together with his endowment schemes. After Holmes left San Francisco, Cottrell wrote him suggesting that the Bureau of Mines accept the patents, for, thought Cottrell, "there are a great many men who would not feel that it was worth while to work out an invention merely to dedicate it to the public in the loose, general way now provided for in our patent law and who have not the time or do not care to work out the full practical application, but who would still be glad to donate their ideas and cooperate to a certain point with a public bureau whose business it was to develop just such problems. This sort of cooperation would greatly strengthen both the Bureau and the colleges and technical schools of the country."

Then Cottrell saw another danger. "Of course," he warned Holmes, "this whole movement, I realize, has a certain socialistic tendency and if you would think it would bring adverse criticism upon you or the Bureau which might do harm, don't hesitate to say so. The time may not yet be ripe for it."

But Holmes, a man of action, moved too swiftly to explore the complexities of such a thought, and replied to Cottrell a month later that the matter had already been brought up before the Board of Regents of the Smithsonian Institution, who seemed sympathetic, and referred to the Executive Committee for action. Cottrell was delighted. Then, with the close of the semester in May 1911, he resigned from the university to take up his new work as physical chemist for the Bureau of Mines, leaving almost immediately for Washington for indoctrination and to find out at first hand the progress of his plans with the Smithsonian. There, through Holmes, he met Dr. Charles D. Walcott, the Institution's secretary—a man of force, decision, and great personality who, like Holmes, was immediately charmed by Cottrell's energy and imagination.

Walcott recalled their introduction four years later: "I recollect one June evening, in 1911, sitting on the porch of my home and seeing two tall men coming up through the dusk, one of them Dr. Holmes. He said, 'Dr. Walcott, I have brought a man here who comes from California to see you. He wants to talk to you about something he has in mind.' Dr. Cottrell sat down and gradually unfolded his conception of turning over to a research corporation the results of his own research work . . . for the purpose of creating a fund from the business development of these patents which could be used for research to carry forward not only these special lines but any lines of human endeavor."

Stimulated by Cottrell's appeal, Walcott spurred the Institution's Executive Committee on to considering the acceptance of the patents. Meanwhile, together with Holmes, they exhibited this curiosity from the West to Alexander Graham Bell and others of Washington's scientific elite. They introduced him to the Secretary of the Interior, who considered Cottrell's plan one which might well become standard procedure for all government employees who wished to dispose of patents and the Secretary promised to bring the proposal up at the next cabinet meeting.

"This," Cottrell proudly wrote Jess, "is getting matters up to headquarters far faster than I had any idea would be possible. In fact, they are going so well that I've got to be very careful not to get the big head and spoil it all at the start."

But Cottrell, in his personal relationships if not in his work, was a man of restraint and nothing was spoiled. In December of that year the regents decided to accept the offer of Cottrell and his associates in a left-handed way, or as stated in their formal report for 1912, "it seemed to the Regents advisable, for various reasons incident to the business management of the patents, that there be organized a stock corporation which could take title to the patents and in which the Institution would be directly represented by the Secretary as an individual, and not in his capacity as Secretary." Thus, in effect, the corporation organized could have the prestige of unofficial sanction by the Smithsonian Institution, which would consent to receive any profits therefrom to further its honored purpose "for the increase and diffusion of knowledge among men."

3

After his first trip to Washington in the summer of 1911, Cottrell returned to Berkeley and set about the business of organizing the office and laboratory of the Bureau in San Francisco. Confident that with Walcott's backing the Smithsonian would approve his scheme, he, Heller, Miller, and O'Neill transferred the precipitation companies to Walter Schmidt. Henceforth these two organizations would confine themselves to business outside of the United States; to smelter and industrial work in the six Western states; and to Portland cement plants throughout the entire country. For these concessions the Cottrell group would eventually receive in the neighborhood of $75,000 to be apportioned among the four of them, although as part of his share Cottrell forsook some of the immediate cash in favor of 15 per cent of the foreign royalties. Their investment in developing the art to the point of maturity it had then reached amounted to over $30,000 so that the balance, when divided and spread over a five-year period, represented only the moderate return they had asked.

With these affairs disposed of, Cottrell plunged himself into the work of the Bureau which almost immediately brought him back into the field of smelter smoke, particularly at Anaconda. By 1911 the Deer Lodge Valley farmers' injunction suit had reached the Circuit Court of Appeals and the records of the case ran to a massive 25,000 printed pages (so voluminous that when the affair reached the U. S. Supreme Court in 1913 the suit was dismissed on the technical grounds that the plaintiffs, in bringing the appeal, had failed to reprint the whole case records for the new trial—an undertaking few groups of farmers could afford). Moreover, by 1911, the executive branch of the United States Government, through the Department of Justice, was actively interested in the affair and had already entered suit, claiming extensive damage to national forest reserves. The Attorney General's representative, Ligon Johnson, complained to Cottrell that the Anaconda management was uncooperative in the extreme and that "in their testimony and in their conferences with me and others they have ridiculed your appliances, the baghouse methods, feasibility of sulphuric acid manufacture, and every other possible solution."

Cottrell's earlier suggestion that a commission be appointed to study that perennially troublesome situation had gained wide acceptance among mining men and metallurgists. Whether or not as a direct result of this, a technical commission was formed in 1911 to arbitrate the Anaconda matter rather than push the suit, and the members of this consisted of Holmes, representing the government; L. D. Ricketts, Arizona's first citizen and a man of great integrity, to represent the smelter; and John Hays Hammond, the celebrated mining engineer of international repute, who was selected to retain an impartial point of view in the case of disagreement of the other two. All three easily and happily agreed on Cottrell, who could be counted on to supervise the actual mechanics of the investigation with complete scientific detachment. It would be the aim of the committee to find out exactly what could be done to lessen the fumes and, after everything possible in that line had been accomplished and if some fume still existed, to determine what could be done to minimize resulting damages to crops and forests. As a first step in the pursuit of these objectives Cottrell was commissioned to set up a station at the smelter in order that a precise study might be made of the "metallurgical balance" in connection with the operation, with particular emphasis on the nature and volume of those materials that created such havoc in escaping via the smokestack.

For four months, during the late summer and early fall of 1911, Cottrell devoted himself to the preliminaries necessary to getting the project started. It had been Jess's first hope that his new work with the Bureau would confine Cottrell more closely to the San Francisco Bay area and home—a hope of which she was quickly disabused by the Anaconda assignment. She barely had time to adjust to the new peripateticism resulting from this before Cottrell, in December of that year, was again called East, this time to attend a meeting of the three smelter smoke committeemen. He arrived in time to find the Smithsonian's Executive Committee ready to act on his patent offer and so it was only natural, therefore, that he extend his visit long enough to found a corporation to receive and execute the patents.

Thus it came about that, having conceived of his duty to the world, having created the instrument through which some measure of that duty could be discharged, he must now, of necessity, also establish the means by which that instrument could effectively be utilized.

4

While still the bearded Leipzig student, Cottrell had made to Jess these declarations of intellectual and moral independence: "If," he wrote her then, "each time that you break away from convention you make sure in your own mind that you are doing it for a really higher ideal, you are perfectly safe. But such ideals you must hunt out and build for yourself. You can't expect 'convention' to furnish such ready to hand. You can get hints for them and lots of encouragement from biographies of people who have been acknowledged in thought or deed, but even here the very best lies between the lines and you must construct for yourself."

And again: "We seldom can trace our ideals all the way back; but if you work toward such an end you come gradually to understand it better and better and it becomes in the same measure possible and real. I've been noticing the really great men I've come across, either personally or through their work, and it becomes more and more forced upon me that this, above all other things, is what they have in common. I don't mean to say it's the only essential, but *an* essential to the highest type of work in any line . . . my real satisfaction [in my work] comes from what I have accomplished, or feel that I have, and not what others may think of it . . . whether anyone else in particular understands my aims and methods and ways of life and whether they please them or not is a matter of pretty thorough indifference to me."

It was a twenty-four-year-old Cottrell who wrote these brave words and now at thirty-four, even though he was conjuring with Names in other fields, there were no signs of diffidence, no apologies for thinking the untried, no inhibitions over broaching his own unconventional proposals to successful men of wealth and solid business achievement, some of whom listened with frank amazement. What he was doing, in Washington, New York, and Boston—although such was far from his aim—could be construed as a flank attack on the dividend. The effrontery of this was the more pointed since it was carried out largely from an office in Wall Street, the very citadel of that system of sharing. That anyone listened was a remarkable tribute to Cottrell's enthusiasm and Walcott's prestige, or, perhaps, even more was it testimony to the fact that, however deeply overlaid with egoism, there is latent in every man an altruism that can respond to that of others and rise where it can be led.

By their decision to patronize but not actively support the patent plan the Smithsonian Board of Regents had neatly tossed the ball back to Cottrell, and he thereby remained, with but one difference, a brash young ex-university professor of whom not many people had heard; who came from out West (some believed they had heard California mentioned); who had a scheme. It had to do with an invention of a sort and if there were profits they were not to go to investors but to someone else. Like hundreds of other unknown inventors, he was looking for money. On the whole, the sound of it was financially unappetizing; the overtones disturbing.

The scheme was a corporation to handle the patents in the manner Cottrell had envisioned, and what chiefly differentiated him from other inventors was Walcott and Smithsonian approbation. Together they set out on what Walcott termed their "missionary work." Walcott recalled later that they "visited practical businessmen, bankers, scientific men, engineers, all classes of men—a hundred or more—and finally succeeded in interesting fourteen of them so that they would be glad to serve as directors of this future research organization. . . . The enthusiasm was not very strong. These men came together as though they were undertaking a somewhat hopeless task, but after Dr. Cottrell talked to them for a half hour they began to brighten up and they decided it was worthwhile for them to put their shoulders to the wheel."

Aside from Walcott, Cottrell had another staunch supporter in Arthur D. Little, whose firm of chemists and engineers was to become one of the largest independent scientific research organizations in the world. Little had first met Cottrell at the memorable San Francisco convention of the American Chemical Society and so was familiar with both his achievements and his hopes. After the meeting of the Board of Regents from which had flowed the Institution's hedged blessings, Walcott and Cottrell adjourned to Harvey's Restaurant where, by coincidence, they met Little. It was the latter's solicited advice that any organization formed should be as representative as possible and confined to no one clique or region as (thought Little) was the Carnegie Foundation. Moreover, he volunteered to steer them to the "right" people, for as a man of polished diplomacy he recognized the importance of a snobbish appeal—altruism or no altruism. Little, as good as his word, put them in touch with T. Coleman du Pont, who eventually replied with flattering enthusiasm that he would serve as a director to "do some good for the country in which I live. . . . If [Dr. Walcott] thinks I can be of any use to my fellow men, it will be a pleasure for me to serve." With this the new organization had gained not its first but one of its staunchest admirers. Little did not stop there but also tapped the imposing Boston field, and it was Little who suggested that the new organization be christened Research Corporation rather than Technical Research Company, the name Cottrell at first proposed.

In the meantime, however, Cottrell on his own had found an unexpected reservoir of support in personnel connected with Columbia University. There he was already acquainted with Milton C. Whitaker, a professor of industrial chemistry, and through this initial contact Cottrell met and interested Frederick A. Goetze, then dean of the Faculty of Applied Science; Benjamin B. Lawrence, a Columbia trustee; John B. Pine, a lawyer and Columbia graduate; and George F. Kunz, a Tiffany vice-president. All were interested and eager to serve the new corporation in one manner or another, and of these none more enthusiastic than Lawrence, a big, bluff, hearty mining engineer with a shrewd sense of humor.

The Smithsonian decision to accept money from the patents had been made on December 14. Throughout the few remaining days of 1911, Cottrell and Walcott knocked and called, talked and listened, traveled and wrote—fiercely inspired amateurs on a practiced salesman's errand. Their proselytizing continued on through January with unabated intensity until early in February when they stopped and savored the swift results with satisfaction. On February 4— only fifty days after the two had set their hearts to the campaign—the Board of Directors of the corporation had been picked and the Articles of Incorporation were ready to be filed. Even the optimistic Cottrell must have been astounded. There were those, as he was to say, who laughed at him as a "visionary," but Cottrell knew well that something far deeper was involved. The success, he acknowledged four years later, was due, more than any other one thing, "to a recognition, not merely in a static but in a dynamic sense, of the amount and uniform distribution . . . of altruism throughout humanity. The only trouble is that we are too timid about asking people to do things for the good of the cause, especially when the cause comes fairly within the purview of business pursuit, as this does. We have taken the attitude that has usually existed in matters far removed from business in our minds and brought it down close to business methods. That represents what there is novel in the plan and method of Research Corporation."

The first Board of Directors—those who therein saw a cause and found it good—were: William L. Dudley, professor of chemistry,

Vanderbilt University; General T. Coleman du Pont, former president of Du Pont Powder Company; Frederick A. Goetze, dean of the Faculty of Applied Science, Columbia University; Elon Huntington Hooker, president of Hooker Electrochemical Company, Niagara Falls, N.Y.; Hennen Jennings, of Sea Board Air Line, a retired South African mining engineer; Charles Kirchoff, president of the American Institute of Mining Engineers; Benjamin B. Lawrence, consulting mining engineer and Columbia University trustee; Arthur D. Little, consulting chemist and president of the American Chemical Society; John D. Pine, lawyer; Lloyd N. Scott, lawyer and Cottrell acquaintance while a student at Berkeley; Charles A. Stone, of the engineering firm of Stone and Webster, and trustee of Massachusetts Institute of Technology; James J. Storrow, of the banking firm of Lee, Higginson and Company, trustee of Harvard; Elihu Thompson, founder of the Thompson-Houston Company, out of which grew General Electric Company; and Charles D. Walcott.

These were the men who, without pay or profit, consented to direct the destinies of a corporation without precedent and (since it proposed to own eventually all its own stock) of suspicious legality. While there were because of geographical difficulties two changes in the membership of the Board immediately after organization, the power of the idea behind its formation was sufficiently faith-sustaining so that several of the original members remained as active directors for the rest of their lives. Significantly, Cottrell declined to become either a director or officer, for, aside from any possible clash with his government position, it was his belief that if his idea—once established—had merit its survival was assured without him and its self-reliance would develop the more quickly in the hands of strangers who, thrown on their own, must rely on their own enthusiasm for success.

Cottrell already had applied this principle in another way. The proposed directors, or such as could attend, held preliminary meetings in the law offices of Scott and Pine at 63 Wall Street, and several questions immediately arose. There was the question of a membership corporation as distinct from a stock corporation. The first was considered impractical by those who feared that, as directors, they would be open to lawsuits in cases where electrical precipitation might fail to work and who favored greater protection afforded them under stock corporation law. The next question was what was to be done with stock which paid no dividends. This, by agreement, was to be endorsed and deposited with Scott as acting secretary. Then came the matter of capitalization. Since many of the members of the Board were accustomed to thinking in opulent terms, the amounts suggested ranged from $200,000 to $500,000. Here Cottrell intervened. Let it, he said, be much smaller, and for this he had several reasons: the less the amount at the outset, the more satisfying the accomplishment later on; but what was more important, by starting in a small way the directors and management would, of necessity, have to be that much more aggressive and alert to overcome the handicap and, besides, there would be no tendency at the outset to hire imposing names commanding even more imposing salaries to manage the company. It must, in short, prosper from hunger.

The Cottrell idea won out. Two hundred shares of stock were issued at $100 per share and when slightly over half of this was paid in (subscribed to mainly by the directors in small lots) Research Corporation, with $10,100, was ready for business. (Just in case this Spartan sum induced any delusions of grandeur, Article 3 of the Certificate of Incorporation read: "the amount of capital with which the corporation shall begin business is One Thousand Dollars.") It was only years later, when the corporation for the same amount bought back its stock, that those who invested confessed that their motives at the time could only have been called charitable.

In the course of his life Cottrell assigned various reasons to his founding of Research Corporation and of these several were stated and apparent at the time. While he was still doing his missionary work during that December of 1911 he spoke before a local meeting of the American Chemical Society in Washington. Here he said that there should be a proper link between technical advances made in universities and their application to industrial needs on the outside. Ideas born in academic laboratories could be turned over to an institution, such as the corporation he proposed, when they reached a certain stage, and through further development by that body be carried over into the industrial field. "There is," Cottrell told the ACS, "a certain amount of intellectual by-products going to waste at present in our colleges and technical laboratories all over the country. There is a great deal of work that is being developed to a practical or semi-practical standpoint that dies right there because the men . . . do not want to dip into the business side of technology and go out into practical fields and the work has not come to the point of economic usefulness that is desired."

Cottrell had another thought that might have derived additional impetus from an extraordinary incident. One of electrical precipitation's pioneers in Germany had been a Dr. Karl Moeller, of the firm of K. & Th. Moeller, of Brackwede, Germany, whose work on the subject roughly coincided in time with that of Lodge in England. Moeller's son Erwin took up the work independently the year the International and Western Precipitation companies were formed and when word of their successes reached Germany the Moeller firm applied for the European rights. Just before Cottrell left for Washington in the summer of 1911, Erwin Moeller made the trip to California to make a deal. There either the benign climate or Cottrell's spell seems to have dazed Moeller. While he left California with loose co-operative commitments, he also found that he had agreed to contribute some Moeller patents, along with those of Cottrell, to whatever endowment organization Cottrell might succeed in establishing. It is true that Moeller, once he returned to Germany and had the star dust brushed off by his family business partners, had a complete change of heart, and it is easy to imagine that he was never again let out of Germany if his itinerary were to verge on Cottrell's orbit.

This episode, together with the possible co-operation of Sir Oliver Lodge and his son Lionel in England, and added to this the opportunity Cottrell saw in co-ordinating his project with that of Robert Kennedy Duncan in cleaning up the polluted air of Pittsburgh, must have helped broaden the scope of his idea. One of the first specific indications of this appears in September 1912 when, speaking before the Eighth International Congress of Applied Chemistry in New York, he said: "[Negotiations on such foreign rights as Moeller's] emphasizes in a most practical way the fact that academic organizations, and particularly the Smithsonian Institution, are international in spirit, and so recognized by scientific men the world over, presenting at once a nucleus from which may well be developed many activities leading toward world consciousness, cooperation and peace.

"The present movement, as stated, had its inception on the far western edge of this continent in very unpretentious beginnings, but has already overrun national borders both in the character of its work and the personnel of its supporters. It is a question which should peculiarly interest this [chemical] Congress as to how far and in what way international cooperation can best be assured in such activities which, from their very nature and aims, should from the outset transcend political boundaries and national pride and be treated by one and all from a standpoint as broad as humanity itself."

Four years after that, in a letter to W. M. Hutchings, the Englishman who had supervised the first and unsuccessful Lodge installation in Wales, Cottrell qualified this initial enthusiasm, saying: "I realized that it would seem too presumptuous to attempt to launch the practical work itself on a fullfledged international scale and even got laughed at as a visionary for trying to start it even on the scale attempted, but you will notice . . . that the international idea is there nevertheless. Whether that finally comes from a reorganization of the present nucleus [Research Corporation] or a coalition of a number of such nuclei or from an entirely new and distinct movement and organization, I care not. Expediency and psychology must determine that, but I hope the steps thus far taken may be suggestive at least and possibly furnish some of the necessary encouragement to those who come after."

It was Cottrell's hope that some patents could be administered for the benefit of mankind without geographical or political limitations. (There was to be one episode later where this was attempted with curious results.) While the broader principles behind Cottrell's thinking were not in any sense new, nevertheless the concept of internationalism circa 1912 was among the most fragile of images, nurtured mainly by dreamers, vulnerable to cynics, and lacking any broad base of popular support. The significant thing, therefore, is not that Cottrell lauded and shared the dream, but that he had pointed to one specific medium through which some phase of it could be translated into reality. Nor did his thought long remain unhitched to action even when such wide hopes for Research Corporation failed to materialize, for he was shortly to attack the barriers of nationalism in still another fashion.

However fervent his supranational aims, no hint of them appears in the Certificate of Incorporation, which lists three purposes of Research Corporation, two of them important. The first declared purpose is to acquire inventions and patents and make them more available in the arts, industry, and sciences while using them as a source of income. (In this category fell the Cottrell patents under which the corporation would license and supervise the installation of the electrical precipitation process. Acquiring the equipment for the process was originally left up to each licensee acting on the corporation's advice.) The second purpose is to apply all profit derived from such use to the advancement of technical and scientific investigation and experimentation through the agency of the Smithsonian Institution "and such other scientific and educational institutions and societies as the Board of Directors may . . . select. . . ."

In Cottrell's opinion one of the most valuable men on the Board of Directors, aside from Dean Goetze, was the mining consultant and Columbia trustee, Benjamin Lawrence, who, said Cottrell, possessed among other attributes "a faculty for resolving tensions during the moments when discussions of policy tended to become heated." When the time came, in preliminary discussions prior to the actual formation of the Board, to draw up the Certificate, it was Lawrence who suggested a broadened application of Cottrell's original idea that the Smithsonian Institution be the sole benefactor. He argued his case so skillfully that Cottrell acquiesced and thus was added the "and such other" phrase—a stipulation that was to be the more appreciated in the years to come and by no one more than Cottrell.

Thus on February 16, 1912, under the corporation laws of the state of New York, was forged a tender instrument for the furthering of scientific and technical research; a new idea of public trusteeship for important discoveries. A one-room office was leased at 63 Wall Street, and an engineer, Linn Bradley, who had had some precipitation experience working under Walter Schmidt out West, was hired as manager. Shortly thereafter Cottrell carried out his intentions and returned to his Bureau of Mines work in San Francisco, leaving the untested Bradley the sole repository of operating know-how in the new corporation. It was the most unpromising of beginnings. Besides his brief Western experience, Bradley had only a set of patents describing what their authors said they would achieve and had not always done. Although continuing royalties were due from some of the original Western installations, there were no other immediate customers. The situation was further complicated by two things. None of the directors expressed any strong desire to become an unpaid president so that most of this responsibility fell to Goetze, who cheerfully served as chairman of the Executive Committee. The second inhibiting factor was that, once having elected such a relatively imposing Board of Directors, it was difficult to assemble them again for policy-making decisions. The bride, in effect, was almost too beautiful.

Nevertheless, a prospectus was printed and Bradley set out in search of contracts, while Scott loyally divided his time between his own law office and the adjacent, and virtually empty, sanctum of Research Corporation. Both Bradley and Scott realized their one tangible asset at the moment was what they referred to as their "high seas fleet"—the names of the board members which were more than casually shown to prospective customers. But for a time the distinguishing thing about Research Corporation was that it tenanted one of the loneliest offices in Wall Street.

5

It had been mid-November 1911 when Cottrell arrived in the East. During December he paused barely long enough (on December 21) to shop for Christmas presents, and these included a fur piece, described as Russian hare, for Aunt Mame. "I should have preferred to have it without the heads," he wrote Jess, "and they offered to cut these off but it would have delayed getting the box off." In return he received several packages from home for which he promptly dispatched "thank you" notes. Then all was confusion. Jess wrote a clarification of the situation and Cottrell explained: "As you know, I always manage to put my foot in it some way and I'm afraid I did it once more in the matter of the book which you say was from Frances. The things were on my desk in Washington when I arrived and I opened them while trying to talk with about three different people at once and threw the outside wrappers away without carefully noting them. I found no card or mark in the book and assumed it was from Aunt Mame and I thanked her for it when next writing and only learned the truth when I later got your letter." The awful truth was that he had completely forgotten to get his sister-in-law, Frances, a present; had thanked Frances for the wrong one; had thanked Aunt Mame for Frances' book.

There were other misadventures. Holmes and Cottrell had many traits in common, one of which was a certain preoccupation that tended to lead them into social quicksand where the amenities were concerned. Holmes, for example, had what Mrs. Holmes considered very disconcerting habits. On one occasion he invited a man and his wife for dinner, forgetting to notify Mrs. Holmes. He did, in fact, forget about it himself and on the night designated took the train to Richmond. Mrs. Holmes, serene in the belief that the evening held a promise of restful quiet, had given the cook a night off. She had been, at the moment the doorbell rang and two strangers presented themselves, in the kitchen preparing herself a cup of tea. . . .

Cottrell, too, had dinner with Holmes, and the aftermath he described to Jess: ". . . coming back to the office in the evening, we stopped in at the Seddons [representative from Texas]. The fun of it was that when I came in from [Holmes's] place the other morning, I had all I could carry in my grip without mussing my suits and left the overflow in a laundry box to bring down later and thought last night in the dark would be a good time to take it. Then Holmes proposed to stop and call on the Seddons and said, 'Oh, leave your box and I will bring it down on the car in the morning.' As I knew he certainly would, now that the idea had been suggested, I didn't dare to leave it so started out with it intending to go straight through to the office and leave him to make his call alone. Nothing would do when we got down there but I must come in too. Mind you, the box was a good-sized manila board collapsible laundry box and I didn't have it so much as wrapped up or even tied with a string. I managed, however, to stow it alongside of the outside door with my overshoes before we rang the bell.

"All went well. We found them entertaining company and had quite a pleasant time and when we came to go I was maneuvering to say good-night in the hallway and pick up my box as the front door was closing, but what does Dr. Holmes do but make a dive for it for fear I was forgetting it and as he picked it up the whole thing almost went to pieces and nearly spilled the whole of my soiled laundry all over the both of us while we were trying to say 'good-night' to our host. I came to the rescue in a cold perspiration although I don't think it would have fazed Holmes in the least if he had to walk off with underwear hanging over both his arms and he would have shaken hands just as complacently with these festoons as without."

That was in January. Then February passed and Cottrell was elated with a sense of fulfillment, a consonant personality functioning effectively and having, as he said later, the "time of my life." If, as he reported, he was laughed at as a "visionary" he also said that he found the "Wall Street fellows" just as good fun as those at Berkeley and "just as willing to play the game if it was presented to them in the right way."

February went and with Bradley's arrival in March to take over as manager Cottrell felt the time was ripe to "shake the dust of New York from my feet and look homeward. Up to now, things were always loading up on me deeper and deeper but now I seem to be fast unloading them and can leave with an easy mind soon." Yet still he hesitated, for his expanding thoughts, nurtured by success, were directed more and more to the international possibilities of the Research Corporation idea. "There is no reason," he wrote Jess, "why the movement we are starting here in this country should not be carried on abroad. This may only be day dreaming. Even if it is, I want you to share it with me as we can certainly have that much out of it, even if it never comes to pass and you know it is part of my creed to lay the emphasis on anticipation, as far as enjoyment is concerned. But then, so many of my dreams have been coming true, in one way or another, that my faith in dreams is increasing in spite of me."

By the middle of March the return to Berkeley could be postponed no longer. In a railroad station he stepped on a scale from which was delivered a card showing 208 pounds. It was an insolent card carrying with it the presumption of omniscience, for on the reverse side it bluntly informed Cottrell: "You spend too much time in regretting the things you have not done."

6

No one could say that Jess had not been warned. From the very outset Cottrell's attitude toward his work and toward what he conceived to be his duty had been an uncompromising one. The very tone in which he wrote of these things was conveyed in flinty words that bespoke a stern implacability. One could make concessions here, exhibit kindness or weaknesses there, indulge in a sense of the ridiculous at the proper time, but that higher ideal of human welfare he held sacred. He did not consider himself a religious man.

From Leipzig he once wrote Jess: "I am not going to justify or explain my doing this or that on the grounds that it is necessary or advantageous as regards getting a place [in the teaching profession] or even an advancement in one, but simply because it seems the straightest road to the highest ideal. It may not be the pleasantest or smoothest road for either of us in the popular sense, but I am going to rely on your being resolute and high-minded enough to grasp and carry through this sort of idealism to the point where it really becomes one's highest pleasure and when this is once accomplished in a way that will wear, I can imagine nothing that will ever come between us."

The same letter said: "If we are to have the kind of home we have looked forward to, I feel that it's absolutely essential that you should come to understand from a good ways deeper down in your heart what my work really means to me and should be able to feel somewhat of the same interest in and duty towards it, for these ideals and habits of thought are the very foundation, I am sure, upon which all that is really good and worthwhile in my nature has grown and when you chafe at their natural and necessary consequences and want me to repress them, you are reaching in a very dangerous way directly at the source from which the other feelings which you prize so highly had their start and from which they still draw much of their strength and purity."

To no one else did he speak on this plane. They were words for Jess alone.

Thirteen years later, in 1915, the wind had not yet tempered. "I realize," he wrote Jess then, "that I am hard and exacting on those about me. Do you remember when we were reading Ibsen's 'Brand.' I said I felt I had a good deal of Brand's particular form of insanity even if dressed in a little less grotesque form . . . it represents a type of selfishness in that, in doing good with one's time and energy in wide general circles where one can command to aid his purpose great external forces, he is almost sure to work hardship on those about him in his most immediate circle and although, as you say, he gets his full return from the satisfaction of the work, it may not interest or appeal to them so much nor, unfortunately, do they get their fair share of credit for the sacrifices for it that they are thus constantly called upon to make. I suppose the difficulty comes from my trying to serve two masters: our home and family on one side and what I conceive to be my duties to the world on the other and that the latter gets the better of it because I take too impersonal a view in judging relative values."

That was the year in which a testimonial banquet was given to Cottrell in New York, and he spoke then on the founding days of Research Corporation. He closed his recollections with a tribute to Jess and told of her encouragement. "In the last analysis," he concluded, "any material sacrifice which had come from us is, after all, very much more Mrs. Cottrell's than mine."

Jess was not at the banquet, for the state of her health kept her in Berkeley. Had those present wished to know what her part had been in the development of electrical precipitation and of Cottrell's endowment schemes, she might, if she cared, have revealed the obverse side of the coin; might have told them, as she did Cottrell, this:

"You must get the atmosphere of our first seven years of married life—the financial struggle and the sickness—the developing of your patent work and I shall never forget what a help and comfort it was to me through that year of agony before son came and that just as I went to the hospital a payment of $500 came in and I know that if I'd had the worry of expense we couldn't afford, that I'd not have pulled through that time and the weary months afterwards. Then it came to our rescue in your sickness and paid the hospital bills and Professor O'Neill helped us out through the rest. Then the next spring the oil work came on, Allen [Wright] took hold and in the summer things were quite promising and I remember that while you were East and I was at Mrs. McFayden's that I dreamed many dreams of things I wanted to do for Kate [sister-in-law of Jess whose husband, Wallace, died in 1902] and [her four] children and others if the work came out as it promised.

"Then came my sickness and Dorothy was taken from us. That was in October and in January . . . the bottom seemingly fell out of the oil work for the time being. Then the adjustment of the oil work by Allen and the Coram [Balaklala] work started and the ups and downs of that were many and varied as we both know, but all of these events and troubles we shared together and your work was a vital thing to me and I felt a real partnership in it.

"All that year you worked at Coram and I was taken sick the next January—four years ago, with the heart trouble. From January to May were very trying months to us both. In May or June you got the offer of this Bureau work. Up to the beginning of that sickness, I was in close touch with every move you made. You had spoken of your wish to do something for the University of California with your patent, at various times, but the struggle to make them go was too hard to put much certainty into dreams of that kind at that time.

"When you accepted the Bureau position you felt the necessity of getting out of that work. Then the Moeller situation was on and you and [Walter] Schmidt threshed matters out. The first realization of just how matters stood was when you came home and tried to tell me of your idea of giving away your patent and of the arrangement you had made with Moeller and Schmidt and the reservation for the research work. I remember my feeling of utter dismay as you told me of the dreams and ideals you had ahead as Dr. Holmes had suggested the Smithsonian. This, of course, was news to me and you told me you thought it was worth the sacrifice it would mean to do it—and I cried out and said something of my wish to do something for [Kate's] children and I think it was the first time you ever vaguely realized how much that subject lay on my heart. Your reply was, 'We can do both.'

"Yes, we have done for them and been able to give them in the last three years the necessities. You will say, if I hadn't taken the Bureau position and made the change then we might not have had anything at all. To be sure, that is true, and I've never been sorry you've made the change—but at the same time don't forget that Heller offered to finance the company more substantially after you had the Bureau offer, and you refused it.

"From that time on, the work with the Bureau and Research Corporation has been wholly yours, and I've had no hand in it whatever. Then you put me under Dr. S.'s care and went East and you left me with all the family's problems while you spent four months in organizing the Research Corporation and nearly killing yourself to make the men willing to accept your patents. I wasn't the only one who felt you were hasty in your project, as Allen and Mr. Schmidt both felt that more time could be profitably taken. I remember one Sunday I had to go to Allen for some money for something.

I can't remember now, but I broke down and cried and it wasn't long after that when Allen talked of future schemes of the oil work that 'Cot's share out of it was going to Mrs. Cottrell for a home'; and I can't help but feel today in our home here that Allen, through Schmidt, has helped us to realize it."
Cottrell's rebuttal was simple: ". . . I presume your accusations are all probably true to a considerable extent and depend upon the fact that I undoubtedly don't feel the ties of kinship in as forceful a way, compared to the ties of humanity as a whole, as many people."
By its very nature the heart must beat, the leaf unfold, the thrush sing, the flame burn. To halt or hamper, to curb or capture these things is in a measure to destroy. With no less serious results can one other than channel the compulsions of a conscience.

ONCE, in conversation with a friend, Cottrell likened his outlook toward his work to a checkerboard. Assuming that the interests of most men tended to be vertical—that is, single ideas pursued more or less intensively for prolonged periods—his varied attentions, on the other hand, could be looked at as well-defined and separate horizontals. With almost everyone he met Cottrell discussed freely, when possible, his causes and concerns of the moment in the hope that his horizontals would intersect with the vertical lines of another. The result might show a pattern. Often this was so. Often too, as he no doubt expected, the crossings were at anything but right angles and the resulting design more distracting than revealing. In the decade 1912–21, following the establishment of the Research Corporation, the checkerboard was composed of some squares and of many other things besides.

The first two years of this period were comparatively well poised although, for Cottrell as for millions of others, far-off events were moving in, crowding closer, touching his life here and there in light, imperceptible ways—zephyrlike forerunners of the shock waves of war whose pressures were now growing, swelling, hovering for the explosion of August 1914.

But of this the omens were few in the placid California to which Cottrell returned from New York in 1912. The state itself was fast losing its remoteness, and when New Mexico and Arizona were admitted to the Union in that year California was no longer separated from the rest of the country for part of its length by territories. Too, the Panama Canal was now almost finished and plans were already under way to celebrate the completion of this epoch-making new sea route to Pacific ports with a magnificent Panama-Pacific International Exposition in San Francisco.

The changes were not all so spectacular. The area between Oakland and Berkeley was now more urban than rural. The University of California lost some of its status as an intellectual colony in 1912 when it won the brilliant physical chemist, G. N. Lewis, away from M.I.T. The advent of Lewis and the several young associates whom he persuaded to follow him marked a milestone in the rise of the university's ascendancy in the physical sciences which Cottrell, handicapped by the fact that he was a local product, had helped pioneer. But in spite of progress and portents, some things remained immutable. East Bay commuters still found themselves occasionally fogbound and ferryboat crashes commanded headlines in the Bay Area press. It was the problem of fog which Cottrell next assigned himself as an exercise in electrical precipitation although not before he had settled himself well into his Bureau of Mines position.

Cottrell's nominal headquarters were an office and laboratory which he had established and staffed for the Bureau in the San Francisco Custom House. It was, however, usually easier to find him on the trains of the Southern Pacific or the Union Pacific railroads; in Great Falls or in Anaconda, Montana; in Phoenix, Arizona; or at the Chemists' Club on East Forty-first Street, New York. For the most part, only strangers or the more naïve among his acquaintances made any serious attempts to reach him at home.

His chief responsibility for these first two years was supervising the investigations of the Anaconda Smelter Smoke Commission, funds for which came from a $10,000 annual appropriation made by the smelter—an immeasurably cheaper alternative to litigation and one from which the smelter stood to benefit through the discovery of new operating techniques. Between this fund and the Bureau were his salary and expenses apportioned. For a man of lesser caliber, it could have been a job handled routinely and for the most part from behind a desk with the incumbent playing a superintending role. It was instead a job that felt the full force of Cottrell's vigor and therein lay snares which it took all of his native tact to avoid. It was a part of the agreement between the Anaconda management and the commission that much of the information developed through investigation at the plant was to be regarded as confidential. Smelting was, after all, a highly competitive business and when it came to matters impersonal Cottrell was not a secretive man. In "riding circuit," as he termed it, on the major Western smelters, it must have been difficult indeed for him to restrain himself from passing on ideas and facts that the altruist in him would consider for the common good, but the injunction was one which Cottrell scrupulously respected. When at one point he became suspect, and an Anaconda official wrote a snappish letter to Holmes, Cottrell calmly pointed to the fact that the information in question was common knowledge published years before. The smelter backtracked with apologies. Cottrell had shown not even the faintest signs of annoyance.

The purpose of the commission was to assist in determining the causes and extent of the damages of which both the farmers and the government Forestry Service bitterly complained. Were arsenic fumes and sulphur dioxide gas the only ones to blame and, if so, which affected plant and which animal life, and under what conditions did these things happen? As quickly as separate phases of such questions could be determined, the commission staff cooperated with the smelter's own investigators in recommending changes in stacks, flues, furnace connections, and methods of operation in order that the various gases and fumes could be better segregated and their treatment undertaken individually.

It was a long painstaking study outlasting by several years Cottrell's active connection with it, but by 1915, Cottrell reported to Holmes that the top smelter officialdom had authorized plant reconstruction and modification to the extent of $6,000,000, a good portion of which was allotted to installations of the Cottrell process.

Of one of these precipitators attached to a leaching plant, one Anaconda official wrote to another, "I think that the Cottrell system is very efficient, more so than Cottrell has any idea of." In the skeptical world of smeltermen this was praise bordering on extravagance.

Cottrell's single-minded attack on the questions posed by the Smelter Smoke Commission lasted about two years. As the signs gradually pointed to the fact that many of the fume problems were amenable to solution, it is more than likely that his enthusiasm diminished correspondingly. Then one day in 1914 at the San Francisco Engineers' Club he lunched with a Chicago manufacturer of electrical equipment and heard of the 350-kilowatt, 1,000,000-volt transformer that was to be brought out for the Panama-Pacific Exposition. Whether or not this furnished the impetus, the diary notes two days later that there was another lunch, more discussion of the transformer and of "fog experiments."

Here again Cottrell was following the path of Sir Oliver Lodge, who had thought, in electricity's earlier days, that he had found a means of attack on England's costly fogs, compared to which those of San Francisco were but exhilarating vagaries of the weather. Lodge's experiments of some thirty years before had been all but forgotten by this time, although one British review of the fog problem in 1909 referred to them as "conclusive tests." Lodge, using a single electrode, had gone so far as to bring his work out of the laboratory and try it on the river Mersey, where the fogs played periodic havoc with Liverpool shipping. The same review noted of this attempt that "under the influence of the electrical current thrown into the atmosphere, the air within a radius of fifty feet around the discharge point was observed to be quickly cleared, the moisture coalescing into small flakes of snow."

When, with bursting civic pride, San Francisco opened the West Coast's first great exposition in 1915 hard by the Golden Gate, the Bureau of Mines was represented with an exhibit. This, if nothing else, gave Cottrell ample reason for a deep concern in the exposition and for spending some portion of his time there. There was, however, a something else. From the Smithsonian Institution he obtained a grant of $2000, and from Research Corporation $957. With this Cottrell engaged assistants and erected a system of grids and horizontal electrodes on the roof of the exposition's Palace of Machinery —a building covering several acres.

Plans for using the 1,000,000-volt transformer were abandoned in favor of one of 350,000 volts, also part of an exhibit by the same Chicago manufacturer. The project then shifted to the electrical engineering laboratories of the University of California, where an air-blast rectifier was designed to be used in conjunction with the transformer. One of Cottrell's assistants who worked on these experiments, in making a formal report, wrote, "The fact that all of the preliminary work had been done at 30,000 to 35,000 volts made the 350,000 volt design a long step into the unknown."

The rectifier was not completed until early September, in the latter-day stages of the exposition, and the long step into the unknown had been made with the usual bits of Cottrell extempore. One, almost inevitably, had to do with an oscillograph. A Cottrell assistant at the time remembered that "we came up against one problem that would have taken most electrical engineers several days to work out. Cot, in less than half an hour, made a glass cell for use with the oscillograph to measure transient voltages." Cottrell by training may not have been an electrical engineer but he had a positive affinity for oscillographs. Two other improvisations gave the rectifier a homemade touch. One was a large tin dishpan of forgotten purpose but still a conspicuous part of the rectifier, and the other a blower from a pipe organ which supplied the air blast.

From the rectifier and transformer in the Palace of Machinery a wire ran up to the roof where it connected with the several types of electrodes. Through September, October, and November, Cottrell and his crew tested and adjusted, rearranged and experimented with the sundry units of equipment. Accentuating their difficulties was the fact that by the time their equipment was in effective operating condition the heavy summer fogs were over and those that did seep in through the Golden Gate blew by on an irritating course over the bay north of the exposition grounds. On a few nights, however, tests proved practicable, bringing Cottrell back across the bay from Berkeley to work well into the morning.

On the whole the results were not promising. A diary entry on October 19 noted "some visible clearing around wire but much insulation trouble." Other observers noticed a clear area of perhaps three-inch radius in a half circle on the windward side of the wire, but eddies of fog particles streamed off to leeward.

After these doubtful results the experiments at the exposition were abandoned in November.

2

The wheeling years brought other things. Of these, one was a new Ford car (with starter) bought for $400 and which, in the parlance of the times, Cottrell referred to as a "machine." This, for a while, proved a real diversion that brought him out of the office at closing time and even kept him away from it on week ends. He took delight in driving around the Bay Area with Jess and others of the family, including Cynthia, now aging and ailing at seventy-one. Almost twenty years had passed since the angry incident at the piano; half that time since his father had died and Cottrell had refused to be "at home" to his mother as a visitor. In the interim, however, something had happened, and the tolerance with which he regarded strangers was now extended to Cynthia. The mellowing may have been due to Jess's patient insistence. If so, the first record of success appears in the diary in September 1915 when Cynthia, no longer a repugnant "Mrs. C," was referred to as "Mother." Although somewhere among his papers Cottrell still kept a package of Cynthia's unopened letters written to him in Leipzig, their relationship warmed to the point where he acknowledged her birthdays with wirelessed greetings and gave her presents at Christmas so that Cynthia had at last been victorious in gaining some overt manifestations of regard, if not affection.

There were other shifts and balances in Cottrell's family relationships. Although he had replied to Jess in a tone of self-justification that he did not seem to feel the "ties of kinship in as forceful a way, compared to the ties of humanity as a whole," such abnegation is not borne out by strict fact. Around 1912 there were wholly dependent on him for support—aside from Jess—Cynthia and Aunt Mame. As her elocutionary powers waned his sister-in-law, Frances, came to lean more and more heavily upon him. The four children of Jess's sister-in-law, Kate, now growing to high school age, needed increasing help beyond what their widowed mother could afford, and the incidentals of adolescence—teeth-fixing; operations, major and minor;

the miscellaneous expenses of education; the more costly items of clothing—came ungrudgingly from Cottrell. But these were not all. Sometime after 1912 the creative wellsprings of his brother Harry dried up and he and his wife, though childless, were added to the growing list of semidependents.

Harry, through flaws either of his own personality or in the laws of economics, had fallen far short of the moderate economic success he deserved. He wrote well over fifty plays, almost all of which were produced. A Los Angeles drama critic once took the better part of a Sunday feature page to wonder, in view of the red-blooded characters Harry created, if he would not be the one to write *the* great American drama. One of his plays had even reached Broadway but the critics there had considered the characterization and plot somewhat too loamy, causing the Los Angeles critic, in turn, to make slighting comments on effete Eastern tastes incapable of appreciating the robustness of Western art.

But if Broadway failed to respond, other parts of the country, and even Australia, accepted Harry and such of his plays as *The Half-breed*. Its success later brought Harry briefly to Los Angeles and filmdom, where he set a precedent for more celebrated playwrights, for even at that early date Harry found the tempo of movie making in Southern California too frenetic for his nerves and returned to San Francisco.

Harry's constant necessity for immediate cash had led him into a disastrous policy of selling his plays outright so that in lieu of royalties he was forced to look to his brother for the rest of his life as a major source of income. This Cottrell accepted. When Harry later decided that he was tired of San Francisco and needed country air, Cottrell agreed that everyone needed a change now and then and bought him a house south of Oakland. Harry's weather-vane enthusiasms then came to a seasonal rest on chicken and rabbit raising as a straight, simple road to the good life. Cottrell financed and encouraged the undertaking but the winter rains proved unusually rainy, the price of feed soared, the chickens sullenly refused to lay eggs, and the rabbits traitorously withheld co-operation. Never, though, was there a reproachful word from Cottrell.

It is, then, difficult to understand wherein Cottrell thought himself lacking in responsiveness to the ties of kinship of which he spoke. It was a self-reproach to which Aunt Mame would never have subscribed. As he made the rounds of Western smelters in the interests of the Bureau and the Smelter Smoke Commission she, in a hand now grown unsteady, wrote him faithfully as of old. She worried, as always, over his forgetfulness in the matter of haircuts and of adapting his clothing to the exigencies of the weather; wished, forever wished, that she could somehow relieve and not add to his burdens; but her heart, no longer as stout as the sentiments it held, finally stopped in July 1914. She left a will, dated 1911, in which she did "give and bequeath this set of coral jewelry to my nephew, Frederick Gardner Cottrell, in part recognition and payment for his expenditures and kind care for me. He can sell or dispose of them as seems best in his own good judgment. (Signed) Mary Sophia Durfee."

3

The Bureau of Mines quickly recognized that in Cottrell it had not only a brilliant employee but also a devoted public servant. Almost coincidentally with Aunt Mame's death he was raised to chief chemist and his salary brought up to $4800. Thereafter his rise was rapid. Although he continued to hold a place high in Holmes's esteem, his progress in the Bureau could in no wise be attributed to the fact that he was a Holmes protégé, for in 1914 the latter suffered an attack of tuberculosis so incapacitating that all administrative work was taken over by his assistant, Van H. Manning, as acting director. Then in July 1915, Cottrell lost a friend when Holmes died in Denver. *The Journal of Industrial and Engineering Chemistry* seemed to reflect the opinion of American metallurgical and scientific circles when it claimed Holmes to be "a victim of overwork" and of "a too great devotion to the duties which had been assigned to him."

With Holmes's demise a situation arose—not always common to governmental bureaus—which was not only a tribute to the esprit de corps Holmes had engendered in his organization but was also illustrative of Cottrell's striking ability to transcend personality issues without disrupting harmonious relations. Manning, as acting director, was in many ways the logical man to succeed Holmes. While he was recognized as an able administrator, he was not a man of scientific training and this, Cottrell thought, might jeopardize the prestige—and consequently the effectiveness—of the Bureau, with which Holmes's connection had so admirably endowed it. He therefore openly considered Manning to be a second choice while pushing the candidacy of H. Foster Bain, a geologist of national repute with intensive mining experience. It had, in fact, been Bain who introduced Cottrell to Holmes in San Francisco. Cottrell's choice of Bain was a matter he discussed frankly with Manning, and in partial justification of this preference wrote Dr. Charles L. Parsons (then a department head in the Bureau), ". . . you know my tendency, perhaps, to over-subordinate considerations of personal justice to those of the general good."

If Manning felt any resentment he failed to show it. Some six weeks after Holmes's death his appointment as director was announced, and it was on Cottrell that Manning came to rely heavily for advice on technical problems.

Even before Holmes's death the emphasis in Cottrell's work had shifted from smelter smoke to the establishment of new experimental mining stations—somewhat on the order of his own San Francisco office and laboratory—for the Bureau. As Manning's dependence on him grew Cottrell's interest in the purely metallurgical aspects of the Bureau's work increased until in 1916 he was appointed chief metallurgist. This, since the fields tended to overlap, did not mean complete abandonment of chemistry, but Cottrell looked upon the change as salutary, for he had strong opinions about both private and governmental organizations, centering chiefly around the tendencies of such departments to ossify, of the thinking therein to become rutted and sterile. Some of this feeling he expressed in a letter to Bain: "The greatest stumbling block which I have encountered in most organizations with which I have come in contact seems to derive from the tenacity with which various officials . . . hold on to what they conceive to be the authority originally delegated to them. It has been my observation that men of real ability are on the whole more often limited in their progress by failure to get rid of their present responsibilities than by the failure of new and larger ones to materialize.

"I have now gotten the smelter fume work and other non-ferrous problems pretty well off my shoulders and I am planning while in the East this next year to give more of my time to ferrous metallurgy because I know so little about it and feel that this will insure my active interest and hard work on it. When teaching at the University

I always felt I did my best work when keeping just a few laps ahead of the class, probably on this same account. I am inclined to believe that it is the best way for some of us to work, providing we are quick enough on our feet. I want particularly to follow up the subject of the use of oxygen, or at least enriched air, in blast furnace practice. This has long been a hobby of mine."

It was decided that, as chief metallurgist, Cottrell would function more efficiently with headquarters in Washington rather than in San Francisco, and it was in November 1916 that he and Jess packed and moved to the city that was to become home for the next twenty-eight years. There, however, they had no sooner got settled than his plans for an extensive investigation into the use of oxygen in metallurgy immersed him in one of the most remarkable and controversial scientific developments of World War I—the commercial production of helium.

For all their air of detachment, scientists, like theatergoers or pigeon fanciers, or any group bonded by a common interest, have their prima donnas, their favorites of the moment, and in the yeasty ferment of the first World War helium rose to stardom. As such, it captivated the feature writers, the less inhibited of whom expansively foresaw the day when lighter-than-air craft would replace the ocean liner and miniature dirigibles become the "poor man's flivver." Cottrell, in such accounts, was nearly always credited with having brought these things into the realm of possibility almost single-handedly, and in some banner headlines he became "Uncle Sam's Wizard of Science." For many years thereafter Cottrell found wizardry a painful source of embarrassment.

Eleven years before Cottrell was born a brilliant English astrophysicist, Sir J. Norman Lockyer, began his investigation of the composition of the sun with a spectroscope. Unable to account for one of the spectrum's lines (which had also been observed earlier by the Frenchman, Jannsen), he daringly assumed that it represented some substance unknown on earth. This he named helium from the Greek *helios,* the sun. There were others who worked in the latitudes of this problem, but helium's presence on earth was first discovered by Sir William Ramsay in experiment that was jewellike in the annals of research. Ramsay announced his findings in 1895, the year the student Cottrell decided Oakland High School science courses were too elemental for him, and five years before he first met Ramsay in London.

Helium thereafter created little stir, as dormant as a popular subject as it is inert by nature. Until World War I perhaps not a total of 100 cubic feet of it had ever been separated as a pure gas, and this at a cost generally estimated at $1700 a cubic foot. Then almost everything seemed to happen at once, and in the frontal attack to bring helium out of its mink-coat status among gases the steps in the campaign became blurred and, understandably, hurt feelings developed among the many men responsible for the eventual success of the undertaking. In fact so many people were so closely involved that it is almost clear why feature writers, under pressure of space, cut the Gordian knot by giving Cottrell virtually sole credit.

Helium's meteoric popularity was the result of its innate characteristics fitting with uncanny preciseness into what was then conceived to be an urgent need. It is colorless, odorless, tasteless, nonpoisonous, non-inflammable, non-explosive. In addition to these negative qualities it has the triumphant virtue of being, next to hydrogen, the lightest known substance—its lifting power being 92.64 per cent that of hydrogen. The fact that hydrogen is lighter, as well as colorless, odorless, and tasteless, was heavily offset for purposes then under consideration by its combustibility, as well as by its more rapid rate of diffusion through fabrics.

The use of hydrogen-filled zeppelins on bombing missions over England had turned Ramsay's thoughts (and undoubtedly, too, the thoughts of many others) toward helium. Ramsay, in February 1915, wrote Dr. R. B. Moore, one of his former American students who had entered the employ of the Bureau of Mines, saying he was trying to locate sources of helium for use in British dirigibles. Moore then recalled a queer episode some years earlier that had led to the discovery of about 1 per cent helium in some natural gases: the little village of Dexter, Kansas, had rejoiced at the discovery, in 1907, of a gas well only to find that when it burned at all it did so in such a poor fashion as to be worthless as fuel. A sample, analyzed by Professor H. P. Cady and a colleague at the University of Kansas, showed the presence of helium—the first time it had been discovered as a constituent of natural hydrocarbon gas. With this discovery Moore was familiar. But the United States was not yet in the war; President Wilson had strongly urged neutrality on the country; and

Moore, as a government servant, felt he would be out of order in reporting the matter to Ramsay.

The failure to locate any adequate sources of helium had apparently discouraged Ramsay from pursuing the matter further and by the time the United States had entered the war in 1917 he had died. His suggestion, however, remained with his pupil, and in the spring of 1917, Moore attended a meeting of the American Chemical Society in Kansas City. There he listened to a paper by a young chemist, C. W. Seibel, who was working with Cady, on krypton and xenon—relatives of helium in the gaseous "inert" brotherhood. It was Moore's recollection that at the meeting Seibel "expressed regret that at such a time, when everyone was thinking of war problems, his paper was of a purely scientific nature and had no practical bearing on the war." Moore rose to disagree, pointing to Ramsay's idea, and, to still the vocal skepticism, called on Cady, who was also present, for support. Cady, according to Moore, agreed that helium had strategic uses, although he, too, was dubious about costs. Later in the day Moore discussed the matter with Dr. Charles L. Parsons (then chief chemist in the Bureau of Mines), who volunteered to return the idea with him to Washington, where it could be taken up by the Bureau and the War Department.

Helium also went to Washington by a collateral route. Another able employee of the Bureau just prior to that time was a chemical engineer named George A. (later Colonel) Burrell, who until 1916 was in charge of the Bureau's gas investigations. In pursuance of that work he had examined samples of natural gas from all over the country. With the United States' entry into the war, Burrell was recalled to the Bureau from private industry to take charge of research work on chemical warfare. His thinking, too, had touched on helium for use in airships—a hypothesis given emphasis one day when a Mr. F. A. Lidbury, general manager of the Oldbury Electrochemical Company in Niagara Falls, called on Burrell to discuss the use of some of his company's chemicals. Lidbury had at one time assisted Ramsay with his helium experiments and told Burrell that Ramsay, before his death, had been looking for a potential supply in coal gas. Burrell knew, as did other chemists, that natural gas containing large amounts of nitrogen might also contain helium. He recalled from his previous work that the gas in the Petrolia fields in Texas ran to about 35 per cent nitrogen and, knowing of Cady's earlier Kansas discovery, promptly had a sample of the Petrolia gas shipped to him for analysis. Cady found 1 per cent helium.

Here, before Cottrell was identified with the project, was the first point of contention still active in scientific publications as late as 1938. Cady claimed he located the gas in Texas (the Kansas field on which he had originally worked was almost exhausted) through consulting a map, finding that there were fully developed gas fields, and then "our isohelium lines, greatly extended, indicated that this supply might contain upwards of 1% helium." Burrell, with equal certainty, felt that Cady's knowledge came from the sample which he had had dispatched to Cady from the Petrolia field.

Whatever the case, Burrell reported the facts on helium to Director Manning and Manning referred him to Cottrell. The logic of this move stemmed from Cottrell's deep interest in the enrichment of air by oxygen in metallurgy. The main step toward the use of oxygen in metallurgy meant the liquefaction of air just as the proposed extraction of helium from natural gases pointed inevitably to the liquefaction of those gases, and ever since he had installed the first liquid air machine on the Pacific Coast in his university laboratory the subject of gas liquefaction had been a Cottrell favorite.

Burrell and Cottrell now mapped out a plan of campaign to excite the armed services. Burrell, in one account, said that he found it "somewhat difficult to interest the Army and Navy in the new proposition to the extent I thought it warranted." Cottrell, in his record of the case, found the Army balloon representative "intensely interested" while the Navy "immediately appreciated the importance of the subject." But if there was agreement on the importance of the objective, there was much and heated discussion as to the best means to that end—how to separate the helium from the natural gas.

Almost a year before the issue even arose Manning had heard of a new process of air separation which he had referred to Cottrell, who had filed it away with other "clues to great inventions." As soon as he had time to look into the scheme he found it the work of one Fred F. Norton, an engineer of wide experience, who had pooled his interests and patents with E. A. W. Jefferies under the name of the Jefferies-Norton process. One version of this process had already been tried out, at a cost of between $50,000 and $100,000, by the General Chemical Company with doubtful results, but the changes and improvements in the process since that time were what particularly interested Cottrell. In a report on the process Cottrell said, "Many of those I talked with seemed to look upon it as a sort of perpetual motion scheme and were sure there was a flaw in the reasoning somewhere, although they had never run it down themselves but understood that this one or that one had done so."

Like other air separation processes then in use, that of Jefferies-Norton would be adapted to the helium problem by liquefying the components of the natural gas—except helium. This presented no great difficulty since helium, to turn liquid, requires a temperature of 267.9 degrees below zero centigrade—the most difficult of all the gases to liquefy. The cycle involved in the Jefferies-Norton process, however, seemed to defy the second law of thermodynamics, which law Cottrell had never really recognized as having been duly legislated by any highly constituted authority. By virtue of its unorthodoxy the new process promised to separate gases—and hence helium —far more cheaply and efficiently than any other known methods. It was this process that Cottrell espoused, and other experts concurred in the opinion that, with experiment, it should prove a practical method.

About this time the word "helium" disappeared from the typewritten page and was dropped from vocal use and in the interests of secrecy the word "argon" was substituted. By either name, its extraction by the Jefferies-Norton process quickly ran into opposition. The Army at first seemed willing to use it, but G. O. Carter, of the Navy's Bureau of Steam Engineering, was strongly opposed and championed instead the better-known liquefaction process of the Linde Air Products Company. Moore, who had first raised the issue of helium at the Kansas meeting, proposed the Claude process of the Air Reduction Company. Cottrell agreeably thought all three might well be tried. With this, the committees sprang up, the conferences started, the National Research Council was solicited for advice, and a bevy of scientific novae, ranging from R. A. Millikan and Harvey N. Davis down to the lesser scintilla, were sometimes amicably, sometimes disputatiously, involved.

The excitement of it all received further stimulation when, in response to a report sent over by Burrell to the Admiralty, the British dispatched a delegation to Washington anxious to obtain 100,000,000 cubic feet of the gas at once and a contract for a further supply of 1,000,000 cubic feet weekly. They, too, favored the Jefferies-Norton process because of its promised cheapness, since the estimated best that could be expected of the two older methods would be about $80 a thousand cubic feet. The British had, at the time, $125,000,000 invested in grounded dirigibles which they hesitated to send up with inflammable hydrogen.

The joint Army-Navy Aircraft Board had already recommended (on the advice of the National Research Council) that $100,000 be appropriated from Army and Navy funds to make helium available —the whole undertaking to be carried out under the direction of the Bureau of Mines with Burrell, as Manning's deputy, in charge. The stimulus injected by the British prompted the Aircraft Board to recommend an additional $500,000 for the project. To this the Navy agreed providing not a penny of it went for the Jefferies-Norton project, and the Army followed the Navy's lead, having designated Carter to represent them jointly. Only after much pressure on the part of the National Research Council and the Aircraft Board was the Navy's co-operation insured. Then came the final decision that all three processes would be used—the Linde and Claude in plants at North Fort Worth (the gas to be piped from the Petrolia field over a hundred miles to the northeast) and the Jefferies-Norton, because of its lesser demands on power and water, in a plant to be located in proximity to the Petrolia field itself.

All this had taken time and it was not until March and May 1918 respectively that the Linde and Claude plants at Fort Worth were ready to operate, and not until October 1, 1918, that the Jefferies-Norton plant began production. Long before that, however, Burrell had gone into the Army Chemical Warfare Service, leaving the Bureau of Mines phase of the helium work largely in the hands of Cottrell, although no written instructions from Director Manning to Cottrell seem to exist in the files of the Bureau delegating to Cottrell that authority. Thus the whole organization of executive responsibility was one of unmuted confusion which continued until August 1918 when all three plants were put under a joint Army-Navy-Department of the Interior Board. No one acquainted with the tangled intricacies of wartime befuddlements ever fully understands how a victory is won, but out of all this came a kind of a victory, for on the day the armistice was signed in November 1918 there were awaiting shipment on the docks of New Orleans the first 147,000 cubic feet of 93 per cent helium contained in 750 cylinders. This at prewar prices would have cost in the neighborhood of $250,000,000. Now, while it was impossible to calculate its worth in view of the unusual conditions under which it had been produced (some claimed ten cents a cubic foot), it did demonstrate positively that cheap helium could be produced in quantities sufficient to realize the dreams of the dirigible enthusiasts—if helium alone could make them come true.

It was not, however, Cottrell's victory but one in which he could (with dozens of others) justly participate. It was not his victory in even a nominal sense because the helium produced at the time of the armistice came almost exclusively from the plant employing the expensive Linde process, which had been strongly advocated and chiefly supervised (from the government's side) by Carter of the Navy. The Claude process at the same time and at the same location was producing about 70 per cent helium while the Jefferies-Norton process at Petrolia was just getting under way. On the other hand, the tardy record of the Petrolia plant was due in a large measure to the objections of the Navy representatives who had delayed its construction in the first place, and, according to the information which Director Manning later passed on to Cottrell, Carter was found to have been in the employ of the Linde company during his connection with the Navy's Bureau of Steam Engineering on the helium project. As its operating quirks were amended and improved in the years immediately following the armistice, the Jefferies-Norton plant gradually produced up to 55 per cent pure helium (the Navy in the meantime having worked up some latter-day enthusiasm for it) and hopes were high for its eventual success when the whole helium program underwent a reorganization and the Petrolia field gases showed signs of giving out.

As the years passed, the wonder of helium lessened and the bright new world of transportation that was to have been opened by the giant dirigibles evaporated to the accompaniment of a macabre obbligato of sudden death. But important uses other than aeronautic were found for helium, especially in weather balloons, in metallurgy and welding, and in medicine. There are, very likely, valuable uses for it still undiscovered. Meanwhile, as a government monopoly, it continues to be extracted from natural gas, chiefly in Texas and New Mexico, by methods that combine the experience gained from the three pioneering plants so feverishly built in 1917–18, and the cost which once stood at the fabulous high of $1700 per cubic foot has eventually been brought down, under Bureau of Mines operation, to as low as one cent for the same amount.

In all probability Cottrell's part in the helium affair would have been one of relative anonymity had not the Affiliated Chemical and Electrochemical Societies of America singled him out for applied chemistry's highest honor, the Perkin Medal. This was awarded him —as its thirteenth recipient since Sir William Perkin originally received it in 1906 for stumbling onto mauve, the first of the aniline dyes—in January 1919 "in recognition of his most original and valuable work in applied chemistry." The presentation speech dealt at great length with the Cottrell process of electrical precipitation and ended with a two-sentence reference to his "more recent work of investigation [which] had to do with the securing of helium gas for war balloons."

Then Cottrell spoke in acceptance. He first made some remarks on the administration of patents after they leave the Patent Office ("The prime object to me in the formation of the Research Corporation was to furnish an experimental laboratory, as it were, in this most interesting branch of economics"). Then he launched into the whole history of the helium development. He minimized his own part in it, struggled valiantly to give due credits but, as closely connected as he was with it, and familiar with the part each had played, the complexities proved too great, the cast in this drama too large to provide a perspective that would satisfy everyone. Moreover, he was at the time preparing to leave for Europe and he sandwiched the writing of the speech in between penultimate chores—some of it being composed in the New York subways while shuttling between appointments.

Here was big news which, classified and cloaked during the war under the name of "argon," was being given its first major scientific airing and the fumes of helium made newspaper city desks giddy. The banquet and speeches took place at the Chemists' Club in New York on the evening of January 17. Something akin to shock and horror must have gripped Cottrell's precise scientific mind on the morning of January 18. In headlines he became the "DISCOVERER OF NEW BALLOON GAS" from which, with growing embarrassment, he could squirm on down to read that "Dr. Cottrell's achievement lies in devising a process by which it is estimated the cost of helium gas will be reduced from $1,700 a cubic foot to etc., etc. . . ." For this, most of the accounts either said or implied, he had received the Perkin Medal.

Whatever the state of his feelings, the diary reveals only one thing —that he spent several days immediately thereafter revising the script before it went to the various technical journals for publication. Then he sailed for Europe in mid-February and a lively intramural squabble broke out in Washington.

On March 15 the Navy News Bureau issued a press release authorized by the department's thirty-seven-year-old Assistant Secretary, Franklin D. Roosevelt. The release, three pages long, dealt with the "important part played by the Navy during the war in the production of helium." The Navy summed up its complaint by saying, "In recent articles on this subject, both in technical journals and in the daily press, the Navy's work has been largely ignored." Justified though the Navy may have been regarding the daily press, the charge was unfounded in regard to the technical journals which carried the revised text of Cottrell's speech.

It then grew very warm for March. According to the Washington *Post*, "Secretary of the Navy [Josephus] Daniels has already called Director Van H. Manning, of the Bureau of Mines, to account for having experts [i.e., Cottrell and a committee] in Europe cooperating with the British in using helium for dirigibles for commercial purposes, and yesterday the Navy Department issued a statement charging the Bureau of Mines with having abandoned the work of producing helium during the experimental stages and claiming credit for having brought about a continuation of this work, which now proves so important."

Manning fired back the charge of "untrue" and added that "the Navy was now attempting to claim credit which it was not entitled to." Manning wrote the news to Cottrell: "Taking up this challenge at once," he said, "I had prepared a painstaking and exhaustive report to the Secretary of the Interior, whereby our files were ransacked for evidence, and practically every statement made was verified by actual exhibits . . . while informal acknowledgment of the Navy's mistake has been made, no formal word of apology or retraction has been received or published."

Three years later there were still off-stage rumblings. The May 1922 issue of *Review of Reviews* carried a story on helium. ("To a second American scientist [i.e., Cottrell] is due the honor of grasping and developing the great possibilities of helium in dirigibles.") This ratio of Cottrell to helium seemed out of balance to a Buffalo consulting engineer who formerly had been connected with the Linde process. In a tone well fitted to dueling protagonists the engineer wrote Cottrell, "I call upon you to make a full and frank statement of the facts of the case and your failure to do so will obligate me to perform this unpleasant duty."

Cottrell patiently replied: "It used to annoy me when the Sunday supplements and the magazines began to 'work' the story of electrical precipitation and insisted on featuring me out of all proportion to my part in it, which after all was not much more than getting other people thoroughly worked up to its importance and fully committed to see it all the way through. I wrote quite a little and talked a good deal more trying to make it clear, but it only seemed to make matters worse by keeping my name before them, some of them even making capital of it by citing it as false modesty on my part.

"I think the same thing is happening with respect to helium matters and nothing would please me better than to see you set this right by getting into the field with more of the story from another angle which would be fresh enough to attract new interest and stand on its own feet, which I am convinced is the only thing which will accomplish what you have in mind. . . .

"If there is any data or help I can give you . . ."

But the burr continued to stick. With every award he received thereafter that commanded coverage by the daily press there crept in—to greater or lesser degree—references to "his development of a cheap process for producing helium." By appearing in some of his obituaries, it even outlived Cottrell.

4

It was the peace to insure peace ending the war to end wars and in it Cottrell participated in a characteristic way. Although, in February 1919, he went abroad as chairman of a three-man Bureau of Mines commission to gather technical information on the condition of European mining and metallurgy following the war, he was still, at heart, much the same prospector who as a student had boarded the old *Waesland* in 1900, seeking, as he sought all his life, the "best hunting grounds along the fissures and contact planes between different massive formations."

In his official capacity Cottrell found himself in charge of just one more American commission that invaded Europe with the advent of peace. Sometimes together, sometimes singly, the commission members investigated the mines and smelters of the Saar, Luxembourg, and the devastated areas of France and Belgium. Had it not been for Cottrell's presence, it would have been a routine junket with the usual reports which the Bureau hoped would be of interest and value to American industry in postwar planning.

But the relative passivity of simple investigation was not Cottrell's forte. "Sometimes," he wrote Jess, "I feel much encouraged at the prospect of what may be accomplished and then again everything seems to go so slowly and, above all, so indefinitely, and there seems so much crying need for real action and you are constantly among men, in uniform and out, who have been doing so much under such trying circumstances . . . that it makes one feel a crushing sense of responsibility to justify his presence here by some steady actual accomplishment or get out of the way and stop crowding the French out of house and home."

However, by the time winter gave way to spring he began to feel needed. The Ordnance Department of the American Expeditionary Force borrowed him to inspect the vast Skoda armament and steel plant at Pilsen, Bohemia (Czechoslovakia), in company with Brigadier General C. B. Wheeler. Aside from the usual report of no great significance, the trip was chiefly noteworthy because the Vienna–Prague leg of the journey was made in the private railroad car of former Emperor Franz Josef—the car in which the Archduke Francis Ferdinand went to his Bosnian death, thereby achieving one of history's most fateful assassinations. In Prague, however, Cottrell met Professor Lincoln Hutchinson, of the University of California and a member of Hoover's American Relief Administration, who requisitioned Cottrell to "look over the question of possible increase in production of raw materials and to lay stress at first on coal as the key to the rest." Cottrell made what few recommendations he could considering the six weeks' brevity of his stay, then proceeded to Italy to check on a report that helium existed in the boric acid springs of Larderello. (It did, in small amounts.)

It was early July when he returned to Paris, his step more eager, his excitement mounting, for now, in an atmosphere of Victory Parades, he was to begin in earnest one of the major campaigns of his life and the stage for this was set in the numerous meetings of national scientific societies that were beginning to gather in hope of reweaving the international ties disrupted by the war. The fact that Cottrell was on the ground in Europe enhanced his already considerable value as a delegate to the extent that it must at times have demanded a high order of alertness to remember just who he was representing where. Earlier in April there had already been a preliminary meeting of allied scientific societies in Paris at which he had represented not only the American Chemical Society but also the National Research Council. This congress helped solidify sentiment to organize two new groups—a proposed international chemical union and the International Research Council. When word of these decisions reached the United States, the American Chemical Society, the American Electrochemical Society, and the National Research Council all appointed Cottrell as one of their delegates to represent them among the chemists whose meetings were to be held in London and Brussels. In addition to this the National Academy of Sciences and the National Research Council nominated Cottrell to attend the inaugural meeting of the International Research Council in Brussels on their behalf. Since all of these groups were to share his expenses (and Hoover's American Relief Administration, not to mention the AEF, had already been assessed for his trip into eastern Europe) the over-all accounting must have been as confusing as Cottrell's several allegiances.

The appointment as a delegate of the National Research Council came from two of America's most distinguished physical scientists, George Ellery Hale and A. A. Noyes. Hale, who had been so instrumental in the development of the California Institute of Technology, was also a strong proponent of the proposed International Research Council. In picking Cottrell, both Hale and Noyes recognized that energy and enthusiasm were of equal importance with sound technical knowledge, and Cottrell was charged by them with "activating" some of the more listless French academicians.

The problems were many: How best to dissolve the prewar and moribund international scientific societies. Should, as the Americans wished, the International Chemical Union become the representative section for that branch of science on the International Research

Council? Should applied, or industrial, chemistry be represented as well as "pure" chemistry? (Cottrell found a "lack of any apparent interest in the applied side of science and rather a questioning even whether it was desirable to have any real representation from that side.") Should countries that had remained neutral during the war be admitted?—enemies, naturally, being beyond the pale.

For Cottrell the international prospector, here was the good hunting ground—the exciting fissures, the adjoining surfaces of strange and different origin, the formations new and potentially massive. Too, for Cottrell the chemist, here was a whole new laboratory in which to experiment—a laboratory still lacking instruments, but he was, after all, a man whose talent for improvisation under such circumstances was unequaled. As with other men, the war had deepened his feeling that new tools must be found, new techniques applied to end the disastrous enmity of nation for nation, of man for man. Even before America became a belligerent, Cottrell, in the testimonial banquet given him in New York in 1915, said: "We have got to come to a larger form, a larger patriotism that will overstep national boundaries, and it is going to be on the shoulders of the scientific men of the country to make the first step in such direction. It will be the duty of scientific workers—and I use the term science in its broad sense—to interest the rest of the world in this idea of cooperation. The present disturbed conditions in Europe bring these things home to us stronger than anything else could. The significance of these movements are very large and reach back into the fundamentals of life and society."

It was, he pointed out at that banquet and later, the very international nature of the Smithsonian Institution that made its close relationship with the Research Corporation so highly desirable "for the furtherance of the broader aims and ideals of the Corporation, particularly as regards the spreading of its activities beyond national boundaries." If, because of the war or for other reasons, the Research Corporation had by 1919 no opportunity to express Cottrell's broader aims, he spent no time in lamentation or regrets, for the new tool he now set out to propagandize and promote was an international auxiliary language.

Perhaps, in Cottrell's mind, nothing better illustrated the consummate need for such an instrument than his experiences at the Brussels conferences to which he was so multilaterally delegated in

1919. At one of the meetings the question arose as to the desirability of publishing a truly international chemical journal of abstracts—an abbreviated compilation of experimental results reported in other journals the world over. Services of this nature existing at the time tended to be incomplete and overlapping. The obstacles to a unified system were all but overwhelming, centering mainly around the costs of translation. Thus it was easily possible that new formulas, new medical discoveries, new techniques of value could either be delayed in reaching the researcher to whom they were important or else be completely overlooked.

There was, at the meeting, general and pleased agreement at the idea of such an international organ. No one denied the need but there followed a discussion of details which immediately raised these points: In which language should such a journal be printed? English, of course, was a favorite. But if it were to be in one language only, how effective could it then be? English and French? Perhaps. If one restricted its scope and practiced the strictest economy, it could then be made to pay. This seemed the most likely solution and had an additional advantage in following the precedent set by the Treaty of Versailles. But now the Italians intervened. If more than one language were to be used, they were strongly of the opinion that Italian should be included. In the arguments that followed the only point on which agreement could be reached here was that such a scheme would never pay and the whole project was abandoned.

Into this Babelic breach Cottrell boldly stepped, for it was a subject on which he held firm opinions backed by some practical knowledge. He had first heard the subject of an international language discussed at one of Ostwald's Sunday student gatherings but at the time he had found it of no more than passing interest. Then one day in 1914 at the San Francisco Engineers' Club (where the scheme to dissipate fog had originated) he sat next to an electrical engineer who was reading a not quite familiar-looking pamphlet.

"What's wrong with that Italian?" Cottrell could not resist asking.

The engineer laughed and replied that it was not Italian but Esperanto—a language he sometimes found of use in corresponding with the engineering staffs of Russian railroads with whom he occasionally dealt. To Cottrell, who had long been baffled by orthodox foreign tongues, the moment was historic. He had, too, he said later, been looking for some time for a subject ("not too academic and preferably of potential use") in which he and Jess could jointly interest themselves, studying it as an antidote to the technical nature of his work beyond her ken. Together he and Jess decided to take up Esperanto.

Although that was the way Cottrell recalled the matter in 1948, it is possible that Jess's enthusiasm for Esperanto was less than burning. She did, for example, write him in 1915, shortly after he had broached the matter to her: "You want me to share with you the things that will be of use to you in your work . . . whether they fit me or not, for example, you think Esperanto will be of use to you and you want me to study it with you." But Jess, like many others, found Cottrell all but irresistible when an idea was upon him and they embarked with determination on the project—with, perhaps, too much resolution, for in May of that year Cottrell noted in his diary: "Read Esperanto to Jess until she kicked."

But the more deeply Cottrell probed the possibilities of an international language the more fascinated he became and he quickly endorsed the first commandment of such a movement: whatever the language considered, it must always be thought of as *auxiliary* or, as he later expressed it, "The project of an auxiliary language may be looked upon as analogous to that of stenography, i.e., as a development of a special tool for special purposes, which has no more bearing on the use and spread of existing national languages than stenography has had on that of printing and longhand."

Although the modern history of an international language goes back to Descartes, who in the seventeenth century confined himself to the theory of the subject, the practical problem of constructed languages only began to receive widespread attention about the time Cottrell was born. The first to achieve anything approaching acceptance was Volapük in 1879 which, after a faddish rise and fall, was replaced in popular esteem by Esperanto. Esperanto, the patient invention of a Polish genius with humanitarian ideals, Dr. L. L. Zamenhof, appeared eight years later and its hardy adherents still flourish despite schisms, wars, cynicism, inertia, poverty, and all the fateful buffetings to which a daring idea falls heir. It has also retained pre-eminence over a hundred or more competitors, including Ido (its closest rival), Interlingua, Occidental, Arulo, Ro, Europal,

Omnez, Kosmopolito, Europeo, Idiom Neutral—not to mention Basic English and at least one other still under laborious construction. Cottrell immediately encountered a balking situation. Almost everyone would agree with him that humanity stood to make immeasurable gains toward mutual understanding if there were a common tongue, yet the emotional cocoon enveloping each national language defied breaching by the most violent tactics of rape or the more subtle blandishments of wooing so that the best one could hope for in an imperfect world was the crutch offered by an acceptable auxiliary tongue. Yet here, too, was something of a paradox. Those who thought well enough of the latter idea to espouse it with any degree of vigor or sincerity were usually imbued with simple good will (although its commercial advantages, too, were obvious); yet such normally mild and thoughtful folk were easily aroused to Tartar-like ferocity if their favorite auxiliary tongue received so much as a critical scratch. Thus, in the view of many experts, nothing has contributed quite so heavily to retarding the growth of such a scheme as its partisan dissenters, whose sectarianism rivals that of Christianity.

Of all this Cottrell was well aware when he took up Esperanto in earnest. He considered Esperanto the most convenient to learn largely because it had the greatest number of disciples and then, too, it was the first on which he had stumbled. His classic open-mindedness, however, never jelled on the idea that Esperanto should necessarily be *the* auxiliary international language if such a language were ever to be universally adopted. Until that day, which he recognized as far off, he was content to espouse it simply as the handiest to learn, while those whose tastes lay elsewhere could practice any other constructed tongue of their choosing as long as interest in the general subject was kept alive.

Never a faddist, Cottrell approached the movement in a mood of serious inquiry. His work with the Bureau of Mines brought him in contact with many campuses where he normally would have confined his business to the scientific departments. Now, however, his newly developed taste for Esperanto led him to seek out also the philologists, the etymologists, and the linguists, where to his vast astonishment he found unmitigated intellectual snobbishness. He first tried the University of California and there discovered that, while nearly everyone had heard of Esperanto, there was no active interest or any real knowledge of it; yet to Cottrell here was just the forward-looking kind of development which one should naturally expect to find in most active ferment behind university walls. It was a shock. He next took it up with members of the American Association for the Advancement of Science at a meeting in San Francisco only to find "mild interest but no real enthusiasm."

"Later," Cottrell said, "I was to understand this apathy on the part of language academicians and why [a constructed language] had made no progress. To linguists it was a language without literature—nothing around which a graduate course could be built. It was as though I were teaching chemistry with an itch to do research work, and it would then be quite a chore to take the initiative in offering a course in the chemistry of cooking to a home economics class.

"The traditional approach of the linguist to established languages is like that of an expert fisherman who believes that trout should be caught on light tackle with a difficult hook. To them, Esperanto is like commercial illustrating to the real artist."

Nevertheless, between the time he adopted the study of Esperanto in 1914 and his trip to Europe in 1919, the subject became one more "horizontal" with which to intercept the "vertical" interest of a friend, an acquaintance, or whatever intelligently sympathetic person happened to be sitting in the opposite Pullman seat. In lonely hotel rooms he read it aloud to himself. Some of his less hurried letters to Jess were in Esperanto, and where there were cities that had Esperanto Clubs, Cottrell established himself as one of the fraternity. At the time he recognized that in the flux of international leavening after the war an opportunity for its serious use would come. He took the matter to Walcott, urging that the Smithsonian Institution "undertake work bearing on the subject of an international auxiliary language." It would, he felt, be well within the province of the Smithsonian to collect a library of literature on and in international languages; to become a natural clearinghouse for information; and to work toward the formation of a responsible international body to guide and stabilize an international tongue. Although Walcott was interested and used Cottrell's appeal as a basis for discussion with Regents Alexander Graham Bell and Senator Henry Cabot Lodge, what encouragement he received is not on record.

This, then, was the extent of his progress at the time he arrived in Europe, where Esperanto was far more widely accepted, largely as a result of the stimuli occasioned by the claustral barriers of many tongues. In spite of his studying, he was not yet a fluent Esperantist so that (he wrote Jess) when he visited the central Paris office of the organization he "tried to talk in Esperanto and it had slipped me badly and [I] got mixed up with French, German, and Lord knows what all until I was thoroughly ashamed of the mess I made of the whole job."

It was, however, a momentary shame, for whatever self-consciousness Cottrell possessed seldom inhibited his gregarious impulses where his work was concerned. He attended the Esperantist meetings and found them such a "fine antidote for the official atmosphere in which I've been swimming around the last few weeks" that he "felt like a new woman." As he also told Jess, "the frank enthusiasm and simple-heartedness of these folks" cheered him so that it gave him courage "to tackle new jobs courageously. It certainly looks," he added, "as if I needed just about so much of these crank hobbies to keep me in good working trim." The mood that followed one of these meetings was, in fact, so buoying that for once in his life Cottrell resorted to downright coyness. A letter to Jess was written on a memorandum form of the American Expeditionary Force. Following the word FROM, he wrote "Wuzzy"; after TO, he inserted "Fuzzy."

But the mood with which he entered into the organizing of an international chemical union and the International Research Council at Brussels was anything but kittenish. His own experience with patents as well as that gained from the Research Corporation had given him something of the standing of an amateur patent expert and he put all his knowledge at the disposal of the chemical union's patent section in furtherance of their plan of an international patent. This he did in addition to fulfilling (in co-operation with other American delegates) his instructions from Hale and Noyes of the National Research Council as well as doing all in his power to see that the applied side of chemistry was brought in and represented on any international chemical body that would be born from the meetings. In both he was successful after endless buttonholing and lobbying, but perhaps his greatest zeal was reserved for taking advantage of any openings that would further the cause of the international auxiliary language.

Such an opportunity seemed to come when the enthusiasm for an international journal of chemical abstracts disintegrated into complete disagreement over the languages in which it should be published. Cottrell tried to get action on establishing a committee to investigate an international language but to such a proposal the membership remained cold. However, three days later at the general assembly of the International Research Council, Cottrell was ready. There he introduced a resolution (drafted on the back of an envelope) that a committee be appointed to "investigate and report to it the present status and possible outlook of the general problem of an international auxiliary language."

The resolution passed, the committee was appointed, and Cottrell was named its chairman. An entering wedge had at last been made.

How deeply the subject lay in his mind is indicated from a Sunday diary entry about a week later in Arnheim and Leiden. "Tried to call on Prof. ———, pres. of Holland Esp. Assoc. but house closed up (probably off on vacation). Called at home of M. Caspers, Editor Ido paper. Found him away in Germany but his wife there and told me of work and conditions (very interesting). Then made call on Mr. Rinders another member of Directors of Nat. Esp. Assoc. and had pleasant visit with him and his wife and tea there. He then accompanied me to my hotel and to 3:50 P.M. train for Leiden. But found after I got under way on train that it made no connection for Leiden direct on Sunday so had to change and go via Hague. Met Catholic priest on board and had quite a discussion over Esp. matters. Reached Leiden about 7 P.M. and to Hotel ———. Evening hunted up local Esperantists. Found first address empty (gone to Amsterdam). 2nd one met young med. student and had interesting visit 10 to 12 P.M. with him."

Much as Cottrell enjoyed this leg work on a precinct-beat level, his aspirations for the movement were already winging their way on and up. There was not only the British Association for the Advancement of Science, to whom he next carried the campaign, but also "in addition," he wrote Jess, ". . . I am hoping I may also get a good chance to talk the matter over with Sir Eric Drummond, Secretary for the League of Nations Committee in London, and see if we cannot start some cooperation, even if only nominal at first, in that direction. If I can get any considerable part of this program going over here before I sail, I believe on getting home I can put a big push behind the Smithsonian nucleus and make each of these boost the other in preparation for the time, a little later in the year, when they are rather expecting (after the Senate ratifies the League of Nations) to hold a big international meeting probably in Washington to formally launch the League, and I hope, if so, at that time we could make a further step in our program."

But his time abroad was running out. There were few Bureau of Mines affairs that would justify his remaining. Word reached him of his mother's serious illness in California and because of this, as well as other affairs of the family that were concerning her, Jess had gone out to California and urged him to return. And so in August he sailed from England on the *Royal George* without having soared to high British diplomatic altitudes from whence he could spread further the gospel of an international language. On departure there was no weight-vending card to warn him that he spent too much time regretting self-defined sins of omission but he embarked, nevertheless, an apprehensive man. Scarcely was he out of sight of the Scilly Isles before he "began to doubt wisdom of early sailing." On the following day there was another diary entry: "More and more irritated at having come off on this boat and left so much to do behind." As he was entering New York Harbor a week later he finished a letter to Jess, saying, "I haven't yet been able to forget all the things I've left behind undone but hope 'time will heal the wound.'"

But time had been busy with other things while he was in Europe. The Chicago Section of the American Chemical Society wrote that it had chosen him for the Willard Gibbs Award for 1919 but this he had declined, from Paris, saying "that to multiply such similar awards on one individual . . . represent [s] a certain miscarriage of justice."

He had left the United States as the Bureau's chief metallurgist at a salary of $6000 a year. He returned as one of two assistant directors of the Bureau at a salary of $5000, having received this contradictory promotion, in July while abroad, with his consent.

It was, though, almost like the old days in Filbert Street—the days of Cottrell the printer/photographer/electrician/publisher, for now Cottrell the scientist/inventor/promoter of international languages returned to take up where he had left off with one of his most curious roles—as a principal investor in and impresario of a lightweight vehicle variously called the Packet car and the Pony truck.

5

Everyone seemed to agree that it was a good idea, although there were dissenters when it came to the fundamental question of whether or not it was good enough to warrant a declaration of faith through the expressive channels of venture cash. The ultimate extent of Cottrell's investment in relation to his income was proof—irrefutable proof if need be—that Cottrell could never be considered a man of little faith.

It was first called the Packet. The Packet, said an early prospectus, "is a Truck, pure and simple, built for a Truck and built as good as a Truck should be to deliver more packages for a Dollar than anything available. The Packet delivers automotive service at motorcycle expense . . . the Packet can be operated at less than a cent a mile. . . . Speed: 25 miles per hour . . . 40 miles to a gallon of gasoline . . . weighs 1000 pounds, carries 100% of its weight. . . . Price: chassis $325.00 (bodies and equipment optional)." It was manufactured in Minneapolis, Minnesota, and had as a slogan: "George Can Operate and Care for the Packet." It had a box body, few parts, and no chrome.

The Packet involved no mechanical innovations. Its originators— principally a skilled mechanic named Frank R. Brasie—had measured the truck market and found a gap in the vehicular field for parcels and light packages for which the motorcycle was not adapted and the one-ton Ford truck considered too heavy for real economy. According to a report on the matter made to Cottrell, "the [Ford] with top, costs nearly $700 which is too high a first cost for many small concerns, and also its operating cost is decidedly high—considerably higher than for the ordinary Ford touring car." This basic assumption on which the Packet was conceived, therefore, seemed entirely reasonable.

But if a need existed for the Packet it was not sufficiently obvious by 1918 to have affected the fortunes of the Packet Motor Car Company in a benign sense. It would be necessary to help create a market through advertising and salesmanship, and the difficulties of trying to manufacture a new car under wartime restrictions had placed the company in the position of having one or two models assembled for demonstration purposes, an excellent, if small, factory located on a railway spur (cost: $30,000) with a capacity of five cars daily, and the most limpid of bank balances.

No Cottrell acquaintance could recall exactly what first drew his attention to the Packet although, since there was a Bureau of Mines station in Minneapolis which he occasionally visited, it could have happened during one such trip. It could just as well have been a chance meeting on a train or, since his was a popular name on assorted mailing lists, it might have come by post. At any rate his diary in May 1917 notes that he spent the evening of the twenty-eighth at home "going over Packet motor literature." His next contact was also stated in the diary when he arrived in Minneapolis in July and called the company on the phone. By November he had received a letter beginning "Dear Stockholder" in which he was advised that several cars had been completed; that fifty more were under construction; and that production plans were sufficiently advanced to justify the establishment of a sales organization and opening a campaign. The same letter also pointedly mentioned that because of the war the company had never been fully financed. The latter fact was given emphasis a month later when he received another letter announcing that the Packet Motor Car Company was on the brink of receivership unless sufficient capital were forthcoming from stockholders to enable manufacture to begin. (The day on which he received this cheerless news also brought a letter from Dr. R. B. Moore, in charge of operations at the Petrolia helium plant, which had just made its first unpromising start at production. Moore advised Cottrell that Norton had "blown up" and that things were generally on the "ragged edge of collapse.")

Then about the time he was receiving the Perkin Medal in January 1919 and explaining the complexities of helium production to the cacophonous accompaniment of aggrieved voices, he was notified that the earlier appeal had brought in only $150; Packet had gone into receivership; steps toward reorganization were being taken and under a new corporate setup the Packet would be named the Pony truck. With this news Cottrell's paternal interest in the dim cause seems to have taken an excited leap and the Pony truck became his stepchild.

By this time the habit of success had nurtured Cottrell's strength and self-confidence. Here, at the age of forty-two, he had been chiefly instrumental in establishing two successful business organizations—

the Western-International Precipitation companies and the Research Corporation, and both had originally been shoestring enterprises. The Packet-Pony—if it could be adequately financed and imbued with the proper spirit of bold initiative—while far from bearing the indelible stamp of a sure thing, held out a reasonable promise and that was often more than Cottrell really asked. Still, the question remains, why bother with such a risk when all his previous machinations had been directed toward absolving himself of business worries and the embarrassing profits that resulted?

One blunt fact was that he wanted and needed money—although it would require an intricate sifting of values to determine which was the want and which the need. With Aunt Mame's death the number of his dependents, full and semi, was reduced by one to ten, but the cost of ill-health and medical attention on the part of nearly every member of the family gnawed alarmingly into his income. The chief family physician at this time was Dr. Walter C. Alvarez of San Francisco, who later achieved a national reputation for his distinguished work at the Mayo Clinic. When, in 1920, the *Saturday Evening Post* marked its discovery of Cottrell by a feature-length article Alvarez was moved to write to Jess: "The country certainly ought to know about him. They would appreciate the sacrifice on the financial side even more if they knew what I know—if they knew of his generosity to any number of sick relatives. I think it's all the more remarkable that he has gone ahead so bravely with his ideals without neglecting claims which others would not have paid so generously."

(Alvarez, in the same letter, had a further tribute to pay. "That article was a great stimulus to me because the temptation now is strong to cut down on the research so as to do the work that comes in at the office. The article helped me to stick by my ideals and to try to keep down my money getting.")

Cottrell's income had some of the attributes of an accordion. Prior to 1919 his Bureau salary ranged in the $4500 bracket. Then, in that year it jumped to $6000, only to suffer deflationary pressures when it was reduced by $1000 on his appointment to an assistant directorship. Too, his income billowed and ebbed with the fortunes of the International Precipitation Company which, along with Western Precipitation Company, had flourished under Walter Schmidt. Here Cottrell received royalties from the foreign rights and this brought him in, during the years 1916–18, over $7000, $6000, and $4000 respectively. The bulk of these amounts represented his share of the sale of the Japanese foreign rights to the Cottrell process, which had been disposed of to Japanese nationals for $150,000. For this Cottrell could be self-congratulatory, for it had been largely his perspicacity that had insisted on Japanese patents—to the faint ridicule of his patent lawyer—when electrical precipitation still functioned more effectively in the laboratory than it did in practice. Aside from these props, he still retained a small residual interest in the Petroleum Rectifying Company which Allen Wright had successfully built on the Cottrell-Speed patent of electrical de-emulsification of crude oil, and in some years during this period dividends from this source amounted to several hundred dollars.

Their wants being simple, the Cottrells led frugal lives, although not for reasons of penury. Thus, in spite of the family responsibilities, Cottrell had by 1919 achieved a state of middle-class financial respectability with a $12,000 equity in real estate in Washington and the West Coast; $5000 in Liberty Bonds which constituted all of his savings (and against which he had borrowed $1700); adequate life insurance; and the foreign precipitation interests.

For this Jess deserved a measure of credit. Although she had never completely shed her early diffidence, she, too, had gained in self-confidence, for Cottrell's long absences from home had increased her responsibilities in the management of family affairs (no doubt, too, as a calculated matter of policy on Cottrell's part) to the point where her opinions became positive, her grasp of finances firm, and her voice in family councils one of authority. In her letters she spoke knowingly of mortgages, notes, insurance, interest, deposits, and taxes. Her lot was not easy. Her husband's offhand way of writing checks, coupled with his occasional absent-mindedness, made the Cottrells' fiscal life while he was away from home one of tortured mathematics. No longer were their letters the youthful and groping expressions searching for an approach to life; his duty to the world, having once been defined to Jess and partially executed, was never again a subject of correspondence; love versus duty was still a matter of conflict but the scars that had formed over this old wound were tough enough to bear constant exposure to reality and the subject rarely, now, came up for discussion by mail. Instead, their letters now leaned strongly on the vagaries of addition and subtraction. Cottrell was, moreover, a man quick to respond to requests for small personal loans—and of some of these he undoubtedly forgot to tell Jess. He seldom tried to collect them but when, at one point, his ready cash balance was low enough to welcome the return of $200, he did face the unpleasant duty of writing to ask for it. This brought in return a heart-rending reply, no check, and Cottrell did not press the matter further.

Finally, however, Jess's patience with Cottrell's tepid interest in the immutable laws of subtraction to which bank balances are subject was strained beyond limits. In April 1920 she received notice that the account kept in the Berkeley bank was $1.39 overdrawn, and the assistant director of the United States Bureau of Mines found the following ultimatum in his mail: "I sent a check for $75 on April 15 which should have reached there yesterday, but what you may have done in the meantime is an open mystery. From now on I'll attend to *all* the family checks—and your job will be to see that I have enough to do it with."

Cottrell's reply was worthy of the man who had dazzled Leipzig with his ability, had ingeniously trained electricity to separate dust from gases, had founded corporations: "I am getting," he said, "to have great confidence in your ability to manage somehow very well for yourself without me and hope you fully appreciate the compliment implied."

But the end of World War I made the capitals HCL part of the day's cant and the high cost of living—as other Americans in other generations were to know—kept the Cottrells' funds at low levels of solubility. Thus, when he set about to resuscitate the Pony truck, Cottrell, in letters to potential friendly backers, made poignant reference to "an anchor to windward in a financial way." Money, however, was not all. At the same time, he said, he was on the lookout for something that would not interfere with his government work and yet would "furnish a little excitement and interest of a personal nature to keep me from becoming stale in the purely impersonal details of my main duties. The fact that my Bureau connections make it improper for me to get personally interested in the technical matters that I am, perhaps, most directly familiar with, increases somewhat the difficulty of finding an attractive and, at the same time, available opportunity."

The Pony truck was such an opportunity. "If," he declared, "it turns out well, with only relatively moderate returns, I want to have enough from this so I will not have to keep chasing similar pot-boilers but can turn full attention to more important public service." As a first step in the assumption of his new responsibility he set about to raise $24,000 to refinance the company. It was understood that if he succeeded in bringing this amount in he would acquire half interest and that control of company policies would be largely in his hands, although he himself felt that he would serve more effectively as an arbitrator between new investors and the older Brasie interests (chiefly Mr. and Mrs. Brasie) who had built and financed the new factory with its equipment. While this plan, Cottrell wrote a friend, "places a rather larger and more definite responsibility on me than I have contemplated, I am willing to undertake it if it will help along the project but do not wish to accept an undue pro-portion of the returns in comparison to services rendered." He would, he said, consider it more "in the nature of a trust."

For some Cottrell friends this was enough. Two of those who responded with unwavering loyalty were both wealthy men who had made respectable personal fortunes in mining and allied fields—L. D. Ricketts, the Arizonan who had served on the smelter smoke com-mission representing the smelter interests; and Benjamin B. Lawrence of New York, who had assisted so ably and enthusiastically in the formation of Research Corporation. A third friend who gave his wholehearted support to the project was a forceful young metallur-gist attached to the Bureau of Mines Minneapolis station, C. E. Julihn, whose regard of Cottrell was second only to his reverence for Lawrence. "I feel," Julihn wrote Cottrell, "it is a rare privilege to further the purposes of such a man [as you]."

But Cottrell's ability to inspire what occasionally amounted to a fierce loyalty was not equal to the task of allaying the doubts of other friends and acquaintances, who tempered their respect for his business acumen by long hard looks at what they deemed to be solid business facts. E. H. Hooker, of Hooker Electrochemical Company, a man who considered himself a shrewd financier, tried to dissuade Cottrell for his own good from "doing anything foolish." Another acquaintance, when approached with a proposal that he invest, had the matter investigated by one of his knowledgeable employees familiar with the automotive field. He reported that although there seemed to be a market for the Pony truck, "with the motorcycle factories, on the one hand, and the Ford Motor Company on the other, both in a position to obtain much lower costs through quantity production, there would be the keenest kind of competition and there seems to be no question that the Packet Motor Car Company could not profitably produce as good an article at an equal price."

It was in December 1918 that Cottrell decided to assume responsibility for financing the Pony—a hazardous feat under the best of circumstances, now rendered doubly so since he planned to sail on his first European junket in February. In Julihn, however, he felt he had a lieutenant competent to handle the job. At Julihn's request Cottrell delegated to him the task of raising $24,000, furnishing him with a list of likely prospects (with some of whom Cottrell had already discussed the project), and the following ethical policy: "In picking the people for this enterprise I have constantly kept this factor [of personal integrity] uppermost in mind rather than the mere question of financial or technical ability. The latter are certainly not only important and necessary, but the former is absolutely *fundamental* for my way of playing the game and whatever I do in this enterprise is based on the assumption that we are going to be able to maintain a good proportion of that spirit in our own group, at least, and in this I include Mr. Brasie as it was the recognition of just this element in him and the early literature of the project that attracted my attention and his subsequent attitude has fully borne out my first judgement."

Jess was not among the more ardent supporters of the new enterprise—at least not to the extent that she shared Cottrell's boundless optimism for its auguries. When, after sailing, he wrote her advising that she allot $1000 to $3000 more of their savings for the venture he justified the request by saying, "These figures look big when written down in cold blood but we are constantly, in a lot of little ways that we don't think of, frittering away just as much without thinking of it and in any case the amount here involved will not completely make or break us and as the very worst that could come, I might have to get out and hustle more again for awhile to make up for any false step now which, in the end, might be the best thing that could happen to all of us. So brace up," he further encouraged her. "Be a sport and get all the fun there is in this as well as the value of these experiences."

But Cottrell's absence abroad was too much of a handicap for Julihn and, despite his earnest hard work, fund raising made little progress. There was much corporate reorganizing during this time with one end result that the amount to be raised jumped from $24,000 to $37,500.

With Cottrell's return in September 1919 the tone of the campaign took on a more resonant timbre. "After carefully thinking over the whole project," he wrote Ricketts, "what I should like to do is to personally take on two-thirds of the present proposition, i.e. $25,000 out of the total $37,500 to be raised at this time and divide the remaining one-third or $12,500 among those from whom I borrow the money necessary to take on the first two-thirds." Here indeed was the old Cottrell who had said, when he founded Research Corporation, that "the only trouble is that we are too timid about asking people to do things for the good of the cause."

Ricketts obligingly took the cue. As a matter of business routine he had a representative go to Minneapolis and on his report that "this is not a cinch but rather a gamble with fair possibilities" Ricketts subscribed $25,000—half for Cottrell, half for himself. Ricketts asked that only $5000 of this be covered by a Cottrell note, the rest to be paid back out of profits. Graciously Ricketts wrote him: "Do not worry about papers and securities and notes and all that kind of thing. Later on we can attend to a note. In these transactions, however, between friends there is no need to be too formal unless the matter develops into an important business negotiation. It is a great pleasure to me to be associated with you in a business enterprise. I have never wished to interfere with your idealism, but I have always felt that if I could make you see a little bit more clearly your duty towards yourself that no harm would be done. I know I could not make you selfish for that would be real harm." Benjamin Lawrence was equally informal. He advanced $5000, saying, "I will place your letter on file, and this together with your acknowledgement of the letter will be the only evidence of the transaction necessary."

There were other takers of lesser amounts so that, by mid-January, 1920, only $2500 of the $37,500 remained to be covered and, according to a contract signed by Cottrell and Brasie, this total amount must be paid in by February 1. Two prospects on whom Cottrell counted for the $2500 would sign up as soon as their finances permitted, but in order to meet the February deadline Cottrell decided to sell some of his Liberty Bonds. The mechanics of this operation met unforeseeable delays so that it was not until January 29 that he was able to mail a check from Washington for the necessary amount. Somehow it failed to arrive in Minneapolis on time.

The fun which Cottrell had promised Jess then began.

"I find it my duty," Julihn wrote Cottrell on February 6, "to report to you that Mr. Brasie attempted to refuse acceptance of the last payment which carried with it control. He deliberately planned to get past February 1 and then repudiate the plain intent of your contract, as well as his expressed promise to me that the actual date of payment would make no difference to him."

Julihn's was a wrathful report. He denounced Brasie's "treason," his "villainy," the "viciousness of his character." Apparently, however, Brasie, in fancying himself as something of a lawyer, had acted without legal aid, for when on Julihn's advice he sought it, he retreated, put the check through the bank, and delivered the stock. Then, wrote Julihn, "he had the unspeakable meanness of spirit to call me up on the phone and say he had not had the heart to go through with his plan, because he got to thinking about you and how much you would be disappointed if things did not go through exactly as planned—though when I had last seen him he had brazenly ridiculed all thought of sentiment and proclaimed the supremacy of self-interest above all else."

The sequel to this illustrated far better than anything else the profound and unshakable faith Cottrell had in the essential goodness of the human spirit and it is a question of which, from this point on, commanded his greater interest: the financial and mechanical success of the Pony truck or the ethical redemption of Frank R. Brasie.

At first Cottrell wrote Julihn that he was "not disposed to be too greatly perturbed over the facts as long as we are fully aware of them." Two days later Julihn, if he never knew before, found out the meaning of tolerance. "With regard to Brasie," Cottrell wrote, "it seems to me our biggest job is to educate him kindly but firmly to the realization that really big business is done, and has to be done, very largely on a basis of personal confidence. His point of view is, after all, not so surprising perhaps, considering his limited opportunities thus far for observation and experience in these things and amongst the men doing them. Until we get him so educated and fully realizing the absolute and fundamental importance of such matters, we must, of course, take no chances with technicalities and I realize this may be a long time but I believe we should firmly approach the problem with the view that eventually we can and will be able to so equip him. Despite all that has happened, and not discounting any of it, I still believe Brasie has good stuff at bottom and is not too old to get these unfortunate elements out of his constitution. It will take some work but am inclined to think it will be very much worthwhile."

This did not exhaust the subject. The following week Cottrell elaborated: "One always has to figure on having to do a good deal of business with people whose business ideals are widely different from his own. Brasie is into the thing with us and I sincerely hope that we can find a way to see it clear through together and I believe I am getting as much interested as in anything else to see if we can't eventually do a good bit to improve Brasie himself in just these matters. That would, in itself, be a real service both to him and the community as well as ourselves." The framework in which this sentiment was expressed was a four-page longhand letter outlining to Julihn a background of tangled finances in which Cottrell now found himself as a result of the Pony venture. It asked no sympathy for himself, made no accusations, expressed no remorse.

All this was preliminary to a stockholders' meeting of the United States Machine Corporation, the expansive title of the new company formed to manufacture the Pony truck. The meeting took place the latter part of February 1920 in Minneapolis, with Cottrell, representing the majority stockholders and as the company's vice-president, attending. "We met some pretty delicate situations," he wrote Jess, "but discussed them with great frankness and everyone behaved finely and the best of relations have been maintained and we now have the situation all worked out to mutual satisfaction of all concerned." (He also used this trip in his plural-minded way to stop off at the Universities of Michigan, Chicago, Wisconsin, and Minnesota to advance the cause of an international language with their respective, although not always responsive, philologists.)

But fate continued in a heavy-handed way to deal with the Pony truck. In Julihn's eyes Brasie failed to respond to the other-cheek treatment. Then Ford prices were lowered. A milling machine, as indispensable as it was expensive, was ordered in the spring of 1920 but failed to leave its factory until late in May. It thereupon met with a railroad strike and in being rerouted got lost, arriving in Minneapolis the last of July. In the meantime, 200 motor blocks had been cast and a Japanese firm showed interest in ordering several hundred cars as soon as they could be produced. By October, however, there were still no trucks and the general tenor of affairs was contained in a telegram from Julihn to Cottrell which, among other things, advised him:

LULL IN DEMAND MOTOR MARKET ONLY TEMPORARY PENDING ADJUST-MENT PRICES RAW MATERIALS. REVIVAL DEMAND EXPECTED AFTER ELECTIONS. STOP. THREE THOUSAND DOLLARS NEEDED TO CARRY TO JANU-ARY WHEN FIRST LOT TWENTY-FIVE MOTORS WILL BE COMPLETE. . . .

Then the postwar world moved into its first business depression in 1921—a state in which it had already been preceded by the United States Machine Corporation. The faithful Ricketts agreed to take an additional $50,000 worth of stock providing it were preferred stock with voting power, but Brasie seemed to favor liquidating rather than have Ricketts acquire control. At this Ricketts washed his hands of the affair and Cottrell sought support elsewhere but many others who wanted to help agreed to do so on the basis of personal friendship rather than as a calculated investment. The idea of exploiting charitable impulses in such a situation was repugnant to Cottrell, yet, according to his diary, he still talked of "need for sympathy re Brasie's point of view and general feeling."

There were endless plans for reorganization. If any of this depressed Cottrell he gave no evidence of it. In March 1921 he wrote Ricketts, "I am taking care of the payroll out of my own pocket week by week to tide over and am making an effort to help in securing orders for the motors or cars. I have fortunately just sold my house in Washington and while I had to take notes and trusts for most of my equity in it, which at best won't keep things going very long, it will help out very opportunely to tide over the gap that may occur in my present canvass of outside resources. The more I go into this thing with people on the outside, the more convinced I am that we are on the right track fundamentally in this enterprise." To add to his troubles, two weeks after this Jess was hospitalized for a severe case of asthma and entered a sanitarium at Pompton Lakes, New Jersey, for an indefinite course of treatment.

The United States Machine Corporation did, however, pass a small milestone in May 1921 when the first car was put on the road. Its chief demonstrator was Herbert Fulton, the eldest of four children of Jess's sister-in-law, Kate Fulton, at the time a student at the University of Minnesota, and to him, as to the other three children, Cottrell had assumed some of the stature of a father since the death of their own in 1902. Cottrell thought the Pony truck venture would be good experience for young Fulton and brought him into the company as secretary-treasurer. In so doing, Cottrell wrote Jess that he had taken the project on "as much for the boys [i.e., Herbert and his brother Eugene] as anything else."

Fulton attempted to make up in conscientiousness what he lacked in experience but by this time the enterprise was beyond the bounds of the most experienced of consciences. Meanwhile, in the summer of 1921, Cottrell had again decided it was necessary to go to Europe, and young Fulton found Brasie's character no more palatable than had Julihn. He could only, as of September, report to Cottrell in Paris that "the plant is absolutely shut down and there is not one cent in the treasury at present."

This was the situation that faced Cottrell on his second return from abroad in the fall and which with matchless tenacity he still did not consider hopeless. To some investors he wrote in all sincerity that the outlook was encouraging if only he could arrange sound financing. Against this theme of hope which Cottrell played came such ominously percussive messages from Fulton as:

BRASIE DECLARES WILL FORECLOSE NOVEMBER 1 UNLESS YOU ARE HERE BY THAT TIME.

As if this were not enough, Cottrell arrived back in the United States as a full-fledged apostle of the international auxiliary language and in addition to a heartbreaking attempt to raise capital for the truck was, at the same time, trying to get large contributions for the propagation of that movement.

"I can't remember a time," he wrote his old friend Walter Schmidt, "since some of the most strenuous days of the precipitation and de-emulsification crises when I have had so many apparently critical, not to say desperate, situations all pressing on me for immediate attention and relief and yet all very well worth while and really doing finely if I can only get over the top with them during the next few months. Next to the Minneapolis matter, perhaps the I [nternational] A [uxiliary] L [anguage] is most insistent also due to my absence and consequent shortage of finances. On the other hand," Cottrell added brightly, "while abroad, I succeeded in getting this squarely landed in the official laps of both the British Association for the Advancement of Science and the League of Nations."

This latter note of triumph did not alleviate Schmidt's misgivings over the Pony truck. As one of Cottrell's closest friends, he thought he saw unfair advantage being taken of his old colleague's good will and good nature. Schmidt was saddened. "The thing that grieves me most about this," he replied, "is that you have jeopardized your next royalty receipt [from International Precipitation Company], for I do not see why it is up to you to individually safeguard the interests of the other stockholders. This does not appeal to me as either business or philanthropy. If the money [to pay off a mortgage Brasie held] had to be raised by a note, why not obtain the signatures of all the stockholders—or at least the principal ones—to this note?"

Then, in what he conceived to be his friend's best interest, Schmidt painted a doleful picture of the international precipitation business outlook; spoke guardedly of a "curtailment of operations" and a "virtual suspension of activities." Actually business, while not brisk, was not wholly bad. In that year Cottrell had over $4000 due him, and which he received, from international royalties but by a judicious use of well-intentioned duplicity Schmidt hoped to paint a sufficiently gloomy picture of future prospects to discourage Cottrell from committing himself further in the truck morass.

If Schmidt felt any guilt on account of this stratagem his sin was shortly expiated. Immediately before the war he had spent considerable time abroad organizing the precipitation business there, arranging for the free exchange of information on all technical developments between the autonomous foreign companies engaged in the precipitation business and his own Western Precipitation Company as well as Research Corporation. Although much of this developmental work was interrupted by the war, Schmidt returned to Europe with the end of hostilities and in mending the fences played a major role in the formation of Lodge-Cottrell Ltd. in England, which, under the direction of Sir Oliver's son Lionel, handled the precipitation business there. On Schmidt's suggestion that the work of Cottrell be recognized by the English firm, Lodge-Cottrell in 1922 obligingly presented Cottrell with 1500 shares of stock (par value, one pound). These gave him, with but few annual exceptions, several hundred dollars in yearly dividends for the rest of his life. The loyalty of his friends repaid Cottrell in the same year in somewhat the same way. Ricketts, in an effort to somehow compensate Cottrell for his out-of-pocket expenses on behalf of the Pony truck, presented him (since Ricketts' business conscience would not permit a further investment) with a gift of 1000 shares of Ahumada Lead Company stock—a venture in which Ricketts was interested. This, too, for many years paid good dividends, and although Ahumada eventually met the exhausted fate of all mines, Cottrell could never in later years, when its value was considerable, be induced to sell it. It was a gift. One did not sell gifts.

Ricketts had already had experience in trying to overcome the scruples which Cottrell steadfastly entertained where money was concerned. No documentation bears the following episode out, although several of Cottrell's close colleagues knew of it for a certainty. Sometime in this period 1912–21 (some thought it was in 1918) several Cottrell admirers believed his value to science and humanity could be enhanced under conditions other than as a government servant, a university professor, or an industrial researcher—the most likely openings for a man of his talents and training. The movement was spearheaded by Ricketts, although Benjamin Lawrence was also thought to support it.

Ricketts called in Julihn and told him of a plan he hoped to put into effect not only for the above reasons but because he also felt he stood in Cottrell's debt. Without Cottrell, he said, a copper mine in southern Arizona called the Ajo would have been relatively worthless. The ores there ran to about 1 per cent copper and, according to the story, in some inscrutable way Cottrell suggested an improvement in reduction methods by which they could be treated in order to insure profitable operation. Ricketts charged Julihn with sounding Cottrell out on what many a researcher would consider a sheer fantasy: Ricketts and a friend, or friends, would equip a laboratory to Cottrell's specifications at their expense. They would, moreover, agree to endow him with $50,000 yearly for ten years and for which no accounting need be made. The laboratory would be his. He could work on whatever he chose.

"We owe him that and more," Julihn remembered Ricketts saying. When, in as diplomatic a manner as possible, Julihn broached the matter to Cottrell the latter demurred. He had already heard of the scheme, he said, "but it's too much like being subsidized."

If, then, Cottrell's enduring faith in human nature was even slightly shaken by the Pony truck enterprise, these other evidences of his friends' interest in his welfare must have been more than compensatory. What he lost in the undertaking he never revealed, and whether he was in any sense duped was not a point on which all his friends agreed. One thing seems certain and that was that he assumed more financial responsbility than was necessary, even allowing for the moral obligation he felt toward those friends whom he had persuaded to join in the project.

In him, faith died hard. For several years after the factory closed down in 1921 he tried vainly to refinance it. He had an engineering friend make an impartial study of the plant, the truck, and its prospects, and the report came back that with alert, aggressive management and sales organization, together with proper advertising and adequate financing, the United States Machine Corporation "can compete successfully and should obtain its share of the established business within two years allotted time after embarking on its active production and sales campaign."

The fact that Cottrell thus sought independent advice displeased Brasie, and his letters to Cottrell, once aglow with the camaraderie of mutual adventure, grew stiff and cold. Cottrell, for his part, knew one moment of bitterness when he referred to Brasie as insisting on "his pound of flesh."

The plant never reopened to manufacture the Pony truck but there were many other plans and projects to take Cottrell's mind off this. There were the international language and the activities of the Research Corporation. There was the directorship of the Bureau of Mines which he had assumed and resigned. There was his new work with the National Research Council. There was a new banking system which he tried to encourage. He thought, too, there were likely business possibilities in Washington, where a new enterprise called the American Coal Corporation had been launched, for, far from being dismayed by the failure of either the Pony truck or its human progenitors, he still seemed to see both in a strange shadowless light of his own.

6

For a brief eight months Cottrell was director of the Bureau of Mines. President Wilson sent his nomination to the Senate on May 5, 1920, and his resignation took effect at the end of that year. It was not a distinguished tenure but then Cottrell did not intend it to be. As one of two assistant directors he had been in charge of the Bureau's Investigation Branch as differentiated from its Operations Branch. There his responsibility covered five divisions—mineral technology (of which he himself had lately been chief), fuels, mining, petroleum and natural gas, and experiment stations. The latter, in turn, brought under his wing the eleven bureau stations scattered between Pittsburgh and Fairbanks, Alaska. For the benefit of any taxpayers who might wonder what kept a sizable staff busy in so many places, the Bureau issued an annual report covering the work of both branches which, for the year 1919, showed in addition to routine work some fifty special projects. These included the training of 9781 miners in first-aid and rescue work, to say nothing of such less obvious things as a comprehensive investigation of the white clays of the United States and the value of these in the ceramics industry. It was a full program absorbing the energies of almost 700 employees under the direction of extremely competent and able chemists and engineers noted in their fields.

This was the organization of which Cottrell took command as a matter of public duty. Manning, his predecessor, left the Bureau to become director of research of the newly organized American Petroleum Institute and in so doing fired a parting shot at a situation that was later to plague Cottrell. Manning lauded the work of government-employed scientists, their "inestimable value" to the government and hence the public. Most of these men, he said, were a fine type who cared little for the commercial field and many held high ideals of public service, yet, he added, "with the marvelous expansion of industry in this country and the growing necessity of science to industry, the scientific bureaus have been utterly unable to hold their assistants against the competition of industry which is taking their highly trained men at salaries the government does not pay or even approach."

Before his resignation, at which time he wrote these sentiments to the President, Manning had made his plans known to Cottrell and urged that he accept the directorship—a matter in which the retiring director usually had an influential voice. "We discussed the situation quite fully," Cottrell wrote in his diary, "and I told him I would, temporarily, if it would help out in the change but didn't fancy looking forward to it permanently." This feeling later crystallized into a definite proviso that he would accept the position only for as long as it took to find a man Cottrell deemed suitable both as an administrator and as a technologist worthy of the high standard which Holmes had set and Manning had perpetuated.

Behind this disinclination was Cottrell's strong antipathy for purely administrative work, a feeling which had been reinforced by his duties as assistant director. The confines of such work definitely cramped his free-wheeling style and it was likely that the directorship would involve a certain amount of politicking and such panoplies of office as speechmaking, indiscriminate handshaking, and entertaining—all of which Cottrell relegated to a nuisance category already congested by haircuts, the trying on of hats, and having his picture taken.

His purpose, therefore, in finally accepting the job, and one which he made clear, was simply to provide a continuity of policy until another choice could be made. After four months' incumbency he admitted in a letter to a friend that, while he had found it pleasant work in many ways and that he had enjoyed it thus far, still "the experience has only confirmed my former conviction that my best field is in less ponderously executive work."

One of his candidates to succeed himself was Herbert Hoover but Hoover had other plans. The results of their discussions he vaguely summed up to Jess, saying, "While [Hoover] has, I rather understand, no personal unsurmountable objection to taking the work . . . and realizes it would be properly understood by those who know him, he feels it might be misinterpreted by others and be the basis for weakening his influence in the other and more important lines."

Hoover got off lightly in another way. Cottrell took advantage of this contact to bring up the subject ("in a lighter vein") of an international auxiliary language but, he confided to the diary, "he shied off very hard so I dropped it." The conversation then got around to broader topics and Cottrell noted: "Hoover felt sure we would in a very few months be in the League of Nations with such modifications as would save face of Republicans. Believed Bolshevism was practically dead outside of Russia."

Cottrell was not the one to overlook a stimulating contact on any level. About this same time the 1920 biographical sketch appearing in the *Saturday Evening Post* elicited the following letter from Portland, Oregon:

Dear Dr. Cottrell:

I am a boy eleven years of age and am interested in chemistry. Your article in the "Post" is very interesting to me, specially because my Daddy often talks of, in some way, taking the oxygen from the air and storing it for fuel and power.

I would like to know if we take the air into the system through the nose, if so, how does it separate the oxygen from the rest of the air and retain it also?

Do you think that chemical sets are much use to experiment with? I am now in the 7B. When I graduate next year do you advise a polytechnical or high school for me? I will be very glad if you will answer these questions.

Yours truly
Ian Mackay

Cottrell noted on the letter that a reply was made. Then on his next Western trip he found Portland on his itinerary and, in spite of a schedule almost avariciously crowded (in San Francisco he had a meeting with Sir Oliver and Lady Lodge, after a drive with the latter, he wrote Jess, "I delivered her Ladyship back to the Palace Hotel 6:30 and then beat it for home"); he bethought himself of young Mackay. This necessitated writing back East for the address, which arrived in Portland in time for Cottrell to invite the boy and his father to breakfast. "Ian is a nice little fellow," he reported to Jess, "and of course I gave him some Esperanto literature."

If, because of the temporary nature of his tenure, his administration of the Bureau was unmarked by any new policies, he did achieve without ever trying a certain popularity as director. His nomination was hailed by a syndicated columnist thus: "In the group of scientists which revolves around the Cosmos Club in Washington, there is much satisfaction over this appointment. Too often the man at the head of a government scientific bureau is more of a politician than a scientist." When word of his impending resignation became public two petitions from Bureau personnel called his attention to his fitness for the post, begged him to think of the good of the organization, and the "unanimous feeling" on their part that he reconsider.

Nevertheless, his mind was made up to leave. By mid-December 1920 he had finally persuaded H. Foster Bain (whom he had in earlier years championed for the directorship over Manning) to leave his more lucrative work in private industry and in the name of public service take over the job—a choice which was quickly approved. And so he terminated his nine years' formal connection with the Bureau, leaving with the usual felicitous messages from the President and the Secretary of the Interior and also with a fine leather traveling bag presented by his staff at a farewell dinner.

7

The traveling bag led a busy, restless life often strained beyond capacity by a demanding owner, sometimes neglected in station checkrooms, handled indifferently in hotels more substantial than swank, although it experienced one high moment of glitter when it crossed first class to Europe on the *Aquitania* and knew the prestige associated in the twenties with sailing under more than two smokestacks.

When Manning left the Bureau and took that opportunity to chide the government for neglecting the financial welfare of its scientists, some of whom placed the public weal above private gain, the prototype might have been Cottrell. As the interim nature of Cottrell's incumbency became known he began to receive bids from prospective employers and among those of a non-academic nature was one from a prominent New Jersey electrical firm offering him as high as $25,000 yearly to assume the directorship of its new research laboratory. Whitney, at General Electric, had apparently surrendered all hope of snaring Cottrell by this time although, even if he had not, it is likely that Cottrell would have shown the same lack of interest that he did by declining the $25,000. Instead he chose to throw in his lot with the National Research Council and for a salary of $6000 became the chairman of their Division of Chemistry and Chemical Technology.

Sired by the august National Academy of Sciences (a group of the scientific and intellectually elite who had not yet seen fit to enroll Cottrell), the National Research Council had come into being during World War I. With an eye to impending hostilities and in accordance with the terms of its own charter, the academy, in 1916, offered its services to the President. Wilson accepted and asked the academy to organize the scientific resources of the country. The academy thereupon established the council, consisting of representatives of the country's scientific societies, research organizations, government scientific bureaus, and businessmen in allied fields of engineering and industry.

Brilliantly administered by such men as George Ellery Hale, R. A. Millikan, Charles D. Walcott, and Gano Dunn, the organization served its country well during the first World War (to say nothing of World War II). It had touched on Cottrell's work by recommending the helium project, including the Jefferies-Norton process, and the council was among the organizations he represented in London and Brussels in 1919 when the International Research Council was formed.

The vigor of the council enabled it to survive the armistice. In adapting itself to peace, it took as its purpose the "promotion of scientific research and of the application and dissemination of scientific knowledge for the benefit of the national strength and well-being." Unlike comparable organizations in other countries, it abjured government money for peaceful purposes and drew financial support from the Carnegie Corporation, the Rockefeller Foundation, and other private contributors.

With $500,000 from the Rockefeller Foundation, the council set up its first research fellowships—in physics and chemistry. In addition to Cottrell, Hale, Millikan, and A. A. Noyes, this fund was administered by Simon Flexner; Henry Bumstead, professor of physics at Yale; Elmer Kohler, professor of chemistry at Harvard; and Augustus Trowbridge, professor of physics at Princeton. It was Cottrell's new job to recommend and supervise the grants in chemistry as well as generally to oversee the routine projects of his division which, in co-operation with the Division of Physical Science, included solicitation of a $200,000 fund for publication of International Critical Tables of Physical and Chemical Constants.

The attitude of the council toward the heads of its separate divisions was one of eminent reasonableness. The appointments to such posts were made yearly and the council recognized that a good scientist, harassed by routine, might welcome such an interlude to shoulder a few light but important duties and use the rest of his time to carry out any cherished project which the pressure of his normal work prevented. At the time of his appointment to the chairmanship of the Division of Chemistry and Chemical Technology, Cottrell was also notified that his vacation period, with pay, was not to exceed two months.

Being a man of cherished projects, Cottrell co-operated wholeheartedly with this council policy. The possibility of working with and for the council had first occurred to him while in Europe in 1919. There he met one of their representatives, a Dr. Henry M. Howe, who, as chairman of the Engineering Division, was also attending the formative meetings of the International Research Council. Howe thought Cottrell would be the man to replace him in that capacity. In telling Jess of this, Cottrell wrote, "I shall be strongly inclined to favor whatever gives me the freest hand to keep in touch with things over here for the next few years." And to Manning he wrote, "I can see that under proper conditions this might open the way to some very attractive opportunities of service, especially in some of the international fields in which I have been getting more and more interested."

When he left England in that year and fretted his way homeward on the *Royal George* some part of Cottrell remained in Europe. Shortly after his arrival in the States the council made him a definite offer which Cottrell found hard to resist, for Manning was already hinting at his own resignation and Cottrell found no pleasure in the prospect of succeeding him. But Manning's appeal stressing the Bureau's greater need won out and Cottrell rejected the council's first overtures.

Then between 1919 and 1921 the international turn of his thinking became so pronounced that for this period at least he functioned less as the scientist than as the man of good will. For this a few of his colleagues took him to task, urging that he return to the laboratory in spirit and forget this nonsense of an international language. Some of those who regretted his frittering away his time on such distractions had had refreshing proof in 1919 of Cottrell's wizardry as a laboratory technician, for in that year the *Journal of the American Chemical Society* published his paper "On the Determination of Boiling Points of Solutions." It is true that the method and apparatus were of his devising while still an assistant professor at Berkeley but somehow he had never gotten around to write them up until urged to do so by another investigator who had a contribution to make to the same problem. While the determination of the boiling point of a pure liquid had always been easily and accurately obtained, getting that of a solution required complicated apparatus subject to aberration. Cottrell's method and apparatus, while hardly of testtube simplicity, was such an advance that on publication it became the basis for standard laboratory practice and found a place in all physical chemistry textbooks in which the subject is treated.

While there were scientists who looked down their noses at Cottrell's refusal to confine himself to accepted affairs, they constituted a small unorganized minority for whom he maintained a tolerant, if bemused, indifference. In the eyes of most colleagues he was fired by a touch of genius which in 1920 led the Chicago section of the American Chemical Society to offer him again the Willard Gibbs Medal. Although, while abroad the year before, Cottrell had refused the honor, this time he accepted.

The attitude of the more progressive men of science toward Cottrell was reflected in the presentation speech made by Whitney of General Electric, whose employ Cottrell had so long and successfully eluded. Whitney said that the *way* Cottrell had done things was more important than the actual things themselves and, he emphasized, "we exalt that human *quality* which insures advanced undertakings of human welfare and interest. . . . You are one who, no matter how wisely you may act, must withstand many rebuffs and disappointments, because, in blazing new trails, countless obstructions must be encountered and surmounted. Herein you have always retained your momentum and your good nature." Whitney concluded his address by saying, "We will be willing to forgive in you many possible errors or mistaken undertakings in the future, if your ideals and your will to be right and the intuition to be constructively dissatisfied with imperfect existing conditions persist as they have hitherto existed."

It did not take Cottrell long to let the assembled and banqueting chemists know the tenor of his thoughts. The thirty-seventh and thirty-eighth words of his acceptance speech were "international affairs." He went on (after mentioning the need of guarding against the ferment of the "wild yeasts of Bolshevism") to say how international co-operation in both pure and applied science could "unquestionably furnish one of the most powerful forces possible against the growth of national misunderstandings"; how a better understanding could be directed toward the "common needs and common good of humanity as a whole." He used the international auxiliary language as an example of one instrument that could bring about this cooperation. Then he said how often the control of raw materials fostered wars and asked, "Who is there better equipped than the chemist to look into the future with regard to the world's needs for raw materials?" Petroleum, he felt, was a particularly important pivot on which an international situation could turn and it alone would serve to emphasize the point of his talk, i.e., how "responsible and important a part the chemist must take in the guidance of new international relationships now rapidly pressing upon us."

This was the responsibility he felt so strongly that it drew him back to Europe in 1921. He felt it so strongly that what was happening there was of far greater consequence than any attempt to salvage his own personal fortunes and the benefit his presence in America could have given the floundering Pony truck. He felt it so strongly that he overrode Jess's objections, for she knew better than he how oblivious he could be to his own physical well-being. "I shall hate very much to see you go," she wrote, "as you have never been yourself since that last trip abroad."

Nevertheless, he went in the middle of June in a capacity hard to define. As a consultant for the Bureau of Mines (a connection he retained after his resignation) he would execute a few miscellaneous missions on a per diem basis. He was, in addition, chairman of the International Research Council's Committee on International Auxiliary Language for which he had, since 1919, been able to solicit only some $3000 to carry on the work and most of which was already expended. As chairman of his Chemical Division of the National Research Council he would represent them at the second conference of the International Union of Pure and Applied Chemistry which he had helped organize two years earlier. The council, however, could only partially subsidize his trip. Too, he thought if he went as a businessman he might carry more weight in approaching other businessmen on the language project and so he solicited and received a $700 drawing account from the Petroleum Rectifying Company to look into their interests in England. Each affiliation understood that he was concerned with the others, but faith in Cottrell's capacity was such that no one seems to have doubted his ability to serve sundry masters conscientiously. But he went also as a free agent, which meant that some of his expenses would be out of his own pocket and, as of 1921, the one reserved for money was a shrunken pocket indeed.

Yet he sailed on the expensive *Aquitania.* When he somehow got word that George Eastman, whose reputation for philanthropy was second only to that linking his name with Kodak, was to be a passenger on the *Aquitania,* Cottrell canceled his budgeted passage on the *Lapland* and submitted to the luxury of the larger liner. He had no introduction to Eastman but he was in a sense an anxious mother with an ungainly, marriageable daughter whose beauty could only be considered as inner, and these have always found the milieu of a transatlantic liner particularly well adapted for adroit maneuver.

It took several days to achieve speaking terms with Eastman but the result was a two-hour talk. He found Eastman "approachable and responsive." Eastman admitted having once bought some Esperanto books but had failed to follow up the subject. Cottrell did not press his luck and tactfully postponed the subject of money.

There were others on board whom Cottrell wooed. Nicholas Murray Butler surprised him by displaying an affable familiarity with his reputation and work and promised to bring the language project to the attention of the Carnegie Foundation, with which he was connected. Marshall Field III ("a fine young fellow, very modest and clear headed") expressed a sympathetic interest in the idea. When, however, he came to Bernard M. Baruch, Cottrell subordinated the international language subject to the Wheeler Banking System, which for several years now had captured his interest as a lesser horizontal.

(Although there is no record of how these attentions were welcomed by the Messrs. Eastman, Butler, Field, and Baruch, there were those who genuinely appreciated his efforts to interest them. Just prior to sailing he had written a rugged and wealthy Chicago individualist, Colonel George Fabyan, enclosing some Esperanto literature to which he received the following reply: "I want to express my gratitude. . . . Any man who has time to do this for a mere chance acquaintance has got time for anything, and his body must be too small for his heart. I am not trying to write a nice letter or pick words; I am just putting down my reactions.")

The *Aquitania,* however, had one disadvantage. Its swiftness handicapped Cottrell in developing his contacts to the fine point of maturity where he felt it meet to solicit outright support. Nevertheless, he thought (he wrote Jess), that "I've earned my extra fare over pretty well by the work I've been able to do but wish I had another week ahead of me with this crowd as I've only begun on the possibilities with them."

Then came the long days, restless nights, lost meals, fatiguing trains; the conferences, meetings, and interviews against which Jess had futilely warned him.

London: ". . . first contact with Lord Robert Cecil out here at Hyde Park where they are holding a big demonstration over League of Nations issues. I caught him on the fly between platforms."

Brussels: ". . . the International Chemistry meeting . . . lunch yesterday at the home of M. F. Cottier, the President of the Board of Directors of the Banq d'Outremer, one of the largest and most powerful financial agencies in Belgium. He has taken quite an enthusiastic interest in the problem and invited me to meet the Director of the new Colonial School in Antwerp, a Col. Le Maire, who was one of the early explorers of the Congo and also took part in the Esperanto and Ido movements."

Paris: "[A session of the French National Academies] gave me a much appreciated opportunity to mill around and propagandize Esperanto among them."

London again: "I asked [Eastman] if he felt sufficiently interested to help us out financially but he said just at present he was overextended."

Prague: "I had hoped to write you but found it absolutely impossible until now as I had to leave on the present trip with Dr. Nitobe, Assistant Secretary General of the League of Nations, to attend the International Congress of Esperantists. . . . Dinner tonight with Dr. Nitobe and Mr. Benes, Czechoslovakian Minister of Foreign Affairs. . . . Am having one of the hottest and most exciting days of the trip dividing myself between the meeting of the Esperantists and the Idists, both of whom are holding meetings here today and who are watching each other like hawks."

Vienna: "The thing I am particularly interested in this trip is to study the relations between the International Labor Office and the rest of the League at Geneva. I get the impression that the two are not in as close touch as they might be and, as these very things are what I am most interested in and believe I can do most service in, it appeals to me as a particularly good clue to follow up just now."

Zurich: "The French Society of Chemical Industry wants to elect me an honorary member."

Geneva: "Am finding the League of Nations Secretariat extremely interesting and running into all sorts of new and old contacts here."

Edinburgh: ". . . A meeting of the British Association for the Advancement of Science. . . . It is nearly 3 A.M. I've been working over papers and writing steadily since breakfast (yesterday) and I scarcely seem to have made any impression on my list of way overdue correspondence. . . . The meeting up here has been pretty good and our report went through o.k. . . . Am too tired to think further tonight."

Geneva again: "The [League] Assembly has definitely placed the question of teaching Esperanto in the schools on the agenda for next year and ordered the Secretariat to investigate the subject thoroughly in the meantime."

Here was Olympus, the high-water mark of his trip. No matter with what futilitarian aura such an equivocal achievement might be regarded in decades to come, it was largely as a result of his efforts that the subject of an international auxiliary language was brought to the League's official attention and official action taken. The representatives of twelve nations moved that the question of teaching Esperanto in common schools be referred to a committee. This, headed by Lord Robert Cecil, recommended that the subject be studied and placed on the Assembly agenda for 1922. The Assembly unanimously adopted the report and while it is true that League resolutions later exerted the force of a withered arm, at the time Cottrell did his language lobbying it was the most promising international opinion-forming instrument through which to work.

This action, together with spirited progress in focusing the attentions of the British Association for the Advancement of Science, as well as other learned groups, on the problem, were results that gave Cottrell a sense of accomplishment, for this time he returned to America less reluctantly. It was work that had taken enormous amounts of faith and massive doses of zeal. He knew, for example, that he would in all probability never live to see anything resembling universal acceptance of one auxiliary language, so that both faith and zeal must have for their rationalization the long point of view. Yet, even if he were to see this accomplished, it would still not be the end he sought. It would be merely one of the tools to bring into being that "larger patriotism that will overstep national boundaries" about which he had, for almost a decade, been both preaching and doing. Impatient of results as he sometimes was, he was also discerning and knew that for the most part massive formations change but slowly, often imperceptibly; that this was particularly so where the factors were human and the momentum of progress took its force from the intellect rather than from the eruptive drive of emotion.

When he did arrive back in Washington in October (pausing there less than two days before rushing off to Minneapolis to salvage the Pony truck situation) he tried again to solicit language funds from Eastman and he wrote of the League action as being the "product of my trip [which] has given just the impetus and moral backing here at home which was needed in order to insure the serious interest and consideration of our own academic and official circles."

The trip also had by-products. In Leipzig, Dresden, and Berlin he saw the eclipse of German pre-eminence in the physical sciences. In Dresden he met Luther, his old teacher and Ostwald's chief assistant, who recognized the symptoms of decline, and Cottrell found him "frankly and tremendously impressed with the progress that the American technical science had made in the last few years, which, coupled with our control of raw materials, he felt would give us the lead over Germany in her present situation for at least many years to come, if not permanently." As if to emphasize this, Cottrell also found in Berlin that the Kaiser Wilhelm Institute, once the greatest scientific pride of imperial Germany, had "an air of desertion and desolation."

These observations on German academic science and technology he included in his formal report to the Bureau of Mines, for which he was acting as a consultant. Absorbing as was the language work, it had occasionally faded into the background, for in between his four visits to London, three to Paris, and two each to Brussels and Geneva, Cottrell managed to investigate and report on the glass industry in Belgium, helium and metallic aluminum manufacture in France, oxygen liquefaction in English mining and metallurgy, and liquid oxygen explosives in Germany.

Since all this had been accomplished in a four-month stay abroad it is small wonder that he returned a tired man. A photograph taken in Geneva with Dr. Inazo Nitobe, the undersecretary general of the League of Nations with whom he had struck up a warm friendship, shows his face to be deeply lined and almost haggard yet still giving an impression of strength. It was not, at this point, a handsome face, for the prominent features—the deep-set eyes, the nose, the strong jaw—that had once been subordinate to a youthful fullness were now exaggerated. But it was, still, an arresting face with an air of responsive kindness that often reminded others of Lincolnesque qualities.

Now, for his health's sake, Jess again took him to task. When he returned in October he made a two-day visit to the New Jersey sanitarium where she was staying, before hurrying to Minneapolis and the Pony truck.

There he received a letter in which Jess summed up her grievances: "It is to be hoped that you can settle down this next year to one spot long enough to get yourself together and get in more normal physical shape, which you are a long ways from at the present time. You are not doing your best work by any means and if you would plan to give up these long and hasty trips for from three to six months, you'd find that life would have different values for you and you would realize what a long strain you had been under. In the last four years you have not been anywhere only a few weeks at a time. In the beginning of 1918 when I came back from my illness in California and we took the little house you were home off and on until the latter part of July and August when you took a trip to California and the West. You returned the last of October and with a few trips to New York, etc. were home until February 23, 1919, when you sailed for abroad. From the 23rd of February until December 1st we were together less than 15 days—the week you spent in California after your return from abroad in August and the five days I was home after my trip to California and before going to Johns Hopkins. The middle of February you started out to the Coast, etc., and from then to June 1st, when you took the Directorship of the Bureau, I don't think you were home two or three weeks at most, off and on. We took our vacation of two weeks in July and the first of August you started off on another trip and it wasn't until about the 12th of December you returned. During the time I was in the sanitarium in Washington to the last week in October you made several trips to surrounding cities. Then you were away all of November while I was trying to get adjusted somewhere. In 1921 you were making trips every few weeks—from a few days to two weeks—from January to June—and June 14th sailed for Europe and were gone four and a half months and now on return, a trip to Minnesota. In the last three years we've averaged about twelve months of being together."

There was truth enough to Jess's complaint, for Paris and Prague had simply replaced Selby and Anaconda. Aside from the vacation which her letter mentioned, there had been few periods of respite between 1912 and 1921. In 1917 they spent several weeks together in Glacier National Park. Here Cottrell found relaxation in climbing up and over a nine-mile mountain pass in two hours and four minutes ("with about fifteen minutes of this used up in stopping to tempt squirrels"). The next year they went to a hotel in the White Mountains where, by no coincidence, there was also a congress of Esperantists. Nor on his trips by himself did he take time out. Occasionally while on the Anaconda-Great Falls circuit, he would go fishing with smelter officials in the Montana streams but one friend claimed he watched unobserved while Cottrell gently removed the hooked trout and released them back into the water. Cottrell recorded in his diary that one evening in 1917 he spent at the Chemists' Club in New York playing Kelly pool with his old friend Buckner Speed. The dissipation of this, however, was lightened by an additional note that at the same time they discussed nitrogen fixation and the overthrow of the second law of thermodynamics. Twice, in a three-year interval, he played golf with Ricketts in Arizona but the process of moving small balls around with either a cue or an iron was not imaginative enough to have captured his fancy.

However, the Wheeler Banking System and Industrial Credit Association did. This was the design of a Washington businessman in the metal roofing trade from whom it took its name. Its chief purpose was to furnish easily available credit to lower-income groups or, to use the term more frequently employed at the time, "the poor man." Deposits were made in multiples of four for which the depositor received a certificate akin to a traveler's check. These, when properly filled out on the reverse, were negotiable either as withdrawal slips from the bank itself or, according to a prospectus, any store would accept them as cash. Deposits drew 3 per cent interest payable monthly, thus combining the features of both a savings and a checking account. All deposits under this system constituted what was, in effect, a joint account available for borrowing by members at 6 per cent annually.

The prima facie merits of the system were such that one or two Washington banks installed it and it seems to have worked for a time. There were, however, people who wondered what would happen if any large number of small borrowers failed at one time to make good on their obligations. Cottrell, in all probability, thought the pros outweighed the cons and, from the time in 1917 when he first came in contact with the system, added its literature to that of others in his briefcase and, not one whit abashed by its unimpressive origins, brought it to the attention of such blue-chip financiers as Baruch and Otto Kahn. There is, however, no record of any staunch converts, although his espousal of this cause lasted a good ten years.

Another obscure organization blended his language and his international interests. Its name was Tuvalia International Amikaro and in the United States section Cottrell held cabinet rank as Minister of Records. The aims of TIA were broadly and vaguely humanitarian, centering around a "cooperative union of the nations of the world." Article IV (Eligibility) of the Constitution stated that a candidate must "be so tolerant that, whatever may be his own ideas regarding political, social or other beliefs or theories, he can concede sincerity in other people holding dissimilar beliefs, and is able to discuss these and kindred subjects with a friendly attitude for the reciprocal receiving of information."

Although the organization was founded several years before Cottrell's affiliation with it in 1916, such constitutional provisions seem so descriptive of Cottrell that they might almost have been drafted with him in mind.

TIA championed an international language and believed that no individual could be part of the social fabric of humanity without sharing personal responsibility for his fellow men. However, several things tended to detract from the nobility of these stated principles, for TIA seems to have borrowed some of the less intelligent trappings of a collegiate fraternity. There was a secret handclasp, a ritualistic initiation ceremony, and its international director was unknown to a membership which was limited to one per thousand of a country's population. Also it was considered unethical to discuss the private affairs of TIA with non-members.

The organization need scarcely have worried over the threat of a bloated membership. It functioned only sporadically during World War I, and when in 1920 an attempt was made to revive it, its 364 American members were circularized by mail. Of these, 64 responded. In spite of this, the Washington nucleus continued to meet for several years thereafter and, in defiance of the earlier Lhasa-like aura of mystery imposed by the elusive chief, discussed the affairs of the world quite openly.

The Wheeler Banking System and TIA were but fringe interests which competed with others such as the town of Lomax in western Illinois—a community to be developed on the principles of the "garden cities" of England—and New Llano, a co-operative colony in Louisiana. These latter did not earn Cottrell's active support but he kept abreast of their multifarious problems, encouraged their backers as he did with any experimenter who engaged his fancy, and considered them as reserve subjects of discussion when other horizontals failed to intersect.

8

If, in a few opinions, these vagrant concerns earned Cottrell a measure of scientific disapproval, his was a valued counsel in many fields and in the matter of patent law his influence was felt in Congress.

The irresistibly sweeping advances of science and technology in twentieth-century America had profoundly affected not only the academic and industrial worlds but had made themselves felt in the federal government, where many departments and bureaus were making important contributions of their own. Here the question of inventions and patents (of which there were thousands) was as complex as it was confusing, for no standard practice existed for their handling and there were almost as many policies and schools of thought on the subject as there were bureaus affected. In general, all inventions and patents developed by its employees on government time and in government laboratories were held by the government exclusively. Greatly embarrassing was the fact that no agency or office was legally authorized even to take title to or administer such inventions. Some bureaus permitted their employees to take out patents provided they were dedicated to the public; some permitted no patenting at all. One of several paradoxes existed in the fact that such bureaus as Mines, Chemistry, Soils, and Standards existed for the benefit of the public, yet it was difficult, and usually impossible, to develop their inventions commercially for the use of the public since no private manufacturer wished to commit himself without adequate protection and a knowledge of what the competition might be. Nor, obviously, was it the proper function of the government to develop and exploit except in the case of some inventions made principally by the Army and Navy. Here was a point Cottrell well understood, for, as with his own precipitation process, seldom does a patent leave the Patent Office in a perfectly marketable condition—both money and time are required to bring it to a stage where a public finds it acceptable.

World War I, by stimulating invention in government bureaus, aggravated this multifaceted problem, and a partial solution seemed pointed to by the Trading with the Enemy Act. This empowered the President to administer enemy-owned or -controlled patents—a power which he successfully delegated to the Federal Trade Commission. The commission acted effectively in the public interest. With this as an example, many government scientists, under Cottrell's leadership, thought the commission would be the logical agency to handle government employee patents, i.e., arrange for their licensing to private industry, determine the government's shop rights, allot some remuneration to the inventor out of the licensing fees, and give over whatever remained (above these and administrative costs) to the U. S. Treasury.

Cottrell, at this time, was still chief metallurgist in the Bureau but his interest in the subject was so great that, in conjunction with E. S. Rogers, a former Federal Trade commissioner, he drafted a bill embodying these features which Secretary of the Interior Franklin K. Lane recommended to President Wilson. Wilson approved the idea, referred the bill to the House Patents Committee, and the ovoid legislative ball began rolling.

This Cottrell cause had had its inception around 1916, and by 1920 he had enlisted the strong support of one of the country's ablest legislators, Senator George Norris of Nebraska. Their acquaintance warmed into a friendship which probably would have become close had either had more time for its cultivation and it was later to result in collaboration on a vastly more important piece of legislation.

Along with other prominent government scientists, Cottrell testified in hearings before the House Patents Committee. After the inevitable revisions the bill was introduced into two Congresses, where it failed of ultimate passage. The last time, it passed both Houses in an amended form, went to conference, passed the House again, but was filibustered out in the closing days of the Senate session. Some senators, backed by elements in industry, contended that the bill would put the government in the patent business (where, inevitably, it was already—the bill was merely intended to bring order out of confusion) and objected to government employees retaining any rights on patents they might acquire.

The defeat apparently depressed Norris but Cottrell gave no sign of disappointment, even though, of the two, his had been the prior interest and his enthusiasm had fired Norris' support. The wealth of his seemingly limitless optimism led him to subordinate any personal feeling of discouragement. After the Senate filibuster ended, Cottrell called at Norris' office to drive him home. At the same time, according to the diary, he gave Norris another kind of lift, for he directed his conversation toward "cheering him up re Patents Bill and things generally." Of himself, he merely noted, "Found myself very tired."

This cheerful fatigue was, in fact, the theme on which the decade ended. The trip to Europe later on in 1921—anything but restful— brought him back home worn and tired. Immediately following this was the emergency call to Minneapolis and the unrefreshing atmosphere of the Pony truck situation. The second appeal to Eastman for language funds, on which Cottrell had laid inordinate hopes, resulted only in the discouraging reply, "The new school of music and theatre connected therewith are taking all of my spare cash."

Yet neither these setbacks nor the attendant weariness could quite quench his optimism. Research Corporation had prospered. The League of Nations had taken official cognizance of Esperanto. He still spoke of the Pony truck as "promising." Then almost coincidental with Eastman's refusal came a bright new turn in his thus far dispiriting attempts to raise money for the international language. Strangely, in this case, Jess patterned the checkerboard.

THE SPIRIT of the times has gone down in United States history as baroque. To describe the changing mores induced by prohibition, the flamboyant touches that characterized murder, the pursuit of happiness to a two-four beat, an ever-rising stock market, roadhouses, synthetic optimism, shortening skirts and lengthening skyscrapers, chroniclers of the period have used such terms as the Jazz Age, the Roaring Twenties, and others. If the stigmata of the era were so pronounced that such nicknames are justified, it is well to remember that there were still other values extant and many men dedicated to them. One of these men, Cottrell, chose this time to return to the laboratory.

Jess's asthmatic condition, which no doubt in later years would have fascinated practitioners of psychosomatic medicine, had kept her under protracted treatment in a sanitarium at Pompton Lakes, New Jersey. This coincided both with Cottrell's 1921 European trip and with the illness of another patient, Mrs. Dave H. Morris. Mrs. Morris was an exceedingly rare combination of spirited intelligence, charm, and considerable beauty, and possessed the further attribute of being a granddaughter of Commodore William H. Vanderbilt. Jess and Alice V. Morris struck up an acquaintance and in chatty feminine fashion discussed their husbands' affairs. Cottrell at this time was sending back letters full of his European doings with the language movement. These, together with Jess's knowledge of Esperanto, caught Mrs. Morris' interest and after her discharge from the sanitarium and before she had had a chance to meet Cottrell she wrote Jess that her doctor had encouraged her to take up the study of Esperanto; that her husband had also become enthusiastic and that through it they could have "some mental fun together." Mrs. Morris did not realize it but with this light commitment she had taken on what, aside from her family duties, was tantamount to a life's work. Four months later, in March 1922, Mrs. Morris wrote inviting Cottrell to visit them on his next trip to New York and discuss language matters.

In the heart of New York's upper East Side the Morrises lived a life of cultured wealth. Dave H. Morris, a lawyer and financier (later appointed by Roosevelt as American ambassador to Belgium), shared his wife's civic-mindedness and humanitarian impulses. Although they had access to the social levels covered by the term Society, their active friends and acquaintances were drawn chiefly from the leaders of solid intellectual and serious-minded movements. They were charmed by Cottrell.

The Morrises, and in particular Mrs. Morris, adopted the international auxiliary language movement with the ardor of elderly parents in need of just one more small child. Together they proselytized their own extensive field of acquaintances. "We wish," Mrs. Morris wrote Cottrell, "we had your wonderfully persuasive powers! Our own are growing, however, through the persuasion of the cause itself." So intense were their efforts that by March 1923 cohesion was inevitable. Two meetings were called, and by invitation Cottrell was the principal speaker at both.

The first of these took place on March 21 in the ballroom ("palatial" . . . Perth Amboy *Evening News*) of the home of Mrs. John Henry Hammond in New York, and this in itself—a far cry from Cottrell's door-to-door canvassing in Arnheim and Leiden—was indicative of the plane to which the movement was now appealing. Over two hundred people attended, and equally revealing was the fact that it was presided over by Dr. Frederick Paul Keppel, then president-elect of the Carnegie Corporation. Publicity for both meetings was handled by Russel Crouse, a comparatively obscure reporter for the New York *Evening Mail,* who had not yet fallen into dramatic collaboration with Howard Lindsay.

Two days later the Morrises entertained more selectly for a group of forty, including three college presidents—MacCracken of Vassar, Mezes of the College of the City of New York, Morgan of Antioch. John Dewey of Columbia and Dean Virginia Gildersleeve of Barnard were there, as were Mrs. Andrew Carnegie and Mrs. Charles L. Tiffany. Unfortunately John D. Rockefeller, Jr., was ill in Florida, but sent his assurances that otherwise he would have been present.

At both meetings Cottrell animatedly pointed out the simple basic needs for an auxiliary international language and urged that impartiality toward the proposed and competitive tongues be maintained. His enthusiasm caught on and, reinforced by that of the Morrises, within a month the International Auxiliary Language Association (IALA, pronounced "ee-yah-lah") was formed. Aside from this, the meetings produced agreement that the way to proceed with the language question was to foster research in the colleges and universities while stimulating interest in the secondary schools through optional courses in one or more of the synthetic tongues. Some results were immediate. Columbia University Extension announced that it would introduce a general IAL course in its fall term, while Antioch College and its socially polar opposites, the very fashionable schools, Miss Mason's in Tarrytown, Miss Spence's and Miss Chapin's in New York, planned full-term Esperanto courses.

When the fund-raising started, Mrs. Morris, after making a sizable contribution of her own, wrote Rockefeller in search of a pledge and said of the meetings: "One of the most delightful features . . . was the reiteration of personal regard for Dr. Cottrell. It was awfully hard to judge which was uppermost in the minds of the educators, admiration for his eminent work as a scientist or affection for his unselfish, dauntless devotion to the cause of humanity shown, among other ways, in his volunteer labors for an auxiliary language." Rockefeller replied that he would match every contribution up to $2500 that was raised.

Looked at from the standpoint of Cottrell's operating technique, all this represented a high measure of achievement. As with electrical precipitation, with petroleum dehydration, and with the Research Corporation, he considered his job all but done in bringing this project to a point where diffused sympathetic interests solidified into an active working force for its development and propagation. Once he had found the instrument to which he could confidently bequeath his ideas and his enthusiasm, that was the point at which he could step aside and with the retention of only a fatherly interest go on to other things. It is true that at the time many organizations existed to further the causes of separate linguistic sects but there was none to sponsor the non-partisan idea behind the movement as a whole.

However, Cottrell's remaining interest allowed him to accept a directorship on IALA's board. Along with General James G. Harbord, president of Radio Corporation of America, and General John J. Carty, vice-president of American Telephone and Telegraph Company, he served also as a member of its General Advisory Committee and nominally retained his chairmanship of the International Research Council's Committee on International Auxiliary Language (which, since its other members were scattered over Europe, had no chance to meet). But the burden of the movement was off his shoulders. Now he could, with less feeling of responsibility toward the language cause, devote his major efforts to the Fixed Nitrogen Research Laboratory in the Department of Agriculture. He had been appointed director of that, at a salary of $6000, in the summer of 1922.

2

There was more than the usual spate of job offers when Cottrell decided to leave the National Research Council on completion of his second yearly term in 1922. Brown University flavored its bid with the highest salary paid on the campus, to which Cottrell replied that he would be happy to help them find another man. Massachusetts Institute of Technology considered making him head of their chemistry department, although they never got around to a formal offer. Columbia and Purdue were equally tentative. Lehigh wanted him for a professorship in metallurgy. The Carnegie Institute of

Technology made proposals, as did the University of Arizona and others.

One thing, however, was uppermost in Cottrell's mind and this he wrote his Japanese friend, Nitobe, in Geneva: "In looking over the positions open and their geographical locations, I expect to be considerably influenced by the possibilities they will offer on letting me see through to a conclusion, or at least a safe landing place, much of this work along international lines for which, in a way, I have already made myself more or less responsible."

If only, he thought, he could land the international auxiliary language in the lap of the Smithsonian with financial backing from the Rockefeller Foundation, the Carnegie Corporation, or the Research Corporation. "I am not sure," he wrote Jess, "we could not work out things so that I might make [the Smithsonian] my headquarters next year with the frank understanding that I devote most of my time to this subject until it was well underway. I am not sure that this may not be the best and easiest solution even if I had to find most or all of the funds to float the whole thing. It would at least give the project a permanent basis which is hardly yet established."

But to this proposition the diary had the answer: "Walcott very wary."

Then he met the Morrises. Shortly after that the directorship of the Fixed Nitrogen Research Laboratory unexpectedly fell vacant and, satisfied that his language cause would be advanced in the capable hands of his newly found friends, he accepted a laboratory offer.

With the possible exception of uranium and its kin, perhaps no element offers more opportunity for wry moral thought than nitrogen. Even more than politics does it make strange bedfellows. It first nourishes the soil that gives man food by which to live. It next serves the industries which economically sustain him. Then, although it promises to be eclipsed by other elements, it is the handmaid of wars that maim and kill. Without it, life is impossible; with it, violent death is commonplace. It is lavishly given in a natural state. Cottrell once figured that under ordinary conditions affecting barometric pressure there were over any forty acres of the good earth approximately 1,500,000 tons of nitrogen in the air.

Either happily or regrettably, man has discovered ways to bring it out of the air and convert it into utilizable forms (or to "fix" it) for his own good and for his own nefarious purposes. There is still a lively possibility that the means by which this can be done with the greatest ease and facility known to date may rest largely on the right shoulder or on the conscience of Cottrell. How this problem of nitrogen fixation became a concern of the United States Government is a story that makes the helium venture one of drab complexities.

Although nitrogen in the air is plentiful, its usefulness as such is severely limited. It is more helpfully, if insufficiently, compounded in the earth. It is found in such things as the humus of the soil, in coal and petroleum beds, and to the great good fortune of the Republic of Chile, in once vast nitrate deposits along her barren northern coast—an arid land whose rainlessness kept the soluble nitrates from dissolving away. Here for the better part of a century was the world's chief source of nitrogen both for fertilizer and for munitions. Chile held a natural monopoly, just as the United States had on helium and Germany had on potash, until World War I, when electrical precipitation helped supply it from cement dust. It was only by curious chance that Cottrell's interest and work had been brought to bear on all three of these.

The fixation of atmospheric nitrogen had long been a subject of scientific study and was recognized as one of vast importance in world affairs. Although up until 1902 man had failed for aeons to achieve this end, less politically nervous organisms had been doing it with secretive diligence—the work of very specialized bacteria underground which managed throughout centuries to combine nitrogen from the air with elements in the soil into nutritive compounds. Cottrell once observed that in a workmanlike season these organisms can fix as much as 100 pounds of nitrogen per acre of soil. He might well have tendered them his applause for thus confining themselves and leaving the explosive field to man. But Nature has other ways of fixing nitrogen, and the intense heat of perhaps every lightning flash permits nitrogen to combine with oxygen in the air, some of which is then absorbed by rain coming down and into the earth as nitric acid.

It was after this latter method that man patterned his first successful process of nitrogen fixation. Based somewhat on its long-known principles, a small plant was set up by two American chemists in Niagara Falls in 1902. Here was made a successful demonstration (although not a commercially successful one) that a powerful electrical arc could under certain circumstances chemically wed oxygen and nitrogen which, through a series of easy steps, could be formed into various nitrates for introduction into the soil. Despite its relative simplicity, this arc process had a drawback that made its use impractical for most countries. In relation to the amounts of nitrogen it could fix, it used enormous quantities of electrical power. It was better adapted to lands both watery and picturesque where hydroelectric power was available in cheap abundance, and therefore it attained its greatest commercial importance chiefly in Norway.

Almost at the same time came the cyanamid process. Although this used only about a quarter as much electrical energy as the arc, it required more raw materials and a greater number of steps to achieve the end result. First calcium carbide must be made by melting coke and lime together in an electric furnace. To this, at red heat, was added pure nitrogen made from liquid air. The resulting calcium cyanamid had only restricted use as a fertilizer so that further treatment was required to break it down into ammonia and urea, which were then adaptable for soil requirements.

If the United States could be said to have had a nitrogen fixation industry at the beginning of World War I (it really didn't: an American company had a cyanamid plant at Niagara Falls, Ontario, whose output was sold in the United States), it was all subterranean, where it remained, dark and uncapitalized, and conducted by bacteria. The country relied for its organic nitrogen on manure, dried blood, slaughterhouse tankage, fish scrap, and other things whose supply was as inadequate as their sundry smells were potent. For inorganic nitrogen there were imported Chilean nitrates and the domestic by-product coke ovens from which nitrogen in the form of ammonium sulphate is recovered when bituminous coal is made into coke. It was a hapless situation for a country on the eve of a great war—a war which, according to one observer, used as much fixed nitrogen in a single day as either Robert E. Lee or Napoleon had used in a whole campaign.

Around the supply of nitrogen centered early naval strategy of World War I. England blockaded the ports of the Central Powers, but German cruisers hovered off the coast of Chile to interrupt the supply of nitrates to the European Allied Powers. In the years immediately before hostilities opened Germany had imported millions of tons of Chilean saltpeter and some of this was being put to her good advantage in raising food to feed her troops, who were also using it to smash their way through Belgium and France. Britain sent a fleet to clear the nitrate route but it was defeated in November 1914. A second and more powerful fleet won a victory off the Falkland Islands a month later, but for a critical four months the supply line had been severed and the cost of saltpeter soared.

From the standpoint of nitrogen, however, the British blockade of Germany was of far less significance than was the German interference of the Chilean route to England and France, for it has often been said and may in some measure be true that Germany would not have started the first World War had she not devised a marvelously ingenious nitrogen fixation process of her own. It was called the Haber process, the Haber-Bosch process, and the so-called Haber-Bosch process. In the United States the less wieldy term "direct synthetic ammonia process" came into official acceptance.

This process developed into industrial being in Germany in 1913 and liberated the art of nitrogen fixation from complete dependence on cheap electric power, since the necessary energy could now be derived from coal. It achieved the direct synthesis of ammonia by compressing a mixture of pure nitrogen and pure hydrogen under a very high pressure and then passing the mixture under heat through a catalyst. Cottrell's old teacher, Ostwald, had already devised an effective means of converting the resulting ammonia into nitric acid, from which the explosives came. The nub of the process, however, was the catalyst.

Chemists have as much difficulty explaining a catalyst as theologians do with the Holy Ghost. It is hard to say just *how* catalysts do what they do, but unaccountable reactions occur in their presence though they themselves seem to take no part in them. Some of the explanation of the cause seems to be contained in the effect. They are delicate and sensitive things. They can be "poisoned" by chemical and thermal changes and on them is lavished great amounts of research. One of the most searching inquiries into this field was that undertaken immediately after World War I by the United States Government in the Fixed Nitrogen Research Laboratory.

By 1916 it was apparent to even the dullest that America was vulnerable in the extreme, so heavily dependent was she on nitrates brought overseas from Chile. When Congress passed the National

Defense Act in 1916 a section of it authorized the President to conduct investigations as to the best, cheapest, and quickest means of producing nitrates. This was carried out by the War Department with the result that two nitrate plants were built near Muscle Shoals, Alabama—the repercussions of which were to echo down congressional corridors, permeate cloakrooms, and discomfit the White House for over a decade. At the time these plants were conceived they were intended for war purposes. When and if peace came they were to be devoted to bucolic ends.

They were called Nitrate Plant No. 1 and Nitrate Plant No. 2. Their histories parallel those of the helium plants in Texas to some degree, and at the time of the armistice the results at Muscle Shoals were about equally conclusive with those obtained in Texas when it came to determining the merits of the separate processes used. Plant No. 1 was to use the direct synthetic ammonia system and Plant No. 2 the cyanamid process. Although it was realized that the latter was possibly not the best, quickest, and cheapest means of fixing nitrogen, still—thanks to the plant at Niagara Falls—chemists and engineers in America knew how to build and operate such a plant. That was important. Plant No. 1, on the other hand, was based on the principles of the Haber process with its subtle catalysts, and almost all expert knowledge of that was in Germany. The Haber process was no secret it itself, yet there was a secret in how to make it work effectively and that had never been mastered in the United States.

Two months before the armistice Plant No. 1 turned out its first synthetic ammonia but that was about all. For anything resembling production in quantity or with efficiency, it had been discovered, the whole plant would have to be redesigned and that on the basis of more extensive probing into the entire process. It had been simply a good try. Plant No. 2, which was to have an annual capacity of 40,000 tons of fixed nitrogen through the cyanamid process, started into successful production a few days before the armistice was signed. In the meantime, other cyanamid plants were under construction and the net effect was that the government spent $107,000,-000 during the war on its nitrogen fixation program, obtaining almost enough nitrogen in sufficient time to celebrate the armistice by firing a few jubilant, booming cannons. It had, after all, been largely the products of Chilean nitrates that exploded American shells.

While that may have been the immediate result and open to

cynicism, the lesson was not wholly lost. True, congressional interest all but expired and the government plants were shut down until it could be decided what to do with and about them—a point that remained unsettled for fifteen years. But two good things happened. A private nitrogen fixation industry began to develop and the government, out of the balance of a war appropriation, began a programed study of the entire problem.

Among the American commissions (such as Cottrell's Bureau of Mines group) that took up the invasion of Europe where the Allied armies left off after the armistice was the Fixed Nitrogen Commission, consisting of four men among whom was Dr. (then Lieutenant Colonel) A. B. Lamb. They visited the various nitrogen fixation plants in England and on the Continent with, of course, irrepressible interest in the two great German Haber works at Oppau and Merseburg. While the commission was shown through these plants, the Germans, conquered or unconquered, allowed them to take no written notes. Nevertheless the commission gleaned much valuable information.

In the meantime, the Secretary of War established the Fixed Nitrogen Research Laboratory and under the direction of Dr. Lamb this began an immediate investigation, among others, of the Haber process based on the information the commission brought back as well as on experience gained from Plant No. 1. Then, as the military importance of nitrogen fixation receded, the laboratory was placed under the Department of Agriculture in 1921 with the emphasis shifting to fertilizers. Lamb had returned to Harvard and was succeeded by R. C. Tolman. Tolman, more a physicist than a chemist, went on to a distinguished career at the California Institute of Technology and Cottrell took over.

3

The beginnings were happy. It pleased Cottrell to be back once more in the laboratory, faced with important problems yet free within a liberal framework to choose some of his own techniques for their solution. He expressed himself on the situation in three ways: with professional gravity to a friend, "This rather appealed to me as it leaves a good chance for initiative and they evidently want me to sit in on the major councils of the Department [of Agriculture] as a whole from the first and take a wider part than the leadership of this particular laboratory in itself would imply"; with enthusiasm to Jess, "I find myself so tickled at having a lab to work in again that I am cooking away at fool things I suppose I could just as well get a boy to do—way up to 6:00 P.M. and then long after everyone else is gone, but I'm frankly indulging my taste for that and recultivating the habit of mine which comes back easier than I thought it might"; with nostalgia to the diary, "Much like the old days in Berkeley."

As in the directorship of the Bureau of Mines, Cottrell had been preceded by two very able men. The laboratory was already established and functioning effectively when he entered it. Its staff numbered in the neighborhood of a hundred and included scientists ranging in capacities from plodding to brilliant. Its program, even to laymen, was exciting. With these solid beginnings stemming from the cumulative efforts of Lamb and Tolman, it matured under Cottrell's administration to the point where scientific leaders, both foreign and domestic, spoke of it as "one of the most important and active research organizations in the world" and even "one of the finest [research] organizations that has ever been developed."

But there were troubles. The first of these came shortly after Cottrell's administration began and had a peculiarly Cottrellian twist. Both at the University of California and in the Bureau of Mines, those who worked with Cottrell (with the exception of newcomers) had by long association come to a tolerant understanding of his inspired, if erratic, ways and regard for his ability as well as the genuine warmth of his ingratiating personality usually softened what otherwise might have been an unrelievedly irritating trait. He would enter a laboratory and in wanting to be of help would throw out so many suggestions that the usual immediate results on the listener were mild symptoms of intellectual indigestion. A case was sometimes rendered acute by the weight of his reputation, for no one knew just which of his ideas might be the exact key they were seeking (he had been known to furnish just that in a matter of minutes), which were false scents, and which were trails that would lead into extraneous fields, distant and forbidding. It was axiomatic that in such a visit Cottrell could easily lay out a long life's work for any researcher in a very short conversation. He could, that is, to those who took him with undue seriousness, but the hardened Cottrell colleague knew that he was just being stimulated, if not actively helped, and returned to his work unperturbed except by such new thoughts as he cared not to reject.

During the latter part of his administration the laboratory took up the investigation of how bacteria, cleverly operating under no known patents, were able to fix nitrogen in the soil. This meant analyzing extremely minute quantities of organic substances—single bacterium, it was hoped, or, at the most, small colonies of organisms. One of the men assigned to this problem was Dr. R. T. Milner, who had finished his graduate work but two years before and was later to become director of one of the Department of Agriculture's regional research laboratories.

Cottrell began his attack on the bacteria problem by suggesting to Milner that they devise a microbalance necessary for quantitative work in weighing small amounts of material with much greater sensitivity than was generally necessary. A very few institutions at the time had such facilities but, as Milner recalled it, "Cottrell did not have the time nor the inclination to search the literature extensively. His own imagination was so fertile that he would propose most of the previous methods of attack that others had thought of." Nevertheless, together Milner and Cottrell constructed a microbalance of their own crude devising which was partially successful. Whatever their success at that comparatively early date for such techniques, Milner remember that "it bore a marked resemblance to the quartz balance developed [almost twenty years later] by Dr. Paul Kirk for the plutonium work." But Milner remembered, too, that once their efforts showed success in conducting their first microanalysis Cottrell's interest lagged.

This modus operandi was all to the good as soon as Cottrell had established himself in the laboratory and his methods and means were understood. In the beginning, however, he was something of a stranger and his uninhibited thought-scattering was almost immediately misinterpreted. Moreover, his informality of approach tended to ignore organizational charts, and since he considered a nice laboratory chat worth twice the time spent administering from behind an executive desk, he often failed to work through channels.

What was apparently his first awareness that all was not going well came one day in the first few months of his directorship when Lamb, his predecessor, visited the laboratory in his emeritus capacity as a consultant, and the diary stated: "Lamb came to my office to eat lunch and tell me of the boys' agitation over my administrative methods in the laboratory. Had long talk with him re this and lab plans. Had another long talk (same day) with Lamb over lab conditions and the 'near rebellion.' "

The next day matters came to a head: "[Lamb] had conference with the boys by himself and called them into office and had good frank talk over lab situation, Karrer leading [the division chiefs] in re grievances consisting chiefly in my dealing too directly and too authoritatively with their respective staffs. Everyone seemed to feel better for it." But the grievances continued to rankle and on the second and third days following the "frank talk" Cottrell again had to explain "re not taking my suggestions as orders."

Slowly, however, the laboratory adjusted to Cottrell, for it is doubtful if the reverse of the process could altogether be true, although he very likely observed organizational amenities with more regard. No amount of rebellion could keep the ideas from bubbling over and out. Cottrell, in fact, probably could have given "the boys" some good suggestions for the conduct of rebellion.

This intramural contretemps had no lasting effect on the serious purposes of the laboratory, chief among which was to devise the most effective catalyst possible for the working of the direct synthetic ammonia process. Like most laboratory research, it was slow, step-by-step trial and error—in this case almost purely an empirical method because of the fact that the exact functions of catalysts were so imperfectly understood. Yet the commercial success of the process depended most heavily upon it. If it were a catalyst that poisoned easily, that meant that the hydrogen and nitrogen used must be as pure as possible, which in turn meant higher purification costs. The type of catalyst—thousands of combinations were studied—determined the size of the catalyst chambers, the circulating system, and the heat interchangers. The temperatures and pressures at which the catalyst used would give the greatest yield of ammonia would greatly affect the design and construction of the plant. There were still other things to be considered but most important was the fact that in addition to satisfying all requirements the successful catalyst must make possible large-scale production.

The pursuit of the catalyst was carried out in the Synthetic Ammonia Division of the laboratory under Dr. Alfred T. Larson. Considering the significance of the catalyst militarily and economically, its progress excited comment only in a small circle outside the walls of an American University building in Washington which housed the laboratory. Soldiers yet unborn might someday meet death because of it. The great nitrate ports of Chile, at times the busiest in the world, would owe their eclipse partly to its development. It could make the difference between success and failure in the crop of an Iowa farmer. But America at the time was not war-minded, the ports of Chile were of no concern, and American agriculture was not fully aware of the necessity of fertilizers—a knowledge in which Europe far outstripped the United States and a fact attested to by the vastly greater produce yields from comparable European soils.

It seems to have stirred no one deeply, therefore, when the Department of Agriculture issued its annual report in 1922. Buried in the section devoted to the Fixed Nitrogen Research Laboratory was the announcement that a "satisfactory ammonia catalyst" had been developed and a method perfected for its large-scale production. Possibly some of this diffidence grew out of the fact that this was the first year of Agriculture's suzerainty over the laboratory, whereas before it had been restrained by certain bonds of secrecy as a War Department captive.

The following year, 1923, the report became almost lyrically bolder. "Probably the greatest single contribution of this laboratory to date is the development of a very reactive and stable catalyst. As far as we have been able to learn, there is no country in the world which has an ammonia catalyst superior to that developed by this laboratory. A method has also been developed for manufacturing this material which gives the necessary chemical control of the product and at the same time makes large-scale production possible. As a consequence, we are now in possession of such reliable information concerning at least one type of ammonia catalyst and its manufacture that one of the principal obstacles to the successful operation of such plants as United States Nitrate Plant No. 1, at Sheffield, Alabama, has been removed." The laboratory had indeed served its purpose well.

But even this failed to make significant news except in such papers as were written by the laboratory staff for the scientific and technical publications. It took another year before headlines blossomed and then by a freakish circumstance.

In 1924, Harvard, to which Professor Lamb had returned after leaving the laboratory, was casting about for funds for a new chemistry laboratory. One of the university's publicity men dedicated to this cause was searching for an angle in the manner of all publicity men and somehow fixed upon Lamb's former work in Washington when he had been in charge of the laboratory during the early development of the catalyst. The publicist wrote a fetchingly lurid account in which he tied Lamb to the catalyst much as Cottrell had been millstoned with helium. Fortunately Lamb had an opportunity to emasculate the release before it was sent out, but still, on February 26, 1924, a Boston paper reported: "A chemical discovery said to be one of the most important of the 20th century has just been made at the Fixed Nitrogen Research Laboratory at Washington, Professor Arthur B. Lamb, of Harvard, announced here tonight." There were more details, none of which explained why a Harvard professor was announcing in Boston an epochal "discovery" that had taken place in Washington several years earlier.

Other papers and news services pursued the story further. Although these never achieved the accuracy which Cottrell could have wished, still, he wrote a colleague, "it has [resulted in] a rather useful stream of general information which has brought us some very useful contacts and intelligent questions and has probably helped the cause, as well, I hope, as helping Harvard in its laudable desire for a new chemical laboratory."

This time, however, Cottrell made certain that his name was disassociated as completely as possible from the reputed discovery. To one inquirer he wrote: "The catalysts which we are relying on are not a new discovery in the last few months but have really been in use at the laboratory for a year or more, having been in steady development which then had to be tested out over considerable periods of time to determine their performance under varying conditions and their longevity . . . this work was all so far under way and completely planned before my coming into the Laboratory that I have had very little to do with it except in a more general administrative capacity."

One feature writer who submitted his copy to Cottrell for editing had written: "The men directly connected with this discovery are F. G. Cottrell, Director of the Fixed Nitrogen Research Laboratory; Dr. Arthur B. Lamb, originally Director of the Laboratory and now of Harvard University and acting in a consulting capacity at the

Laboratory; and Dr. Alfred T. Larson, Head of the Division of Synthetic Ammonia Process." Cottrell ran a heavy pencil through the reference to himself and made the marginal note "out." Sometimes thereafter Cottrell referred to it in a general way as "Dr. Larson's work."

By 1923 the United States had made a start on a nitrogen fixation industry and in that year produced a few thousand tons, or enough to rank it ahead of Switzerland although behind Yugoslavia. Most of this was in the form of liquid ammonia and was used almost entirely for refrigeration purposes. Germany in that year produced 200,000 tons of fixed nitrogen, 80 per cent of which went into fertilizer. But the rush to nitrogen fixation was on. Other countries developed their variations of the Haber process and the stimulus of these, together with the knowledge of the art gained from the Fixed Nitrogen Research Laboratory and the private laboratories of such firms as Du Pont, sent the world off on a nitrogen spree that was to bring fertilizer prices tumbling and temporarily result in a glutted market when the years of the Great Depression set in.

Since the investigative possibilities of nitrogen fixation were potentially infinite, the work of Cottrell's laboratory did not stop with the development of a good catalyst. It went into the study of hydrogen production—how to cheapen and purify it—for the production of hydrogen, which united with nitrogen over the catalyst to form ammonia, was one of the most expensive steps in the synthetic process. Other mechanical and chemical methods of fixation were probed, and an intensive attack was made on the secrets smugly held by azotobacter and radicicola bacterial organisms. In most of this the laboratory co-operated and pooled its knowledge with the Bureaus of Soils and Chemistry so that it served not only industry as a clearinghouse for information on nitrogen fixation processes but also agriculture which, in America, had not yet felt the pressing need from a population standpoint of replenishing elements necessary to the health of its soil. Any farmer who doubted such necessity—and there were doubters—could reflect on any year's corn crop of which America was so fabulous a producer. In 1923, the year the United States fixed 4120 tons of nitrogen—none of which went to agriculture (for this we relied mainly on imports)—the country's corn yield was 3,054,395,000 bushels. In so yielding, agronomists calculated, the soil also relieved itself of 3,054,395,000 pounds of nitrogen by virtue of bearing that crop alone. Yet the doubters then had something of a point; myopic, perhaps, but still a point. Why pay for costly fertilizers to raise more corn—or tobacco or cotton or potatoes, all heavy soil depleters—when the market could not absorb what was already produced?

Yet for the sake of the future, aside from any question of national defense, a need for a nitrogen fixation industry existed in the United States. As this became established through the twenties it touched on the laboratory in an unforeseen way that brought out one aspect of Cottrell's theory of public service. When Manning resigned the directorship of the Bureau of Mines and complained of the government's inability to keep good scientists because of inadequate salaries, he did so at a time when it was almost no problem at all compared to that the government experienced in the twenties, for now expanding industry and high wages affected almost every bureau employing trained technical men. Because of the burgeoning nitrogen fixation industry the Fixed Nitrogen Research Laboratory was particularly handicapped. There, $5000-a-year men could and did get double that amount outside, so that, by 1924, Cottrell had lost twenty of his most important staff members. Even though a bill was passed raising the limit on such government salaries, things gradually grew worse, until in 1929 the laboratory had four positions open for every man available. (Private industry was also feeling the pinch. When the personnel manager of the laboratory consulted the Bell Telephone Laboratories he was advised that they had openings for a thousand young electrical engineers of which they managed to get three hundred after a vigorous campaign.)

All this had a double effect on Cottrell. Even before the situation became acute it sapped the efficacy of the laboratory so severely that he wrote, "With these continual defections in personnel steadily going on I am almost beginning to wonder whether there is something the matter with me or my point of view that keeps me at it and makes me see it still as an attractive opportunity." If that was how he felt about it in one moment of annoyance, a larger point of view generally pervaded his thinking—one he expressed frequently in urging his men to accept better opportunities both for their own good and for that of the nitrogen fixation industry, which looked upon the laboratory as a prime reservoir and training school for experienced personnel. He felt that some government service helped a man's perspective and for this he gave his reasons to the Senate Committee on Agriculture and Forestry when testifying in hearings on proposed Muscle Shoals legislation: "I think . . . the Government is doing useful work in getting into the minds of these young men . . . more of a spirit of public service. And in talking with them it has seemed to me they have got a little clearer view of public service and the rights of the public than the average man who has grown up purely in industry, with a purely commercial view. I don't mean to say that there are not just as public-spirited men in industry that have not come out of public service, but it is a good plan to carry out to have a constant exchange between the personnel of industry and the Government. It makes for clearer and more sympathetic understanding on both sides and I believe more than pays for the cost of employment turnover involved."

In one respect Cottrell was fortunate. Many who knew him agreed that his reputation and personality (despite the "near rebellion" that had been precipitated by his early impulsiveness in the laboratory) had a strong attraction for good men, and one colleague described him as "a brilliant picker of men as long as he was not trying to salvage humanity." As a picker of men, some thought he made his greatest contribution to the laboratory, bringing it thus to the high point of prestige it enjoyed. His enthusiastic impartiality made him an excellent salesman of science, and if there were worthy men available Cottrell usually stood a good chance of getting them.

But the hegira from the laboratory added to his burdens and these were further increased by a fitful controversy over one of the basic purposes of the laboratory itself. The laboratory had a mandate to study the fixation and utilization of nitrogen so that the knowledge gained could be used for the encouragement and intelligent guidance of industry. The development of the catalyst, for example, fulfilled a laboratory purpose but in so doing it was also inevitable that a certain amount of technical and engineering knowledge was gained that was useful in the design and construction of fixation and fertilizer plants. How far, then, was a government laboratory justified in extending its services beyond the field of pure research and into engineering, where it met with private competition?

The laboratory had its Engineering Division, in addition to its Divisions of Physics, Chemistry, and Synthetic Ammonia, but the personnel of the laboratory took sides as to what extent such a unit was justified. The difference of opinion extended beyond the laboratory and aroused the ire of some elements in industry. The president of one nitrogen fixation company pointed out to Secretary of Agriculture Jardine how this function of the laboratory worked unfairly. The Engineering Division had been instrumental in aiding in the design and construction of at least two privately owned synthetic ammonia plants in competition with his plant, which had been designed by private enterprise, and so, he wrote the Secretary, "we feel very keenly having to compete with a branch of the Government who designs ammonia plants for others." Let the government, he added, stick to its research on fixation and fertilizers and leave engineering to industry.

The issue was one of honest opinion with no personalities involved, for the same man who complained had previously testified as an expert before the House Committee on Military Affairs and had said: "I think out here in Dr. Cottrell's laboratory you have got concentrated more knowledge of a practical kind than in any laboratory that I know of, and they have worked out what I consider, and what my experts tell me, is the best catalyst that has ever been developed in the world." The manufacture of ammonia through this catalyst, the witness assured the committee, would virtually halve the cost of fertilizer to the farmer.

The reply of the Secretary to this protest of industry was placating and mentioned a laboratory reorganization "with a view to placing much greater emphasis on research. The difficulty, of course," the letter continued, "is to determine in particular instances how far it is necessary or desirable to carry each investigation in order to effectively connect with industry and insure adequate development in the broadest public interest." The hand that signed the letter may have been the hand of the Secretary, but the rhetoric and the split infinitive had the sound of Cottrell's voice.

A full year before the question arose Cottrell had already stated his belief in the purpose of the laboratory in a letter to a colleague: "My feeling is that the permanent and intensive aim of our lab as a part of Agriculture should be the very fundamental chemical and physical studies reaching more toward the biological than the engineering as an *initial* aim but being followed up as they develop far enough into chemical technology and engineering to make firm and useful liaison with the industry either directly or thru other departments of the Government whose business it is to work specifically with and for the going industries as it is Agriculture's [business] to, with and for the farmer."

Thus, although Cottrell saw some room for the extension of government laboratory technology and engineering into the industrial field, his primary and often stated sympathies were bound up in physicochemical and biochemical research. It had been his purpose, he said when he finally summed up his career with the laboratory, "to salvage at least a considerable portion of this temporary organization, making from it the nucleus of a much-needed new development within the Department of Agriculture; viz., an attempt to study those parts of modern physics which are most intimately fundamental to agricultural science."

But for almost a year a schism bitterly divided the laboratory's key men and exacted a toll from Cottrell's nerves. ("If it is the last act of my life," one anti-Engineering Division chief wrote Cottrell, "I intend to go as far, and to do anything and everything that may be necessary, to eliminate certain conditions at the Laboratory and prevent the absolute wreck of one of the finest organizations, etc.") The engineers lost, partly as a matter of principle and partly because in 1926 the laboratory's war-given appropriation ran out, and after a series of reorganizations among several of the Department of Agriculture's bureaus, the laboratory was absorbed into the newly merged Bureau of Chemistry and Soils.

Although the conflict was resolved and the laboratory settled into its smooth routine once again, its pressures had been instrumental in sending Cottrell into a sanitarium in Massachusetts for three weeks—a health resort he described as a "school for tired nerves."

However, as far as Cottrell and fixed nitrogen were concerned, his administration of the laboratory was only an apprenticeship.

4

"The American Coal Corporation," said a 1922 prospectus, ". . . establishes a closer relationship between the Corporation and the consumer along lines which will abolish credit and collection departments and very materially reduce selling and delivery costs." These benefits, the prospectus went on to say, were to be realized by bringing the consumer in as a preferred stockholder, and on the basis of this credit residential coalbins could be stocked in the spring and summer months when coal prices were at their lowest. The American Coal Corporation held a further advantage over its Washington competitors in that its yards were fully mechanized and a fleet of trucks, rather than horse-drawn wagons, were used for delivery.

"I shall have no fears," wrote Cottrell to the corporation's president, "for the success of the venture as long as you maintain the same high level in the integration of competent, honest and energetic personnel which is today your chief asset, and I hope will always be a dominant feature of the organization."

"The organizers and directors," he explained to Jess, "would receive some of the common stock for their work and in turn this should begin to pay some dividends." But he added, as though anticipating her fears, "I shouldn't figure to put in any money myself at the outset." Although it seems likely that, aside from a $1000 loan he made the corporation and which was repaid with 6 per cent interest, Cottrell never did invest in this organization, nevertheless by 1923 he had accepted a directorship. There may have been several reasons for so doing but one seems clear: it gave him an opportunity to bring two people into the corporation—his nephew Herbert Fulton, who had been pitted against overwhelming odds in the Pony truck situation, as well as Cottrell's secretary, Ward Nichols, who had assisted him in the affairs of the now inactive language committee of the International Research Council. Nichols, a former president and general manager of a Philadelphia brewing company that had suffered the fate of all respectable breweries during prohibition, was made secretary and treasurer.

By early 1924 the American Coal Corporation reported to its stockholders that regular distribution of coal had begun, that there were 1500 customers, ten motor trucks for delivery, an undeveloped coal mine had been acquired, as well as patents on a coal briquetting process, a Baltimore plant was to be opened, and a "successful" New York investment house had agreed to take over marketing of the corporation's securities. In spite of this, the chief unmortgaged assets of the corporation seemed to remain the competent, honest, and energetic personnel which Cottrell had praised. Although the corporation claimed that it was doing the largest business of its kind in the city of Washington in 1924, such things as coal strikes and overexpansion on the basis of easy financing common to the era eventually brought this news to stockholders, bondholders, and general creditors five years later: "The affairs of this company have reached a state where it has become necessary to foreclose the deed of trust, given on its properties located in South Washington, to secure a bond issue."

The demise of the American Coal Corporation which followed was in no wise attended by the unpleasantries that had marked the latter-day stages of the Pony truck, for the failure seems largely to have been the result of good ideas and intentions failing to survive unsound financing—a charge to which many business concerns of the period were vulnerable. Although this time Cottrell escaped unscathed, the corporation's president, C. G. Gilbert, had a less happy experience. The $2,800 mortgage on his Washington home was foreclosed and the realty company had posted a notice at the residence that it was TO BE SOLD AT AUCTION, TUESDAY—followed by the date. On Monday, although neither Mr. nor Mrs. Gilbert had seen it go, the sign disappeared. The bewildered Gilbert hurried to the real estate office where a secretary described a tall, unpressed-looking man, wearing glasses, who had assumed the mortgage and who, she supposed, would get in touch with Gilbert. The name was Cottrell.

Cottrell had succumbed to the glasses in 1922 at the age of forty-five and thereafter few things furnished his acquaintances with more amusement than to dwell on the subject of Cottrell's glasses. Although at first he underwent the usual optical tests and had a pair prescribed that met with optometrical approval, he subsequently must have decided that such a practice showed a dearth of originality with no outlet for improvisation. Henceforth he became a devoted customer of the F. W. Woolworth Company and acquired what was probably one of the most amazing private collections of ten-cent-store glasses in America. Of these he had his favorites—compounded, halved, and the lenses reshuffled in accordance with theories that unfortunately have gone unrecorded. He usually carried three or four pairs of these in a roomy second pocket inside his suit coat, and while it was not unusual to see him wear one and a half or two pairs, there are those who claim that he sometimes put on two and a half or three. This had a peculiarly disconcerting effect in meetings where Cottrell could sometimes be counted on to vary dull routine by removing a set of the glasses he had on, diving into his coat pocket, and emerging with a new combination to meet whatever optical exigencies were involved.

Obviously such a situation called for improvement and often, during what he would consider an idle moment, Cottrell devoted thought and effort to this end. One extended experiment involved gluing together the edges of two pieces of common mica the size of silver dollars. From a minute opening on one edge ran a small tube several feet in length to which was attached a rubber bulb containing water. The basic idea was simply that by pressing on the bulb the hollow lens could be filled to change the focus at will. What a pair of those could do to a meeting has never been demonstrated, but Cottrell carried the experiments to a point where he referred them to his patent lawyer. The latter found seven patents already covering the idea in one way or another, and Cottrell's later judgment was that if plastics and glue had both reached more advanced stages of development at the time he might have experimented further.

These dabblings were carried out in a small laboratory which he set up in the sun porch of a house at 3904 Ingomar Street—a house he bought in 1924 and in which he and Jess lived for their remaining twenty years in Washington. He referred to the laboratory as "a crude little shop" but, he wrote a friend, "it is surprising what one can do in this way even with very primitive equipment. There has always been a genuine fascination to me in the Robinson Crusoe sort of work where you have to make improvised things for yourself as you go along."

The house on Ingomar Street at times also had some of the features of an aviary. Cottrell had left the New England sanitarium with the strong recommendation of the doctors that he take up some hobbies of an innocuous nature, and this led him into a few years of birdbanding. No sooner had the suggestion been made, however, than the variety of his adventures with the lame, the halt, and the blind in the kingdom of birds exceeded anything he had ever experienced with oscillographs. It must have seemed to Jess that injured birds deliberately picked Ingomar Street as a haven, to which she had no objections, although she was extraordinarily sensitive to their sufferings, except when Cottrell went outside the bird realm to bring home a particularly unfriendly bat.

On June 7, 1925, Cottrell (according to the diary) "found young robin hung by foot in tree and with broken leg. Climbed tree and got him down. Took him home. Amputated and dressed leg and spent good part of day feeding and playing with him." Two days later: "Robin failing and apparently hurt internally so chloroformed and buried him." After that came the bat, abandoned baby thrushes, wrens, and more robins, all of which he tended and befriended. They in turn learned to perch confidently on his shoulder and eat from his hand. To reach this rapport he devised a method of feeding them when their natural bird-wariness still made it advisable for him to remain some distance away. For the purpose he adapted a test tube which had a small opening at the rounded end. The test tube was filled with peanut butter and into this he inserted the end of a stripped-down umbrella shank, controlling the tube by means of wires stretched to the umbrella handle. He could then sit several feet removed from an outdoor table and by drawing on the wires squeeze out peanut butter worms which, the results indicate, were well received by the birds.

These winged adventures were not all confined to home. One morning on arrival at the Fixed Nitrogen Research Laboratory, Cottrell heard some faint chirpings coming from a vent in an unused experimental blast furnace. These led to a nest of very young wrens, and for several days thereafter Cottrell nursed them by various means, waiting for a legitimate parent to claim them. When no mother bird showed up Cottrell spent the better part of a working day devising different types of syringes for their feeding and eventually took all four of them home for rearing, making occasional foraging sorties out into the neighborhood in search of grasshoppers. But one of his colleagues remembered that on the day Cottrell devoted so much laboratory time to the syringes he left instructions that that day was to be applied against his annual leave, for Cottrell's sense of responsibility toward things animal and human was so encompassing that it even included taxpayers.

5

When in Europe, beginning with his student days abroad, Cottrell occasionally diverged from official paths into picturesque byways, during which his letters to Jess would wax descriptive and tell her of his wish that she could be there too. In 1919 and 1921 these expressions took the form of promises that when the time was ripe and her health permitted she should accompany him and they would enjoy the thrill of mutual discovery. It was not until Cottrell was nearing, and Jess had passed, fifty that such an opportunity came. It is questionable if by that time travel for its own sake held many inherent joys for either of them.

In 1926 large German and British nitrogen producers, who were eyed askance by their American competitors, called an international meeting of nitrogen fertilizer producers to be held in Biarritz in April. An invitation was extended to the U. S. Department of Agriculture, which accepted by naming Cottrell as one of two to represent it, although the tendency of the United States nitrogen industry itself was to remain aloof. It took the peripatetic Cottrell but a very short time to realize that here was a chance to visit the main nitrogen fixation centers throughout all of Europe and, en route, also take in the meetings of the International Institute of Agriculture in Rome, the Faraday Society in London, the International Research Council, the British Association for the Advancement of Science, and whatever other stimulating gatherings (there was always some kind of an Esperanto meeting if one knew where to look) might be going on. But in redemption of his earlier promises and because her previous experience had proved that it was only a kind of ghostly Cottrell who returned from Europe, it was decided this time that Jess should also go.

The trip started out at a relaxed pace. On the voyage over he scarcely mentioned either an international language or birdbanding to fellow passengers. Part of this uncommunicativeness may have been due to the fact that Cottrell sailed as a delegate, if not under a cloud, at least under a light haze, for while the American nitrogen fixation industry had a full and ungrudging respect for his scientific ability, there were a few expressions of apprehension that what was considered Cottrell's ingenuousness would bring him as a knowledgeable lamb into a pack of cunning foreign wolves. Since the discovery of the Haber process the industry had invested itself with great secrets in America as well as Europe, whereas it was Cottrell's charged duty and habit to unlock scientific secrets and disseminate the results. "Some of the ammonia and fertilizer producers over here," wrote Dr. S. C. Lind, whom Cottrell had left in charge of the laboratory as associate director, "were not over-enthusiastic about your attending this meeting in the fear that the Europeans would get more information from you than they would be willing to give in return."

But Cottrell was by no means an easy mark and could be sharply aware of dubious motives when his suspicions were once aroused. Moreover, it is sometimes true that it takes a confidence to gain a confidence and frankness to breed frankness. While there is no way of knowing what the proportions of give and take were in this particular instance, Cottrell's letters back to the Department of Agriculture were frequent and full, one of them running to twenty-seven handwritten pages of nitrogen news. He said that the Badische people, who held the Haber-Bosch patents, had "been very communicative and are evidently planning to show us a good deal pretty freely at Merseburg and Oppau," the two huge German fixation plants. Other producers, too, were co-operative, but at one German plant he found the director "at first quite frankly hesitant to talk of their work because he looked upon the Fixed Nitrogen Research Lab as a competitor"; the manager of a French plant "did not offer to take me through the works"; in England, "Brunner-Mond seem to be the only people who are doing anything in ammonia and their policy of secrecy seems to be as tight as ever"; and the director of a Belgian plant thought "it was not a particularly good time to show it to visitors." Nevertheless, a day or so later, Cottrell passed the latter plant on a train and reported: "I could easily recognize and analyze it into its elements from the aerial photos of same which [the director] had shown me."

But before encountering this and immediately following the Biarritz conference, Cottrell and Jess put in two weeks in southern France and northern Italy as pure tourists. At Nice they spent the evening at the casino having supper and watching what Cottrell described as "vaudeville." They also took in the Monte Carlo Casino, where he won fifty francs. They visited cathedrals, museums, art galleries, châteaux, an assortment of ruins, Carcassonne, and Lourdes. The diary entries are too cryptic for any conclusions as to what measure of enjoyment these doings may have brought either of them, but somehow Lourdes reminded Cottrell that he had forgotten to describe an installation of electrolytic cells at Pierrefitte in a previous letter to Lind.

Then, as if this sight-seeing had discharged some measure of his duty as a visitor on European soil, the tempo of the trip changed. After Italy came Germany, France, Belgium, the Netherlands, England, and Norway, where there were nitrogen fixation plants, meetings, universities, and laboratories to be dealt with in varying degrees of concentration. Sometimes Jess went along but often, too, they would establish a national headquarters, such as Paris, where she would remain while Cottrell did his patrol work in the provinces, so that, in spite of the restraint Jess had hoped to exercise, five months after their departure from New York Cottrell wrote Lind, "With the growing shortness of time and the realization which is again forcing itself upon me that beyond a certain point of fatigue (mental or otherwise) a person does not accomplish anything no matter how hard he tries, I can see I shall probably have to cut out much of the above list and try to do what is left more effectively."

They returned to America in November. In the following May, Cottrell was notified that he was granted a leave without pay until September 15 and letters of explanation from the laboratory regarding his absence mentioned "an effort to recover his health" and his "run-down condition as a result of overwork." He and Jess had decided to go to California for a complete and unadulterated rest. Business was to be forgotten, cares laid aside, correspondence postponed, laboratories by-passed, meetings ignored. It was, except for family affairs, to be a total vacation.

Perhaps the initial error had had its inception three years earlier in 1924—a year in which Cottrell again found honors pressed upon him. A committee of the American Chemical Society had included his name in a list of thirty-three Americans who had achieved eminence in chemistry. The Gold Medal of the Mining and Metallurgical Society was awarded him for that year for his electrical precipitation work and Research Corporation activities. (Cottrell had demurred about accepting but the society's president brushed this aside with: "Please let me assure you that our Society . . . made no hasty or ill-considered selection. I do not misinterpret your modest disclaimer of merit for the work you have done. It is not a matter of opinion; the facts speak for themselves.") Then W. W. Campbell of the University of California asked that he attend ceremonies in Berkeley and receive an LL.D. at the time of Campbell's own inauguration as president. Cottrell wired his thanks but pleaded that business matters would prevent his going. The offer was repeated in 1925, but that was the year Cottrell found his nerves bad enough to attend the Massachusetts sanitarium. But no amount of refusing could deter the university when it came to honoring a native son, for the invitation was repeated in 1926 and again in 1927, when Cottrell finally accepted.

This may, as was said, have been the first misstep, the newly re-formed tippler's first visit back to the warm inviting atmosphere of his favorite bar. "I was surprised to see how many old friends were still here," Cottrell wrote back to F. A. Ernst, whom he had left in charge of the laboratory (Lind having gone on to direct the University of Minnesota's chemistry laboratory), "and how cordial and natural everything seemed." What, after all, was more natural when among old friends than to discuss one's problems, and the most acute of these—the shortage of personnel in the laboratory—seemed to integrate with a happy fitness into the present situation, for the universities of the Coast were far enough away from the Eastern labor market to offer some recruiting possibilities. The result was that Cottrell set out on a campaign and, in order that his travel expenses might be covered for this, had his leave of absence tem-porarily revoked. That was in May.

"We have now been gone from Washington a little over two months," Cottrell wrote back in July, "and Mrs. Cottrell insists that the vacation proper has not yet commenced, as I have found so much of technical interest and work to be done all along the line that it has kept me pretty busy."

For after the University of California had come Stanford and California Institute of Technology and if the graduates of these did not fit into civil service requirements, Cottrell, a loyal alumnus, tried to steer them into openings at Berkeley. It is easy to imagine that somewhere about this point Jess issued an ultimatum, for the uni-versity activities ended abruptly and they set off for a six weeks' stay in the Sierras. It is also easy to conjecture that this took addi-tional pressure from Jess, for on the eve of their departure for the mountains a trio of crises occurred: Ernst announced that he was leaving the laboratory to take a $10,000-a-year job with the Atmos-pheric Nitrogen Corporation; the laboratory itself, which had al-ready been put under the Bureau of Soils, was now being brought into the new Bureau of Chemistry and Soils; and Arthur A. Ham-merschlag, the president of Research Corporation, died.

But Cottrell (or Jess) was firm. "I am, however, going forward with our camping plan essentially unaffected," he wrote back, "as I feel that all these changes make it all the more important that I come back in the fall feeling thoroughly fit and fresh for the new problems now piling up ahead." It was a firmness perhaps bolstered by such letters as one from Harry A. Curtis (professor of chemistry at Yale and a Nitrogen Laboratory consultant who was later to become a director of TVA). In a testy if well-intentioned report on affairs in Washington, Curtis chided him for not vacationing as he had planned, adding, "At last report you were a laboratory director *in absentia,* of no known address, buzzing away at some three thousand miles . . . going to start a vacation some day and maybe come back some day after that." Even the report of a stockholders' committee of the American Coal Corporation announcing a "program of reorganization toward the end of caring for pressing obligations and providing adequate working capital" did not imperil the resoluteness of Cottrell (or Jess), for he again wrote, "I [am] determined to go the limit in trying to freshen up and see how much of the old boyish enthusiasm and staying quality I could bring back with me to the work."

As a vacation, the longest and most elaborate the Cottrells ever planned, the trip to Parcher's Camp in the High Sierras was not an unalloyed success. Shortly after their arrival Jess became ill. Cottrell managed to get in some fishing, tramping, and horseback riding until Jess recovered. Then they started on a pack-train trip, but another member of the party was thrown from her horse a few hours from camp, seriously injured, and the whole trip was abandoned. Cottrell, undaunted, struck out alone with two horses and apparently enjoyed it. For five days he roamed in the direction of Kings River, improvising in a laboratory manner on his diet (the diary shows a breakfast of "fritter pancakes" made with canned minced clams), and one cold night he draped his hammock and slept over some rocks heated in a campfire. "A little overdid it," murmured the diary next morning of this.

But it was enough fun to have his leave-without-pay extended, and it was October before the Cottrells returned East.

6

The press of business which Cottrell pleaded in first declining California's honorary degree was no shallow excuse. Congress, at the time, was involved in the fifteen-year controversy over the disposition of Muscle Shoals—one of the deepest conflicts ever to disturb it on the fundamental question of government in business. Muscle Shoals, by 1924, included not only the unused Nitrate Plants Nos. 1 and 2, as well as two steam power plants, but also the massive, nearly completed Wilson Dam. It was therefore capable of producing two commodities—great power and (in peacetime) significant amounts of fertilizers. The power had a ready market while fertilizer did not, and so the problem was not only how to keep them linked as an entity but also how to keep them from being divorced from the broader considerations of conservation, flood control, and navigation on the Tennessee River and its tributaries. While private enterprise wanted the power and might be tempted to take on fertilizer, it could not relate them to a larger program of development which had long been called for in the public interest.

When the Fixed Nitrogen Research Laboratory was established one of the responsibilities with which it was charged was to study the best methods for the peacetime utilization of the Muscle Shoals nitrate plants. This responsibility Cottrell inherited when he assumed the directorship of the laboratory, and it was this that inevitably drew him intimately into the Muscle Shoals dispute, where he was a popular expert witness in House and Senate committee hearings and where his name was sometimes bandied about in congressional debate.

It was generally agreed by all who knew him in Washington that Cottrell was an expert lobbyist. On this point Harvey N. Davis, president of Stevens Institute of Technology, wrote him in 1925: "You can pull more wires in Washington than any man." While Davis was hyperbolizing, the fact remained that when Cottrell approached policy and opinion makers he was not only vigorously persuasive but, consciously or unconsciously, created the impression that he was above the ordinary run of politics; that he pleaded no special causes except those he conceived to be in the common good; that he asked nothing for himself and knew what he was talking

269

about. This last uncommon trait alone endeared him to many in Congress, and one of his greatest admirers was a senator whose integrity matched Cottrell's—George W. Norris.

The central figure of the Muscle Shoals debate was Norris, who had long concerned himself with flood control and public power and was an avowed enemy of what, in those days, was sometimes referred to as the "Power Trust." Norris made himself a student of the whole question of power ownership and operation and in so doing became more than conversant with electrochemistry. In developing his knowledge along these lines he came to lean heavily on the tutorial powers of Cottrell in shaping his Muscle Shoals legislation, for he had already developed a respect for Cottrell's opinions during their earlier collaboration on patent matters.

Norris led the fight, almost singlehandedly, against disposing of Muscle Shoals power to private interests even though the dominant trend of political thought at the time favored such a course. He was supported in his view by the terms of the original Defense Act under which the Shoals project had been created and which called specifically for government construction and operation. Yet each session of Congress between 1919 and 1933 saw a rash of new bills introduced, most of which offered to relieve the government of about 250,000 horsepower on terms not always flattering to the taxpayer. One of the most publicized of these bids was that made by Henry Ford, who thought in terms of a hundred-year lease and who also promised to make fertilizer, but some who analyzed his figures declared them to be outrageous even for government war surplus plants.

It was this question of power and how to dispose of it that particularly concerned Norris. In the matter of Nitrate Plants Nos. 1 and 2 with their potential fertilizer production, he was for the most part content to follow Cottrell's advice. In this he was not alone, for the authors of other bills had also looked to Cottrell as a mentor and some of his rhetoric was recognized by a congressional committee in the wording of a presidential message.

This fertilizer phase of the Muscle Shoals problem centered around the fact that the country needed more and better fertilizers; these needed to be developed; private industry found the job of developing them too big for the market at hand and farmers tended to regard any newfangled fertilizers offered by a private concern with wary suspicion as being probably not worth their considerable cost. It was Cottrell's belief that in the national interest the government should shoulder this job in its initial stages. This would mean experimenting with all types of fertilizers (including phosphoric acid and potash as well as nitrogen), cheapening their production through improved techniques, distributing them on a controlled basis to certain farm areas (not all fertilizers are adaptable to all types of soils), assessing the resulting yields, and furnishing private industry with the knowledge so that they could eventually take over and bring the United States to a point where it was at least on a par in the use of fertilizers with advanced European countries.

Such a program would have represented the largest, most expensive experiment in the production, distribution, and application of fertilizer that had ever been undertaken in the history of the world. Norris wanted $10,000,000 appropriated for it, but Cottrell was more conservative. Because the two nitrate plants at the Shoals had largely become outmoded since their completion in 1918, Cottrell suggested that only a small unit of Plant No. 1 (using the Haber process) be remodeled and set up for experimental purposes. Other pilot plants would be built in other sections of the country where soil problems were different. This he figured could be done for $2,000,000 (an amount which Norris later used in his Muscle Shoals bills) but for the most part the project could be financed by the sale of surplus power from the Wilson Dam to private companies.

There were, inevitably, those who feared that this would put the government in the fertilizer business, even though Cottrell stressed the fact that the program was temporary and experimental and the resulting benefits would eventually accrue to industry as new manufacturing techniques and a greater knowledge of fertilizer utilization were amassed. Nevertheless, in spite of the opposition, this plan which Cottrell advocated, and which other scientists in the Department of Agriculture had been instrumental in forming, was perhaps the most favored in congressional circles as far as the fertilizer aspect of the Shoals problem was concerned.

Inevitably, too, in view of the nature of the proposals he advocated, Cottrell had to face the question in committee hearings as to his opinions on government in industry. In one such session he was asked: "On the great broad question of the Government vs. private ownership, you are for private ownership and control?"

Cottrell answered: "Wherever it is possible. I do not feel that government operation for the most of our economic needs is as efficient as private operation and I think the energies of the Government can better be spent on other types of work." When encouraged to amplify this statement, he added: "It is my opinion that the general tendency to keep the Government out of business is a good one." The extent of Cottrell's influence in shaping Muscle Shoals legislation was reflected in two statements. One of these was made by Norris in a Senate debate on his resolution (which in amended form ultimately passed both Houses but was vetoed by President Coolidge). "In the preparation of the resolution," Norris said, "I did not consult with the Secretary of Agriculture himself. I went to the people whom I knew were going to handle this problem. I went to Dr. Cottrell . . . and to a great extent it is his language and my resolution. I put in everything he thought we would need. If we direct the Department of Agriculture to perform an experiment . . . there is no question on earth that Dr. Cottrell will have charge of it, and everybody who knows him knows that he would do it absolutely in good faith and give everybody a fair show regardless of what he may think personally."

Norris referred, of course, simply to the fertilizer provisions of the resolution, since Cottrell tended to avoid the broader power issue as one outside the scope of his expert knowledge. It was this same fertilizer issue that came up for discussion in hearings on the Morin bill on Muscle Shoals in the House Committee on Military Affairs, and Cottrell, a witness, was asked whether he preferred that to the Norris resolution. His part in the drafting of both was so well recognized that one of the members of the committee spoke up to interpose, "Do you think it is fair to have a parent forced to discriminate between two twin babies?"

It was in the hearings before this committee, too, that Cottrell was told by a member: "Norris says you are the man who is going to have charge of all our [fertilizer] plants there."

To this Cottrell replied: "He is surer of it than I."

He had reason to recall such doubts later when these Muscle Shoals plans, vetoed by Coolidge and Hoover, were dwarfed by the gigantic concept of the Tennessee Valley Authority which embodied almost all of Norris' and much of Cottrell's thinking. That was five years later, in 1933, when Cottrell was called but wasn't chosen.

The rising wind of the 1920s did not leave him untouched. Between 1925 and 1929, Cottrell's income more than doubled and in the latter year he reported over $30,000 as a gross income figure. This handsome sum was accumulated in a variety of ways, mostly unpremeditated, and a small percentage was owed to the fact that, in common with millions of his fellow Americans, Cottrell had discovered the stock market.

When, years earlier, the process of electric de-emulsification of crude oil had, after an initial success, failed to work in certain oil fields, the Western Precipitation Company sold most of its interests in the venture to Allen Wright and a group of backers who formed the Petroleum Rectifying Company. To the chagrin of the sellers, this branch of electrical precipitation proved unexpectedly profitable and Cottrell's residual interest brought him tidy dividends yearly. On his 1927 visit to the Coast the affairs of Petroleum Rectifying were in such good order that they decided to set up their own research laboratory and offered Cottrell $7500 yearly to act as consultant and advise them on a program of research. This Cottrell accepted after clearing the matter with the Department of Agriculture on the understanding that his duties as director of the nitrogen laboratory came first. The fee, in itself, was larger than his government salary, and in 1929 the same company underwent a merger and reorganization that proved another bonanza for Cottrell. He held 50 shares of stock in the original company of which he sold 25 when the reorganization took place and for which he received $12,627. His remaining 25 shares were converted into 1000 shares of new stock, but of these windfalls Cottrell wrote the president of Petroleum Rectifying Company that he did not know what to do with the money. He had only to wait until 1930, when the new backers of the company gave him some help with such problems by reducing his consulting fee from $7500 to $1800 a year, and Cottrell agreed that this was more in keeping with the services he could render.

The foreign business of the Western Precipitation Company, in which Cottrell had retained a small share, was also contributing substantially to his income, averaging in most years of the late twenties about $4000, but these were strange years in which assorted sums, like his disabled birds, came home to roost on Ingomar Street. One of these, amounting to $6000, was for a time a mystery. From the diary February 2, 1928: "3:00 P.M. to see Dr. Abbot at Smithsonian and told by him that some anonymous donor had offered to finance the Smithsonian investigation on plants and animal radiation work on condition I should be retained as an advisor in the matter at honorarium of $6000 per year. Told him I would be interested to cooperate and help them in such work in any case, whether there were any honorarium or not, and was willing to consider seriously honorarium only if party endowing the work was ready to give them enough to do it in worthwhile ways to give them very free hand. Left it with him thus to further pursue with prospective donor."

In March, Cottrell accepted from Abbot a check for $6000 "re photochemical project sponsored and backed by some wealthy man." Warily the diary added: "Jess and I both seriously question advisability of accepting this. I shall have to take it up carefully with Dr. Abbot." Then for a year the matter lay dormant. In June 1929, Abbot wrote him that "the anonymous party of whom I informed you last year has expressed so much pleasure with our cooperative agreement that I am desired to turn over to you a second honorarium of $6,000." But somehow or other Cottrell had by this time divined the source of these mysterious blessings and Abbot confessed.

In 1928 Research Corporation decided that it was, for the first time since its founding, in a position to set aside an appreciable sum for grants. Of the $25,000 so allotted, $15,000 went to the Smithsonian for Abbot's project, enabling the Institution to establish the Division of Radiation and Organisms for the study of the effects of solar radiation on living organisms. It was the feeling of Research Corporation that the time was also ripe to make some gesture of recognition to Cottrell, but no one knew of a way to do so openly that Cottrell would find acceptable. After all, he was at times a difficult man to reimburse, particularly when he refused to recognize the debt. They had therefore taken Abbot into the plot. "He feared that should I decline to accept it," Cottrell wrote in the diary, "this might cause a withdrawal of some, at least, of R.C. support from Smithsonian. He evidently felt embarrassed in trying to handle the matter so I told him I would take it up directly with R.C. people in a careful way so as to do no violence to anyone's susceptibilities." That ended the honorarium, although Research Corporation's support of the radiation investigations continued for over a decade.

But Cottrell had found a use for the $6000. Abbot had assigned a room in the Smithsonian for his use whereupon Cottrell engaged C. G. Gilbert, the former president of the American Coal Corporation and an engineer by profession, and set him to work on a project that was to lead into a whole new enterprise before Cottrell's days as an organizer were over.

Aside from creating an atmosphere of unaccustomed prosperity, this miscellany of income had seemingly one other effect on Cottrell. This he discussed with the head of the Bureau of Chemistry and Soils and, according to the diary, reached "a tentative agreement to gradually withdraw from full-time Government service and eventually act in a consulting capacity as soon as the proper personnel changes would be effected." The prosperity also led him to buy a new Chevrolet, acquire a broker, and the diary references to late evening studies of stock market reports increased. There were purchases of I.T.&T., Standard Oil of New York, Johns-Manville, a mining stock, a chain-store stock, and stocks that were soon to lose all identity. Cottrell did not plunge, but the dividends from all sources, including his Petroleum Rectifying Company holdings, amounted to $1650 in 1929, and that fateful October that ended an era found Cottrell in Japan.

The year before the Japanese trip the Cottrells made one more attempt at a vacation. In discharge of his obligations as a Petroleum Rectifying consultant he again obtained a leave without pay from the laboratory in 1928 and together he and Jess set out for the Coast. This time they had what seemed to be foolproof plans. He would spend a month or two on petroleum research, mainly in coaching the new laboratory staff in techniques, then he and Jess would board an intercoastal ship and return to New York at a leisurely pace as passengers, well insulated by large areas of salt water from any diversionary crises. It almost worked. Even though he got an urgent summons from Washington suggesting that he return for budget hearings and Muscle Shoals legislation he refused to be "stampeded" and recalled that "I have hurried home before only to kick my heels about after I got there." And so he replied that he would give up the ocean trip only if it were an ultimatum or the Secretary of Agriculture himself requested it.

With this, everything was set for a relaxing sea voyage when Jess suffered a severe asthmatic attack at the last moment and had to be carried on board. She recovered in time to make two brief shore excursions before the vessel reached New York four weeks later, but for the most part she had been confined to her cabin or a deck chair. As for Cottrell, he managed a few side trips where the ship touched port, but Jess's illness made it less than the anxiety-free adventure they had planned. One thing did happen that should have awakened in Cottrell memories of his first transatlantic voyage and served to remind him that, though twenty-eight years had passed, he apparently had lost none of his earnest demeanor, for on the first Sunday out of San Francisco the purser approached him with the suggestion that he conduct services. Cottrell's excuse was noted in the diary: "Begged off on basis of incompetency."

Untimely though Jess's attack may have been, it did not daunt her from again boarding a ship when they set out a year later for Japan. Now Cottrell went as a delegate to the World Engineering Congress to be held in Tokyo and, in his usual role, as a collector of information and ideas in whatever other ways might open up. (A British delegate to the Congress was Sir Alexander Gibb, consulting engineer to the Admiralty. On the day of his arrival in Tokyo the *Japan Advertiser* took the lead paragraph of its right-hand, front-page column to express Sir Alexander's opinion that the British naval base then under construction at Singapore constituted no menace to Japan.)

The name of Cottrell carried with it a certain familiarity in industrial and scientific Japan. One of his correspondents there in 1927 wrote him, "The 'Cottrell process' is now recognized by the public as the mysterious dust abating process and all over Japan everyone call the name 'Cottrell' only, omitting electrical precipitation." With this as an entree, it was well that he had not gone for a vacation, for not long after his arrival he wrote back, "The Japanese Precipitation Company (Cottrell Corporation of Japan) is under the management of the Mitsui Mining Company. The Japanese in general and the Mitsui interests in particular have been wonderfully helpful and, in fact, embarrassing in the extent of their hospitality." The hospitality manifested itself in an endless succession of lunches, garden parties, dinners, teas, and inspection trips that eventually drove both Cottrell and Jess to Nikko for a week's rest. Thus fortified, Cottrell returned to Tokyo and there, in the Institute of Physical and Chemical Research, thought he had at last found an instrument which, through co-operation with the Research Corporation in the free exchange of patent rights, could enhance the international character of science—a cause he had given so much in thought and energy to advancing. "The plan suggested by me," he wrote in the diary, "was for each to send quite freely to the other, patents or data on which patents could be taken out in the other country, and that when these were exploited, the cost of such foreign development and exploitation should first be deducted . . . and the . . . profits should then be put in a separate fund and from this fund, from time to time, by mutual consent . . . appropriations should be made to aid meritorious research anywhere in the world." He noted that this plan also appealed to Dr. M. Okochi, the director of the Institute, who promised to forward to Research Corporation the full details on some projects in which the Institute was interested and which might offer the opportunity for reciprocal exploitation which Cottrell envisioned.

The richness of this concept gave the voyage home in December a piquancy that for Cottrell far overshadowed the presence of Mary Pickford and Douglas Fairbanks, on board as fellow passengers. Whatever the latter used as conversational fodder during the long reaches of the Pacific passage, Cottrell found sustenance in discussing his new plans for co-operation with other engineering delegates also returning home.

The furtherance of this idea was one added reason why Cottrell again felt it advisable to give up his directorship of the nitrogen and fertilizer investigations and continue his connection with the Department of Agriculture only on a consulting basis, for his interests were once again broadening and diversifying according to old familiar patterns.

In March 1930 after his return to Washington he made preparations for resigning to take effect in October. It was a time when most men were hugging whatever security they could find. The years of the plague had set in and now the filling of jobs was the least of the worries of his or any other laboratory. It was not the time when a man of caution sat down to compose a resignation, but then

Cottrell's reputation for caution had never excited the admiration of most businessmen, many of whom were now holding collections of stock certificates whose value might lie in their fine gilt seals. And that was a strange thing. Those who did not expect orthodox business acumen from Cottrell might have been surprised to learn that he escaped the stock market crash with barely a bruise, for before sailing for Japan on October 10, 1929, he had left stop-loss selling orders with his brokers and the wind that uprooted mighty oaks passed lightly over Cottrell.

COTTRELL'S few geology courses in the university had already led him into occasionally thinking of himself as a prospector. Had he been a botanist he could have looked upon his activities as cross-pollination not only of the sciences but of other fields of human endeavor in which he discerned relationships. Being a physical chemist, he most often thought of himself as a catalyst— a quickener of reactions of which he did not precisely become a part but which left him free and utilizable for still other reactions. He sometimes described himself as a catalyst and as such thought he rendered his greatest service to science and to mankind generally. Those who knew him best agree that this was so, although one colleague profanely extended the thought by remarking, "Catalyst, hell! He's a detonator!"

"We are today far over-specialized," Cottrell wrote in 1932. "What is most needed is more overlocking at the critical joints. The specialist working in any particular field must become more willing to work over the boundary line of the next adjacent field and encourage the workers there to do the same for his. It is only by this cooperative interlacing of knowledge, sympathy and experience over the joints between the fields of endeavor that we can get the full benefit of the most intelligent human endeavor in the present age. . . . That is one of my hobbies."

This was something more than catalysis and something more than a hobby. For the balance of his life it was virtually his vocation, for in his prospecting, pollenizing, catalytic way he would seek out new ideas, interest himself in their development, spark new reactions where possible, and then attempt to relate the results to other studies, other projects, and other industries. Since both the scientific and non-scientific worlds were becoming unusually full of challenging ideas, it was enough to make a busy man very much busier and it was Research Corporation that made it possible for Cottrell to fulfill this concept of himself and his endeavors.

For two years after its founding the corporation subsisted almost entirely on fees for engineering services in connection with installations of Cottrell precipitators and, while royalties were in the offing, as of July 1914 the corporation had in its treasury a total of only $1200. There was indeed a fine note of incongruity present during these early years when the directors, combining the varied unpaid talents of such industrialists and financiers as T. Coleman du Pont, Otto Kahn, George W. Perkins (a retired Morgan partner), and Elon Huntington Hooker—when these impressive gentlemen met among their peers to scan the corporation's financial report and to discuss bank balances that might fittingly resemble those of the nearest corner cigar stand.

But there were large installations in progress. There were, among others, those at the Raritan Copper Works at Perth Amboy, New Jersey, the Hooker Electrochemical Company at Niagara Falls, and the American Smelting and Refining Company at Garfield, Utah, so that by January 1915 the directors had reason to feel more at home among the figures of the annual statement. By then the corporation was able to buy back the $10,100 in stock originally subscribed by seventeen men. When this was repurchased one of the seventeen perhaps typified what was the general spirit of the others by remarking, "When that $500 came back to me it was a revelation that had never come to me in my long life. I have often helped altruistic movements, but this is the first time the money I gave was ever returned."

In addition to buying back its own stock (a procedure later regularized for this specific case by a special act of the New York State legislature during the governorship of Franklin D. Roosevelt) the corporation had, by January 1915, other reasons to feel self-congratulatory. In that month the treasurer was able to announce that royalties paid on precipitation installations had brought into the treasury some $65,000 ready cash, as well as $100,000 in secured notes. In reaching this satisfactory point, slightly less than three years had elapsed.

(In one sense these amounts represented a tangible yardstick by which to measure the value of the electrical precipitation process. Although very small installations were made on the basis of a flat sum paid to Research Corporation, the more important usually paid according to a percentage of the "values" recovered. Thus at the Duquesne Reduction Works in Pittsburgh [a small-to-medium installation] the precipitators treated 11,000 cubic feet of gas per minute from waste metals furnaces. By the Cottrell process 5000 to 10,000 pounds of dust were recovered each week, almost a quarter of which was good usable tin, and 10 per cent of the value of this went to the corporation as a royalty. Even more elegant values were recovered. The Cottrell precipitator at the U. S. Assay Office in downtown New York not only abated a dust nuisance as it did in the case of the tin reduction works but also processed 5000 pounds of fume per year which yielded some 250 ounces of gold then worth about $11,000.)

Ordinarily the management of a new corporation would have rightfully found a ruddy glow of satisfaction in such a treasurer's report. There might, over the cigars, have been talk of a small dividend which would be postponed; a salary raise here or there (also postponed); a cautious round of back-patting. The problem at Research Corporation was not quite so simple. By the articles of incorporation there could be no dividends and by agreement top salaries were limited to $5000. Instead it was the purpose of Research Corporation to acquire inventions and patents and make them more available in the arts and industries while using them as a source of income, as well as to apply all earnings derived from such use to the advancement of technical and scientific investigation and experimentation through the agency of the Smithsonian Institution and such other scientific and educational institutions and societies as might be selected by the directors.

The first of these purposes, including the pursuit of the art and business of electrical precipitation, was what the corporation lived by and the second was what it lived for. Both means and ends were more difficult of achievement than they sounded.

Within the first three years of its founding Research Corporation had several patents and inventions offered to it for development. After a certain winnowing process two or three of these were thought to have commercial possibilities sufficiently good to warrant the corporation's interest. One, for example, was a reinforced concrete railroad tie to replace the wood tie and this was to be tested in co-operation with a group of railroads. The railroads, after an initial enthusiasm, decided against the idea. Then there was a meat concentrate unappetizingly called "Meatox." Research Corporation itself finally doubted the wisdom of becoming involved in this, for it was the feeling of most of the directors that there were grave dangers in branching out too broadly into unknown fields at such an early date when much still remained to be done in refining the art of electrical precipitation itself. Moreover, preponderant sentiment had it that the corporation should protect itself more cautiously in the matter of building up financial reserves before setting out to satisfy the second purpose of the organization, i.e., the distribution of profits to the Smithsonian and other institutions for scientific research.

(Until 1918 only one gesture was made in the latter direction when, in 1915, $957 was granted to Cottrell to add to the sum allotted him by the Smithsonian Institution for the fog experiments he conducted at the Panama-Pacific Exposition in San Francisco.)

While the views that guided the corporation's policies during its early years were wisely conservative from a business point of view and did not violate the letter of the charter, it cannot be said that they conformed to the spirit of it in the manner Cottrell conceived that spirit to exist. It is very doubtful whether most of the members of the board, by the very nature of their training and experience, could ever have captured that spirit. It may also be possible that had they embraced that spirit with too much enthusiasm the corporation would not have survived an infancy of scattered energies. Then, too, the management soon decided that the first logical step in the growth of the corporation was to engage actively in the design, manufacture, and sale of some precipitation equipment rather than to act merely as consultants and engineers to plants installing the process. Such a move not only offered a better prospect for profit but gave the corporation a firmer control over equipment employed as well as a greater responsibility toward the successful operation of precipitating equipment and plants.

Nevertheless, in the matter of disposing of profits either to the Smithsonian or in exploiting new inventions, the ultraconservative (or, "let's-wait-till-we-have-more-money") viewpoint dominated Research Corporation thinking until 1922. For most of this period the unpaid presidency was held by Elon Huntington Hooker (also, but not unpaid, president of Hooker Electrochemical Company). Hooker was a hardheaded, driving businessman of acknowledged ability who held Cottrell in a great admiration that stood up under all tests except that of the disbursement of corporate funds. For his part, Hooker could point to two war years during which the corporation had successfully weathered operating losses thanks to reserves his administration had saved. He could point, too, to a policy of beginning charity at home by which some of the profits were spent in furthering research in electrical precipitation itself and in building up and expanding the physical assets of the organization.

Although there was never any real friction, this was not exactly the way Cottrell had hoped things would be. He was at heart a non-amasser (except for such things as ten-cent-store eyeglasses and bits of equipment that would come in handy in future experiments) and the idea of waiting until a sizable sum had been accumulated and then spending the interest on research appealed to him not at all. Yet, since he had from choice no formal connection with the corporation, his influence was largely a moral one that exerted itself only intermittently in the odd moments he found time to devote to the corporation's affairs.

("It was my feeling that the Research Corporation had a big chance to do something different," Cottrell said years later. "Instead of building up a big fund, it was my idea to give grants right at the start and this, I hoped, would obviate the tendency institutions have to become ossified. If Research Corporation were to operate on the basis of 'spend as you go' it would be running on its own momentum and *have* to keep alive whereas big foundations tend to get wooden and lose drive.")

But ten years elapsed between the corporation's founding and the point in 1922 when Cottrell at last felt that his original aims were beginning to be put into practice. This came about when Hooker retired from the presidency (while retaining his board membership) and Dr. Arthur A. Hammerschlag was elected the corporation's first paid president—a post for which the $5000 salary limit was ignored.

Hammerschlag had previously been one of Andrew Carnegie's bright young men and before that a promising Morgan employee. Despite this rock-ribbed background, his outlook was essentially progressive and his administrative ability was such that he was picked as first president of the Carnegie Institute of Technology. In this capacity he was frequently in touch with the Bureau of Mines, through which he had met Cottrell and where the latter formed the opinion of him as "a good organizer, a good leader, and a mixer who was a master of good fellowship." Moreover, his interests were not confined to science but extended over a wide range, including art and music. The personalities of Hammerschlag and Cottrell were in splendid concordance, and Hammerschlag readily grasped the spirit Cottrell thought he had breathed into the organization on its founding. Some of Hammerschlag's enthusiasm for his new work crept into a press statement published in conjunction with the corporation's 1924 report, in which he was quoted as saying: "This work of discovering, helping, and conserving American inventive genius is without parallel. It is an experiment in social economics and business which promises results of far reaching importance.

"Men come to the Research Corporation with innumerable so-called patents. Hundreds must be discouraged because they only rediscover old devices. Others contemplate new uses for old inventions. But every now and then some startling, unexpected invention is discovered. In a single year we have uncovered a marvelous calculating machine that can compute algebraically; a printing machine that dispenses with type, electrotypes, and halftones, and instead of printing from a design which carries the ink, prints more rapidly and better from a pattern which never comes in contact with the ink.

"Thus, this unusual clearing house has begun to function in the public interest and offers a marvelous opportunity for the inventor who is a pioneer and needs a business organization to safeguard his interests and to bring his patents into commercial use."

Hammerschlag had other ideas that met with Cottrell's approval. He thought of moving the corporation's offices to Washington and associating part of its activities more closely with the Smithsonian. In 1923, when this possibility was considered, the corporation made its first grant to the Institution—$5000 to forward the rocket experiments of Albert H. Goddard. Goddard, who is sometimes credited with being the father of the modern rocket (he developed an early form of the bazooka in World War I, and his first successful liquid fuel rocket, fired in 1926, is sometimes said to be the direct ancestor of the German V-2), had already received support from Smithsonian funds but, curiously, this single grant was the only one made in the furtherance of pure research during Hammerschlag's five-year regime.

Nevertheless, both Hammerschlag and Cottrell were bold thinkers and together they conceived an ambitious idea. Since the whole Muscle Shoals controversy revolved sharply around the issue of government versus private operation of the power and fertilizer facilities, it was their idea that Research Corporation, a private business organization operating for profit but not for private gain, was admirably adapted to act as trustee for the Shoals in the public interest. The matter was suggested to the Secretary of War in 1923, but Congress adjourned before hearings could be held on such a proposal and somehow the idea died before Congress reconvened.

Despite Hammerschlag's zeal in pursuing the corporation's aims, he found the job of administering an admixture of business and philanthropy even more besetting than that of presiding over an institute of technology. More often than not, when patented devices that caught the corporation's interest were given exhaustive tests, they failed even to approach preliminary glowing promises. Sometimes, too, as in the case of the algebraic calculator and some surgical apparatus, the corporation undertook further development fully aware that no profitable market existed but that such projects were worth while and the expenditure justified if there were only a reasonable expectation of science or the public benefiting. To be president of such a corporation did indeed seem to call for a man who could walk even-gaited with but one foot on the ground and there must have been times when Hammerschlag had doubts, for in the second year of his administration Cottrell wrote Jess, "[Hammerschlag] said frankly that if he had realized how tough the R.C. problems really were he didn't think he would have tackled it but now that he was in he was going to make a go of it."

Yet he handled the job with ability and imagination until his death, following an operation, on the eve of Cottrell's departure from Southern California for the Sierra vacation in 1927.

"One aspect of the work that was particularly close to Dr. Hammerschlag's heart and in which I thoroughly sympathized with him," Cottrell wrote to Howard Andrews Poillon, who succeeded Hammerschlag, "was the correlation . . . of the work of Research Corporation with that of the scientific bureaus of the Government, and in particular the Smithsonian Institution. I feel that the passing of Dr. Walcott and Dr. Hammerschlag, both within a few months, has laid a special duty on those of us left behind to study and carry forward . . . these particular ideals which form so intimate a part of the original conception of the Research Corporation, and to which these two both separately and jointly devoted so much earnest thought and work."

This concern that the corporation abide by the policies that Hammerschlag pursued followed Cottrell on his vacation that year and led him to write a declaration of his views to be read before the directors: "[Hammerschlag] never lost sight of the fact that the development of new projects was, after all, the ultimate object of the Corporation and even in the hardest times of making both ends meet kept also driving ahead on new lines. In the early history of the Corporation a feeling grew up that perhaps it was most expedient to concentrate nearly the entire attention on the precipitation work, viewing other and newer projects as distinctly incidental until a surplus or reserve of, say half a million to a million should be built up, and then turn more definitely to the projects of new inventions.

"Personally I was always a half-hearted supporter of this policy but time has since demonstrated that if we are to make the Research Corporation serve the central purposes for which it was created, we must not let the mere running of its established and already income-producing lines of activity absorb all or even the larger part of the interest and attention of the management. In fact, if it seems wise from a purely business standpoint, I should not hesitate in the least to approve of the R.C. disposing of the precipitation business as a whole if thereby it could be assured of even as good an income as it could reasonably expect under its own operations and be not only free to—but in a sense forced to—concentrate its energies on newer fields."

Now Poillon, the new president, was a mining engineer and dedicated to the not unreasonable principle that the way to run a business was to do so efficiently and profitably. Once this duty was discharged, one could indulge in a feast of idealism to heart's content but such idealism should not compete with his concept of sound business principles. Poillon was a deliberative thinker and a man of great personal integrity; he held Cottrell's scientific ability in detached esteem, but when it came to business as Poillon understood the term, Cottrell was something of a man on a flying trapeze. Nevertheless, shortly after he took over the presidency and Cottrell had returned East, the latter made the following diary note: "Had phone from Poillon emphasizing desire to follow along lines or suggestions from me in R.C. matters."

It was primarily this interest in using his influence toward directing the philanthropic aspects of Research Corporation back into the channels he had originally conceived for it—particularly with reference to the Smithsonian Institution—that led Cottrell to resign as chief of the Fertilizer and Fixed Nitrogen Investigations (a title he had assumed when the Fixed Nitrogen Research Laboratory lost its independence in the Department of Agriculture and became a unit of the Bureau of Chemistry and Soils). Besides, since an American nitrogen fixation industry was now firmly established, one of the original purposes of his government work had been fulfilled. Then, too, his contact with the Institute of Physical and Chemical Research in Tokyo had stimulated him further toward broadening the activities of Research Corporation.

After all, there was something of a parallel between nitrogen fixation and Research Corporation. In establishing the latter, Cottrell had found an abundance of altruism in the atmosphere. Indeed, the corporation was in itself a fixation process that combined that altruism with earthy profit-making elements to produce a compound that would prove nutritive to science and invention. But the process needed a good catalyst. And there was Cottrell.

2

The plan was this: Poillon would devote himself to conducting the precipitation business of Research Corporation along orthodox business lines in the manner of one responsible to a board of directors and as though dividend requirements were to be met. When it came to the other purposes of the organization—the development of new inventions and ideas, the acceptance of new patents for the corporation to administer, the granting of funds for institutional research—he would be guided largely by Cottrell. Cottrell's official status with the corporation would be that of paid consultant—thus establishing his third consultative position, for he retained such a connection with the Department of Agriculture and still acted as such for the Petroleum Rectifying Company.

The fifteen-year relationship of Cottrell and Poillon that ensued was one of a conflict of basic points of view. Since the latter was a man of tempered, reasoned patience and Cottrell a man of intense, intuitive enthusiasms, both in degrees that measured toward the extremes, the surprising thing was that the conflict never rose above the surface but produced instead some remarkably fine results, as well as some errors, by a series of successive compromises.

Perhaps few things better illustrate what Cottrell conceived to be one of the basic functions of Research Corporation than a series of investigations in which he and Poillon first became interested in 1931, not long after the beginning of Cottrell's consulting activities.

From Cottrell to Poillon
Long Beach, Calif.
July 7, 1931

"The main situation I want to cover in the present letter is the various developments at the University of California. There have already been so many interlacing that it is a bit hard to select just where to begin. . . . The case of Prof. E. O. Lawrence is looming up as of possible particular interest. If this latter really works out to be anything, it may prove to be very big indeed. . . .

"Prof. Lawrence is a young man originally from South Dakota, I believe, who later went to Yale and got his Ph.D. a few years ago there under Swann and then came out to Berkeley. He, Brackett, and young Loeb were all on about an equal footing in Physics Dept., U. of C. . . . After I took Brackett [to the Fixed Nitrogen Research Laboratory] I got better acquainted with Lawrence and became very much impressed with him and later got him put on our [F.N.R.L.] consulting staff and have had him visit the lab on his trips East. Also had him visit the Research Corporation on his way through New York but don't remember whether he met you at that time. I have looked upon him as a man we should keep close track of. He is young enough and with a sufficiently good early start to go far. He not only does good work himself, but I have been particularly impressed with how much he manages to get out of his graduate students on the research problems of which he keeps a surprising number going full blast.

"The two reprints enclosed herewith will give you an idea of *one* of the most interesting and promising lines he has been developing over the past year or more. I have followed this from the beginning with a great deal of interest. It has a good many possible applications and lines of development, but two especially which are of immediate obvious interest to many and may be rather spectacular and important in their early developments, viz:

"(1) the production of high voltage *protons* (charged hydrogen atoms) for use in disintegrating the nuclei of other heavier chemical atoms.

"(2) the production of high voltage *electrons* for generation of very penetrating X-rays, gamma rays (like radium, etc.) and even up to 'artificial cosmic rays' etc."

From Lawrence to Cottrell
Berkeley, Calif.
July 20, 1931

"I telegraphed you last night asking if it is convenient for me to come down [to Long Beach] to see you Wednesday or Thursday . . . on my way east.

"As you probably have surmised, I want to get your advice on the present best procedure towards raising some more money for the high speed proton experiments. The present developments in the work make it practically certain that we will be able to produce ten or twenty-million-volt protons when the large magnet and a powerful high frequency oscillator are made available to us. With the present experimental setup we have exceeded one million volts and the proton currents are very much more intense than we had expected; these new results give me great confidence in the practicability of going to much higher energies.

"It seems to me that at least $10,000 and possibly $15,000 will be needed to cover adequately the expense of all the equipment needed for the work, and the money must be found somewhere. . . . It appears that our difficulties are no longer of a physical but of a financial nature."

MASSACHUSETTS INSTITUTE OF TECHNOLOGY
CAMBRIDGE, MASSACHUSETTS

October 23, 1931

Mr. Howard A. Poillon, President
The Research Corporation
405 Lexington Ave.,
New York City.

My dear Mr. Poillon:

President [Karl T.] Compton has communicated with you in regard to my proposed work in developing a very high voltage direct current source of considerable power output. . . . I beg now to make formal application for a grant from the Research Corporation to enable me to continue the development of this project. . . .

Once the generator is built a number of interesting lines of practical and theoretical interest are opened up for investigation. It is perhaps premature to discuss them here in detail, but they are briefly suggested as follows:

(a) Operation of X-ray tubes for extremely penetrating rays . . .

(b) Development of an electrostatic motor . . .

(c) It is certain at any rate that a whole new range of scientific problems dealing with the constitution of the atomic nucleus could be investigated with this source of high voltage . . .

In view of these considerations it appears that an appropriation of $10,000 should be adequate. . . .

Very sincerely yours,
R. J. Van de Graaff

Poillon to Cottrell
October 26, 1931

". . . It appears to me that Van de Graaff's project might offer an excellent vehicle to establish Research [Corporation] with M.I.T. in the same manner as you have discussed with the University of California. . . . My reasoning was that we are already interested in the project in California; if Van de Graaff has something of value that is important, might we not, first, assure him of our willingness to assist him in obtaining his patents and consider giving him a grant through M.I.T.; by doing this we show our attitude toward helping out intelligent inventors, and second, also our willingness to give funds for important research when carried on by a recognized institution. . . ."

Cottrell to Lawrence
November 11, 1931

"Since my return to the East, another matter has come up to the Research Corporation for support in this development through Compton and the M.I.T. This is the electrostatic generator of Dr. Van de Graaff. . . .

"The Research Corporation has undertaken to help them out to a certain extent both in their next stage of construction and also in the development of the patent situation. The whole thing looks very interesting and supplements in many ways the approach to this general field which you are already making. Of course, there will be some parts of the general field in the two lines of approach which will in all probability develop some competitive features, but this should only add to the general hilarity and spice of friendly cooperation. In fact, it may serve to illustrate and give us practice in showing how the Research Corporation can be of service in bringing about such cooperation and acting as a buffer and safeguard against any undue commercial competition between related projects of this kind originating in different universities."

292

Headlines in the New York Times
Sunday, November 15, 1931

SCIENCE LAUNCHES NEW ATTACK
ON THE ATOM'S CITADEL

Millions of Volts Made Possible by Van de
Graaff Invention Are to Disrupt the Nucleus
in the Hope of Wresting From It Secrets of
the Universe

Physics' Most Stupendous Task
Clearly Set Forth

*From the "Annual Report of the President
of Research Corporation for the Year 1931"*

"Acting on authorization by the Board of Directors at the 1930
Annual Meeting, the Executive Committee reports the following
grants. . . .
Smithsonian Institution, $20,000 . . .
International Auxiliary Language Association, $4,000 . . .
Leland Stanford, Jr. University, $2,500 . . .
Columbia University, $3,000 . . .
Harvard University, $2,750 . . .
Smithsonian Institution, $1,000 . . .
Kaiser Wilhelm Institute for Medical Research, $1,500 . . .
Stevens Institute of Technology, not to exceed $10,250 . . .
Massachusetts Institute of Technology, $10,000 for defraying the
cost of equipment to permit Dr. R. J. Van de Graaff to con-
struct an electro-static high voltage generator with spheres
fifteen feet in diameter.
University of California, $5,000 for defraying the cost of recon-
ditioning, moving, and installing a magnet of eighty-five tons
to permit Dr. E. O. Lawrence to continue his research and investigation in high speed protons. . . . At the suggestion of
Research Corporation, the Chemical Foundation made a grant
of $2,500 to the University of California to assist Dr. Lawrence
in his research on high speed protons, and has since given assurances that he can expect further contributions to aid him
in his work."

From the "Annual Report of the President
of Research Corporation for 1932"

"The work of both Dr. Lawrence of the University of California and Dr. Van de Graaff of Massachusetts Institute of Technology, being done under grants made to their respective institutions, is being followed as closely as possible in an attempt to cover the patentable features as they develop. The great difficulty that is being encountered in this program lies in being unable to reduce their ideas to a form which will be understandable to our patent attorneys and the Patent Examiners. We are confronted with the problem of locating the person, if such exists, who can grasp, and having grasped, transmit their concepts into something sufficiently definite to establish claims that can be protected."

From a "Brief Summary of the Work
of the Radiation Laboratory
of the University of California for 1932"

"The original grant of funds by the Research Corporation for the installation of the electromagnet offered by the Federal Telegraph Company and for the purchase of accessory equipment has more than given the University of California the largest magnet in the world devoted to physical research. The support of the Research Corporation is virtually responsible for the rapid development of a new experimental technique in research in the domain of the nucleus of the atom and the establishment of a new kind of laboratory, the Radiation Laboratory of the University of California. This laboratory is devoted to the study of the properties of very high speed electrons, protons, ions, and atoms, with particular regard to the study of the atomic nucleus and the disintegration of atoms. It has long been recognized that many more of the secrets of the atom will be unlocked when high speed particles are available in the laboratory. . . .

"One cannot predict what the experiments in the Radiation Laboratory will bring forth during the coming year, but it is at least certain that the experimenters look forward to the work with intense enthusiasm and with confidence that most interesting things will emerge. Everyone connected with the laboratory is deeply grateful for the support of the Research Corporation which has made it their privilege to carry on this work."

From the San Francisco Examiner
January 27, 1932

"With the recent installation of one of the largest magnets in the world in their laboratory, two University of California scientists are setting about their task of trying to break up the atom and release its terrific energy.

"The magnet, weighing 85 tons, was one of four built for globe-girdling radio communication during the war.

"Working only with a two-ton magnet, the scientists, Professors Ernest O. Lawrence and M. Stanley Livingston, say they have been able to penetrate the outer husk of the atom. With the greater magnet, they hope to shatter the atom completely with an ultimate 25,000,000 volt impact.

"What wonders will result if they are successful, not even they can tell."

From Lawrence to Poillon
August 18, 1932

". . . As you know, our funds are getting low and if we are to do much more work some more funds will have to be made available. . . ."

From a "Report on Progress on Construction
of the 10,000,000 Volt Direct Current Generator at M.I.T."
(for 1932) by Robert J. Van de Graaff and Karl T. Compton

"It was in order to make possible the construction of this generator that the Research Corporation made its grant of $10,000 and the Massachusetts Institute of Technology undertook to contribute an equal amount. . . .

". . . In addition to the immediate objectives of atomic nuclear investigations, this generator, or modifications of it with subsidiary apparatus which has also been designed, may open up a new field of practical applications of electricity at high voltage, and the investigation of this new field is a second objective of the work. . . .

"In conclusion we wish to express our sincere thanks to the Research Corporation without which this generator would not have been built. This assistance has consisted not alone in the grant of the funds, but also in the very generous and helpful donation of time by officers and employees of the Research Corporation, who prepared the engineering drawings, secured the bids, let the contracts, and contributed many valuable ideas to the design."

From the "Annual Report of the President
of Research Corporation for 1933"

"University of California, $1,000 for the construction of a Wilson Cloud Chamber in connection with the researches of Dr. E. O. Lawrence.

"University of California, $800 for special equipment to be used in connection with the researches of Dr. E. O. Lawrence in the field of atomic disintegration.

"Massachusetts Institute of Technology, $2,500 to be used in connection with the development of the Van de Graaff generator and transmission system."

From the Washington Star
November 29, 1933

WORLD'S STRONGEST ELECTRIC BOLT
SMASHES ATOM IN EXPERIMENTS

South Dartmouth, Mass., Nov. 28 (AP) . . . It was a day of triumph for 32-year old Dr. Robert J. Van de Graaff, research associate in the department of physics of the Massachusetts Institute of Technology, who for the last six years had worked on the development of a machine which would wrest from the atom the secret of its internal construction. . . .

From the "Annual Report of the President
of Research Corporation for 1934"

"Massachusetts Institute of Technology, $4,000 to be used in connection with the development of the Van de Graaff generator and transmission system.

"University of California, $2,000 in aid of the researches of Dr. E. O. Lawrence. The Chemical Foundation is cooperating in the support of this research project."

From Poillon to Cottrell
March 30, 1934

"I have just received a letter from Dr. Lawrence in California. He writes me regarding his requirements for the coming academic year and as there is no immediate rush about this and the letter is quite lengthy, I can give it to you to read when you come to New York and get your advice then . . . it is my feeling that he will be a Nobel Prize winner very shortly. . . ."

From a "Report to Research Corporation
on the Activities During 1934 of the Radiation Laboratory,
University of California," by E. O. Lawrence

"When we undertook the development of experimental methods for the study of the nucleus of the atom, we were entering a virgin field of investigation with little knowledge of what to expect; but we felt sure that important things would come from the study of the nucleus, as we knew at least that more than 99% of the atom's mass and energy was in the nucleus and that indeed the very nature of the atom was determined by the nucleus. During the past year there have been several discoveries that have already demonstrated the great importance of nuclear physics, and in my report this year I wish to single out for mention the one which perhaps is the most important, namely, artificial radioactivity.

"Early in the year Irene Curie, the daughter of Madame Curie, and her husband, F. Joliot, discovered that some substances are rendered radioactive by bombardment with the alpha rays of radium. This discovery suggested that perhaps protons and deuterons, the high speed atomic projectiles produced by the apparatus in our laboratory, might be able to make various substances radioactive in a smiliar way. Following this lead, we bombarded various substances, and to our amazement discovered that almost every substance bombarded was rendered radioactive. We were able to manufacture in the laboratory radioactive atoms. This indeed was something new under the sun. . . .

"Again I wish to express my deep feeling of gratitude, and in this my colleagues join me, to the Research Corporation for the generous support which has made possible the work of the radiation laboratory."

From a "Report of the Nuclear Research Project at Round Hill for the Year Ending January 1, 1934," by Dr. R. J. Van de Graaf

"The object of the Nuclear Research Project at Round Hill is to apply the voltage from a large electrostatic generator to a specially designed vacuum tube for the bombardment of atomic nuclei. This would make available to nuclear research a tool of greater voltage, power, control, and flexibility than has hitherto been used."

From the "Annual Report of the President of Research Corporation for the year 1935"

(*page 23*) "As [the] Corporation had insufficient cash to finance its [precipitation] contracts, it borrowed on its thirty-day to ninety-day unsecured notes from the Bank of New York and Trust Company."

(*page 24*) "The Executive Committee reports that the following grants, amounting to $30,009.74, have been awarded. . . .

"Massachusetts Institute of Technology, $4,000 to be used in connection with the researches of Dr. R. J. Van de Graaff."

(*page 25*) "University of California, $2,000 in aid of the researches of Dr. E. O. Lawrence. The Chemical Foundation is cooperating in the support of this project.

"University of Rochester, $1,000 in aid of its project to construct a small cyclotron to advance the study of nuclear physics."

From a "Report on the M.I.T. Nuclear Research Project at Round Hill for the Year Ending December 31, 1935," by Dr. R. J. Van de Graaff and Associates

". . . Since the necessary voltage is now available, the primary problem is that of constructing a vacuum tube which will withstand this voltage."

*From a "Report to the Research Corporation
on the Activities During 1935 of the Radiation Laboratory,
University of California," by E. O. Lawrence*

"In my report last year I stressed the discovery made in the pre-
ceding few months in our laboratory of the production of various
radioactive substances by bombardment with high speed deuterons.
During the past year this work has been vigorously carried forward
with results of great importance. The cyclotron, the apparatus that
accelerates the atomic projectiles to very high speeds, has been improved to the point where it works satisfactorily at a voltage of
5,000,000, a voltage five times higher than that used in any other
laboratory in the world for similar purposes. With this high voltage,
we have been successful in transmuting a large fraction of the
known elements to radioactive forms, and it now seems that all of
the elements of the periodic table are susceptible to attack with our
present apparatus.

". . . one of the results of the process is the conversion of platinum into gold. . . ."

[From *Time* magazine, November 1, 1937: "In altering atomic
structures, Dr. Lawrence has even created a few atoms of gold, thus
technically at least realizing the old dream of the alchemists. But the
raw material for this transmutation was platinum, and the few gold
atoms were not worth a fraction of the energy used in manufacturing them, although the electric current necessary to run the cyclotron for an hour costs only $1.50. 'Anyway,' as Lawrence remarks
with a grin, 'the information we are getting is worth more than
gold.'"]

"The importance of the possible medical applications of the work
of the Radiation Laboratory is widely felt, and as a result many institutions are undertaking extensive programs of research along
these lines with large expenditures of funds. The Rackham Fund has
given to the University of Michigan Department of Physics and
Medical School $25,000 a year to carry forward an extensive pro-
gram of research. They have undertaken to follow closely the
methods developed in our laboratory, but with their larger fund
plan to build a cyclotron and other equipment on an even larger
scale. A similar project is under way in England. The University of

Rochester has a cyclotron nearing completion; one is under construction at Princeton; another, primarily for medical purposes, is being built in Philadelphia, and others at the University of Chicago, the University of Illinois, Purdue University, Cornell, Columbia, etc. Several of these new laboratories will be under way within a year, and doubtless discoveries in the field of nuclear physics will go forward with accelerated rapidity. We in the Radiation Laboratory, of course, are gratified that our methods are being so widely accepted. . . ."

"Nuclear Physics Research Program.
A Report of Progress" (*to Research Corporation, 1935*)
by Dr. L. A. Du Bridge

"Following a long period of laying plans and securing financial support, actual construction of the apparatus for the research in nuclear physics at the University of Rochester was begun about October 1, 1935. . . ."

From the "Annual Report of the President
of Research Corporation for the year 1936"

(*page 30*) "Again your Corporation has had insufficient cash to finance its [precipitation] contracts. It borrowed . . .

"The Executive Committee reports that the following grants, amounting to $42,400, have been awarded. . . .

"Massachusetts Institute of Technology, $6,700 . . .

"University of California, $3,000 in support of the researches of Dr. E. O. Lawrence. The Chemical Foundation is cooperating in the support of this project.

"The Johns Hopkins University, $6,000 in support of Dr. Fowler in his work on a method and apparatus for obtaining large quantities of neutrons, and also in support of Dr. Franck for the construction of apparatus to produce neutrons and the study of their kinetics.

"University of Chicago, $1,000 for the construction of a cyclotron to advance the study of nuclear physics.

"University of Rochester, $1,000 in aid of its project to construct a small cyclotron to advance the study of nuclear physics.

"On this, the twenty-fifth year of your Corporation's existence, the

President wishes to express his sincere appreciation to the members of the Board of Directors . . ."

From a "Report on the M.I.T.
High Voltage Nuclear Research Project
for the Year 1936" by R. J. Van de Graaff and Associates

". . . Having brought the [electrostatic] generator to a satisfactory state of operation, we have concentrated during the year on the development of a suitable vacuum tube to make possible the application of the generatory voltage to the bombardment of atomic nuclei."

From a "Report to the Research Corporation
on the Activities During 1936 of the Radiation Laboratory,
University of California," by Ernest O. Lawrence

"The cyclotron has been further improved, many new radioactive substances have been discovered, and much other work in nuclear physics has been accomplished; and there have been important developments in applying the new discoveries in nuclear physics to the medical sciences. . . .

"We are particularly glad that through the generous continued support of the Research Corporation, the Chemical Foundation, and the Josiah Macy, Jr. Foundation, and through a gift from Mr. William H. Crocker for a building, we are to have a new Laboratory with much better facilities for carrying on the work. The Laboratory will be equipped with a much larger cyclotron, weighing about 230 tons and capable of generating atomic projectiles with energies up to 50 million volts."

From a "Report on Research Done
at the Johns Hopkins University During the Year 1936"
by Dr. J. Franck and Dr. J. A. Bearden

"The grant given to us by the Research Corporation was intended to be used to build up an ample source of neutrons which will enable us to attack several problems connected with energy exchange and reactions of neutrons with atoms. One of our goals will be to measure the velocity of neutrons more exactly than has been done heretofore."

From "Nuclear Physics Research Program
[at the University of Rochester] A Report of Progress
for the Year 1936" by Dr. L. A. Du Bridge

"The program involved the construction of a 'cyclotron,' of the type developed at the University of California by E. O. Lawrence, which is capable of accelerating charged particles of energies of from three to six million volts. . . .

". . . a regular program of research is now getting under way."

From a "Report on Research in Nuclear Chemistry
(at the University of Chicago)
During the Year 1936" by Dr. W. D. Harkins

"The grant of one thousand dollars contributed by the Research Corporation has been expended as part of the cost of a seventy ton magnet, which is being set up as a cyclotron, similar to that of Professor Lawrence of the University of California, and is to be used in obtaining atoms of very high velocity; that is, velocities of ten thousand to twenty thousand miles per second."

From the "Annual Report of the President
of Research Corporation for the year 1937"

"The Executive Committee reports that the following grants, amounting to $65,000, have been awarded. . . .

"Massachusetts Institute of Technology, $5,500 of which $500 was used for research assistants under the direction of Dr. R. J. Van de Graaff . . .

"University of California, $5,000 in support of the researches of Dr. E. O. Lawrence, at the Radiation Laboratory.

"Cornell University, $3,000 to be used for research in nuclear physics, under the direction of Dr. R. C. Gibbs.

"University of Chicago, $1,000 to purchase auxiliary equipment for the cyclotron, under the direction of Dr. W. D. Harkins.

"Purdue University, $2,400 to assist in the construction of a cyclotron, under the direction of Dr. K. Lark-Horovitz.

"University of Rochester, $2,250 to purchase auxiliary equipment for the cyclotron, under the direction of Dr. L. A. Du Bridge.

"Stevens Institute of Technology, $5,000 for technical and scientific investigation, research and experimentation. The Institute distributed this sum equally between Dr. Percy W. Bridgman of Harvard University and Dr. Ernest O. Lawrence of the University of California, in order to permit them to continue their respective researches.

"Columbia University, $5,600 to support four projects in the Departments of Physics and Chemistry (under the direction of Dean G. B. Pegram, Drs. L. P. Hammett; I. I. Rabi; H. C. Urey, S. L. Quimby and H. W. Webb)."

From a "Report to the Research Corporation on the M.I.T. High Voltage Nuclear Research Project for the Year 1937"

"The previous annual report described a vacuum tube 24 feet long for use in connection with the . . . electrostatic generator for the acceleration of positive and negative particles. Only very preliminary tests had been made at that time. The tube has since been improved by the addition of annular corona shields and found to withstand successfully a voltage of 2.6 million volts. It has been used successfully for the acceleration of both protons and electrons."

From a "Report of Progress Made at the Radiation Laboratory of the University of California" (for 1937) by Dr. E. O. Lawrence

"The cyclotron has been further improved, many new radioactive substances have been discovered (there are more than 200 of these synthetic radioactive materials now known) and . . . the applications of nuclear physics to problems of biology and medicine have gone forward with most gratifying results, indicating an abundant future for the medical radiation laboratory, the establishment of which was begun during this year.

". . . The cyclotron delivers 100 microamperes of 5 million volt deuterons, 20 microamperes of 7.6 million volt deuterons, and .2 microamperes of 15.2 million volt helium ions. Thus new records of both voltage and current have been established.

"These high outputs of atomic projectiles have resulted in the production of nuclear reactions on a correspondingly large scale. The cyclotron delivers neutrons now in sufficient intensities for extensive medical research, and indeed medical therapy, and it produces radioactive materials equivalent in temporary radioactivity to about one gram of radium."

From a "Report of Progress . . . at Cornell University
[during 1937]
with the Support of a Grant . . . from the Research Corporation"

"The cyclotron has been in almost continuous operation since the beginning of the school year, supplying deuterons for disintegration and for producing induced radioactivity and as a neutron source."

From a "Report of Progress in the Construction
at the University of Chicago
of a Seventy-ton Cyclotron" by Dr. W. D. Harkins

"The construction of this cyclotron has now progressed so far that it is practically ready to operate at a low energy, that is, to give protons of about two million volts.

"The University has contributed fourteen thousand dollars for the construction of the cyclotron. . . . The Research Corporation has contributed two thousand dollars, and the Chemical Foundation, one thousand dollars to aid in the construction."

From a "Report on Progress of Cyclotron Research
at Purdue University" (for 1937) by Dr. K. Lark-Horovitz

"At present three groups are working on the completion of the cyclotron and auxiliary equipment. . . ."

From a "Report of Progress
on Nuclear Physics Research Program
at the University of Rochester" by Dr. L. A. Du Bridge

". . . During the months January to June, 1937, a large number of elements were found to become radioactive under the bombardment of our proton beam whose energy had by this time been increased to 4 million volts. The ability of protons of this energy to produce such a large number of nuclear disintegrations was quite unexpected since many of the observed radioactivities could not be explained in terms of the types of reactions which had been previously observed with protons. In the previously known reactions either the proton was directly captured by the nucleus which it struck or else it caused the ejection of an alpha particle from this nucleus. The results of our studies showed that in addition to these two reactions, a new type of reaction must take place in a large number of cases in which the proton causes the ejection of a neutron. . . ."

From a "Report on Chemical and Biochemical Investigations with Artificial Radioactive Indicators at Columbia University" by Dean G. B. Pegram and Dr. L. P. Hammett (for 1937)

"In developing the research program on the use of artificial radioactive isotopes, the ground work has been laid for the completion of the projects originally submitted, and a number of new researches in addition have been made possible.

"1. The measuring and detection equipment and the methods have been developed for quantitative studies of the radioactive isotopes. . . ."

From a "Report of Progress Made at Columbia University on Molecular Beam Research" by Dr. I. I. Rabi (for 1937)

"The object of the experiments to which the Research Corporation loaned its support was the measurement of the magnetic properties of the atomic nucleus. Although it has long been supposed that the nucleus of the atom has the properties of a little magnet in addition to its property of mass and electrical charge, this magnetism had not as yet been demonstrated directly, except possibly in the case of hydrogen. Furthermore, no satisfactory way existed of measuring the strength of this nuclear magnet.

"A method of accomplishing this desired result was devised by the writer. . . ."

From the "Annual Report of the President of Research Corporation for the Year 1938"

"The Executive Committee reports that the following grants, amounting to $85,000, have been awarded. . . .

"Massachusetts Institute of Technology, $11,000 to support two projects: (1) researches of Dr. R. J. Van de Graaff and Dr. L. C. Van Atta . . .

"Columbia University, $9,550 to support five projects as follows: (1) research on isotopes, under the direction of Dr. H. C. Urey; (2) research on the use of isotopes, under the direction of Dr. L. P. Hammett and Dr. J. R. Dunning; (3) experiments on the cyclotron, under the direction of Dean G. B. Pegram; (4) equipment of molecular beam research under the direction of Dr. I. I. Rabi. . . .

"University of California, $7,500 in support of two projects: (1) research in nuclear physics, under the direction of Dr. E. O. Lawrence . . .

"University of Rochester, $2,500 in support of researches on the cyclotron, under the direction of Dr. L. A. Du Bridge."

From a "Report to the Research Corporation on the M.I.T. High Voltage Nuclear Research Project for the Year 1938"

"The production of radio-silver and radio-sodium has been accomplished with a deuteron source and a beam of 10 microamperes. We hope to have considerably higher beam currents shortly, so that we can begin supplying radio activity for research in medical and other fields."

From a "Report of Progress Made at Columbia University on Molecular Beam Research" by Dr. I. I. Rabi (for 1938)

"In our last report I indicated that we were in the process of developing a new method of measuring the magnetic properties of the atomic nucleus directly and with high precision. You will be pleased to learn that the results of this method have exceeded our expectations. Since January 18, 1938, when the first edition of our apparatus went into operation, we have measured the magnetic moments of thirteen different nuclei. . . .

"During our investigation of hydrogen and heavy hydrogen (deuterium) we discovered that, contrary to current views, the electrical charge distribution in the deuterium nucleus is not spherical in form but elongated in the direction of its spin (cigar shaped). This discovery profoundly alters our views of the nature of the forces which hold the nuclear constituents together. . . ."

From a "Report on the Cyclotron
at Columbia University" by Dean G. B. Pegram (for 1938)

"The allotment made from the generous gift of Research Corporation to Columbia University last March for experiments with the Columbia cyclotron has been of great aid in the employment of assistance to complete the cyclotron and to enable us to begin to supply artificial radioactive materials for use as tracers in biochemical processes."

From a "Report on Research Program
Carried on at Columbia University
Regarding the Use of Artificial Radioactive Isotopes"
by Dr. L. P. Hammett and Dr. J. R. Dunning (for 1938)

"The development of the research program on the use of artificial radioactive isotopes in various fields of scientific work to date has been marked by gratifying success. One investigation of a general method of concentrating certain radioactive isotopes has been completed, one research on metal diffusion has been practically finished, and a third problem of general type of molecular compound for concentrating radio-isotopes is well under way. . . ."

From a "Report on the Activities During 1938
of the Radiation Laboratory, University of California," by Dr. E. O.
Lawrence

". . . Most gratifying results.

"Many further investigations of artificial radioactivity have been made, and certain fundamental processes in nuclear reaction have been elucidated, such as the capture of orbital electrons by nuclei and the internal conversion of gamma rays.

"Of special interest, indeed of historic interest, is the clinical work of the laboratory during the year. It will be recalled that Dr. John Lawrence observed that radioactive phosphorus is in large measure deposited in the bones of animals, and also in the case of mice which have the blood disease leukemia, the radio-phosphorus is preferentially taken up in the leukemic cells. This suggested the possibility that radio-phosphorus might be of value as a therapeutic agent in the treatment of leukemia in human beings. Accordingly, early in the year he decided to begin in a small way experimental treatment of leukemia with radio-phosphorus, and these treatments have been proceeding regularly on a small number of patients with interesting results. The radio-phosphorus produces at least a temporary remission of the disease, much as results from X-ray treatments. It is, however, much too early yet to arrive at any conclusion as to whether radio-phosphorus is definitely superior to radium or X-rays in the treatment of this dread disease."

From a "Report of Progress
on Nuclear Physics Research Program
at the University of Rochester" by Dr. L. A. Du Bridge (for 1938)

"About 50 nuclear reactions not previously reported have been found to occur with high energy proton bombardment. About 30 of these reactions result in the formation of radioactive isotopes which have also been produced by other methods, and about 20 lead to new isotopes."

From the "Annual Report of the President
of Research Corporation for the Year 1939"

"The Executive Committee reports that the following grants, amounting to $47,900, have been awarded. . . .

"Massachusetts Institute of Technology, $5,800 to support the high voltage nuclear research project of Dr. R. J. Van de Graaff and Dr. L. C. Van Atta.

"University of California, $5,600 of which $5,000 was to support research in the Radiation Laboratories under the direction of Dr. E. O. Lawrence . . .

"Columbia University, $4,500 to support three projects in the Department of Physics under the direction of Dean G. B. Pegram, Dr. L. P. Hammett, Dr. J. R. Dunning, and Dr. I. I. Rabi."

From a "Report to the Research Corporation
on the M.I.T. High Voltage Nuclear Research Project
for the Year 1939"

". . . The high voltage installation at the Institute now affords intense beams of electrons at greater bombarding voltages than have previously been available for research. This opens up a rich and relatively untouched field for pioneering investigations in high voltage X-rays, in nuclear disintegration by both X-rays and electrons, and in nuclear electron scattering. Some preliminary measurements have already been taken on X-ray production in this new range. Also experiments in nuclear disintegration have been begun, both indium and beryllium having been disintegrated by intense beams of X-rays."

From a "Report on Activities of the Radiation Laboratories at the University of California" by Dr. E. O. Lawrence (for 1939)

". . . Perhaps the three most outstanding pieces of work accomplished this year were (1) the discovery by Alvarez and Cornog of light helium (helium 3) as a rare constituent of ordinary helium, (2) the discovery by Alvarez and Cornog of radioactive hydrogen (hydrogen 3) which as radioactively labelled hydrogen opens up a tremendously wide and fruitful field of investigation in all biology and chemistry, and (3) the measurement by Alvarez and Bloch of the magnetic moment of the neutron with an accuracy of better than one per cent.

". . . The treatment of leukemia with radioactive phosphorus is continuing with encouraging results . . . it is still too early to draw any conclusions other than that the radio-phosphorus treatment appears to produce at least as good remissions in the disease as X-rays and has the advantage of not producing any of the unpleasant symptoms called radiation sickness, which sometimes results from X-ray treatments."

From Cottrell to Lawrence November 11, 1939

"Hearty congratulations and best wishes on the supremely well-merited award to you of the Nobel Prize. . . . I am particularly happy to think that coming just at this time, the award is bound to help greatly in your further program for even larger expansion of the field which I know lays so close to your heart."

Lawrence to Cottrell
November 30, 1939

"Beginning to get back to normalcy after all the excitement with the Nobel award, this is just a note to say how much I appreciated getting your grand letter.

"Needless to say, I appreciate the fact that this great recognition was made possible by the joint efforts of many people, not the least of which was your own early interest and support. As you say, the Nobel Prize could not have come at a better time, as doubtless it will give the laboratory and the program of work added prestige which will help us get the funds to build the hundred million volt cyclotron. . . ."

From a "Combined Report on Cyclotron and Connected Researches in the Department of Physics at Columbia University" by Drs. G. B. Pegram, L. P. Hammett, John R. Dunning (for 1939)

"The grants from Research Corporation have aided our whole program of physical, chemical and biological research that is being developed in connection with the cyclotron and the use of radioactive isotopes. This report will therefore present a number of parts of this research program, each of which has been materially aided through the assistance provided by Research Corporation.

"It is not inappropriate to record here that on the side of research personnel this has been a very fortunate year for the progress of these researches. The coming to the Department of Physics of Professor Enrico Fermi, whose work in nuclear physics won him a Nobel Prize, has been a great inspiration to all of our group. . . .

"The radiation of neutrons and gamma rays is so large that the present barriers of masonry and water are inadequate to protect the staff from overexposure. Some of the funds granted by Research Corporation are being utilized to pay part of the cost of 12 steel tanks, three feet thick to provide an additional water barrier which will completely enclose the cyclotron. . . .

"A startling development in nuclear physics occurred last January, and immediately became a major phase of our research program. The news that Hahn and Strassmann in Berlin had discovered chemical evidence which indicated that uranium, when bombarded by neutrons, forms new radioactive substances which behave like ordinary barium and rubidium, rather than the so-called trans-uranic elements, as had been supposed, was first brought to us by Professor Niels Bohr last January.

"It seemed clear to us that if this occurred, there must be a real splitting of the uranium nucleus into two light fragments and that the nuclear explosion which produced this process should liberate a tremendous amount of energy.

"Detecting equipment had already been highly developed in our laboratory and the cyclotron had just begun operating, so our research group immediately investigated this possible energy release by placing a thin uranium layer in an ionization chamber connected to our linear amplifier detecting systems, and bombarding the uranium with neutrons from the cyclotron. Large energy releases of about 180,000,000 electron volts were immediately observed, a new order of magnitude from what had hitherto been produced by terrestrial methods. Other laboratories in this country soon verified the observations, and it was later learned that the experiment had been performed in Copenhagen a few days earlier.

"It was immediately realized that this process, soon called *Fission*, was of such importance that much of the effort of the laboratory was directed toward its investigation, and the grants from Research Corporation for operation of the cyclotron and for radioactive isotope research have both been used in part for this purpose. . . .

"A very important phase of the fission problem is the identity of the fragments themselves. Hahn's brilliant chemical work identifying ordinary barium and rubidium as products of the bombardment led to the deduction of the fission process itself.

"Dr. G. N. Glasoe and Dr. J. Steigman, a very able chemist who has done most of our previous chemical work on radioactive isotope applications through the support of Research Corporation, have combined ingenious physical and chemical techniques to attack this problem. Aided by the large intensities of neutrons from the cyclotron which can be used to produce fission, they have been able to solve many of the questions.

"The fragments formed in the uranium nuclear explosions are very highly excited, and highly radioactive. Neutrons and gamma rays are ejected quite instantaneously, and fragments are so excited they continue to eject beta and gamma rays and form a number of whole series of radioactive isotopes. The situation is much more complex than at first thought, but Drs. Steigman and Glasoe are making good progress on it. . . .

"The work of Anderson, Fermi and Hanstein . . . ; Anderson, Fermi and Szilard . . . ; and Zinn and Szilard . . . in the Pupin Laboratories was not done with the cyclotron, but it is important to note that their results, together with the earlier work of Joliot and his co-worker in Paris, show that two to six additional neutrons are liberated quite instantaneously by the excited uranium fission fragments. This might result in the excess neutrons producing still more fissions with a cumulative liberation of atomic energy on a large scale, the so-called 'chain reaction.' Nevertheless, an understanding of the appropriate conditions for such a reaction, if it is possible at all, has not yet been attained. A number of experiments have been in progress here to obtain information bearing on this chain reaction question. . . .

"A number of other research projects are in progress in which the general aid of Research Corporation toward operating the cyclotron is of great aid."

*From a "Report on Researches Carried Out
in the Molecular Beam Laboratory at Columbia University" by Dr.
I. I. Rabi (for 1939)*

". . . The results obtained by . . . two totally independent methods agree to one part in two thousand. We can therefore say that, to within this accuracy, there are no forces between the nucleus and the electrons because of their spins, other than those arising from the fact that the nucleus, as well as the electron, is a magnet. . . ."

*From the "Annual Report of the President
of Research Corporation for 1940"*

"The Executive Committee reports that the following grants, amounting to $119,550, have been awarded. . . .

"University of California, $55,100 of which $50,000 was set aside as a contribution to the construction of a cyclotron, under the direction of Dr. E. O. Lawrence . . .

"Columbia University, $15,500 of which $10,000 was to be used for enlarging the cyclotron in the Department of Physics . . .

"Massachusetts Institute of Technology, $7,000, of which $4,000 was to support the high voltage nuclear research project of Dr. R. J. Van de Graaff . . .

"Cornell University, $2,500 to assist Dr. R. F. Bacher in carrying out experiments with mono-energetic slow neutrons."

From a "Report to the Research Corporation on the M.I.T. High Voltage Nuclear Research Project for the Year 1940"

". . . nuclear bombardment experiments in a new field."

From a "Report on Activities of the Radiation Laboratories at the University of California" by Dr. E. O. Lawrence (for 1940)

"The outstanding event this year has been the beginning of construction of the great cyclotron, designed to attack the domain of energies in the atom above 100 million volts. . . .

"The laboratory has undertaken a considerable amount of work for the National Defense Research Committee. . . . Naturally, details of the work should not be given. . . ."

From a "Report on Molecular Beam Research, Columbia University," by Dr. I. I. Rabi (for 1940)

"Our chief result was the successful completion of an apparatus to study spins and nuclear moments of radioactive elements. . . . Unfortunately, further progress of researches along this line and the publication of this significant result was interrupted by the course of international affairs."

From a "Report on Enlargement of the Columbia University Cyclotron" by Dr. G. B. Pegram (for 1940)

"The enlargement of the Columbia cyclotron is now nearly completed. This program, which has been made possible through the generous gift of $10,000 by the Research Corporation and the contributions of the University amounting to approximately $15,000 will increase the effectiveness of the cyclotron. . . .

313

"The aid of the Research Corporation toward operation of the old cyclotron assisted many researches since the last report, and is gratefully acknowledged. Because of defense implications not all researches have been published as yet. Among the researches aided may be mentioned the following: "1. Nier, Booth, Dunning and Grosse. A number of papers have been published dealing with the separated isotopes of uranium. It has been shown conclusively that a rare isotope of uranium, U-235, is responsible for slow neutron fission, and that the abundant isotope of uranium U-238 is responsible for fast neutron fission but inhibits a 'chain reaction' because it captures secondary neutrons through a resonance process.

"It may be concluded, with what other experiments have shown, that self-sustained liberation of atomic energy on a large scale is now possible if sufficient quantities of U-235 can be separated. The realization of such liberation, however, presents a very serious long term problem because of the enormous technical difficulties involved in isotopic concentration. . . .

"Grosse, Fermi and Anderson carried out the first experiments showing quantitatively the relative production of the many elements resulting from the fission of uranium 235."

From "The Smyth Report (A General Account of the Development of Methods of Using Atomic Energy for Military Purposes under the Auspices of the United States Government, 1940–1945," by H. D. Smyth, Chairman of the Department of Physics of Princeton University, Consultant to Manhattan District U. S. Corps of Engineers. Written at the request of Major General L. R. Groves, United States Army. Publication authorized as of August 1945)

INTRODUCTION

"The purpose of this report is to describe the scientific and technical developments in this country since 1940 directed toward the military use of energy from atomic nuclei . . .

EXPERIMENTAL PROOF OF THE EQUIVALENCE OF MASS AND ENERGY

". . . Rutherford's work in 1919 on artificial nuclear disintegration was followed by many similar experiments. Gradual improvement in high voltage technique made it possible to substitute artificially produced high-speed ions of hydrogen or helium for natural alpha particles. J. D. Cockcroft and E. T. S. Walton in Rutherford's laboratory (in England) were the first to succeed in producing nuclear changes by such methods. . . .

METHODS OF NUCLEAR BOMBARDMENT

"Cockcroft and Walton produced protons of fairly high energy by ionizing gaseous hydrogen and then accelerating the ions in a transformer-rectifier high-voltage apparatus. A similar procedure can be used to produce high-energy deuterons from deuterium or high-energy alpha particles from helium. Higher energies can be attained by accelerating the ions in cyclotrons or Van de Graaff machines. . . .

PRACTICABILITY OF ATOMIC POWER IN 1939—PERIOD OF SPECULATION

"Although there were no atomic power plants built in the thirties, there were plenty of discoveries in nuclear physics and plenty of speculation. . . . The discovery of a few . . . nuclear reactions . . . suggested that a self-multiplying chain reaction might be initiated under the right conditions. There was much talk of atomic power and some talk of atomic bombs. But the last great step in this preliminary period came after four years of stumbling. The effects of neutron bombardment of uranium, the most complex element known, had been studied by some of the ablest physicists. The results were striking but confusing. The story of their gradual interpretation is intricate and highly technical, a fascinating tale of theory and experiment. Passing by the earlier inadequate explanations, we shall go directly to the final explanation, which, as so often happens, is relatively simple.

DISCOVERY OF URANIUM FISSION

". . . The neutron proved to be the most effective particle for inducing nuclear changes. This was particularly true for the elements of the highest atomic number and weight where the large nuclear charge exerts strong repulsive forces on deuteron or proton projectiles but not on uncharged neutrons. The results of the bombardment of uranium by neutrons had proved interesting and puzzling. First studied by Fermi and his colleagues in 1934, they were not properly interpreted until several years later.

"On January 16, 1939, Niels Bohr of Copenhagen, Denmark, arrived in this country to spend several months in Princeton, N.J., and was particularly anxious to discuss some abstract problems with A. Einstein. . . . Just before Bohr left Denmark, two of his colleagues, O. R. Frisch and L. Meitner (both refugees from Germany), had told him their guess that the absorption of a neutron by a uranium nucleus sometimes caused that nucleus to split into approximately equal parts with the release of enormous quantities of energy, a process that was soon to be called nuclear 'fission.' . . . Immediately on his arrival in the United States Bohr communicated this idea to his former student, J. A. Wheeler, and others at Princeton, and from them the news spread by word of mouth to neighboring physicists including E. Fermi at Columbia University. As a result of conversations between Fermi, J. R. Dunning and G. B. Pegram, a search was undertaken at Columbia for the heavy pulses of ionization that would be expected from the flying fragments of the uranium nucleus.

THE CHAIN REACTION

"In June 1940, nearly all the work on the chain reaction was concentrated at Columbia under the general leadership of Pegram, with Fermi and Szilard in immediate charge. It had been concluded that the most easily produced chain reaction was probably that depending on thermal neutron fission in a heterogeneous mixture of graphite and uranium. In the spring of 1940, Fermi, Szilard and H. L. Anderson had improved the accuracy of measurements of the capture cross section of carbon for neutrons, of the resonance (intermediate speed) absorption of neutrons by U-238, and of the slowing down of neutrons in carbon.

"Pegram, in a memorandum to [L. J.] Briggs on August 14, 1940, wrote, 'It is not very easy to measure these quantities with accuracy without the use of large quantities of material. The net results of these experiments in the spring of 1940 were that the possibility of the chain reaction was not definitely proven, while it was still further from being definitely disproven. On the whole, the indications were more favorable than any conclusions that could fairly have been claimed from previous results.'

WORK ON PLUTONIUM

". . . In the summer of 1940 the nuclear physics group at the University of California in Berkeley was urged to use neutrons from its powerful cyclotron for the production of plutonium, and to separate it from uranium and investigate its fission properties. Various pertinent experiments were performed . . . at Berkeley . . . prior to 1941, and were reported by E. O. Lawrence to the National Academy Committee [on Atomic Fission] in May 1941 and also in a memorandum that was incorporated in the Committee's second report dated July 11, 1941. It will be seen that this memorandum includes one important idea not specifically emphasized by others, namely, the production of large quantities of plutonium for use in a bomb."

3

When the world awoke in an atomic age it was inevitable that, for popular understanding, such an epoch be assigned a birthplace. Among the localities mentioned for this title, Berkeley, California, has been rightfully included. The atomic age has also had its architects and among these are several members of the university's Radiation Laboratory whose development of techniques for subatomic investigation has been matched in importance by such of their discoveries as the element plutonium, to mention but one.

There is one further claim to be made: in the thirties, when the period of intensive study of atomic energy began, the earliest diversified support and encouragement of the development of the techniques of nuclear physics in America came from Research Corporation. This relatively unknown organization, successfully amalgamating business and philanthropy, had moved some years earlier from a once lonesome office in Wall Street to the more aspiring Chrysler steeple, where it unostentatiously went about the work of precipitating the smoke and fume of others for reasons that it had not always been sure of itself. Now, after a long period during which there had been questionings and self-doubt, the corporation had finally begun to find a métier.

At the time Cottrell made his 1931 visit to Berkeley and first solicited Research Corporation's support for Lawrence's work, the latter had already built an experimental cyclotron using a small magnet with six-inch poles. It worked sufficiently well for Lawrence and his co-workers—David Sloan, M. Stanley Livingston, and Niels Edelfsen—to hope and plan for a model both bigger and better. What they got next exceeded all their expectations and came about by pure chance.

The chairman of the department of electrical engineering at the university was Dr. Leonard F. Fuller, who was also vice-president of the Federal Telegraph Company, the headquarters of which were in Palo Alto. This organization was originally a radio telegraph operating company on the West Coast and around 1910 some of its officials happened to read in the *Electrical World* (the same publication that had amiably agreed to put itself on a reciprocal exchange basis with Cottrell's *Boys' Workshop*) of the invention of the Poulsen arc in Denmark. They proceeded to acquire the American rights. When this device developed successfully, although it was later to be replaced by the vacuum tube, Federal branched out into manufacturing the arc as a radio transmitter.

In the 1920s, Federal planned an ambitious system of transpacific communication with one of the main stations located in Shanghai. It already had, left over from the war, two giant Poulsen arcs of 85 tons whose casting measured fourteen feet long, ten feet high, and whose magnet poles were forty-five inches in diameter. However, financial complications developed with the Chinese and the plan fell through, leaving Federal Telegraph Company with the better part of two huge electromagnets lying uselessly in back of its Palo Alto laboratory where they were occasionally considered as being of scrap value.

Fuller, who was familiar with Lawrence's work, called his attention to the magnets and offered, on behalf of Federal, to give one to Lawrence. There were, however, drawbacks. The coils were incomplete and needed rewinding and some changes and remachining were necessary to adapt the magnet to Lawrence's purposes, to say nothing of transporting an 85-ton piece of machinery the forty miles to Berkeley, where it must also be housed. A note of urgency was added by the fact that Federal Telegraph Company was moving all its facilities East.

It was the problem of financing the adaptation and transportation of the magnet that was called to Cottrell's attention while he was in Berkeley, with the result that he, Lawrence, and Livingston drove down to Palo Alto to inspect it and discuss the proposal further. This visit was enough to fire Cottrell's already considerable interest in the cyclotron work to an enthusiastic pitch, but since he had no authority to commit the Research Corporation to any financial support, he wisely scattered his efforts. He, Lawrence, and Professor A. O. Leuschner, chairman of the Committee on Research of the Academic Senate, obtained President Sproul's agreement to the university's paying the cost of housing the magnet; partly as a result of Cottrell's pleading, the Chemical Foundation contributed $2500 to the project; while his own solicitation of Research Corporation brought $5000 from that source. With Federal's gift of the magnet and with this backing, the first big cyclotron was born and a new technique in atom-smashing given its first substantial support.

Lawrence, for his part, acknowledged the help Cottrell had given by assigning his cyclotron patent to the Research Corporation in 1934—two years after the annual report of the corporation's president plaintively remarked that there were difficulties in finding patent lawyers who could understand the device well enough to word such a document.

It had been twenty-two years before this assignment of Lawrence's that a young Berkeley scientist had used his own patents on a process of electrical precipitation to create an agency to receive the patents of others "to render the same more available and effective in the useful arts and manufactures and for scientific purposes and otherwise." The Cottrell and the Lawrence patents, however, differed in a way that would have been important to a dividend-bearing organization, for in furtherance of the Research Corporation's aim to render inventions more available for scientific purposes, the Lawrence patent had, by 1949, been licensed free of royalties to twenty-eight universities and scientific institutions to build cyclotrons. More than that, it was income from the precipitation patents that helped in several instances to build or operate these cyclotrons which the corporation licensed.

It was, then, fitting that Berkeley be considered among the American contenders for the title, birthplace of the atomic age.

C OTTRELL the scientist could imaginatively probe a disembodied idea but that was not a wholly satisfying experience to Cottrell the man of good will. It is true that, to whatever degree an idea presented challenging difficulties, the more active was likely to be his response. Still, as he grew older an abstract challenge was not always enough. An idea much more readily acquired form and dimension, became an experience with which he could identify himself, if there were a personality behind it. Then when he found a man with a venturesome idea *and* problems, either personal or technical, the combination was all but irresistible.

The credo of Cottrell in dealing with men embraced some well-formulated tenets. First of all, he believed that eccentricities of character often retarded many men from achieving their fullest potentialities and so it behooved the intelligent man to exercise a tolerant understanding of such traits in others if the fulfillment of more desirable capacities could be realized. He held, too, that a man must always be dealt with in good faith and there is nothing to indicate that his experiences with the Pony truck ever aroused much latent skepticism. But most of all he believed in the productivity of diverse personalities reacting to each other provided you knew your men. The results here might range from mild stimulation to pyrotechnics —a principle recognized by any knowing dinner-party hostess who, with pixyish intentions, juggles her seating arrangements for effect.

On this latter point, one of the men in whom Cottrell became most deeply interested in the thirties had this to say: "When [in 1927] the Bureau of Chemistry and Soils was formed to replace the Fixed Nitrogen Research Laboratory, Dr. Cottrell was given a free hand to conduct research on the production of the three fertilizer elements—phosphorus, potash, and nitrogen.

"Dr. Cottrell, with his widespread contact with government, university and industrial research, promptly began proselyting for research personnel. [Dr. C. H.] Kunsman had been associated with [Dr. C. J.] Davisson in the Bell Telephone Laboratories on the technically useless discovery of electron diffraction. Davisson got a Nobel Prize for this scientific achievement and Cottrell got Kunsman. I am certain that Cottrell did not have the foggiest notion of how Kunsman could contribute to the production of cheap fertilizer. I am also certain that he did not in the least care. The incongruity of tossing a skilled experimental physicist into a research on the production of guano seemed sufficiently fantastic to appeal to his sense of the inappropriate.

"[Dr. F. S.] Brackett on the West Coast, exploring into the byways of spectroscopy, had uncovered the world-famous Brackett series in the infrared spectrum of hydrogen. Because it was apparent that there could never be discovered any use for infrared spectra in producing fertilizer, Dr. Cottrell promptly added Brackett to his research group. [Dr. F. E.] Allison and [Dr. Dean] Burk, being primarily biochemists, seemed as necessary to him as was [Dr. O. R.] Wulf, one of Farrington Daniels' young protégés in the quantum theory of chemical kinetics. [Dr. Sterling] Hendricks was equally indispensable since he was, and is, in all likelihood the outstanding research physical chemist in the field of X-ray spectroscopy and crystallography."

This account of Cottrell's penchant for mixing aptitudes and personalities was made by Percy H. Royster, who also might have mentioned Cottrell's belief that special fields could beneficently overlock at the critical joints. Royster for many years stood in relation to Cottrell as protégé to mentor and, as such, evaluated his own position thus:

"Dr. Cottrell's fancy for the fantastic was perhaps most patently grotesque when he brought me into the fertilizer research in the spring of 1927. I was not a new phenomenon to him. I had first met Dr. Cottrell when he was Chief Metallurgist of the Bureau of Mines in 1916, and the absurdity of my educational and technical background had remained in his mental card index for more than a decade. I was then a rookie Junior Physicist in the Bureau's Pittsburgh Station. A glance at my personnel file, which disturbed the Civil Service savants, seemingly made a lasting impression on Dr. Cottrell.

"From the official record, it appeared that I had graduated from the University of North Carolina at the mature age of 18 with an outstanding scholastic record in Comparative Philology. I had studied both Latin and Greek for a dozen years each, with less consequential ventures into Anglo-Saxon, Gothic, Modern Greek, and Sanskrit. I had acquired a gold medal in Latin, a cash prize in Greek, as well as the Old English Text Society award for the best student in Anglo-Saxon. I was, in 1916, probably the only engineer in government service who had read all of Homer, both the *Iliad* and the *Odyssey*, in the original Greek. I had a Phi Beta Kappa key and had won the *University Magazine* short story prize for three consecutive years and was poetry editor of the magazine primarily for the purpose of seeing my own poems printed. The only inappropriate engineering characteristic which did not appeal to Dr. Cottrell was my having played French horn and bass fiddle for five years in the Harvard Symphony Orchestra."

But this was only one phase of the education of Percy H. Royster. At about the age of nineteen he became an instructor in electrical engineering (which he had not studied) at the University of North Carolina and thereafter settled on a career in the physical sciences. This brought him to Harvard for six years, where he accumulated scholarships and fellowships, developed his techniques on the French horn and the bass fiddle, and did graduate work on the thermodynamic properties of gases. Then came a period of industrial research, following which he entered the service of the Bureau of Mines and met Cottrell.

Of Royster, Cottrell once wrote, "I look at him as a most exceptionally brilliant and capable man." Although most people conceded Royster's brilliance, not everyone subscribed to this opinion in its entirety, for Royster had been tagged with the term "impractical." However, Cottrell's faith in Royster and his works—dubbed by him the "Royster techniques" and "bag of tricks"—was an unassailable thing that mounted at times almost to a crusade. It was a faith that Cottrell took with him to his death, and there is room for a growing belief that in some measure he was more right than wrong.

The hub of these "techniques" was the Royster stove, which was not a stove in the household sense of the word but still a stove in that it generated and stored heat. "The object of my invention," states Royster's patent, "is to provide means for heating a variety of industrially important gases, including particularly air, to higher temperatures than have heretofore been practical, and to a more nearly uniform temperature than can be obtained by such methods and devices as have been used or proposed; at the same time my invention permits the realization of a high efficiency in the use of fuel, and a saving both in cost of constructing the heating apparatus and in the cost of its upkeep and repairs. As examples of the use to which I propose to apply my process I may cite the preheating of air for combustion in blast furnaces; for preheating of air and gases for open-hearth furnaces, for heating the air or fuel for coke ovens, soaking pits, lime kilns, gas producers, and in general for any industrial furnace or process operated at elevated temperatures."

The function of the Royster stove was to transfer and store heat on what those concerned with thermodynamics refer to as the "regenerative" principle. This principle was not new with Royster. About a century before Royster began the development of his stove, Cowper in England had made a workable stove based on the same principle and modifications of it were, and still are, widely used in metallurgy, particularly in the production of iron and steel. According to Royster, Cottrell thought one phase of the fundamental principle even more ancient. The American Indian, this version goes, lacking cooking utensils that could withstand high temperatures, would find a hollow indentation on top of a rock next to which he would build a fire. Into the indentation went water, into the water went corn, and into the fire went pebbles. When the pebbles were hot enough they were scraped into the indentation which boiled the water which cooked the corn. This, Royster said, appealed to Cottrell as an admirably ingenious method on the part of primitives for the transfer of heat in two operative steps; i.e., the heat from the fire was transferred and stored in the pebbles, by which agency it was then transferred to the water and thence the corn.

Although no one ever attempted to cook corn on a Royster stove, it came closer in a mechanical sense to the alleged Indian technique than did that of Cowper. In fact Royster's ingenuity would seem to justify Cottrell's delight in an academic background of Anglo-Saxon, Sanskrit, and the bass fiddle as a prelude to a career in the thermodynamic properties of gases.

As pointed out by Royster, the Fixed Nitrogen Research Laboratory, in becoming part of the Bureau of Chemistry and Soils, took up, besides nitrogen, the investigation of two other vitally important fertilizer ingredients—phosphates and potash. Royster's first job, on coming to work for Cottrell in the laboratory, centered around researches having to do with the production of phosphate fertilizer material by smelting phosphate rock in a blast furnace. Ordinary blast-furnace practice involves the use of regenerative stoves of a conventional Cowper type. In the smelting of iron ores, for example, these stoves work somewhat in this way: the blast furnace itself is an enormous vaselike container holding the ores to be smelted, coke, and limestone. This furnace is, in fact, the cooking utensil. Attached to its base are the conventional air-blast stoves for the introduction of one of the principal smelting ingredients—very hot air, for it takes four tons of air to produce one ton of pig iron. It is the function of the stoves to preheat the air for introduction into the furnace at over 1000 degrees Fahrenheit—the temperature depending on the material to be smelted.

Both the conventional and the Royster stoves work in the same fashion to produce similar effects. When in operation, the blast furnace produces hot gases that, rather than being discharged simply as waste, are piped down into a combustion chamber in the stoves. Here these gases are mixed with air; they burn; and the resulting hotter gases are forced through whatever materials are in the stoves, put there to absorb and store the heat. In the conventional stoves this material is checker-brick deviously arranged in a rigid pattern.

The brick absorbs most of the heat and in so doing cools the gases which, being unsuitable for the smelting process itself, are then allowed to pass out the bottom of the stove. This is Step 1.

Next, valves are shut, and air—the wanted gas—is admitted into the stove, where it absorbs the heat stored in Step 1. The air, greatly expanded by this heating, then rushes into the blast furnace at a speed of several hundred miles an hour and at a temperature of over 1000 degrees Fahrenheit to become an integral part of the smelting process in the blast furnace. Several stoves are employed working in tandem so that some are storing heat from the gases while others are releasing theirs to the incoming air and thence to the furnaces, and one stove is usually in the process of being cleaned or rebuilt.

This, roughly, was the conventional technique with which Royster began his experiments on a small scale for the smelting of phosphate rock in the laboratory. It quickly developed that for phosphates he would need to work with temperatures far in excess of the 1100–1200 degrees Fahrenheit normally employed. Much higher temperatures could not be produced by the conventional types of stove for a variety of very technical reasons centering chiefly around their use of checker-brick as the heat-storing agency. Royster then had an idea and ordered a Washington sand and gravel company to dredge up a load of pebbles from the Potomac. These he screened for size, dispensed with the intricate checker-brick altogether, and simply dumped them into the stoves as heat-storers, which led a foremost expert in thermodynamics, Harvey N. Davis, to call the Royster stove with descriptive accuracy a "bucket of hot rocks." Royster, it might be added, had never previously discussed the matter with any primitive Indians.

It was not long before the pebble-bed stove was producing temperatures up to 2600 degrees Fahrenheit, which of itself brought new problems in its wake but at the same time the advantages, for some purposes, of using pebbles in place of checker-brick were becoming more apparent. The latter frequently became fouled and filmed from the hot gases, lost their thermal efficiency because of that, and had to be torn down, cleaned, and painstakingly rebuilt with tiresome and expensive regularity. When the Royster pebble-bed stove became clogged or dirty the pebbles were simply dropped out of the bottom, easily cleaned, and a fresh batch dumped in at the top. This was quick (fifteen minutes) and this was cheap (the price of pebbles). The exciting thing, though, was that Royster began discovering some amazing relations between pebbles and heat, and the more he found out the more efficient his stove became, for heat to a metallurgist is like money to the ordinary citizen—extremely difficult to store and spent with a lamentable ease.

As the experimenting continued Cottrell-Royster co-workers and colleagues began to hear the word "rheoclastic" creep into their conversations about the stoves. Those who had the courage to ask its meaning found that Royster the philologist had been at work alongside of Royster the physicist. In describing the pebble-bed for patenting purposes, Royster had used the phrase, "a bed of gas-traversable promiscuously-deposited refractory particles of relatively small diameter." Any repetitive use of this tended to give discussions a stilted turn so that Royster went back to the Greek *rheo,* to flow, and *clastic,* as an adjective meaning "broken," to convey the idea of a bed of broken solids through which a gas or other fluid could flow.

Indeed, the intellectual conjunction of Cottrell and Royster was sometimes an awesome thing for the casual bystander. Both were superbly gifted in extraordinarily diverse fields; both had highly impregnative minds; both talked with competitive swiftness. Some who saw them thus occasionally wondered which was talking and which was listening. Each had a faculty for stimulating the other, and together they often soared into rarefied technological realms where terrestrial obstacles existed only as unimportant details to the fruition of an idea. This sometimes brought results; it was sometimes just a physicist's idea of antiseptic fun.

One such discussion dwelt on Royster's stoves, which worked in pairs—one being in the process of absorbing and storing heat while the other absorbed and utilized the heat it had stored in the previous cycle. Cottrell and Royster dallied with the idea of how often such a cycle could be reversed, and a talk took place in the former's car, which Royster described as "a dilapidated device which he naïvely called an automobile."

"Royster," Cottrell inquired, "how often can you reverse valves with a pebble stove?"

Royster said evasively that it was customary to change the conventional blast-furnace stoves every hour, that open-hearth regenerators were ordinarily reversed every twenty minutes, and that water-gas checkers were reversed every five minutes.

To Cottrell this was aboriginal and a type of ingenuity unbecoming anyone except an Indian cooking corn.

"What I had in mind," he said, "was how many *thousand* times a minute could it be done?"

Royster, who for the moment assumed the conservative side of the case, replied with tact that such an idea was absurd.

Cottrell showed patience. He pointed out that he had been offered $50 for his car—more, he thought, than it was worth—and how many times did Royster think a $50 automobile engine could reverse valves? Royster quickly reached for his shoulder holster. From this he whipped out a slide rule, to which he was incurably addicted, made an adjustment with a practiced trigger finger, and gave Cottrell the news that with six cylinders at 2600 revolutions per minute his engine was reversing 15,600 valves per minute.

"Ha!" said Cottrell in triumph. "If an old $50 car can do it 15,600 times a minute you should, if necessary, be able to work your stoves up to 100,000 times a minute."

"Ha!" said Royster.

2

The letter that Cottrell wrote Poillon on July 7, 1931, describing the promising work of young Lawrence in Berkeley, might well have been one of the most important letters written in that doleful year. This may be true not only because it initiated Research Corporation's support of varied researches in nuclear physics but because it also set forth other ideas of major and minor importance. One of these in the latter category had to do with an application of Royster's stoves.

"While at Berkeley," Cottrell's letter continued after making several suggestions for the subsidizing of Lawrence's work, "I got into another promising development for Research Corporation. [The university has] in their new Life Sciences Bldg. an incinerator built in to burn up everything from waste paper and the animals' bodies to waste human anatomy from the dissecting rooms and naturally, being designed by the architect and building engineers, it gives them a good deal of annoyance from imperfect combustion and the white cloud of stench blowing down into the office windows. They asked my advice as a reputed fume 'expert' since I was 3,000 miles from home and could therefore qualify as such. It struck me that here is one more place to apply Royster's regenerative principle and if it works as I hope on this as an experimental unit, perhaps it can be applied to municipal incinerators and a host of other nuisances which arise from imperfect (or rather lack of) combustion such as oil refinery fumes, rendering kettles, paint and oil boiling, etc."

Once more Cottrell was called upon to abate a nuisance, and the Cottrell-Royster Deodorizer was born.

The Deodorizer utilized a pair of Royster stoves connected by a crossover—each stove being in its most simplified form a "bucket of hot rocks." The odorous fumes were admitted at the bottom of one stove, where they passed up through the hot pebbles, acquiring a high temperature that destroyed their malodor. These gases then went to a combustion chamber where the addition of a small amount of fuel restored heat lost in the system. They then passed downward through the second stove, where the heat was lost to that pebble bed, and in an odorless, comparatively cool state were released into the atmosphere. This second stove then received the next batch of smelly gases through its bottom, which, in rising through the pebble bed, acquired the heat left by its predecessor, lost its smell, passed through the combustion chamber, and released its heat to the first bed.

Because it was thermally efficient, inexpensive to construct, and cheap to operate, the device lived up to its name and successfully deodorized about 10,000 cubic feet of gas per minute by a method that, had the ordinary regenerative type of stove been used, would have cost too much in fuel alone to make it economically practical, to say nothing of construction and maintenance. The Deodorizer was hailed by sanitary engineers as a brilliant piece of work, and one expert—Professor Charles G. Hyde of the University of California—called it "the most notable contribution which has been made to the general art of odor destruction in recent years." This evaluation was never gainsaid but only one commercial Deodorizer was ever built, and it had a ten-year record that was enviable in the limited field of smell suppression.

Royster's patent on his stove was assigned to Research Corporation. As a legal protective device the patent had little to offer. In prosecuting the application for the patent, Royster found that the idea of the pebble-bed stove, as such, was not new. A German patent had been issued in 1880 and United States patents in 1913 and 1917; a French patent in 1925 and a British patent in 1926. Nothing much had ever been done about these, however, and his claims varied sufficiently so that he was granted a new one in 1933. It followed that if Royster's patent were to have any value at all additional patents must be taken out covering the specific applications of the stove in each case, i.e., blast-furnace smelting, oil cracking, the Deodorizer, or any of the other thirty or forty industrial processes to which it was hoped the stoves could be adapted. The writing and prosecution of thirty or forty patents, however, is consumptive of large amounts of time, energy, and money.

In the case of the Deodorizer patent Cottrell and Royster discussed the matter and it was agreed that while the stoves themselves were Royster's idea in a loosely patentable way, this particular application was a Cottrell idea and therefore the patent was taken out in his name. It was, in any case, a small point since it was assigned to Research Corporation with provision for Royster's reimbursement in the event any profits accrued.

It was not the energy and it was not the money that concerned either Cottrell or Royster when it came to patents. It was simply that both resented the time required to sit down and write about the device in a form suitable to patent lawyers and the Patent Office. Royster sometimes found it hard to describe a process without including a hypothetical but indispensable little man, name of "Joe," who watched temperatures, turned valves, and read gauges. In Cottrell's case there was a difficulty that caused his Washington patent attorney, R. E. Parker, to age more rapidly than was considered normal as a result of the hazards of his calling, for in the mere act of setting forth his patent specifications Cottrell automatically generated new ideas faster than prior ones could jell. Thus, although it was in 1931 that he first conceived the Deodorizer idea, it was four years before Cottrell found time to actually file the patent application, just beating by one year the first commercial installation, which was built in the city of Pasadena by Western Precipitation Company under a license from Research Corporation.

Pasadena had what was known as an activated sludge sewerage plant that served itself as well as three smaller adjacent towns and produced foul smells that were exceedingly impolite for so genteel a community. The complete success of the Cottrell-Royster Deodorizer here was what elicited critical raves from the sanitary engineering journals ("One of the most completely successful pieces of equipment in sewage work history") and as usual its success was a contributing factor to Cottrell's subsequent lack of interest in it. No intensive campaign of merchandising ever seems to have been undertaken for the Deodorizer, although it is also true that not many other sanitary districts had quite the same problem as Pasadena and the treatment of sludge by methods of bacterial digestion became more widespread.

Cottrell had, however, visualized a host of other uses for the Deodorizer but between the time of its conception in 1931 and the successful installation in 1936 so many other things had imprisoned his time that, far from trying to adapt it to the relief of other civic and industrial odor problems, he virtually forgot all about it. In Pasadena the Deodorizer performed cheaply and expertly until the late 1940s, when a change in the methods of sewage treatment there rendered it no longer necessary.

The Deodorizer was not by any means the only outlet for Cottrell's ingenuity in 1931. The president of Petroleum Rectifying Company, for which organization Cottrell acted as consultant, was interested in developing an American iodine industry—the iodine to be recovered from a water mixture occurring in oil wells. Cottrell took out two patents covering processes for extracting iodine and bromine from dilute brines but before these could be adequately tested the American market was saturated with Chilean iodine and the Long Beach iodine plant was shut down.

Nineteen thirty-one was a year replete with Cottrell's ideas. While still in Long Beach, he played long and lovingly with one for the conversion of salt water to fresh water, using Royster's stoves—this to be done on a scale suitable for the needs, say, of the city of Los Angeles. But this he finally admitted to the diary was impractical. He planned a sensationally new method for the fixation of atmospheric nitrogen. He returned East from the Coast in the fall excited over many things—the possibilities inherent in Lawrence's work; the new applications for Royster's stoves; and almost immediately on his return got in touch with Van de Graaff to see what help and encouragement he could give in the development of the electrostatic generator. But these were not enough and these were not all. On his trip back he stopped off in Salt Lake City and there visited his old friend J. O. Elton who, as metallurgist for the Anaconda Copper Mining Company, had helped in designing the great Cottrell precipitator installed at Anaconda. Elton, along with many other Utahans, had a proposal for damning off the Great Salt Lake in front of the mouths of two of the chief rivers in order to convert an area of 150 square miles into a fresh-water reservoir for industrial and agricultural purposes. It was a concept of a magnitude to which Cottrell was partial, and he added this to the repertoire with which he returned East. It was, Cottrell thought, the type of idea which Research Corporation could well back, at least to the extent of financing the preliminary surveys.

This was Cottrell, still effervescent, at the age of fifty-four; a man with a kindly air of intense preoccupation, his face seamed but healthy; the glasses, singly or in combination, a permanent accessory; the hairline receding and untrimmed; still wearing suits that had the look of having been removed in too many upper berths. If there was any diminution of energy it was all but imperceptible—perhaps not entirely imperceptible, for on this last visit to Berkeley he failed to take his favorite hike back of the university up through the Berkeley Hills to Grizzly Peak, where so often, beginning with his undergraduate days, he had climbed to sit and look out over the plain below, the bay beyond, the San Francisco peninsula beyond that, and the Pacific in the distance. But he did go up to the Peak, although this time he was driven in a car. Perhaps the energy was still there and the car was just a weapon against time, an ancient, remorseless enemy of Cottrell's, whose persistent attack was now waxing.

The close of the year brought a stocktaking, and on January 1, 1932, he wrote in the diary: "Had a good heart-to-heart talk [with Jess] on the plan and outlook for the years to come and I concluded that what I most needed to do was to take a more positive attitude and especially in my non-professional activities and recreation, that is, that I had probably already overdone the policy of mental relaxation that I had been trying to practice for the last couple of years. I must try to develop more (even if transient) positive interest in recreation and the little things of life."

This is a perplexing entry. There is only one piece of evidence pointing to any policy of relaxation, mental or physical, aside from some surf bathing in Long Beach, and that occurred on September 5, 1931, when he sat on the porch of the Faculty Club in Berkeley and thought enough of the experience to note in the diary that he enjoyed it and relaxed. But if that constituted a policy of the past, his new decision to accent the little things of life accounts, perhaps, for a diary entry some twenty days later during a trip to New York. He left the Chemists' Club in the evening for a walk and returned to the Chemists' Club a few hours later. He had, in the meantime, been to his first burlesque show.

3

The New Year's resolutions shared the common fate of most of the other resolutions made on the morning of January 1, 1932, by most other men, and the little things in life continued to elude Cottrell. The year passed. January 1, 1933, came and went and if he even recalled his resolve between then and the following spring it could only have been with nostalgia, for on April 10, 1933, President Roosevelt sent a special message to Congress urging the creation of the Tennessee Valley Authority and for several months Cottrell out-did even himself in a whirlwind of activity during TVA's early organizational period.

This was natural enough. Few men understood better than he the entire concept of TVA, growing as it did out of the old Muscle Shoals controversy. Too, there were few more knowledgeable men in the science of fertilizer production—the improving and cheapening of which was one of the Authority's purposes. Very likely Cottrell's experience would have been called to duty in any case, but with the appointment of Dr. Arthur E. Morgan, president of Antioch College, as Chairman of TVA, Cottrell's involvement became almost a certainty.

Morgan had long been friends with Mr. and Mrs. Dave H. Morris, who had taken over the leadership of the international auxiliary language movement from Cottrell, and when IALA was formed Morgan was appointed to its advisory board. Through this first contact Cottrell and Morgan developed a rare respect for each other's capacities. Both were too busy ever to derive much enjoyment of the friendship that followed, but of Cottrell, Morgan once wrote that "for very few persons have I had a more unalloyed admiration."

Morgan called on Cottrell for advice and help and Cottrell responded with alacrity, for it meant the fruition of many of the plans he and Senator Norris had dreamed of. A news story appeared announcing Cottrell's appointment as TVA's chief consulting chemist —a job which for Cottrell never did materialize. By his own account this had been a premature announcement and such an appointment might have conflicted in policy with his consultancy in the Department of Agriculture. Others have suggested that Cottrell's modus operandi was not always acceptable to the other two directors of TVA, Harcourt A. Morgan and David Lilienthal. In any event Cottrell was called upon for help and he gave of it freely—and this sometimes in a literal sense, for he often neglected to take the time necessary to sit down and write out an expense account. He did, in fact, only charge the Department of Agriculture $632 for four months of continuous services—services which ended when almost the entire TVA staff transferred from Washington to Knoxville. "It was," Cottrell wrote a friend, "great fun while it lasted and I felt rather lost for awhile when it rather abruptly terminated."

Royster's version of some episodes that occurred in connection with the early planning of TVA's fertilizer program indicates that Cottrell's evaluation of his TVA work as being great fun was no understatement provided one had steely nerves, the capacity to subsist on hasty sandwiches, and was disinclined to sleep. At six-thirty one morning Cottrell phoned Royster and asked him to meet with Chairman Arthur E. and Director Harcourt A. Morgan at the Willard Hotel three hours later. Cottrell, to whom few difficulties were insurmountable if one only applied oneself, also asked Royster to come prepared with a complete outline of a fertilizer production program for TVA incorporating all the techniques that had been amassed by the Department of Agriculture's Fertilizer and Fixed Nitrogen Investigations unit. In three hours, minus time for a quick shave, a hurried breakfast, and transportation, Royster drew up a tentative outline for the distillation of potash from New Jersey green sand; for the blast-furnace production of phosphoric acid from Tennessee phosphate rock; and for the fixation of nitrogen by a pair of his own stoves. He even had time to outline a chart complete with colored pencilings.

Royster was first to arrive at the meeting, followed by the two Morgans, who had not yet had a chance to meet each other, and Royster performed the introductions before Cottrell appeared. Royster then thumbtacked his chart on the wall and launched into an hour's lecture. The fact that *all* details of the program were not worked out was explained by Cottrell in an open admission that the preparation time allotted Royster had been "somewhat brief."

Between 1918, when Nitrate Plants Nos. 1 and 2 at Muscle Shoals were completed, and 1933, when the Tennessee Valley Authority was launched, the situation with regard to the production of fertilizer in the United States had changed considerably. So had the knowledge of the use of fertilizers evolved and, indeed, so had the science of soil chemistry. In the case of nitrogen, the country had developed a fixation industry that because of the depression was now producing more than farmers could buy. Emphasis, since supplies of nitrogen were adequate, had shifted to the production of phosphates, of which the United States used (circa 1940) 665,000 tons per year in the form of phosphoric acid, or more than all the nitrogen and potash—the other two essential soil nutrients—combined.

Most phosphate fertilizers are produced by the chemical treatment of phosphate rock—a commodity with which the United States is even more amply endowed than Chile was with nitrates. In the hope of cheapening production, the Department of Agriculture had once or twice taken up the smelting of rock phosphate by blast-furnace methods with some success. One of these experiments had been undertaken in 1927, when Cottrell's laboratory had broadened its scope to include phosphates and potash as well as nitrogen fixation, and he had hired Royster to carry on smelting investigations with phosphorus and potash. It was here, in trying to achieve higher temperatures, that Royster hit upon the "buckets of hot rocks."

(Cottrell and Royster in 1927 had gone even further than the mere production of phosphates. On paper they dovetailed the smelting process for that into a whole series of other production processes including that of ammonia. This seemingly had possibilities since the blast-furnace production of phosphorus and phosphoric acid produced carbon monoxide considerably in excess of the amounts needed for piping back down into the Royster stoves for combustion purposes. This excess, once one mastered the tricky step of separating it from the phosphorus vapor mixed with it, had fuel value usable as a by-product source of power to run a boiler plant which would generate enough electric energy to run carbide furnaces which would produce cyanamid which could be turned into ammonia which is the source of many other important things. Such were the concepts that abounded in the kingdom of Cottrell and Royster and no one could say they wouldn't work if only there was the money in abundance and the time in greater abundance to tinker with them in the experimental stage.)

Although Royster had achieved promising results with phosphate smelting, the Department of Agriculture lost some interest in his investigations after Cottrell's resignation as head of the laboratory in 1930. It was, however, a project Cottrell cherished and, on being consulted by TVA three years later, he convinced them that phosphates could be more cheaply produced using Royster's stoves. Moreover, he was largely responsible for arranging a contract between TVA and Research Corporation by which the latter would design and supervise a program for blast-furnace production of phosphates. From this there was not much to be expected in the way of profits for the corporation. TVA would underwrite the cost of the furnace up to $50,000 and allow the corporation 5 per cent of costs to cover overhead. It was simply Cottrell's idea that because Research Corporation held the Royster patent it stood in a good position to be of service to TVA (allowing the patent to be used royalty-free), which in turn promised to be of great public service. TVA wanted cheap fertilizers. Production by blast-furnace methods using the Royster stoves held the hope of manufacturing phosphoric acid cheaper than any other method. (The corporation did, however, have a dual interest in the development in that electrical precipitators would be necessary to collect the phosphoric acid by this method, but this consideration was one that Cottrell would never have permitted to influence his thinking.)

During 1933 and much of 1934, Cottrell and Royster with a crew of operatives worked fiercely on the construction and operation of an experimental plant on the grounds of the American University in Washington, adjacent to the laboratories where the fixed nitrogen researches had been carried out. As they managed to increase the temperatures which the Royster stoves were capable of producing far beyond those used in regular blast-furnace practice, so did they also run into problems with refractory linings for the stoves capable of tolerating such heat. Their problems were complicated by neighboring residents who complained of the occasional explosions and even fortified one complaint with threats of a warrant. But imaginations as well as coke and phosphate rock were on fire and the work went on relentlessly.

TVA, in the meantime, had gone ahead with concentrated super-phosphate production at Nitrate Plant No. 2, experimenting with electric furnaces. When Research Corporation came up with a design for a large-scale blast furnace based on the Cottrell-Royster experiments, TVA chemists and engineers found technical objections to the blast-furnace process and proceeded with the construction of more electric furnaces. If Cottrell was annoyed he left no record of petulance, although Poillon in his annual report spoke of "our ideas of operating methods to be used to reach a mutually desired end are so divergent from the methods now in use by the Authority that we find ourselves entirely divorced from the sympathetic understanding essential for future cooperation."

Cottrell's assistance to TVA was more than technological. Within a few months after the Authority's organization had been announced it received over 60,000 applications for employment—a startling index of the state of the nation. Cottrell had always been known for his willingness to help place unemployed scientists or scientists in search of a change. This he did with the utmost conscientiousness, carefully weighing each man's aptitudes and character as he knew them, balancing the man against the demands of the job. His letters to prospective employers were no hosannas but fairly pointed out weakness as well as strength. Many men, both in and out of academic circles, were indebted to him in some degree for their jobs. Since his connection, unofficial though it was, with TVA was well known in scientific circles, Cottrell gave a good deal of his time toward helping Chairman Arthur E. Morgan pick the technical men he required for such a mammoth undertaking. One of his recommendations for the important post as head of the fertilizer department was one of the country's outstanding chemists, then chief of the research and development laboratories of Vacuum Oil Company. This was Dr. Harry A. Curtis, who accepted the TVA offer and later became one of TVA's three directors.

The affairs of TVA occupied most of Cottrell's attention during 1933 and, with diminishing intensity, the early part of 1934. Great as were its problems and his application to them, it did not preclude his perennial interest in men with other problems. One of these was Dr. Morris S. Kharasch, of the University of Chicago, who was to provide Research Corporation with the first patents (since Cottrell's precipitation patents) to return appreciable royalties and which in turn heightened the corporation's interest in a field new to it, biologicals and pharmaceuticals—a turn of affairs that was later to have highly important results.

Cottrell and Kharasch were old acquaintances. They had first met in 1922 during Cottrell's chairmanship of the Division of Chemistry and Chemical Technology of the National Research Council. Kharasch then received the council's first fellowship in chemistry, and when Cottrell arrived in Chicago at that time to look over Kharasch's work for the council the latter had made up his mind to desert the university and go into industrial research.

Cottrell spent a half day dissuading him.

"What," he inquired of Kharasch, "would be the minimum grant that would induce you to stay?"

Kharasch remembered that he asked "a fantastic $3,000 and he told me to let him worry about it. What's more, he got it for me."

The paths of Cottrell and Kharasch next crossed when the latter, while at the University of Maryland, accepted a consultancy in Cottrell's Fixed Nitrogen Research Laboratory.

"We talked a great deal then about Research Corporation and the necessity for it," Kharasch recalled. "He thought anyone who made any money out of science should put something back into it, and he thought also that the younger men should get the support rather than the older ones who were established and had better chance of getting it. He not only helped me to get the right slant on research in general but also taught me the responsibility of the scientist to the community."

In such matters Kharasch proved an apt pupil. In 1932, Cottrell recommended to Poillon that Kharasch receive a grant from Research Corporation for his researches in ergot which, although in universal use to control hemorrhage and contract the uterus in childbirth, had deleterious properties and deteriorated with age. Kharasch developed ergotrate and, in recognition of Cottrell's spiritual and the corporation's material aid, assigned his patent to the Research Corporation, which in turn supervised its licensing. Royalties from this coming to the corporation have in some years been as high as $35,000, which go out to a newer generation of hopeful young researchers. Kharasch did not stop there. When he later developed the antiseptic merthiolate, this patent, too, was similarly assigned with the resulting royalties amounting to almost as much as those for ergotrate.

The restless, helping hand of Cottrell next stretched farther west than Chicago, beyond Berkeley and to Japan. At the time he attended the World Engineering Congress in Tokyo in 1929 he met a Dr. Herbert H. Greger, a Czechoslovakian about thirty years old, then professor of fuel technology at the Akita (Japan) Mining College. After five years of research Greger had, or thought he had, reduced the principle of the gas fuel cell to a point where it might be possible to adapt it to industrial uses. If Greger was right, and Cottrell was enthusiastic enough to think there was a chance he might be, a practical fuel cell would have great potentialities especially in electrochemical and electrometallurgical fields. Gas cells had long been dreamed of as a means of converting fuel gas (e.g., natural gas) directly into electrical energy and doing so with an efficiency that would render electrical power cheaper than steam power. A workable gas fuel cell, in short, would be a prime power source—a fact of intense interest to a world as voracious of energy for its machines as it is of food for its population.

The status of research in Japan at that time was too tightly hitched to the requirements of the Army and Navy for Greger to arouse any degree of interest in industry there, and so about a year after their first meeting he turned to Cottrell for advice. Cottrell promptly added Greger's reports to the other projects in his crowded briefcase which invariably accompanied him to meetings of the American Chemical Society, the American Association for the Advancement of Science, the Electrochemical Society, into conferences, into laboratories, into offices, and into homes. Whenever he met anyone who might have a companion interest in a briefcased item the material came out, the talk flowed.

Greger had also forwarded a working model of his cell, and on one of these occasions Cottrell persuaded Dr. Arthur B. Lamb, of Harvard, to test it. At another meeting he got Willard H. Dow, of Dow Chemical Company, interested and submitted Greger's reports to him for investigation. There were others, too, such as the laboratories of Union Carbide, who began to hear of Greger's fuel cell, but the returns were not of a single mind. Lamb's laboratory verified Greger's claims in a general way and appeared very much interested in the results, but Dow's researcher, on checking without benefit of the model, replied, "As a whole, one cannot help but have a high regard for the intelligence of a person who can write such a clever report. It is either the work of a slick promoter or of an impractical theorist."

Greger, in truth, was neither, nor did such a reply have any dampening effect on Cottrell, who kept the project in the briefcase stage until 1933, by which time he thought well enough of the idea and Greger to invite him to America. At first Cottrell was hopeful that this could be done through a Research Corporation grant to some such institution as Stevens Institute of Technology which might in turn use it to employ Greger for further development of the fuel cell. But Poillon had objections or, as Cottrell cautiously stated the matter to Greger, "the fact that several from among the numerous scientists and especially inventors whom I have in the past brought the Corporation in contact with have proved unreasonable or otherwise impossible to work with, and even the entire closing out of our relations with them including return of the patents or ideas they brought with them has not always terminated the complications they got us into."

There had been such inventors. To Cottrell, they simply furnished the normal hazards one encountered in dealing with such precocious people. A scratch beneath their surface peculiarities might reveal gold. But to Poillon, who in the end had to bear the brunt of the administrative migraine they could cause, they were anathema. Never having met Greger, Poillon was wary.

The solution to the problem of financing Greger lay in an action taken earlier in 1933 by the Executive Committee of Research Corporation, which voted that a sum of $7500 be set aside for the joint use of Cottrell and Poillon to "further the purposes of the Corporation" in any way they might see fit. With this support Cottrell wrote Greger, who surely became one of the happiest scientists in Japan when he found out that a monthly salary of $300 would be guaranteed him in America for one year.

It was Greger who solved the mystery of why Cottrell's plans, laid with the Institute of Physical and Chemical Research in Tokyo in

1929, had not succeeded. As a trial, Cottrell had had Research Corporation offer the Institute the patent rights on a method for testing the sharpness of razor blades by means of a corona discharge from the blade. It was a trivial thing but possibly useful as a beginning. What he could scarcely have realized was that there were delicate oriental overtones to the achievement of scientific internationalism inextricably mixed with national sensibilities. The Japanese, Greger explained, considered shaving an intimate matter of the toilet. Particularly because of the hairy aborigines in northern Japan, the mere suggestion to a cultured Japanese that shaving might be a necessity was almost an insult. For months Cottrell had wondered why Okochi of the Institute had never acknowledged receiving the razor-blade patents. In answer to a second letter Okochi had cabled back a terse reply that said only that they had arrived. The razor-blade scheme died there, although Cottrell found the idea of such international co-operation too tempting to forget and later tried again with a much more important discovery.

The range of Cottrell's major interests in the early thirties included one other project, and this centered around the laboratory in the Smithsonian which had been allotted for his use and in which he had installed Chester Gilbert, the former president of the American Coal Corporation. Gilbert, prior to his unhappy experience with merchandising coal, had been a consulting engineer of wide experience in fuels. When Cottrell received the mysterious $6000 "honorarium" for which Abbot of the Smithsonian acted as go-between, he used most of the money to set up a laboratory in connection with the Smithsonian and assigned Gilbert the job of investigating the production of a lime-gypsum plaster based on some patents which the Research Corporation had accepted from a particularly irascible inventor. Gilbert's tests showed these patents to produce no particular economies or improvements over other plasters but, as so often happens in the course of experimenting, he became interested in another idea which had to do with a nuisance called fly ash.

Of all the myriad items snatched from smokestacks by Cottrell precipitators, one of the least dramatic is fly ash. This unwelcome commodity comes as a result of blowing and burning powdered coal in a furnace, particularly as is done in steam power plants, and one result—if such plants have dust-collecting installations—is the burden of collected fly ash. Along seaboards, the practice usually was to take it out to sea for dumping, but inland its disposal was a nagging problem.

The Gilbert-Cottrell problem was what to do with fly ash—a mixture of minute particles of various sizes, many of which are tiny, thin-walled, hollow bubbles of glass. Other investigators had been and were still working on this nuisance, but Gilbert and Cottrell thought they could devise a method of eliminating unburned carbon and iron, recover the particles of less than 1/5000th of an inch, which would then have the smoothness of a talc, and use it as a filler in cements and plasters, thus imparting lightness without loss of strength to concrete; lightness and increased workability to plaster.

The talclike quality of the finer particles of fly ash gave rise to another possibility. Most of the household cleaning powders and cleansers on the market at the time depended for their scouring properties on a vitreous grit loaded with soap—the grit usually being either volcanic ash or silex. In spite of advertised claims, these scratched some surfaces, as could be determined easily if used to clean microscope slides which were then microscopically examined. The processed fly ash, Gilbert and Cottrell found, did not scratch glass. While this was no earth-shaking discovery that would revolutionize scientific thought, still, as long as they were on the problem of fly ash, the collection of which was directly related to the process of electrical precipitation, it was worth looking into.

Gilbert had made enough progress at the Washington laboratory so that when Cottrell declined the second honorarium Research Corporation felt justified in allotting a sum to maintain the laboratory partly for its own sake, partly as a means of providing facilities for testing out other ideas submitted to the corporation, but largely as a focal point for Cottrell's energies. They did not foresee it as the mote, the speck of dust around which Cottrell's ideas and those of his protégés, like so many particles of moisture, would begin to coalesce to form the drop of rain. The result was a new and ill-starred venture called Research Associates Inc.

4

Without any suspicion of what the end might be, Research Corporation embarked on one of its most spectacularly successful policies in 1931 and 1932 when it began to support various researches in the field of nuclear physics. If, at that point, it had paused to reckon the results of its previous twenty years of existence, it must have done so with misgivings. Although it had in most of those years successfully operated an electrical precipitation business, that was the means and not the end. True, it had given the Smithsonian Institution enough money to establish and help maintain its Division of Radiation and Organisms. It had, in those twenty years, made a total of almost twenty-five grants (of from $500 to $23,000) for scientific studies at the Smithsonian and other institutions. But while it had made sincere efforts to carry out another of its purposes—the acceptance of patents and the development of inventions as had once been done with the Cottrell process itself—the results to date had been negative. It might seem in theory that the country harbored thousands of lone inventors in search of an altruistic organization willing to help him apply his idea commercially. But those devices that were perfectable and marketable within the corporation's means were so few as to be almost non-existent. The corporation had spent thousands of dollars on many of these, but none so far had paid for itself. Cottrell himself had admittedly lost by this time some of his enthusiasm for the service he had hoped Research Corporation could perform in this way.

His enthusiasm may have waned temporarily but that did not mean that he had lost hope. Nor did it mean anything akin to despair when, in 1932, the precipitation business all but died amidst the funereal dirges of most other American businesses during the depression and the corporation began to subsist off its reserves. In fact, thought Cottrell brightly, just such circumstances might furnish the corporation with the opportunity to proceed with the development of new products and new processes while its energies were temporarily deflected from the usually all-consuming precipitation work. The establishment of the laboratory in Washington to study the possibilities of utilizing fly ash had already been a step in this direction, and as the years of the depression deepened and Cottrell's collection of men with techniques and ideas grew, so did his conviction that the time had come to undertake new developments both for their own sake and because he had always thought that in such a course lay one of Research Corporation's greatest opportunities.

There was a difference now, though, in his thinking. This may have come about both as a result of the corporation's experiences with the lone inventor (which he himself had once been) and because in the years that had intervened since the corporation's founding research both pure and applied had grown and evolved to a point where the most promising and effective work was being done not by an isolated individual tinkering away in a basement but in universities, in research organizations, and, in particular, in the industrial research laboratory. In 1935, the year Research Associates Inc. was formally organized, for example, Du Pont announced a new type of rayon to be used in tire construction; Eastman Kodak described the "Kodachrome" process for making amateur motion pictures in color; the B. F. Goodrich Company announced a new plastic called "Koroseal"; lithium chloride solutions of high concentration were successfully used in the drying and conditioning of air; Libbey-Owens-Ford marketed a tempered glass. Perhaps most striking of all as an index of inventive development was the fact that in that year the Patent Office issued its two millionth patent—its millionth having been issued only twenty-four years earlier at the time Cottrell was forming Research Corporation. In that brief interval the U. S. Patent Office, if it had allowed itself no holidays, had decided on an average of about 114 times each day that a new idea, or a modification or adaptation of an old idea, was deserving of legal protection. These waters were too warm and turgid, the sun too bright, the air too winy to keep a man of Cottrell's temperament from riding such mounting waves of technical thought.

The first plunge came in the fall of 1934 when Cottrell acted as host at a dinner at the Cosmos Club in Washington. The Cosmos Club, along with the Chemists' Club in New York, had long served him as a spiritual home, redolent as it sometimes could be with the tang of ideas bruited about by Washington scientists on whom its membership heavily depended. Cottrell's proposal to form a new corporation separate from Research Corporation had of course been much discussed and finally approved by the officers and directors of the latter, the understanding being that Research Corporation would underwrite the infant organization. Accompanying this decision was a stern parental admonition that the fledgling make every attempt to become self-supporting at the earliest opportunity. The very fact that Research Corporation was willing to assume such a risk at such a time spoke well for both Cottrell the salesman and the filial sense of responsibility in the corporation he had sired, although Cottrell openly suspected that he was being supported in the movement largely "to protect their nerves against too direct impact from my varied enthusiasms."

There were gathered then as Cottrell's guests on the night of November 6, 1934, in the worn leather-chair atmosphere of the Cosmos Club: William McClellan, president of the Potomac Electric Power Company; Gardner Jackson, a newspaperman and writer prominent in early New Deal Washington; C. E. Julihn, a Bureau of Mines engineer who had been Cottrell's deputy in the Pony truck affair; F. S. Brackett, the physicist whom Cottrell had lured from Berkeley into the Fixed Nitrogen Research Laboratory; Chester G. Gilbert, former president of the American Coal Company, who was now investigating fly ash in the Smithsonian laboratory of Research Corporation; Dr. William C. White, a prominent physician identified with medical research; a Professor Charles S. Collier; James M. Landis, of the Securities and Exchange Commission (later chairman of the Civil Aeronautics Board); and Watson Davis, director of Science Service.

The decision was to organize. Collier dropped out and two mildly obscure government men were brought in. Landis, while not a member of the Associates, agreed to draw up a charter.

The charter, in spirit, was not very much different from that of Research Corporation. There was no capital stock (wherein it differed from its parent) and no profit was to accrue to any member. The accent was to be on research with a view to bringing the subjects investigated into practical, everyday use. Any earnings would be distributed in much the same manner as in Research Corporation, although the emphasis would be on spending surpluses in still newer developments through the Associates' own organization rather than through the Smithsonian and the universities.

The language of the charters of Research Corporation and Research Associates Inc. did differ on one point that, in retrospect, seems more a matter of semantics than of actual fact. This point accurately reflected both the thinking and jargon of the time when the term "social-economic" was more popular than clear, and true to this the charter refers to the new organization as "this social-economic experiment." Exactly what was meant by this was not concisely stated, although a press release (written by Gardner Jackson) called particular attention to that phase of the charter and stated that the Associates "can foresee the possibility of an immediate and increasing field of usefulness in that direction. We cite the subsistence homestead problem as an example and the possibility of developing new industrial operations beneficial to areas in which subsistence communities may be established." The thought was not further elaborated either in this or in any other document bearing on the activities of Research Associates Inc. Probably this aim of the Associates was embodied in the idea of bringing worth-while products out of the laboratory and into the market with a minimum time lag, thereby creating new industries to employ more men.

Eleven days after the first meeting at the Cosmos Club, and before the organization was legally born or had a chance to establish itself in a new laboratory, the Associates had their first customer. This was the very important Freeport Sulphur Company of New Orleans, which sought Cottrell's advice in the manner of many who had found it useful to "ask Cot." Freeport was having trouble in its Grand Ecaille (Louisiana) field, finding the sulphur deposits discolored by oil and coaly matter. While this was nearly always true of new deposits, and a condition that gradually cleared up, the problem at Grand Ecaille had persisted for over a year. Freeport had developed a method for reducing the carbonaceous matter but were still unsatisfied with the resulting color of the sulphur. Cottrell told his inquirers of the proposed research organization, and Freeport authorized a tentative $1500 to investigate. This was not exactly social-economic in spirit but it undeniably was income.

The Freeport bid for services may have been the touchstone that, even before the charter was drawn up, stretched Cottrell's elastic imagination to the point of critical vibration, for within a month of receiving the query he was seriously considering the advisability of establishing not one but two new corporations. The first of these would attend to such problems as Freeport's, but the second would handle power matters exclusively and in this category Cottrell included Greger's fuel cell, a gas turbine of Royster's which interested Cottrell as one of the "Royster techniques," and possibly some applications of Van de Graaff's electrostatic generator.

However, before these elaborated plans became anything more than embryonic, the Articles of Incorporation of Research Associates Inc. were signed on January 3, 1935, and three weeks later an election produced Cottrell as president, Gilbert as vice-president and general manager, Brackett as secretary, and Julihn as treasurer. This meeting also brought out some other important facts. Of the $25,000 Research Corporation had allotted to subsidize the Associates, almost half had already been spent in forming the new organization and in setting up a downtown Washington office as well as laboratory facilities at American University—the quarters in the Smithsonian being too small and the Institution's officials unhappy about a small fire that had started during the course of Gilbert's experiments with fly ash. The state of the treasury led the Associates to decide to make themselves self-supporting within four months since the payroll alone amounted to $2817 monthly. This was a brash and ambitious program for any new organization in any year. In 1935 it wore the face of madness.

Yet Cottrell had always favored and had often succeeded in the bold course, and the initial luck which had attended many of his ventures did not desert him now. On a trip to New Orleans early in January he had convinced Freeport of the applicability of the Royster stoves as one approach to the solution of their sulphur problems, and the result was a contract with a retainer of $1250 a month plus certain costs. Copies of this agreement had scarcely reached the new files of the Associates when Atlantic Refining Company approached Cottrell with one of their worries—some four thousand miles of pipe line were showing serious signs of corrosion owing to minute quantities of water held in true solution in gasoline and other distilled products. For a fee only slightly less than that charged Freeport, the Associates undertook to design a dehydrating plant capable of removing about half a ton of water daily from some 25,000 barrels of gasoline.

Here were two contracts that would ordinarily have delighted most new research organizations. Together they guaranteed an income of $25,000 for one year—the first year of the Associates' existence. It brought some cheer to Research Corporation, which at the annual meeting of the Board of Directors urged Cottrell to continue such consulting assignments as a means of making ends meet until new products could be developed and marketed. The Board was gratified by the fact that between these two contracts and the original gift of $25,000 it had itself authorized, the Associates were able to show for 1935 an excess of income over outgo of $15,012.60. From the standpoint of money, the start was promising.

But Cottrell had other views. Although he was willing to accept contracts of that nature if they came along, such was not the main purpose of Research Associates Inc. He considered it dangerous to start off as a firm of consulting chemists and engineers when the organization had really been formed to pursue projects he thought of as having great potential industrial significance and into which social values could also be read. Cottrell was far from disappointed, therefore, when early in 1936 both Freeport and Atlantic decided against renewing their contracts. This did not come about because of any flaws in the work of the Associates. For the sulphur problem the Cottrell group had come up with two solutions to the discoloration, one of which involved Royster's stove and the other a method of direct filtration. Both worked in laboratory practice. In the meantime, however, Freeport had devised its own distillation process, which seemed to cure the trouble, and favored spending its money and energy on that. Almost the same thing happened with Atlantic. The dehydrating plant which the Associates devised met with the competition of Atlantic's own method of using chemical inhibitors. Both Freeport and Atlantic expressed themselves as well satisfied with the work that had been done for them, then set about to pursue their own ways.

5

"People with money," Poillon once wrote Cottrell, "seldom have imagination and people with imagination seldom have money." If Research Associates Inc. had ever felt the need of a motto, this could have served. They faced, in 1936 and subsequent years, nothing but troubles and yet the laboratory staff, at least in retrospect, was a relatively happy group possessed of an esprit de corps and able to work part of the time with a complete sense of freedom. The defects of this organization were most apparent at the end of each accounting period when, after 1935, the income side of the ledgers was (with the exception of grants made by Research Corporation) an interesting study in small but very round circles that made decimal points a luxury.

To Cottrell the men in the laboratory were his "zoo," a term in which the staff itself found relish, although in the offices of Research Corporation in New York some of them were simply referred to as "Cottrell's black cats." There was the erratically brilliant Royster, in whose stoves alone Cottrell found a *raison d'être* for the formation of Research Associates Inc. It was Cottrell's hope that these stoves, when properly developed, would act as a mainstay for Research Associates Inc. just as his own electrical precipitation process had once done for Research Corporation. Then there was Greger, the Czechoslovakian from Japan, who had a feel for the artistry of experiment and who contributed a continental technique to the laboratory. There was Brackett the physicist, as gifted as he was unamenable to regimentation. There was Chester Gilbert, who as general manager of the organization tried to strike a balance between conducting the Associates' business and pursuing his own engineering assignments in the laboratory. To these principals were added four junior chemists and technicians, as well as a small bevy of secretaries.

With the termination of the two consulting contracts in 1936 the Associates undertook with a show of earnestness to develop some marketable products. To the $15,000 surplus from the previous year Research Corporation added $37,100 dollars, parceled out in smaller amounts that were granted with increased misgivings as the year wore on. For these doubts there were many reasons but it was a curious turn of affairs since Research Corporation, once an untested organization radical of concept and unsure of itself, was now in the position of a conservative parent whose headstrong and profligate offspring was in danger of exhausting its resources.

One frankly experimental aim of Research Associates Inc. was to see if research-development could become self-supporting. This purpose had been deflected in the first year of its existence by the consulting contracts, which left only 5 per cent of its time for other projects. The program for 1936 was different. Development would concentrate on Royster's stoves as a long-term project while immediate attention would be given to several products which the Associates thought would have income-producing possibilities in a matter of months.

One of these was the Brackett headlight for automobiles and trucks—a headlight which was constructed to concentrate its beams below the horizontal and, it was hoped, reduce glare to a minimum.

While it was called the Brackett headlight, the suggestion for such had actually come from Poillon, and Brackett—whose specialty in physics was in the field of spectroscopy—was assigned to produce it. Brackett did design a very good headlight that satisfied most of those who tested it in night driving but, as the Associates already knew, a good product was not necessarily a commercially successful product. To the problem of patents was added that of having the headlight meet the requirements of different states whose motor vehicle bureaus were not always in accord. Moreover, the field was found to be highly competitive and other headlights were being developed that promised to do just as much using fewer parts. The question then arose, should the design of the Brackett headlight be frozen as it stood in order to get into production which might mean sales which might mean badly needed revenue, or should Brackett continue to improve it to meet threatened competition?—a fundamental production question that Research Associates Inc. was by no means either the first or last to meet and not to answer.

The headlight was not the only product the Associates thought susceptible to immediate merchandising. In conducting his researches on the utilization of fly ash, Gilbert had found a preponderance of the material made up of tiny thin-walled hollow spherules, or bubbles, of glass. As a less important use, he thought of such spherules as an ingredient of soaps and cleansers instead of the commonly used splinterlike particles of such materials as volcanic ash which, his researches indicated, tended to have an abrasive effect on sensitive skins. From the fly-ash spherules came the idea of using scrap glass itself, ground up and put through a burner to create minute spherules. These, when mixed with a detergent, should produce a really efficient, heavy-duty hand soap. When this was tried the resulting product (according to a report made by the Associates) was found to have "rather more of a decided odor than might be permissible for a boudoir or even a general family soap or cleaning preparation but this would not be so much of a handicap in most of the places where mechanics' hand soap is contemplated."

It was evident that there would be no money in the beginning years of the organization to do any intensive work on Greger's fuel cell, so Greger was assigned to the spherule-soap program. In the process of working on a detergent suitable for combining with the glass spherules Greger compounded a pure jellylike material that had many of the properties of old-fashioned glycerin soap. It had an organic base, was free of alkali, and, together with a solvent, was found to have a remarkable cleansing effect. This was christened Dermagell and minus the spherules was thought to be marketable as a cleansing cream in the cosmetic field. Then, when used with spherules, it was considered adaptable to the manufacture of high-grade toilet soap. There was also talk of a shaving cream and, inevitably, a shampoo.

This, perhaps, was progress but it was not a direction of progress of which the Associates were particularly proud. They had started out two years earlier with high hope to match a high ideal. They had succeeded after two years in producing a good headlight whose competitive value was dubious and a possible line of soap products. True, they knew that this was potboiling; that their immediate concern was revenue to pursue more significant findings; that these were merely means to an end. But, aside from the headlight, what they had stumbled into was about the most competitive merchandising field in America, and while there were among them salesmen of ideas, it could not be said that any of them were peddlers of soaps.

Aside from the soaps and the headlights, there were two minor income-producing possibilities. One was a process for roasting fuller's earth (used as a filtering agent) which had in turn grown out of an earlier and independent development—the Briggs clarifier. The Briggs clarifier was an oil filter primarily designed for auto engines, and of this Gilbert was a co-patentee. In return for certain developmental work done in the Associates' laboratory they were to receive stock in the Briggs Clarifier Company. While years later this filter met with some commercial success, it was not in time or under circumstances that would have brought any cash benefits to the Associates.

The disparity between their hopes and their achievements led the Associates to consider another move. They decided that it would be best to form still another corporation, Research Products Development Corporation, to be financed in the same way Research Corporation had originally been financed, and this concern would handle the potboilers while Research Associates Inc. itself would go on with more important work. Articles of Incorporation were drawn up, ways and means were discussed, but before any further action could be taken it became all too apparent that, when viewed from the offices of Research Corporation in New York, Research Associates Inc. had the most doubtful of futures.

There Poillon, too, had a genuine interest in scientific research and in the beginning had given the Associates his modulated blessings. His job, however, was to run Research Corporation at a profit and from that profit science could be subsidized. If you had no profit and subsidized no science there was not much reason in having a Research Corporation. To overlook this fundamental point was, in his opinion, openly to court disaster. By the end of 1936 he thought he saw such an ominous possibility in Research Associates' draining off the corporation's assets to a point where the corporation itself was in danger. In this the Executive Committee of Research Corporation concurred so that at their September 1936 meeting a resolution was passed by the committee to the effect that future support of the Associates would be determined by the results accomplished as of January 1, 1937. The Executive Committee appointed a special committee later in December 1936. This, composed of five directors, was named the Committee on Research Associates Inc. and was instructed to go down to Washington to see what was going on and report back to the Board of Directors at the annual meeting in January 1937.

It was a worrisome situation. No one, including Poillon, was anxious to cut off Cottrell's project from the support of the corporation he had founded. "I am," Poillon wrote Cottrell, "in a very uncomfortable position. . . . Please believe me when I say it is giving me sincere concern and worry." Cottrell's attitude on this point was, superficially at least, one of relative serenity. This he had earlier written to Gilbert: "I'm perhaps less hesitant than you to rely, if necessary, on turning to Research Corporation to help us through the first couple of years . . . and in fact am not sure that it is not a perfectly good policy to establish such a precedent ahead of time when we may need it more drastically and in a hurry much as one does in establishing business credit at a bank. They certainly have larger cushioning resources than we, and we are all pursuing the same ultimate end closely enough so I don't feel disposed to stand on ceremony or technical distinction too much if we are really convinced that the money is definitely *needed* for the *best* interests of the project as a whole."

The five directors of Research Corporation who formed the committee to look into the Associates' affairs were under the chairman-ship of Karl T. Compton, then president of Massachusetts Institute of Technology. The other members were Elon Hooker, of Hooker Electrochemical Company; Charles A. Stone, of the engineering firm of Stone and Webster; Isaiah Bowman, president of Johns Hopkins University; and Joseph W. Barker, dean of the faculty of engineer-ing at Columbia University. Their trip to the laboratory of Research Associates Inc. early in January 1937 had some of the atmosphere of a parents' visiting day at Central High.

By and large the committee was impressed, mainly with Royster's stoves, although some of them had not heard of its very successful application to the Pasadena Deodorizer. (When Cottrell later pointed this out to Poillon the latter replied that it was the usual situation with directors who were not in day-to-day touch with ac-tivities of the corporation.) Royster and Cottrell were, at this time, experimenting with linings for the stoves that they hoped could withstand temperatures up to 1980 degrees centigrade and described to the committee some of the myriad ways in which they thought the stoves could be used industrially once the problem of finding materials tolerant of such temperatures was solved.

Although the committee was impressed, still it was disturbed by the inability of the Associates to bring any single line of investiga-tion to a point of application. Nevertheless when the annual meeting of the Board of Directors took place two weeks later the directors allotted $30,000 to the Associates for the year providing the Associ-ates would program their projects efficiently, properly budget their money and time, and adopt a priority plan of development—the Royster stoves to take precedence. Cottrell, who attended the meet-ing, noted that Hooker was "most drastic in demand for control of our work and plans . . . Barker and rest of committee more moderate . . . Poillon came to our rescue insisting on a 'sympa-thetic approach.'" The result was that Barker was appointed to supervise the plans and finances of the Associates, visit Washing-ton once a month for that purpose, and report back the progress made to the corporation's Executive Committee.

For a time the horizon cleared. A large lime company with plants in Missouri and Illinois showed an interest in the stoves and talked with some enthusiasm of building a pilot plant at Hannibal, Mis-souri. Then another optimistic touch was added when some of Cottrell's friends interested the Detroit Edison Company in Greger's fuel cell, and Detroit Edison agreed to underwrite its development for a limited period in their own laboratories. But the arrival of mid-summer still brought no refreshing revenue, so emphasis was switched from the investigation of Royster's stoves to sales of the Brackett headlight and Dermagell in an effort to meet the pay roll. But production of the headlight met delay in the delivery of parts and mirrors, and it was Dermagell, the product of which they were least proud, that reached the market first.

Dermagell, reported the women's page of the Washington *Daily News* on August 19, "is neither a cold cream nor a soap but a cleanser which has certain characteristics of both." The *Daily News* went on to describe how Dermagell's properties had been discovered when, during "routine tests" in the Associates' laboratory, a certain basic compound was found to have cleared up a chronic case of acne with which one of the staff members had been afflicted for years (it *had* seemed to clear up a rash on a relative of one of Cottrell's friends). Two days before this announcement Cottrell had written Poillon that "the boys have turned my office into a soap factory and have thus far filled and largely labeled and packed between 2,000 and 3,000 jars of Dermagell." An advertising agency was given the account and via both press and radio Washington began to hear of Dermagell. Distribution, too, got under way, and on the evening of August 22, Cottrell took a drive down Massachusetts Avenue to see a Dermagell display in a drugstore window.

Many of those who used Dermagell praised it highly, and it does seem to have been a superior product in its field. It reached the New York market in minute quantities, and at one time or another several large drug houses evinced a preliminary interest in taking it over. The advertising agency, however, got too ecstatic about Dermagell and ultimately the Federal Trade Commission issued them a cease and desist order in regard to some of the claims made.

As a David of a product matched against the Goliaths of the cosmetic industry, it was almost doomed from the start and the merchandising miracle that could have saved it did not materialize. Before it died it furnished one moment of pathos when an order came in from a Madison Avenue druggist in New York replacing his dozen jars of Dermagell, which had been sold out. This aroused Cottrell's curiosity, and on his next trip to New York he visited the pharmacy on the upper East Side to see what had caused so promising a flurry in such a rich market. The druggist had no need to consult his records, for the twelve jars had all gone to one customer —Cottrell's old friend in the International Auxiliary Language Association, Alice Vanderbilt Morris.

The headlight, too, ran into difficulties in addition to those of production. Brackett and Poillon disagreed on some points as to the way its development should proceed, as well as over the handling of the patent. The headlight died.

That left Royster's stoves of the major projects, and the promise here, too, gradually faded. It was Research Corporation's claim that, despite solemn agreement on the part of both Cottrell and Royster to proceed with the experimentation on the stoves in accordance with a definite schedule and budget, neither schedule nor budget was adhered to for any coherent periods of time. The corporation felt that Cottrell and Royster, instead of concentrating, were trying to apply the stoves in too many ways at once. Cottrell, for his part, complained at least once that Research Corporation had saddled the Associates with such a closely supervised schedule that there was no time either for him or Royster to work up plans and estimates to be furnished to those industries (Marblehead Lime, Humphreys Phosphate, and Freeport Sulphur) that had shown themselves willing to consider an installation.

The end, or almost the end, came on December 21, 1937, when Research Corporation called a special meeting of the directors to consider the fate of the Associates. Cottrell was not present but later Poillon phoned him that the decision had been to grant an additional $4500 to give them time to arrange for alternative support. This news Cottrell reported in a letter to a friend that same evening and if in that decision he read the failure of Research Associates Inc. it did not leave a sufficiently bitter taste to quench his appetite for organizing. "I think I talked to you when here last," this letter continued, "about my idea of forming a Power Method & Equipment Company as one might call it, which would develop, license, and probably eventually construct and install new inventions in power production, distributing and applying devices. . . . [The] chief, if not exclusive, stockholders might well be the public utility companies and scientific endowments, universities and other welfare and educational endowments. Some of these of late have been casting about for new forms of investments and have shown a willingness to consider a much wider and less conservative or at least orthodox range of securities than formerly." Here Cottrell thought again of the Greger fuel cell, of reaching further into Royster's bag of tricks for a radiation boiler and a gas turbine, of some of Van de Graaff's contributions to electrostatic generation and transmission, and of a more recent Cottrell interest, the Southgate rectifier.

But defeat did not come easily to Cottrell, and as 1937 merged into 1938 he still clung to the idea of an alternative means of support for the Association for whom the $4500 granted by Research Corporation offered a brief lease on life. Operating expenses had been reduced to about $1700 a month and when by February 1938 these had all but exhausted the grant Cottrell pulled a last ace from the hole. Several years earlier Western Precipitation Company had reorganized into Western Precipitation Corporation, and as Cottrell's share of the surplus resulting from the new financial setup he was given a promissory note. This note, representing his own assets, he endorsed over to Research Corporation and against it he drew as the dwindling business of the Associates required. "I am sorry," wrote his old friend Walter Schmidt, "that you felt it incumbent on you to sell the Western Precipitation Corporation note to Research Corporation in order to meet obligations to your men. However, you no doubt find more happiness and satisfaction in giving it away than in keeping it, so there is no reason for our having any objections."

Cottrell's shredding optimism held out through February, through March, and into April, although the strain was beginning to show in diary references to "nerves," "restless night," and "feeling very tired." As the hot Washington summer set in, little heat flashes of hope occasionally flickered on the horizon and kept him in a tantalized state of expectancy that a last-minute reprieve for the Associates was in sight. Most of these were generated by the consciousness with which America was then beginning to view its shortages in strategic metals. (Headline in the Washington Post, April 11, 1938: "Hitler Wins 99.75 of Vote in Austria for 'Greater Reich.'") In this situation Cottrell saw opportunities for Royster's stoves, particularly for the smelting of run-of-the-mine manganese ores into ferromanganese— a project on which he and Royster had been experimenting intermittently for several years. The Cuban-American Manganese Corporation (an affiliate of Freeport Sulphur) thought they would be interested in such a project, but Cottrell objected to some monopoly suggestions that came up in preliminary discussions. Anaconda Copper Mining Company went so far as to ship six tons of manganese ores to Washington for tests but by the time they arrived Cottrell found himself "much embarrassed over the position we find ourselves in with this project" since there was no money left to conduct experiments and Anaconda did not feel disposed to underwrite the project. A titanium alloy manufacturing company also made overtures, but the only arrangement that ultimately developed was with Pickands Mather & Company of Cleveland, operators of iron ore mines and blast furnaces, who engaged Royster for studies on the production of ferromanganese from low-grade ores using his own techniques.

This was the end of Research Associates Inc., an enterprise of which Gilbert had written Poillon in 1934, during the early stages of its formation, that Cottrell looked upon it as "the one genuine opportunity remaining open to his life." Its dissolution did not necessarily prove that scientific and technical research could not be made to pay its own way. If it proved anything at all, it was that the success of such an objective was highly improbable unless adequate time and capital were both supported by skillful, disciplined administration. Too, from its experiences one could also conclude that research-development and merchandising-distribution are two separate fields and the twain are loath to meet in the atmosphere of a laboratory. But no one of these points had Cottrell really set out either to prove or disprove. His primary interest had been to show that some industries had much to gain from using Royster's stoves.

The year for that, however, had not yet arrived.

6

As the fortunes of Cottrell ebbed the greater was the public recognition he received as a scientist, although no connection existed between these two sets of conditions.

In 1937 he was notified that he was to be the recipient for that year of the Washington Award "for his social vision in dedicating to the perpetuation of research the rewards of his achievements in science and engineering." This award, first given to Herbert Hoover, was made by the Western Society of Engineers, acting on the recommendation of several national engineering groups. The award was given him not primarily for engineering achievement but for the "social contribution made by his work," and it would have shamed all competitors as Cottrell's outstanding recognition if there were any correlation between weighty bronze-marble plaques and prestige.

Taking the social theme as his cue, Cottrell's topic as an acceptance speech was the "Social Responsibility of the Engineer," and here again he spoke out for the merging of interests in separate fields. "What I want to bring out," he told the engineers, "is the crying necessity and splendid opportunity for the young engineer of creative imagination and moral courage to join forces with his brother specialists from the humanitarian side and thus insure a really comprehensive picture of what *homo sapiens,* in this year of grace 1937, should be driving at as the immediate and conscious goal for the species."

Cottrell sometimes considered this speech his most important public utterance, even though it expressed only his usual blend of radical conservatism. In it he stressed the sanctity of human values as being as important as the sanctity of property rights. In it he adjured the engineer to hold the ideal of service to society on a plane at least equally elevated to that of the profit motive. He cited Research Corporation and Research Associates Inc. as examples of how legitimate profit had been sacrificed in some cases when a more important public service could be rendered. He also pointed out, as had others before him, how greatly American technological success depended on speculative pioneering on the part of both the American engineer and the American financier and manager. In essence, however, it was a call to the engineer, and particularly the young engineer who would be responsible for much of our future material progress, to consider the goal of use or service rather than to be dominated solely by the motive of profit. It was a challenge which he said Thorstein Veblen had earlier "and perhaps most clearly sounded" in his *Engineers and the Price System.*

The address was delivered at a Chicago banquet and the reaction was mixed. The many who admired Cottrell applauded enthusiastically; the indifferent were polite—a response he himself had foreseen in preparing his speech, when he wondered if the sympathies of his audience might not be too conservative to appreciate what he felt he had to say.

In formal oratory of this kind Cottrell was not rated an inspiring speaker unless he chose to digress, at which time some of the zeal and fervor that drove him rose to the surface above the generally stilted tone of his prepared remarks. He had an active dislike for speechmaking under such circumstances. The very thought of it he once described as "an ordeal." But if his delivery did not inspire, his ideas could. On the occasion of the Washington Award, for example, he invited a young Chicago chemist, whose acquaintance he had earlier made, to escort Jess to the banquet while Cottrell mingled with the dignitaries at the speakers' table. It was this chemist who could say, thirteen years later, that it had been Cottrell who was chiefly responsible for showing him that "the finest values in life are our intangible assets and not the tangible, such as the acquisition of vast material goods. To me, he was one of the truly great men of the era."

It is possible that this award came at a time when Cottrell's morale benefited despite his stated disregard for public acclaim. In accepting it, he wrote the Western Society of Engineers, "There was a time when youthful modesty would have caused me to shy at such an audition, but modesty, like other youthful disciplines, often seems gradually to atrophy with advancing years and I find myself getting more satisfaction and frank pleasure out of this award than any other that has ever come to me."

He had not long to wait for another morale booster. In November of the same year the American Society of Mechanical Engineers bestowed on him its Holley Medal which, in the words of the society, was for "some great and unique act of genius of an engineering nature that has accomplished a great and timely public benefit." To Cottrell's vast gratitude, this required no answering speech. The following month he declined the presidency of the Electrochemical Society, and in March 1938, as Research Associates Inc. began closing its doors, he was named medalist of the American Institute of Chemists—a medal given for "noteworthy and outstanding service to the science of chemistry or the profession of chemist in America."

As usual the news stories accompanying such honors did little to increase Cottrell's regard for the accuracy of the lay press. In reporting the Washington Award, for example, the Washington *Star* followed its lead paragraph with the news: "Dr. Cottrell's name is chiefly associated with the perfection of a process by which helium gas was reduced in cost from about $1,700 to 10 cents a cubic foot"— figures which had been roughly usable twenty years earlier and an association which was not chief at all. Then when he became the chemists' medalist the Washington *Post* gave Cottrell a distinct surprise by announcing that "he has been ranked by Mme. Curie and Sir Oliver Lodge as one of the world's three greatest chemists." There was no explanation of how this evaluation was arrived at, and it left the unfortunate impression that Madame Curie and Sir Oliver had the identity of the others of the triad pretty well fixed in mind.

For the chemists' medal, Cottrell partially prepared a speech which he did not deliver and which bore the somnolent title: "Academic Research and the Patent System." It was, as far as it went, a dull speech and would have curdled no digesting creamed chicken as he had feared that his address at the Washington Award banquet might do. But it did give one paragraph reflecting a measure of his temporary discouragement over the failure of Research Associates Inc.

He wrote: "I started out a third of a century ago with considerable youthful enthusiasm concerning the promise of patents as self-starters for financing research in the universities, but today, although I am well contented with the aggregate results of what this led me into, I have become increasingly convinced that financial profit on the average and of itself, even in university ownership of patents, is far more apt than not to prove at least tardy in arrival and disappointing in magnitude. It should from the outset be considered almost or wholly as incidental and purely speculative, the fundamental justification for attempting any such procedure being clearly recognized as service to the public, not only in more surely and effectively getting the results of both pure and applied research into general use, but by using the mechanism of so doing also as a sort of laboratory in applied economics, thus helping to work out some of our remaining problems in this much-to-be-improved corner of our system of recognized public monopolies."

He had, he seemed to be implying, no objection to profits as such but only to the uses to which they were sometimes put; when profits

were an end in themselves and not an instrument for social better-
ment. Even so, his experience with Research Associates Inc. seems
to have told him that an organization of that nature should exist
primarily for public service and secondarily, if at all, for profit.
While this automatically raised many questions, Cottrell was either
too tired or too unwilling to pursue their complexities, for the
manuscript of the speech ended on page six.

Although in Royster's stoves and Greger's fuel cell Research
Associates Inc. had two projects that were potentially of great value
to industry and therefore indirectly to the public, it cannot be said
that the public response to such an organization produced anything like the reaction Cottrell had probably hoped for. The gulf
between the lofty aims of the Associates and the ideas that were
offered to them for development made it almost a certainty that if
genius were at work in the country's anonymous basements it intended to remain hidden.

The organization of the Associates was accompanied by considerable publicity not only because as an idea it made news but also
because it had the force of Gardner Jackson's wide acquaintance with
the working press behind it. The news story was covered by the
large metropolitan dailies and reached as far as the Ketchikan
(Alaska) *Chronicle,* which treated it handsomely in 15 column
inches. Favorable opinions crept into editorial columns and letters
to the editor. The majority of literate American inventors probably
heard of it but the net result was a thin stew of technological dross
if one had in mind an ideal of public service.

Letters to the Associates began to pour in, offering a variety of
toys and gadgets, a machine that cured cancer, a simplified mailing
device, a new type of dishwasher reflecting the aspirations of a disgruntled husband, a foolproof fire-alarm box, and a mechanical
banking machine. Many of the letters were typified by one beginning "I have just perfected and have not filed application for a patent
as I am not financially able to do so on a remarkable device. . . ."
There were many who said that they understood the altruism moti-
vating the Associates but exhibited a pathological fear of revealing
what their invention was. Others railed against the cupidity of patent
lawyers. One astonishingly fertile mind (Philadelphia) listed some
fifteen ideas that had either achieved or were approaching perfection. (Idea 10 did have a certain social significance: "New variation

or feature to belt buckle for men's trousers. Grips trousers to prevent
the unsightly sagging visible in a considerable portion of belt users.
Model made and worn with satisfaction. Photos of same witnessing
physical reduction to practice in my possession. Model in possession
of [a patent organization] who, after failing to exploit the invention,
conveniently found an excuse to fail to return the model. 'Enough
said.' ") Jackson Heights, New York, submitted a cosmic world
truth, and "the truth is that the Genesis, or source of the human
cancer are $-14E/2$, the like opposite equal halves of the like equal
human world blood cells, $14(+P = -E)$." This was not clearly
explained.

But the fact still remained that Cottrell was often his own best
source of ideas, and his support of one of them helped to bear
fruit entirely independent of Research Associates Inc.

The torrential supply of scientific literature generated by the twentieth century has long overtaxed libraries and baffled some of their
conscientious librarians. Libraries alone do not suffer. Scientific and
technical publications cannot begin to cope with either the cost or
the task of printing the papers on scientific studies submitted to them.
Important papers have sometimes had to wait months and even years
for publication, retarding among other things the recognition due
the discoverer. A researcher in some fields has difficulty in knowing
where to begin his work because of the inability to find out what
has already been done and what the results were. These various
problems, in short, can be lumped under the term "documentation"
to cover the process of getting the results of an investigation into
print, of having this record classified bibliographically, and of having both the record and the bibliography easily available to the researcher. While the various scientific societies publish journals of
abstracts at costs running into the millions of dollars to take care
of a large part of the bibliographic problem, it still frequently
remains difficult to obtain full reports, including tables and illustrations, of an investigator's findings.

The idea of using microfilm as one solution to these problems has
been credited by such authorities as Watson Davis, president of the
American Documentation Institute, to Cottrell. As with many such
ideas there were precedents. In 1870, during the Prussian siege of
Paris and the early days of photography, excellent reductions of
military dispatches were made on film and flown out of the city by

pigeons. Now, however, it was Cottrell's suggestion that all worthy scientific papers be transferred to 35-mm. film for a permanent record, this film, cheaply and simply made, to be deposited in one or more central libraries whence copies could be inexpensively mailed to those interested.

This in essence was the plan brought by Cottrell in 1924 to Dr. Edwin E. Slosson, director of Science Service, and Davis, then an editor of the same organization. Science Service Inc., although only a little over three years old at that time, had been established for the popularization of science through the lay press and had the support of the most imposing scientific societies (such as the National Academy of Sciences) as well as of the journalism profession itself. Science Service Inc., as represented by Slosson and Davis, thought Cottrell's idea eminently practical and tried unsuccessfully to enlist the co-operation, which is to say the financial aid, of some of the country's leading photographic and optical companies.

Both Science Service and Cottrell kept the idea sporadically alive over the next decade while others in America and abroad began developing plans along the same lines. One of these was Dr. R. H. Draeger, a United States Navy medical officer, who constructed a camera for copying the pages of printed texts on microfilm, and when this came to Davis' attention in 1934 he called a meeting of those around Washington who had become interested. The meeting took place at the Cosmos Club, the same place and the same year that saw the birth of Research Associates Inc., with the ultimate result that the American Documentation Institute was organized in 1937 as a non-profit companion to the non-profit Science Service Inc. There was, it would seem, a hormone or an enzyme in the atmosphere of the Cosmos Club that stimulated organization but inhibited profit.

While Draeger was developing his camera Cottrell, too, had been busy in his home laboratory on Ingomar Street trying to work out a viewer for the 35-mm. film. There he devised a pair of spectacles, to be worn as any pair of glasses is worn, through which the reader would roll and study the enlargement of the film at will. He constructed the prototype of such a pair, but when the microphoto plan was put into effect a separate reading machine about the size of a typewriter was thought to be more effective.

After submitting the microfilm idea and assisting in the primary stages of its development, Cottrell, true to form, took no further active interest in either the American Documentation Institute; its government brother, Bibliofilm Service, set up by the library of the Department of Agriculture in co-operation with the Institute; or any of the manifold similar services that subsequently came into being. He must, however, have found some satisfaction in other uses to which the idea was ultimately put—in V-mail during World War II; in the 1,500,000 feet of 35-mm. film the Navy alone used weekly for recording and preserving ship and ordnance plans during the war; and finally in what Watson Davis envisioned with the coming of peace: "Microfilm . . . allows us to contemplate the possibility of assembling in comprehensible size and at reasonable cost the great literature and factual material of the world—the creation of what H. G. Wells has called engagingly a 'world brain.'"

7

The most common attitude with which Cottrell's close friends and few intimates regarded him was threefold: respect for his achievements and capacities, humor at his foibles, and concern for the constant attack he waged upon his own health through overwork. Over the latter Poillon worried, Walter Schmidt worried, and Jess worried, and of these the greatest worrier was Jess. Jess over the years had come to replace Aunt Mame in his life. The depth of the devotion of each was measurable in the same terms; Jess, like Aunt Mame before her, in her genuine desire to be a helpmate, had come to subordinate her life to his work and there is perhaps some parallel to be found in the attitudes of the two women in that both were denied children.

Unlike Aunt Mame, to whom Cottrell's every word was law, Jess could be firm and insistent, qualities she had developed under Cottrell's own tutelage. She, if anyone, could temper his extravagance of energy, could make him relax and rest, and sometimes Cottrell paid heed. When the disheartening business of Research Associates Inc. was closed out, it was on Jess's insistence that they took a California vacation where for three weeks Cottrell consented to lounge among the redwoods. But it was a swift, driving current against which she struggled, one that had slackened scarcely at all since he had written her from Leipzig thirty-five years earlier: "The man who can complacently say to himself, 'Yes, I've won a firm foothold and earned a rest; I can now sit down comfortably and attend to other matters that touch me nearer' will never be able to hold that 'scientific spirit' in its purest and highest form long enough to exercise much influence therewith."

It can reasonably be wondered whether at any point Cottrell was satisfied with the influence he was exercising in the mid-thirties just as it can be wondered whether, being its source, he could hold a sufficiently proper perspective to be aware of the extent of it.

During this period he was deeply wrapped up in the operations of Research Associates Inc. Yet in spite of its fearsome problems, in spite of such minor concerns as microfilm, a sampling of his activities over any few months would reveal something like this:

At the request of the assistant co-ordinator of TVA he investigated a new method of cracking petroleum on which his opinion was wanted.

He was a fond attender of scientific gatherings. These might be the Farm Chemurgic Council in Detroit or a meeting of the American Chemical Society in New York, where he got so involved talking to acquaintances in the hotel lobby that he failed to get to the meeting in session.

He revised Draft No. 6 of the International Auxiliary Language Association's wordy "Plan for Obtaining Agreement on an Auxiliary Language."

He maintained his status as an amateur employment bureau and was both successful and unsuccessful in placing those who appealed to him for help.

He placed the consul of the Irish Free State in contact with the U. S. Bureau of Fisheries regarding the commercial use of kelp.

He read and criticized a long unsolicited manuscript on economics sent him by a stranger on the recommendation of a Cottrell acquaintance.

He established liaison between a reputable man with a contraceptive idea (in which Cottrell saw social implications) and the Josiah Macy Jr. Foundation which seemed to see merit in it.

He addressed a Rural Electrification Administration luncheon.

He endorsed a University of Chicago study on the importance of cholesterol in the problems of old age and recommended that the Macy Foundation grant $5000 for its study.

Tidewater Oil Company asked his advice on some of their problems to which electrostatic dehydration might apply.

Those were but a few.

With Poillon's consent he used part of their joint $7500 fund (granted by Research Corporation for things either or both saw fit to investigate) to have a preliminary survey made of the Salt Lake Diking Project in which he had earlier become interested. The survey, made by a nationally known planning consultant, found the project feasible and the report was turned over to state officials, who took no action.

With the same fund he and Poillon subsidized the growing of ephedra in California. America, at the time, was threatened with shortage of ephedrine because of Sino-Japanese hostilities in Asia, the chief source of supply. The experiment itself was conducted by the U. S. Department of Agriculture which, being short of funds for such purposes, accepted the Cottrell-Poillon subsidy. While it was found that ephedra could be successfully cultivated in California, about the same time other researchers discovered that ephedrine could be synthesized in the laboratory and so the growing project was abandoned.

He had become a national counselor, and was later named a director, of the Purdue Research Foundation.

From time to time he encouraged, both spiritually and financially, an aging and decaying inventor who had once been wealthy and whose name had once been luminous in the electroplating industry. To Research Corporation this was another of Cottrell's "black cats," who to their intense relief missed by the narrowest of margins being invited to work in the Associates' laboratory.

Nor were these things all.

There were unpaid consultancies on government boards, and membership on such things as the Committee on Patents, Copyrights and Trade Marks of the American Association for the Advancement of Science. To most appeals for his services and advice Cottrell responded where he felt his knowledge and experience could be of use. That all these things sapped at and deflected his energies was recognized by the worriers-over-Cottrell. They led to the heart-to-heart talks with Jess wherein he arrived at firm decisions to concentrate more on the "little things of life." On one occasion when he accepted a committee membership which even he felt he should have refused, Poillon was prompted to tell him a story:

"Emmet Boyle," Poillon wrote, "was for a number of years Governor of the State of Nevada and a young man when he died. When he took office he had some money and after being Governor for several terms spent all of his own money as well as his salary and in consequence had to refuse the office when his last term expired.

"He started into private practice as a mining engineer and he promised his wife that he would not accept any more quasi-public, public or society positions. One day he came home and Vida, his wife, thought he looked a little sheepish so she insisted upon his telling her what he had done. Under cross-question he broke down and made the following statement: 'I have accepted the Presidency of the Reno Chamber of Commerce,' and then he added, 'Vida, it is very fortunate that I was not born a girl, for if I had I would certainly be in the Florence Crittenden Home. You know I can never say no.'"

THE FOIBLES of Cottrell had long been considered as something apart from his scientific work and were thought of as adding much to the charm and color of his personality. Included here were his glasses; the dilapidated condition of the automobiles he successively owned; the frightening way in which he drove them, subordinating all operating procedure to the demands of conversation; the Pony truck; his pride in catching trains within sixty seconds of a scheduled departure; the international language; his unfailing kindness to everyone including one or two who violated all recognized codes of decency in taking advantage of his generosity; his disregard of orthodox meal hours; his capacity for outraging a gourmet's sensibilities by such combinations as wheat germ on pie; his dress (with much pride he had shown Jess a new patching technique in readying his evening clothes for the Washington Award banquet)—all these and more were often recounted with affectionate amusement by those who knew him and were recognized as reflecting separate parts of Cottrell's character. Sometime during the late 1930s, however, the boundaries of this classification began to disintegrate in the eyes of many of his colleagues, who with increasing frequency linked his scientific interests with his whimsies. The indications are that Cottrell was aware of this progressive subtle shift but was undeterred by it. He was then in the neighborhood of sixty years old.

Of course it is true that some of his professional activities had always been regarded askance by the narrower scientific purists, and in spite of the other honors he received he had continually been weighed and found wanting by the Chemistry Division of the National Academy of Sciences. To be elected to the academy, one must pass through the narrowest of needle eyes—a feat which Cottrell might have accomplished more easily had he not been burdened with his bulging briefcase filled, as it always was, with projects scientific and projects profane. The critic of long ago who, while Cottrell was a graduate student at Berkeley, complained that he "danced all over the lot" had long since passed on to a plane beyond criticizing but in his place was a Washington contemporary who grumbled with equal triteness that Cottrell wouldn't "stick to his knitting."

While Cottrell could be oblivious to such attitudes, Jess could not. Her concern was a wifely one that he might appear as something less than was his due in the eyes of the scientific world, and it was sometimes a matter discussed by them. One of these talks took place in June of 1939, and Cottrell recorded its gist in the diary: "Had long and very earnest discussion with Jess about my interest and possible future activities in such matters as I.A.L.A., cooperatives, etc., and the drastic differences of appeal of these subjects to her and me and how we could best treat such subjects and adjustments in the years to come. She spoke with particular feeling of her worries in, say, the years 1920–1925 over my activities in international language matters, for fear of its undermining influence on my standing and prestige in my more orthodox and accepted fields of activity."

His standing had been affected, for in April 1939 when he was notified that he was elected to the National Academy it was as a member of the Engineering Division and not of the Chemistry

Division to which he more properly belonged. When his membership had been proposed to the engineers they had accepted him eagerly, whereas the chemists had haughtily dawdled over his name for years, unable to muster the two-thirds majority necessary for his nomination to the entire academy.

This, if nothing else, afforded Cottrell an opportunity to evaluate his own position in the scientific world. To a congratulatory message from Vannevar Bush, president of the Carnegie Institution of Washington, Cottrell replied: "I wonder if many of [the academy] really sense the full chances they were taking. However, I do, and I promise you I will try to do my best not to disgrace the Academy. I always enjoyed attending the Academy meetings that were open to the public and never felt the least hesitation or embarrassment in thus playing around the fringe for I've felt that was really my characteristic place." To another well-wisher he wrote: "What real claim I may have to service or distinction in *creative* science is frankly along borderlines, and even there as a sort of promoter or catalyst of others' work and opportunities rather than in my own name and right."

The lure of the border line still lay strongly upon Cottrell after the closing of Research Associates Inc. Even though Research Corporation had withdrawn its support of the Associates, Cottrell was "not disposed to be too censorious" and, far from bearing any ill will, resumed his old status as consultant, which was, in practice, liaison man between the corporation and the world of ideas in which he moved so fleet-mindedly. Jess had been successful in inducing him to join her in a Western vacation as a transition between the affairs of the Associates and his return to an active consultancy, but three weeks among the redwoods proved enough for Cottrell and, moved by old urges, he turned to the California field for his next ventures in organizing. These sent vibrant waves of apprehension among some who knew him but he considered the potentials great enough to warrant spending nine months between August 1938 and May 1939 on the Coast.

For almost three years prior to this Cottrell had intermittently nourished his interest in two developments in California which he thought might well be integrated. One of these was hydroponics— the name given to soilless gardening, or gardening by means of water culture and chemicals, by Professor W. F. Gericke of the

University of California. Plant water culture had long been a matter of laboratory practice, but Gericke brought it out into the garden with such seemingly sensational results that the subsequent avalanche of publicity embarrassed the university and almost automatically made Gericke a controversial academic figure. (In 1938 the *Saturday Evening Post* ran a story by Frank J. Taylor on Gericke's hydroponics and received in reply one of the greatest responses in its history—so many thousands of letters that it advertised the fact as evidence of its readership.) Until later experiments by others showed that some of Gericke's results could be duplicated by proper plant nutrition in orthodox gardening, it looked as though he had worked miracles in water tanks that yielded luscious tomatoes, for example, on a scale equal to eighty tons to the acre. Among the many impressed by such wonders was Cottrell.

About the same time Cottrell's help was solicited in patenting some features of air-conditioned greenhouses. The development of these—a mild indictment of a climate that is sometimes considered beyond improvement—was being carried on in Southern California by an independent investigator, H. O. Eversole, and by a young U. S. Department of Agriculture physicist, Lauriston C. Marshall. While this project carried with it none of the sensationalism of Gericke's hydroponics, it was nevertheless producing such things as superior, long-lasting orchids whose blooms could be timed for the right markets. In orchids Cottrell, as well as Eversole and Marshall, saw a parallel with aluminum, which was once an expensive chemical curiosity, and one of the implications of air-conditioned greenhouses was this: what could be done for orchids could possibly extend to the entire hothouse industry, making it a scientifically controlled factory operation. Moreover, Research Corporation was at the time becoming involved in the air-conditioning business, which appealed to Cottrell as a further reason it should interest itself in helping with the Eversole-Marshall patents.

Thus, when Cottrell received the medal of the American Institute of Chemists for 1938, he partially prepared and abandoned a speech on "Academic Research and the Patent System," marched straight to his new border line, and spoke instead on the "Complete Control of Plant Growth." In this he stressed how, through such developments as hydroponics and air-conditioned greenhouses, "Man in his growing control of natural forces is steadily breaking down for his own advantage [the] age-old fixity in the conditions of nature." The Gericke and Eversole-Marshall experiments might show, he later pointed out, that special dietary properties could be developed and controlled in grains, fruits, and vegetables to conform more closely with the mineral substances needed by the animal body.

In comparison to the reaction of the rest of the country, to which hydroponics-water culture had become a nine-day wonder, the approach of Cottrell was conservative and experimental, for the whole subject had got completely out of hand. Since the hydroponics idea was not patentable, dozens of wispy businesses sprang up and at exorbitant prices sold nutrient salts to be added to water in the growing tanks in complete disregard of different plant requirements. Sunday-supplement stories pictured a housewife opening a closet door to pluck unbelievably fat tomatoes growing under electric lights. Gericke, something of an innocent victim of all this, stood in disfavor with University of California officials, and out of this chaos Cottrell tried to bring some order.

He first approached Stanford University through Herbert Hoover, one of its trustees, who had a historic interest in food production, in an attempt to locate Gericke and his work there. According to the diary, both Hoover and Stanford's president, Ray Lyman Wilbur, were sympathetic to the idea provided a means of financing the project could be found. For this Cottrell had an answer: "A good deal of what I am working on hardest out here this trip," he wrote a friend, "[is the] plant culture and hydroponic work and the possibility of building up around that . . . both a purely business corporation on the one hand (analogous in some ways to Western Precipitation Company) and a non-profit organization (analogous to Research Corporation) with probably Stanford University sitting in very much the similar place that the Smithsonian did in the earlier example. One attractive aspect of this set-up is that Stanford has a strong graduate school of business administration which I am figuring on getting interested in the non-profit organization from the angle of a social-economic lab, a phase I've always had in mind for Research Corporation which has never worked out very systematically thus far but in a new set-up might get a definite place from the start."

Although there is no record of Cottrell's having broached the subject of the Eversole-Marshall greenhouses to Stanford, his thoughts here ran to establishing a $100,000 fund to be raised through the luxury item of orchids and this money would be used to extend the study of food production in air-conditioned greenhouses with special attention to superior dietary qualities which might be fostered under controlled conditions. In some manner, he hoped, such investigations could be teamed with those of Gericke in a whole new enterprise.

The plan went awry. Stanford biologists rebelled at accepting Gericke. Then the Eversole-Marshall patents proved too complicated and expensive to pursue even though Poillon and Research Corporation looked on them favorably. But here, as in some other cases, the value of Cottrell's catalyzing—if value there were—is impossible to assess and probably amounted only to the information he spread widely on both subjects. Yet, while partially discredited by blue-sky publicity, the employment of hydroponics under certain restricted conditions is still open to study (Gericke's methods were used successfully by the U. S. Army Air Forces in a few localities during World War II), and the art of plant culture in air-conditioned greenhouses became established and commercially successful in a highly specialized luxury market.

This attempt to organize the Gericke and Eversole-Marshall forces kept Cottrell busy from September 1938 through March 1939, although during that time Jess again was able to urge on him the necessity of another short vacation which they took in the desert near San Diego. It had been work that kept him shuttling up and down the partial length of California between San Francisco and Los Angeles but its attention-absorbing properties had not precluded certain other concerns. By his own schedule he was long overdue in Washington, yet the wayward border lines he pursued had a tendency to become almost continuous and, rested by the stay in the desert, he went north to Berkeley for a final survey and round of farewells before he and Jess returned East. It was a leave-taking that lasted two months and out of it came other exploratory meetings to discuss another plan.

This plan was for a Western equivalent of Research Corporation to be centered, in the beginning, around three developments on the Berkeley campus. One of these was vitamin K (antihemorrhagic), which Dr. H. J. Almquist, of the university's College of Agriculture, believed he had succeeded in isolating as a pure vitamin. Another was a magnetostrictor (a supersonic mechanical vibration generator), the invention of Dr. W. W. Salisbury of the Radiation Laboratory. The third was the high-frequency oscillator of Dr. David Sloan and Dr. Lauriston C. Marshall, who had left the Department of Agriculture and air-conditioned greenhouses to join the electrical engineering department at Berkeley. This device, known as the "resnatron," produced ultra high-frequency radio waves at higher continuous power than had previously been possible.

Cottrell called two meetings which were attended by many of the university's ranking professors and influential department heads, but the memory of Research Associates Inc. must still have been with him, for he wrote Poillon, "I have purposely urged them not to attempt to crystallize the movement even in their own eyes too early, but to work just as a voluntary and informal committee at the start." But there was an echo also of Research Associates Inc. in a statement made in the diary in which he defined the movement as one "to assure that useful practical application of research originating in the academic laboratories of the State and Pacific Coast would reach the public promptly, efficiently and without unreasonable cost for development, promotion and other overhead." Then, six months over the expiration date of their return-trip railroad tickets, Cottrell and Jess set out for Washington, leaving behind at Stanford and at the University of California the germinant seeds of two organizations that died unwatered and untended.

The planting of those had still left time for minor chores having mainly to do with Cottrell's gratuitous placement services. One whose case he was pressing was a Dr. Ladislaus Marton, a primary developer of the electron microscope, who spurred its success by first applying it to the biological field. Marton, a Hungarian working at the Université Libre de Bruxelles, had written Cottrell in June 1938 to ask his advice on ways and means of coming to America for more intensive pursuit of the electron microscope's development. Cottrell recommended him to Poillon as eminently worthy of consideration but meanwhile carried Marton's name to every university he visited that might have an opening. "I cannot tell you how grateful I am to you," Marton wrote Cottrell in 1941. "If my dream [of getting into academic work in America] comes true it is entirely due to your help and encouragement." As it later turned out, Marton

had no difficulty in finding a place in an American industrial laboratory but when he decided, in 1941, to return to academic work he
found that Cottrell's earlier missionary work and recommendations
had helped pave the way toward his heading the development staff
of Stanford's Division of Electron Optics which, under Marton's
direction, designed and built a 100,000-volt electron microscope during the war.

While Marton's reputation and achievements in his field made his
case one easily pleaded, Cottrell had at the same time three other
candidates for academic jobs whose plight was a familiar one in
those days—familiar but none the less tragic. As with most Americans who had studied in Germany, Cottrell was petitioned by a
number of former German fellow students seeking a haven in American universities from Nazi persecutions. Unfortunately those from
the laboratories of van't Hoff and Ostwald who had known Cottrell
were now of an age group extremely difficult to place but that did
not deter him from more than routinely conscientious efforts on
their behalf.

Of the three whose causes he espoused, one was disqualified because he spoke no English; for a second, whom he remembered only
indistinctly, Cottrell set aside part of his time during his redwoods
vacation to write letters of appeal. These ended when he finally
received a fearsomely terse and final note from the man's wife
saying: "I wrote you the 7th of December with the request that
you aid my husband to immigrate from Germany. I did not know
that he already, since November 14, is no longer living." The third,
a Dr. Fritz Weigert, who formerly held the chair of physical and
photochemistry at the University of Leipzig, was the subject of over
fifty Cottrell letters and innumerable conferences. Despite an im-
pressive scientific background, Weigert was handicapped by his age
as well as a degree of deafness, and Cottrell's efforts were fruitless.
Weigert did manage to obtain a British post only to be interned as
an enemy alien on the outbreak of war, but the lengths to which
Cottrell was willing to go to aid him were revealed in a letter to
Poillon in February 1939: if, he said, Research Corporation could
see its way clear to make a grant to some institution that might then
hire Weigert, "I would prefer to make my own personal contribution to the project in the form of a decrease in the stipend now
coming to me from Research Corporation. . . . I have had it in mind

for some time that it would be appropriate to reduce that stipend as my more active work for Research Corporation slackens."
If the work was slackening, the conscience was still taut.

2

Once again the time had come, as it occasionally had in years gone by, for Cottrell to worry about himself. His work *was* slackening but in an ominous way that had none of the characteristics of a terminable interlude such as he had been able to recognize on his listless return from Leipzig back when the century was still new. From this present state there could be little hope of a bright reprieve, for he was growing old, the roster of the years was lengthening, the signs were unmistakable.

In the summer of 1940, Jess returned to the West Coast for a visit, leaving strict instructions for Cottrell to follow for a prolonged rest. Yet the summer wore on with Cottrell in a vague and temporizing mood, unable to reach a decision to go West yet fretful at remaining behind. To Jess's entreaties that he join her, he spoke of the "pressure of other matters" that kept him in Washington, although there was little to validate such an excuse. He was, it is true, serving on one or two committees appointed by the National Research Council to advise on such items of national defense as metals and minerals, but the meetings of these were intermittent and his duties consisted mainly in studying and making recommendations on various reports. It was really inertia that gripped him and he spent much of his time around the house rigging up an alarm clock to turn on his radio, puttering again with his adjustable-focus glasses, and trying out a new scheme for a microfilm viewer.

But these were scarcely enough to warrant the "pressure" of which he spoke. He was, rather, overwhelmed by a sense of tiredness. ("I'm so tired tonight I can hardly hold my head up," he wrote Jess in September, offering to compromise on the California journey and meet her in Chicago.) Too, his memory was no longer the sure, sharp thing from which obscurely related facts could be drawn, associated, and assembled with an infinite and pleasurable swiftness. (To Jess: "If my diary notes go a day now I can't seem to remember anything. It seems as if there were a number of things on my mind in between my last letter to you and now that I was going to comment on, but that's just like everything else. I certainly am getting more and more absent-minded.")

In September he got as far west as Chicago.

The inertia in all probability had been sharpened by disappointments. The Detroit Edison Company, which had taken over the development of Greger's fuel cell, had dropped the project partly because it promised to involve too much time and money and partly because the company's researcher who was most interested died. A similar fate attended Royster's three years' work in Toledo with the Pickands Mather group. Although Royster's results had seemed promising on a long-term basis, the growing pressures of defense production made experimentation too much of a hazard and his project was discontinued. The international auxiliary language movement, in which Cottrell still maintained an advisory interest, shriveled at the hot blast of war. Each day's events, which kept him tied to his radio during the despairing summer of 1940, mocked IALA's hope of a common voice.

Then there was another project in which Cottrell had long been involved and one that at times was a subject of daily correspondence. This was headed by a Chicago engineer, R. J. Gaudy, who had elaborate plans for establishing a new aluminum manufacturing company to apply the untried French Seailles process to low-grade Arkansas (instead of high-grade imported) bauxite. Gaudy intended also to employ some of Royster's techniques, and Cottrell favored Gaudy's plan. But Gaudy acquired the reputation of a "visionary" and a "promoter" among such government agencies as might have financed the scheme as a defense measure, and Cottrell's championing of it joined the list kept by those who delineated Cottrell's foibles.

There were these things that happened but there were also compensatory moments. In February 1940, amidst much press-agentry, the National Association of Manufacturers celebrated the hundred and fiftieth anniversary of the American Patents System. They had earlier called upon industrialists, engineers, and scientists to name Americans who could receive the association's awards as being "Modern Pioneers." Over a thousand were nominated. Of these 572 were picked for regional honors, and from these the crème de la crème were sifted for nineteen national awards. On this latter choice list—among others—were Henry Ford, Orville Wright, Lee De

Forest, William David Coolidge, Irving Langmuir, Charles F. Kettering, and ranked among these great by his contemporaries was Frederick Gardner Cottrell.

There were other things from which he could, had he wished, have taken heart and pride, and chief of these was the success of his most memorable corporate product, Research Corporation. In some ways this had not lived up to his expectations. The corporation had, for example, found it exceedingly unwise to undertake development of inventions in its laboratories and shops, using its own funds and personnel, and Cottrell's experiences with Research Associates Inc. had emphasized some of the pitfalls that were inherent in any such program. For one thing, the times had changed since Cottrell first embodied his ideas in the corporation's charter and the need for developmental laboratories had been met with startling success in most cases by industry itself. But in one corner of this field a need existed for Research Corporation—a need which because of its public-service status the corporation was uniquely fitted to satisfy.

This need was patent management. If the corporation found it unwise to invest its own monies and energies directly in an invention or development, that still did not preclude its acting as an intermediary or clearinghouse between inventors who were patent-holders, and industries that were interested in developing inventions relating to activities in which they were already engaged and experienced. Largely through Cottrell's activities Research Corporation was in constant touch with many of the larger centers of university and institutional research out of which came patentable ideas. Few such institutions generated enough patentable ideas to warrant maintaining their own experienced staff to handle the complex business of obtaining patents; of then managing the patents, which includes finding the manufacturer willing to undertake their translation into commercial reality; of arranging for licenses and, if profits are involved, of receiving and accounting for royalties. Although Research Corporation had already succeeded in its purpose of conducting an electrical precipitation business and had succeeded in granting most of the earnings therefrom (with no obligations devolving on the recipients) in ways that had achieved highly successful scientific results, it then, during the 1930s, had broadened the scope of a third service—patent management.

This, with Cottrell's encouragement, had been largely Poillon's achievement, although more often it was Cottrell who performed the specific function of locating the patentable idea. The idea did not necessarily have to be profit-bearing as was true in the case of cyclotrons. Or it might mean limited profits shared with an institution or a commercial firm such as the Van de Graaff group of patents on the electrostatic generator. These were assigned to Research Corporation under a general agreement with Massachusetts Institute of Technology and in turn were ultimately licensed back to the High Voltage Engineering Corporation formed by Van de Graaff and his associates. (As of 1951, this engineering corporation had found very practical uses for the Van de Graaff type generator as a high-energy X-ray instrument for medical purposes; in industrial radiography for detecting flaws in metals and machined pieces, particularly for the military; in nuclear research by helping, in conjunction with a cosmotron, to produce some of the highest artificial energies ever achieved; and in the sterilization of foods and drugs by cathode rays.)

The Lawrence cyclotron and the Van de Graaff type generator, both of which added so greatly to man's knowledge of the atomic nucleus, were but two examples of Research Corporation's usefulness in the field of patent management. More significant from an income-producing point of view were the contributions of Dr. R. R. Williams and his associates, who in 1935 assigned to the corporation their tremendously important patents on the synthetic production of vitamin B_1 and its intermediates. These patents covered a process that made thiamine a household word, took some of the curse off American tastes for overrefined wheat flour, and promises to lower the oriental death rate from beriberi. Williams' public-spiritedness complemented Research Corporation's policy and worked admirably in the public interest to bring the 1936 price of thiamine of $10 a gram down to sixteen cents a gram by 1945. Even this steep reduction meant some earnings both for the licensees and for Research Corporation—50 per cent of the income going into a special fund, the Williams-Waterman Fund for the Combat of Dietary Diseases. Grants from this fund alone, which derives its income only from the B_1 patents, have amounted to about $200,000 annually since the end of World War II.

The B_1 patents, with Williams' endorsement, gave Cottrell another chance to test his aspirations for closer international scientific co-operation for which he had laid the groundwork in 1929 with Okochi of the Institute of Physical and Chemical Research in Tokyo. These plans whereby Research Corporation and the institute would exchange certain patents and patentable ideas—the profits from which would go to aiding scientific research regardless of national boundaries anywhere in the world—had earlier stumbled clumsily over the matter of a simple device for testing razor-blade sharpness. But the B_1 patents were immeasurably more significant and of especial interest to oriental countries where widespread use of polished white rice invited malnutrition and beriberi.

In May 1937, therefore, Poillon, on behalf of the Research Corporation, officially offered the institute the B_1 patents as a friendly gift with the single reservation that they be used only in those oriental countries not controlled by European nations. There followed a suspicion-breeding delay of several months with no acknowledgment of the gift, until the institute finally replied that they had already discovered a method of synthesizing B_1, which Williams agreed might well have been the case since work of significance in the field had been under way for some time in Japan.

The successful administration of the vitamin B_1 patents and the Williams-Waterman Fund supported by those patents brought Research Corporation into prominence in a field as divorced from its industrial activities as such a drug house as Parke, Davis and Company might find itself were it to go into the business of licensing patents in electrical precipitation. Yet this trend, already established earlier by Kharasch's ergotrate and merthiolate, was to continue and received further impetus at mid-century when E. C. Kendall of the Mayo Clinic (whose investigations in cortical steroids had been supported in part by Research Corporation since 1942) developed cortisone, a promising biological wonder, and the Kendall patents on this are managed by Research Corporation on a non-exclusive basis.

If, therefore, Cottrell found disappointment in the evaporative nature of his organizational schemes after 1935, most people would agree that through his original concept alone Cottrell had discharged in a large measure that duty to the world he had conceived so many years before. Yet, if his latter-day dreams failed of embodiment, some of their components met with important successes.

The corporation's growing emphasis on patent management after 1930 was a trend that fulfilled one of Cottrell's hopes, for he had said in one speech that the purpose of Research Corporation was not merely to earn money to support scientific research but was also "to act as a sort of laboratory of patent economics and to conduct an experiment in patent administration. It was not entirely easy to win the first board of directors to a full appreciation of the relative importance of the second object of the project. They saw the possibility of money being provided from the [precipitation] activities for scientific research: as business men it was quite easy for them to grasp that fact, but it was a little difficult to stress the other side; namely, that in the end the more important thing might prove to be that they were aiding in a laboratory experiment in the public administration of patents."

Of the hundreds of patents which eventually came to Research Corporation for administration (a mere handful of which provide any royalties) the last of potential importance to arrive as a direct result of Cottrell's influence was the Sloan-Marshall ultra high-frequency oscillator, the resnatron. This was one of the inventions around which Cottrell had hoped to build a Western Research Corporation—the project conceived during his 1938–39 visit to California. Although that plan failed to materialize, his endorsement of the resnatron led Poillon to favor a grant to Sloan and Marshall, who in turn assigned their patents to Research Corporation.

It was not until after the war, however, that Cottrell was fully aware of what his catalysis here had helped in a measure to produce. In 1940, because of its suspected military potential, the resnatron and its inventors went to work for the Office of Scientific Research and Development—one of the first such projects to be taken over by the OSRD. It was subsequently farmed out to the Westinghouse laboratories, where its further exploitation was undertaken by Sloan and Marshall, working in conjunction with Dr. W. W. Salisbury. Together they found a means, through the resnatron's capacity to produce vast amounts of high-frequency power, of jamming Nazi radar during the closing months of the war so that over certain portions of German territory Allied planes could fly undetected. While, as of 1951, some of the resnatron's uses were still military secrets, its application to the other fields seemed most likely in nuclear physics, in frequency-modulation radio, and in television.

Thus, although Cottrell's work was slackening in 1940, some of the ideas he had previously encouraged and scattered were potent and germinating even though his attention had come to be distracted by a frustrating lethargy. He had returned East after the 1938–39 trip to the Coast laden, among other things, with the idea of the resnatron, vitamin K, Gericke's hydroponics, Eversole-Marshall air-conditioned greenhouses, and with new knowledge of how Lawrence was putting his cyclotron to use. His return trip took twenty days and if his erratic eastward course bore a striking resemblance to that of a pollinating bee it was because the spores he bore must be spread at the University of Chicago, at Purdue, at the University of Wisconsin, and wherever else he stopped. It was the kind of thing Cottrell liked well and thought he did best. At Madison, Wisconsin, he visited with Dr. Farrington Daniels, one of the world's outstanding experts in the field of nitrogen oxides. It was more than just a pleasant visit and out of it came the likely possibility of a new phase for an old industry. But that may not have seemed quite so important to Cottrell as the fact that another opportunity had been opened for a major application of Royster's wonderful stoves.

3

As was said before, the letter that Cottrell wrote to Poillon on July 7, 1931, may well have been one of the most important letters of that year. Pages one to six described the stirring things young Lawrence was doing with toylike cyclotrons at Berkeley. A page was next devoted to Cottrell's offhand idea of using Royster's stoves to still the complaints of professors in the university's Life Sciences Building who were offended by an incinerator. This problem he brushed off with the Deodorizer in one long paragraph, and with scarcely a pause for breath continued:

"Out of this line of development and thinking has also come to me still another very important application of Royster's system if it can be made to work and that is in the nitrogen fixation line and directly along a line I have long watched to see a possibility like this open up. It might even prove the next step beyond the Haber System just as that was one beyond cyanamid. I refer to making the oxides of nitrogen directly from the air but without the use of the electric arc, at least in its conventional form, in that process. The idea is just an extension of the 'combustion completer' for the incinerator, for what you do in the arc process is merely to heat air up to a temperature where some of the N_2 will burn in the O_2 and then cooled off quickly, recovering as much of the heat as you economically can, but the open arc process is excessively wasteful of 'high grade' energy. My scheme is . . ."

Cottrell's scheme had come to him a month before writing to Poillon, suddenly and in an almost complete form as most of his schemes did. Such ideas occurred to him at all hours of the twenty-four-hour day. For example, on February 6 of that same 1931 the diary notes that he woke up early with this idea: ". . . of making phonographic records on thread (probably of rayon-like material) by passing it near a glowing metal filament such as used in the Dutch filament telephone receiver investigated some years ago by Union Signal Co. and using the variably blackened or scorched filament running as a shutter before a thermo-element or photoelectric cell to reproduce the sound. Also conceived the alternative idea of using a stream of chemically active gas from orifice against moving sensitized paper with the suction behind the paper to pull gas through and vary flow of gas on principle of manometric flame for reactions. . . ."

Sometimes the ideas came in midafternoon. In April of the same year, while relaxing from his consulting work with the Petroleum Rectifying Company, he took a swim at Long Beach: "Got idea of making AgCl by blowing Cl through molten Ag. Also idea reconverting AgI back to AgCl by melting or strongly heating AgI and running Cl over or through it dry and condensing the I_2 dry. Also idea use vol-hydrocarb. or SO_2 instead of water vapor (steam) to sublim. I_2 to reduce drying problems. Worked on various ideas re spraying AgCl molten to droplets. Also worked on idea of rolling up agar agar through sheet corrugated on one side with a thin flat metallic foil to serve as an oil and water separator either by itself or in centrifuge."

Or sometimes they bubbled up into consciousness in the evening as on June 5, 1931: "Got first hunch re scheme of nitrogen fixation as NO by running air counter-current up against descending mass of fine-grained refractory as heat interchanger with center heated either by electric cond. or discharge by gas combustion at this point."

This last was the nub of the idea Cottrell took to Daniels at Madison eight years later on his return from the Coast in 1939. It was not the first time Daniels had heard of it for, on the dissolution of Research Associates Inc., Cottrell had spared himself neither time nor expense over a period of weary months trying with all the fervor and persuasiveness at his command to locate Royster at the University of Wisconsin, where Cottrell thought there was an optimum environment for the development of Royster's techniques. Cottrell had in mind particularly the metallurgical applications of Royster's stoves and at one point was convinced that if only Royster could continue his work on pebble-bed stoves at Madison the previous experiments of Research Associates Inc. would not have been in vain. Wisconsin officials wavered over the proposal, some favoring the idea, others being fearful of faculty sentiments if an outsider were to be placed in charge of an ambitious research program. This indecision, meanwhile, was adding nothing to Royster's income, and although he would have preferred an academic connection, he took the offer of the Pickands Mather group instead.

During these negotiations—in Madison, in Chicago, in Washington, in New York, or wherever Cottrell could locate any peripatetic Wisconsin official—the subject of nitrogen fixation using the Royster stoves wove in and out of the conversations as a secondary theme, but it was one in which Farrington Daniels showed intense interest. When the metallurgical aspirations Cottrell held for the Royster techniques failed to weigh against Wisconsin's objections, he again broached the nitrogen fixation project to Daniels, and Daniels acted. Shortly after Cottrell's 1939 visit to Madison, Daniels applied to the graduate school of the university for $1200 to start a research program and hired Nathan Gilbert, a graduate student, to assist him.

What captured the interest of Daniels and had long fascinated Cottrell were some of the things both Royster and Cottrell had found out about pebble-bed stoves. Even when dignified by the name rheoclastic they have connotations less than exciting but some amazing things happen in them—these over and above any advantages such stoves may have because of the relative simplicity of their construction. The surprising things come from the use of loosely deposited pebbles instead of the conventional rigid checker-brick, and the heart of the matter is contained in the swift responsiveness of such pebbles to changes in temperature—a responsiveness directly related to their size. For example, in heating a "pebble" four inches in diameter, Royster found that it took thirty-two minutes to bring the center of the pebble to within 90 per cent of the temperature of the pebble's outside surface. Yet if you took a half-inch pebble, the same thing could be accomplished in thirty seconds. Still, the pebbles couldn't become too small lest they fail to provide proper channels for a turbulent flow of hot gas and hence efficient thermal contact.

Certain-sized pebbles, then, could do two things. They could acquire and store very high temperatures with split-second rapidity. They could also, and as a matter of equal importance, release such heat at a comparable rate. Thus, if one were to take a pair of Royster's stoves connected together, the first move would be to build up, by means of ordinary combustion in a combustion chamber, the heat of the gases moving through the stoves to the temperature wanted for a given operation. With the desired high temperature attained (and maintained by continuous combustion), the hot gases from one stove pass over into the other stove where their heat is transferred and thus saved by the pebbles there but, in passing down through this pebble bed and storing their heat, they do so and cool at a rate that can approach 100,000 degrees Fahrenheit per second—and this in the short course of passing through only two to three feet of pebbles.

Into this second stove then, with its pebbles hot at the top and relatively cool at the bottom, is admitted the next batch of cool gas, which, in rising up through the pebble bed, acquires the heat left by its predecessor (at approximately the same rate of temperature change); passes through the combustion chamber where it is heated higher; then flows down through the second stove where the pebbles store the heat and "quench" the gas in the same swift manner as in the previous cycle. It was this combination of elevated temperatures, quick chilling, and high reversibility that led Cottrell to apply Royster's stoves to fixing nitrogen from the air in the form of nitric oxides.

Actually the old arc process of nitrogen fixation which found practical use mainly in Norway also produced nitric oxide by using elevated temperatures, but because Norway was hydroelectrically rich it could under certain conditions afford the waste of 97 per cent of the electric energy which the process devoured, for only 3 per cent of it was utilized in the actual reaction that produced nitric oxide.

Cottrell's scheme, however, promised high temperatures cheaply attained and stored in Royster's stoves. In blowing air through the hot pebble bed and igniting it in the combustion chamber, small amounts of nitric oxide were formed. If conventional regenerative stoves were to be used, this nitric oxide almost immediately would decompose, but in Royster's stoves, when passed down through a second pebble bed, the extremely rapid chilling—a fundamental necessity to the process—preserves most of the nitric oxide formed— a phenomenon roughly analogous, in a purely literary sense, to the manner in which food flavors are preserved by quick-freezing. (In his patent Cottrell cited some curious relations between high temperatures and the formation of oxides based on earlier German experiments. "The time required to form one-half of the equilibrium oxide concentration is 82 years at 1800 degrees F. and only 30 hours at 2730 degrees F. This half-time requirement decreases to about 120 seconds at 3450 degrees F. and is only 5 seconds at 3800 degrees F.") This nitric oxide then goes through a recovery process after leaving the second stove in a comparatively cool state and is ultimately converted into nitric acid—a source product of many uses.

Neither Cottrell nor Daniels was naïve enough to suppose that simply by constructing a pair of Royster's stoves and getting the air to react to the intense heat the problem would be solved. Both knew, as did Royster, that ordinary Potomac River type pebbles were all right for early experimenting but under conditions of extreme heat would fuse and melt. A more suitable pebble must therefore be found. Moreover, the linings of the stoves themselves and the crossovers between the stoves would have to face the same hot conditions of stress, and even when these problems were solved there was still the matter of devising a method of recovering the nitric oxide which would constitute only about 2 per cent of the flue gases to leave the stove.

Nevertheless, Daniels, like Cottrell, was confident that it could be done, so with $1200 and an assistant Daniels started to work, even though he was free to admit that he knew little about large-scale chemical operations. But at least a beginning had been made.

4

In the year 1942 the state of California was no longer an American outpost and while Oakland had acquired much in the way of population it still remained the state's third city and stood in the same relation to San Francisco that it had a half century before. The function of the old vaudeville stages of San Francisco had been taken over in some degree by the city's newspaper columnists, who could occasionally command a smile by a well-timed reference to Oakland although Los Angeles was now preferred as a foil. There were still commuters. The older of these spoke with nostalgia of ferryboat rides as a more exhilarating way to start the day than by the trains and cars that streamed over one of man's most superb bridges—a bridge whose obsolescence almost coincided with its completion.

The fog was still there during certain seasons of the year. On many days it would lie banked—low, massive, and oyster-white— along the mountainous coast outside the Golden Gate—lie there until midafternoon when, like a shiftless husband whose wife is the wind, it poured in through the Gate, through the draws and the valleys, following courses of least resistance around the hills that ring the bay. The problem of fog dispersal by electrical precipitation had engaged Cottrell's attention during the Panama-Pacific Exposition in 1915, but those experiments had shown the idea to be of very doubtful practicality. Nevertheless, twenty years later, during the course of construction of the Golden Gate Bridge in 1935, he thought the advances made in the interim by the electrical precipitation process warranted a look into the possibility of minimizing the fog hazard on the bridge. This, on one of his jaunts to the Coast, he brought to the attention of the bridge's chief engineer, Joseph B. Strauss. Strauss asked that a project be submitted, but when Western Precipitation Company figured that in a ten-mile breeze some 100,000,000 cubic feet of fog-laden air would have to be treated per minute, the idea was deemed too expensive to make further consideration worth while.

The changes in Oakland were those of any growing city. The houses around Filbert and Myrtle streets in the neighborhood of Twelfth were no longer the targets of prosperous homing commuters, for the area had passed from one of gentility to shabby gentility to shabbiness and Miss Horton's school, which had long since shunned these surroundings, had failed to survive the depression. Nevertheless, Oakland was still a home of free enterprise. The days of Cottrell the landscape photographer/electrician/job printer/publisher/chemist were part of the distant past but in Oakland now was another figure of driving energy and imagination who also gave Prompt Attention to All Orders—Henry J. Kaiser, builder of dams and ships, manufacturer of cement, magnesium, and other things. In 1942 the paths of Cottrell and Kaiser crossed.

Pearl Harbor had brought Cottrell out of his lethargy. In the war shock that followed he saw a chance to show the importance to production of Royster's bag of tricks. This importance, Cottrell wrote, "seems to me not so much merely in the stoves as such, as in the application of the principles and consequences they embody to a whole range of surprisingly diversified and important techniques." The principles could, thought Cottrell, be applied advantageously to the production of metallurgical coke, of manganese, of magnesium, of ferrosilicon, of iron. Take iron for example. If Henry Kaiser were to use Royster's stoves at his projected Fontana steel plant, this was what might happen: many Western deposits of iron ore are considered of too low grade for smelting in ordinary blast furnaces. But blast furnaces using Royster's stoves could achieve sufficiently high temperatures to burn out the high sulphur content of the poorer ores and render them usable. Higher temperatures from Royster's stoves should improve the quality of pig iron produced even by the better-grade ores. Also, the higher temperatures available from Royster's stoves would reduce the amount of coke necessary in smelting and thus lower production costs. Now, if in addition to blast furnaces Royster's stoves were used in the production of metallurgical coke also, it might mean that Kaiser's Fontana steel plant, instead of burning only good coal hauled eight hundred miles from Utah, could use some subbituminous types of coal within three hundred miles of Fontana which, blended with the better grades from Utah in a 25–75 per cent ratio, would theoretically save 118 ton-miles per ton of steel ingot produced. Based on an annual steel ingot production of 600,000 tons at Fontana, this transportation savings would amount to the fancy figure of 70,800,000 ton-miles a year.

All this and cheaper pig iron and steel, too, was only a paper promise but that was not the trouble. Trouble also lay in the fact that Cottrell's was not the only lethargy shaken by Pearl Harbor and in the tornadic rush to produce that followed there were not many who were willing to take chances on untried processes; the moment was urgent and demanded reliance on tested manufacturing practices. This urgency also militated against the time and manpower (for once cost was no great consideration) necessary for experiment unless the promises were even more sensational than those Cottrell believed inherent in Royster's stoves.

It is quite probable that Henry J. Kaiser never knew of the esteem in which he was held by Cottrell. Kaiser's energy, his bold and imaginative attacks on the problems of production, had so earned Cottrell's admiration that he read avidly all published reports that came his way of Kaiser's activities, clipped and saved great quantities of these, carefully underscoring in red pencil the points that aroused his interest. In the Kaiser organization, with its spirit of daring, Cottrell thought he saw just the right loamy soil, not only for Royster's stoves, but if they worked in metallurgical production there might also be a chance to adapt Royster's gas turbine to Kaiser's ships.

The opportunity to meet Kaiser came about unexpectedly. Kaiser had managed to get a loan of over $9,000,000 from the Reconstruction Finance Corporation to build a plant near San Jose, California, for the manufacture of magnesium using the Hansgirg process. Although this method had never been tried in America, Dr. F. J. Hansgirg, an Austrian refugee, had already put it into successful practice in two foreign plants, one for the Japanese and one for the British. It was such willingness on the part of Kaiser to pioneer on an opulent scale that so appealed to Cottrell, just as America's urgent need for light and strong magnesium appealed to the RFC to the point where they were willing to underwrite a loan on Kaiser's magnesium venture.

Kaiser built his plant in less time almost than it takes to get a $9,000,000 loan, but the early results were disturbing to RFC, for there were days when production was measured in ounces and pounds rather than in tons. Instead of appointing a committee, RFC's chief of self-liquidating loans decided Cottrell alone would do to investigate the matter. Two days after he decided to "ask Cot," the latter was happily winging his way westward on a priority order. Cottrell had left with a parting warning from RFC to beware of Kaiser's salesmanship, to which he had replied (he wrote Jess), "I threatened to go [Kaiser] one better."

At that time Kaiser's magnesium production was stumbling over such things as the insulation of furnace electrode glands and here was an entree to the councils of Kaiser that set Cottrell's heart singing. It was the most fortuitous of opportunities to introduce the subject of Royster's techniques, for there in California Cottrell met Kaiser as well as several important Kaiser lieutenants and research chiefs. During a week's stay on the Coast he paid RFC its due by investigating and reporting on the subject of the electrode glands (leaving no record of submitting a bill for his services to RFC), then launched forthrightly into the subject of Royster—of his stoves for blast-furnace production of pig iron, of the coking process, of Royster's stoves as adapted to the nitric oxide process, and of Royster's gas turbine for Kaiser's ships. Cottrell was not pleading that these processes be adopted outright but simply that they be investigated with a view to testing them out in pilot plants that in some cases might possibly also serve as small production units.

What followed is subject to varied interpretation, and if judgment is to be made several things must be kept in mind. Outside of the single and unimportant instance of the Pasadena Deodorizer, Cottrell could point to no successful commercial application of the Royster techniques. Furthermore, Royster himself had gone into the Office of Production Research and Development of the War Production Board, where he was serving as an extremely busy division chief to Harvey N. Davis, the director. This had the disadvantage of making Royster unavailable for consultation most of the time but, what was still more of a handicap, left him little or no time to pursue the tremendously important work of writing up the patents on his varied processes. Without these for protection, not even an entrepreneur of Kaiser's caliber would dare proceed very far, war or no war.

And then, one more fact must be mentioned. As his years had advanced Cottrell had grown garrulous. What had once been considered his capacity for an uninhibited and effusive flow of stimulating ideas was now more often thought of in the light of a man wordily tracking a fixed idea. Cottrell the salesman had lost his effectiveness, his memory was failing him, his talk sometimes grew desultory. The days when he had been sought out and commanded the attention of a group around the Cosmos Club in Washington or the Chemists' Club in New York had gradually given way to these, when he was sometimes avoided by old colleagues, particularly those who were caught up in the swirl and hustle of wartime Washington.

Yet here is what happened both on that first short trip to California and on a longer one which he also made as an RFC consultant in November 1942 and which lasted through January 1943: he was warmly received by all Kaiser officials, particularly those on the side of research and development—many of whom found Cottrell's cause one well worth considering. To this the chronic optimism of Cottrell, which for some time past had been desperately seeking an outlet, reacted with a renascent vigor. An old classmate whom he visited then, wrote Cottrell that he was "glad to rediscover that the effervescence of youth is still with you." To Poillon, Cottrell reported glowingly that he was having the time of his life and mentioned an "especially cordial response." To Royster he wrote: ". . . the more I see of the situation and possibilities on the whole, the more I am impressed with the set-up here as ideal for our long hoped-for opportunity of getting a favorable and broad field for developing the whole group of ideas we have been so long hammering on." With Jess, too, he shared his new-found euphoria, and in between the two trips to the Coast he discussed with her "the pros and cons of going back to California as a headquarters of an eventual real retirement program but based at the outset on a nucleus of University of California and Kaiser background." Then in December he wrote her, "The more I've seen of things out here this trip, the more I have seemed to feel once more at home out here and that we could drop back into residence here comfortably and naturally. . . . It is all very exhilarating and encouraging from current outlook."

Yet Jess knew from long experience that he must be overexerting himself and entreated him to return to Washington. How firm a grasp she had come to have of his work and interests is revealed in one letter in which she relayed all pertinent news with the composure of an old scientific colleague: "Just called Mr. Royster up and read him part of your letter telling of the blast furnace project for Fe Si [ferrosilicon] and its progress. He told me that Harvey Davis is interested in the N[itric] O[xide] project at TVA and that Robert Pike and Blanchard were talking with Davis today about the NO and he talked with [Donald] Nelson . . . regarding the matter. Also, Copson from the [Tennessee] Valley [Authority] was in and

Royster says he talked about six hours with him about the work. Farrington Daniels is in town and is to see Davis Friday. To make it long and short, Davis is much interested in the nitric oxide and wants to go ahead with the work there in the Valley."

Cottrell's plans for Kaiser reached two points of climax. One of these came in February 1943, the other a year later. In 1943 the Kaiser Development and Engineering Division printed a prospectus for an experimental blast furnace (estimated cost: $267,000) to be built at the Kaiser Fontana steel plant which, while having production possibilities, would mainly be to make a "study of the use of the higher blast and furnace temperatures made available by the Royster pebble stove." Then in February 1944, Kaiser's Iron and Steel Division prepared the draft of a proposal for a $64,000 pilot plant for Royster's coking process to be located also at Fontana.

To Cottrell these were the most promising of developments in many a long month and he determined to handle them wisely, for (as he wrote a friend) "I actually have a good deal of a problem at present deciding between the relative efforts and interest I ought to spend on the things I'm busy with for I've got so spread out that at my time of life I realize I've got to now concentrate more and in fact move rather drastically in that direction."

But the harder he concentrated the more illusory became the promise and there are divided opinions among Cottrell's acquaintances as to the reasons for this. Some maintain that in his own enthusiasm he greatly overestimated and presumed on Kaiser's interest. There are others who say that Kaiser was simply too involved in production results to risk much experimenting at such a time. In the opinion of one Kaiser wartime employee certain Kaiser officials took advantage of Cottrell in some degree by feigning an interest in order that his good will might be maintained as a consultant for RFC.

In Washington, Cottrell strove with all his remaining vigor to keep his plans alive through contact with Kaiser's office, with the Office of Production Research and Development, and with others who might prove financially co-operative. But everyone was busy with his own job, too busy for the loquacious outsider knocking to come in. It took weeks to arrange a luncheon at the Cosmos Club to bring a Kaiser official together with one from OPRD. The diary shows phone calls Cottrell placed that were not returned. One old colleague curtly rebuffed him in the Cosmos Club but phoned the next day in appeasement. "Everyone is so busy and hurried nowadays," he wrote Jess on one quick trip to the Midwest, "and I find my own strength and 'stay-with-itiveness' so limited that it takes much more than the usual time to get things done." Again he wrote: "I am doing my best, like the drummer and/or utility man in the orchestra to fill in the gaps that the more orthodox musicians haven't the time or interest or training to be bothered with and trust my wind will hold out until help arrives."

Either Cottrell could not or would not see what was happening, but it is likely that Jess did. From all reports, it was she who made the final decision that they must forsake the frustrating Washington atmosphere and move back to California where Cottrell could begin the retirement to which he had often paid lip service. Actually there was little enough to keep him in Washington. The proposal for the experimental blast furnace at Fontana using Royster's stoves was at deep rest in Washington file cabinets. OPRD refused to consider a grant for a Kaiser plant to try out Royster's coking process, and Kaiser had more important applications for loans before RFC to bother with one for the coking process. Cottrell was tired. Jess was ill. A diary note for April 2, 1944, briefly states: "Decided to drop practically everything but packing and get off to California."

So after twenty-eight years of Washington residence the natives returned to live out the balance of their lives where they had begun and where their children were buried. Yet even in this move Cottrell optimistically compromised with retirement, for he decided to live in Palo Alto, which he felt would be convenient both to the University of California in Berkeley and to Kaiser's Oakland office, as well as to Kaiser's magnesium plant at Permanente.

The Washington leave-taking carried with it traditional Cottrell touches. To Greger, who had accompanied them to the station, he wrote back that he had "made the train with *over* a minute to spare much to the surprise of the red cap." The surprise was merited, for it wasn't until they arrived in the station that Cottrell discovered that Laddie, their collie dog, "had carelessly forgotten his muzzle and rations and so couldn't come along in the baggage car" and Cottrell had to arrange for him to follow by Railway Express.

Laddie, of course, knew nothing about this absent-mindedness of a once alert, exuberant Cottrell, who forty-four years earlier had left

California galloping down to the railroad station in a grocery wagon and, with all the world before him, bade his farewells while Miss Horton's orange candies oozed in his pocket.

5

Despite his jesting boast that he might go Kaiser's salesmanship one better, Cottrell had failed. That failure, however, still did not diminish the fact that Cottrell as a quickener of reactions was still without peer. For example, one of the distinguished members of the University of California's faculty who had, years earlier, been influenced to a large degree by Cottrell in accepting a Berkeley post was Dr. Joel H. Hildebrand, chairman of the university's chemistry department. When Cottrell made his first visit to Kaiser's Permanente plant in 1942 he was shown an interesting phenomenon: it had been found that a certain type of magnesium dust immediately took fire on exposure to the air. Cottrell was asked what best might be done with this piece of information—which had immediately suggested incendiary uses—and he recommended that it be brought to the attention of Hildebrand, who had then gone into the Chemical Warfare Service. Hildebrand in turn took the idea to Washington and subsequently abroad, where he also interested the British Petroleum Warfare Department in it. The eventual result was a new incendiary or "goop" bomb and mortar shell, both of which, according to Hildebrand, played an important part on several occasions in the Allied advance through northern France and was also credited with devastating 160 square miles of industrial area in Japan. When Permanente Metals Corporation, a Kaiser enterprise, received a 1945 Army-Navy "E" award for producing such bombs, the general manager of the corporation wrote Cottrell, enclosing an "E" pin: "I know that without your able assistance and guidance in the past, it would have been impossible for this organization to have attained the results in the development and production of the munitions of war, to earn the coveted Army-Navy 'E' which was bestowed upon our company. . . ."

Other reactions, too, were pulsating. Up in Madison, Wisconsin, Farrington Daniels had managed to enlist the financial support of the potent Wisconsin Alumni Research Foundation for Cottrell's adaptation of Royster's stoves in the nitrogen fixation process. With this money he enlarged his staff of investigators and drew plans for bigger stoves, having already worked temperatures up to 2075 degrees centigrade and found minor traces of nitric oxide. In April 1942, Daniels wrote hopefully of "getting nitric oxide off the assembly line by the 4th of July" and the outlook was bright, adding to Cottrell's jubilant sense of well-being at that time over what he considered the Kaiser prospects. Despite his desire to remain in Washington and push the Royster techniques with Kaiser's office there as well as with the OPRD, he found time for intermittent trips to Madison where, content to let Daniels go on with the major work on nitric oxide, he experimented with metallic magnesium production. He used the old stoves while Daniels proceeded with the installation of the newer and larger ones made possible by his grant from the Wisconsin Alumni Research Foundation.

All this was bolstering Cottrell's feeling during the early years of the war that he was wanted, that he was needed, that he was contributing, that he was happy. "Really," he wrote Jess from Madison, "I'm beginning to feel more genuinely at home here than almost anywhere else I've been for quite a while back and I'm still burrowing in." In Daniels' laboratory he was "hugely enjoying" himself and his sense of accomplishment was heightened when chemical engineers from the TVA visited the laboratory and thought the nitric oxide process worth trying in their own laboratories.

Even as early as 1942 both Daniels and Cottrell felt certain that the new process in its simplicity could eventually win out over the Haber process, and it was a courageous thought when one contrasted their relatively small laboratory apparatus with the half dozen or so giant Haber plants the government was then building at costs running between $20,000,000 and $40,000,000 each to meet the wartime need for nitrogen.

It was a courageous thought also because, while Daniels and his crew had succeeded in proving that nitric oxide could be produced, even the newer, larger stoves failed to show the process practical, for the stoves and pebbles could not withstand the high temperatures produced. Something would burn out, some things would melt, others would fuse. Thus it was decided that because of their more extensive facilities the TVA experimenters would concentrate on this problem of refractories while the Madison group would put their emphasis on the recovery process—that is, capturing the minute quantity of nitric oxide after it was formed so that by successive steps it became nitrogen dioxide in sufficient concentration for practical conversion with water into nitric acid.

The ordeals that faced Cottrell in the early days of electrical precipitation in California all had their counterparts in the development of the nitric oxide process at Madison with this exception: in the latter case no great need existed, for the Haber process could furnish in the form of ammonia all the nitrogen necessary even for a global war whereas electrical precipitation in its early years had had no real competitors. Moreover, the nitric oxide process involved the perfection of two processes—that of producing the nitric oxide and that of recovering it after it was produced. And so it was that by 1944, when results were still doubtful, no American commercial companies could be interested in financing the experiment further and the Wisconsin Alumni Research Foundation, already considering itself teetering on the fringes of its charter in giving the support thus far granted, thought of abandoning the project entirely. True, Daniels and his co-workers were producing as high as 1 per cent nitric oxide; the stoves and pebbles were standing up moderately well; but the supply of fuel gas in the city of Madison was running short and threatening to limit experimentation, the draft was requisitioning Daniel's aides, and the morale of the group was not heightened to learn that TVA, after a year of work on the process in their own shops, had decided to give it up.

This was the situation as it presented itself to Cottrell about the time he and Jess moved to California, in 1944, and shortly thereafter Daniels himself was called into government service on atomic energy, leaving what remained of the work in charge of a capable, hard-working lieutenant, Dr. William G. Hendrickson.

As with Research Associates Inc. in its closing days, it seemed that once again Royster's stoves had failed to live up to Cottrell's promises. One Chinese commercial company did invest in the Wisconsin experiment and helped to keep it alive, for it was thought that the cheapness and simplicity of the stoves would prove a boon to Nationalist China and serve as a means of furnishing them nitrogen without the great installations and expert techniques necessitated by the Haber process. But after several months the Chinese, too, lost heart.

It was from Palo Alto that the next resurgent note of hope came—

a note sparked by the curious chance that Cottrell had at last found the leisure to indulge in some reading.

6

An almost demoniacal combination of circumstances conspired against a graceful retirement. Jess had been taken ill of old maladies even before they left Washington and in Palo Alto she was partially bedridden. Cottrell himself was ailing. Prior to a visit to his doctor, he listed his symptoms: numbness in toes for last two or three years; cramps in feet and calf of legs and varying incidence of seizures thought to correlate with low blood pressure; visibility of crow's-feet light pattern in eyes on pressure; dizziness; arthritic pains in hands; nervous eczema; weight down to 162.

These infirmities had been compounded by an accident. Cottrell and Jess first stopped at a Berkeley hotel while the house they had bought in Palo Alto was being vacated. When the time came for them to move, the Kaiser company thoughtfully sent a large car complete with chauffeur to drive them from Berkeley to Palo Alto. Midway on the ride, what Cottrell described as "an old crate of a Dodge" lunged suddenly onto the highway from a crossroad and collided with the Kaiser car. Both Cottrell and Jess were badly bruised, Jess cracked her jaw, lost several teeth from a dental plate, and Cottrell suffered a fractured ankle.

The dispiriting shock of this was abetted by the fact that the freight car carrying their household goods west was involved in a railroad accident so that almost half of their furniture arrived damaged. Then Jess's condition necessitated domestic help—about as rare a commodity during World War II as helium during World War I.

All these irritations, ills, and frictions Cottrell could have survived without stress but another blow awaited him. In considering his move West, he had laid unwonted emphasis on furthering his campaign with Kaiser's main office in Oakland, particularly with regard to Royster's coking process. By the time he had partially recovered from the automobile accident he learned that Kaiser's research and development program was undergoing such sweeping and thinning changes that scarcely a single important contact, so carefully nurtured and tended on his previous visits, was left.

A reaction set in, for the truth was that in Palo Alto Cottrell was lost. His personal troubles, coupled with the limitations of wartime transportation, made even the short trip to the Berkeley campus a hardship. He had but few acquaintances at nearby Stanford University and the Kaiser bubble had been pricked. Of this latter he wrote Royster, ". . . things seem so much in transition . . . I feel a little foolish and at a disadvantage to start once more taking up our pending projects for discussion even in a very general or tentative form." Along with disillusionment came a sense of aloneness. Royster, never an ardent letter writer, was so occupied in Washington that by December 1944 he had not found time to write Cottrell and Cottrell started a hurt letter to him saying that he was ready to assume that Royster's silence meant that their long-existing co-operation was no longer practical or desirable. The letter was unfinished and unmailed but when some months later Royster did find time to send him all the Washington scientific news and gossip Cottrell was eager to forgive. "You can hardly imagine what a breath of fresh air your present letter seemed to bring with it," he replied. "I've certainly pined for the stimulation of our get-togethers both over the phone and across the table." But to Greger, another of the old colleagues in Research Associates Inc., Cottrell wrote: "I scarcely recognize myself in some ways and am more or less puzzled to know how much of it is due to current living conditions here now and how much is a reaction from the conditions, strain and changes of the past year . . . and how much is just the progress and natural process of aging."

When the postwar United Nations conferences began in San Francisco, Cottrell looked hopefully toward those as an opportunity to bring up the subject of an international language as he had done so successfully on the formation of the League of Nations, but his status was unofficial and the best he could manage was a one-minute conference in a hotel lobby with Chinese delegate Wellington Koo, whom he had known in Geneva in 1921. He tried to write some of his sentiments about the international auxiliary language to his old friend Mrs. Morris but after a dozen trial introductory paragraphs the letter joined his other unfinished correspondence.

But Cottrell's usefulness was not over. In the February 1945 issue of *Fortune* magazine he saw an article on the postwar outlook for the eleven Western states and read therein that some officials of the enterprising Food Machinery Company in San Jose, California, had just bought a large ranch near Merced. A peculiar thing then happened. No sooner had Cottrell finished the story than a Dr. C. P. Segard, of the Wisconsin Alumni Research Foundation, phoned him from San Jose where Segard had been born and had returned to visit. It was perhaps the last reaction of note that Cottrell was to quicken. He suggested to Segard that he call on the Food Machinery people and see if they might not be interested in some nitric oxide stoves on the chance that the nitric oxide could be used directly in the irrigation ditches of the ranch, where it would be absorbed and carried along as a fertilizing element. Food Machinery, in the person of Paul C. Wilbur, director of research, evinced an immediate interest and reacted so quickly that Cottrell was in conference the following morning.

Again it was almost good to be alive, for, after investigating the results of the process to that date, Food Machinery agreed to take further development out of the eagerly relinquishing hands of the Wisconsin Alumni Research Foundation, some of whose technical staff would go along to San Jose and give assistance. As inventive processes go, it was a very long shot. Cottrell had conceived the idea in 1931. It was 1939 before Daniels and his assistants started actual work on the problem in Madison. Cottrell had applied for a basic patent in 1942 but because of wartime secrecy and because of an interfering patent Cottrell's was not granted until June 1947. Meanwhile, the Wisconsin Alumni Research Foundation, a Chinese chemical company, and TVA had spent well over $100,000 trying to make it work by overcoming the problem of stove linings and pebbles that would withstand high temperatures and at the same time devising an adequate recovery process.

It was not until 1951 (or over $1,000,000 and eighteen patents and patent applications later) that the nitric oxide process was ready for commercial production—a tribute to monumental faith on the part of Cottrell, Daniels, Royster, Hendrickson, Wilbur of Food Machinery, and those at Wisconsin who worked so patiently over its development. In all probability this degree of success would never have come about if a collateral development had not taken place in the improvement of refractory materials. It had been discovered at Madison that if magnesium oxide of 96–97 per cent purity were used as pebbles and linings the stoves would stand up under

4200 degrees Fahrenheit and produce what was considered to be a commercially practical 2 per cent nitric oxide. Moreover, it was found that this high-grade magnesium oxide (and hence the stoves) improved with age—the intense heat driving off some of the few impurities remaining in the refractories.

As of 1951 these developments—a culmination of Cottrell's idea twenty years before—had stimulated the War Department to undertake the erection of a $2,500,000 plant for the production of nitric acid at DeSoto, Kansas. As of that date, too, it was the expectation of both Wisconsin Alumni Research Foundation and the Food Machinery and Chemical Corporation (the "Chemical" was added in 1948) that the Cottrell-Daniels, or Wisconsin, process would prove competitive with the Haber process, even though the latter was in some cases producing ammonia in war-surplus plants—plants that had been bought from the government at roughly 50 per cent of their wartime cost. But the Cottrell-Daniels/Wisconsin process had this advantage: in all likelihood the Haber process had reached its apex of perfection, whereas the newer process through continued engineering could even cheapen its own production costs and eventually render obsolete the older one that had stood Germany in such historic stead during World War I.

Cottrell did not live to see this success of his most important idea since hitting upon the electrical precipitation process. As early as 1939 he had written Poillon that the possibility of not surviving until Royster's stoves became a practical reality wasn't "of much significance" even though the nitric oxide process represented the possibility of a new era for an important industry, and this at a time when nitric acid looms as additionally important in the field of propellents for guided missiles. To Cottrell the possibility of such success was of less moment as a vehicle of personal satisfaction than the steps that had led to it. Another duty to the world had been discharged.

7

Frederick Gardner Cottrell died on Tuesday, November 16, 1948, at about 9:30 A.M., at the University of California in Berkeley. Unlike his birth, his passing was widely noted. On his death the local papers could have said again, as they had seventy-one years before, that rain was needed, the public schools were crowded, and San Francisco Bay was rough. The end had come suddenly.

Although, since 1946, Cottrell had been relatively inactive, he did spend some time trying to promote what for many years had been a minor cause—the Southgate rectifier. This was a mechanical device for converting alternating to direct current and had been invented by an engineer whose acquaintance with Cottrell was of long standing. The interest of several electrical manufacturing firms had alternately waxed and waned over the rectifier and when Southgate died in 1946 his widow wrote Cottrell that her husband had always "recognized you as a great man, admired you and enjoyed your companionship keenly, and was proud of your friendship. There was no one who knew so much of his dreams, his hopes and fears as you did." She asked Cottrell's advice on how best to follow up the invention's further development and to this plea Cottrell responded.

In the Southgate rectifier Research Corporation saw an opportunity to supply an outlet for whatever energies Cottrell felt able to summon at this point. Poillon had retired as president because of ill-health, and his place had been taken by Dr. Joseph W. Barker, who prior to his election as president had been dean of engineering at Columbia University and a Research Corporation director.

Barker entered into an agreement with Stanford Research Institute in Palo Alto to proceed with the rectifier's development in a manner that would utilize as much of Cottrell's attention as he wished to give, but this project collapsed before it could be started when it was discovered that a successful rectifier of a similar nature had been invented in Germany during the war and had already been put into commercial use.

Research Corporation made other attempts to occupy Cottrell. One of these was a proposal to set up a Palo Alto laboratory, equipped as he might wish it, and in which he could work as he chose, but Cottrell seemed to lack the energy necessary to organize such an undertaking. Then again Barker tried to prompt him to write his memoirs as being of value in themselves to science and as a means of preserving a record of electrical precipitation's development. This proposal, however, was partially thwarted by the fact that in the disorganizing process of moving into the Palo Alto home and because of Jess's continued illness Cottrell's collections of files and papers (running into tens of thousands of letters and documents) had never been properly rearranged so that he had easy access to them.

One thing Research Corporation's efforts did accomplish in tribute to Cottrell. Although it granted the government royalty-free license on any of its patents for use in wholly owned or operated government plants during the war, it still managed to accumulate sufficient earnings so that $2,500,000 was set aside in a special fund for the Frederick Gardner Cottrell Grants to supplement the regular grants program over a five-year period. The Cottrell-named grants would concentrate on projects in smaller colleges and institutions to foster and encourage the spirit of research and would go especially to those younger men whose opportunities to establish their professional reputations had been interrupted by the war.

This program was to be announced at a special meeting of the corporation's board of directors in October 1945, and an urgent invitation was sent Cottrell asking him to attend, although no clue was given him as to the reason for the meeting. Cottrell accepted and set out on his last trip East. Just before departure, however, he had received an invitation, delayed in being forwarded from Washington, to take part in the Atomic Energy Control Conference called by Robert M. Hutchins, chancellor of the University of Chicago, and attended by some fifty prominent educators, scientists, and businessmen. This Cottrell considered more important than the corporation's board meeting and, in stopping over in Chicago, unwittingly spoiled the surprise Research Corporation had prepared for him in announcing the grants program that would bear his name—a program which Barker later wrote him he hoped would be "one well worthy of the ideals of your conception and formation of the Research Corporation."

This last trip East finally proved one thing to Cottrell. He tired so easily that it was hard to meet people effectively. Still, in the atmosphere of the Cosmos Club he found a powerful stimulus and from there he wrote back to Jess that "This Cosmos Club is certainly the crossroads of the world for me."

Back again in Palo Alto he spoke wistfully of making another trip East in 1947 but the difficulties were too many, the inertia to overcome was by now too great. Those who wished to see Cottrell came to Palo Alto. There were not many of these but one visitor was Lloyd N. Scott, the lawyer and one of the few surviving founders of Research Corporation. This was the Scott who had loyally given so much of his time to that untested concept during the days of the lonely Wall Street office. Scott was neither a voluble nor a sentimental man, but after he left Palo Alto he was moved to write Cottrell a final testament of what could arouse such abiding loyalty: "I don't suppose you realize your great strength of mind and personality and what an inspiration you are to others. I have always considered you something of a superman. I told someone not very long ago that I thought you were one of the most valuable men the country has ever produced. An inventory of what you have accomplished, and are even now accomplishing, is monumental, and your latest project [the nitric oxide process] . . . will be a tremendous thing for the nation and the world, if it works out as you expect."

Jess died in February 1948, so there was only about one thing left for Cottrell to accomplish and that followed nine months later in Berkeley while he was attending a meeting of the National Academy of Sciences. It was a morning business session and about nine-thirty he slumped in his chair, his head back, an audible rattle in his throat.

He died among friends. Hildebrand, of the university's chemistry department, helped Farrington Daniels lay him on the floor, and it was thought that death had come instantly. A doctor arrived and after the body had been removed it was the sentiment of those attending that Cottrell would have wished the meeting to go on. The session continued.

A ritual of cremation consumed the mortal remains of Cottrell just as his own fires had already burned out the fabulous energy that had been only one of his many distinguishing characteristics. But there are some things fire cannot destroy. To those who would evaluate such a life—who would weigh its defeats against its achievements, its pleasures against its rebuffs, its fulfillments, and its despairs—one thing is of paramount consideration. It was a life lived fully in the manner of him who fashioned it, a man unafraid to think and walk alone. Cottrell could express this lightly as he once did, saying, "This chasing of scientific visions which are just on the borderline between hooey and history is a great life if you don't weaken." He could say it gravely, as he did in writing to Jess from Leipzig, telling her of his ideals and of their independence from what others might think; of how he must pursue the ends he envisioned whether or not they had any effect within his own lifetime; for "scientific life and methods of work have fortunately reached such a degree of organization already that one can feel quite sure that nothing which is really of value can ever be wholly lost."

INDEX